THEORY BUILDING IN
DEVELOPMENTAL PSYCHOLOGY

ADVANCES IN PSYCHOLOGY

36

Editors:

G. E. STELMACH

P. A. VROON

NORTH-HOLLAND
AMSTERDAM · NEW YORK · OXFORD · TOKYO

THEORY BUILDING
IN
DEVELOPMENTAL PSYCHOLOGY

Edited by

Paul VAN GEERT

Department of Developmental Psychology
State University of Groningen
The Netherlands

1986

NORTH-HOLLAND
AMSTERDAM · NEW YORK · OXFORD · TOKYO

ISBN: 0 444 70042 0

Publishers:
ELSEVIER SCIENCE PUBLISHERS B.V.
P.O. Box 1991
1000 BZ Amsterdam
The Netherlands

Sole distributors for the U.S.A. and Canada:
ELSEVIER SCIENCE PUBLISHING COMPANY, INC.
52 Vanderbilt Avenue
New York, N.Y. 10017
U.S.A.

Library of Congress Cataloging-in-Publication Data

Theory building in developmental psychology.

(Advances in psychology ; 36)
Based on a symposium held at the Inaugural European
Conference on Behavioural Development in Groningen,
28-31 Aug. 1984.
Includes bibliographies and index.
1. Developmental psychology--Research--Methodology--
Congresses. 2. Developmental psychology--Philosophy--
Congresses. I. Geert, Paul van. II. Inaugural European
Conference on Behavioural Development (1984 : Groningen,
Netherlands) III. Series: Advances in psychology
(Amsterdam, Netherlands) ; 36.
BF713.T46 1986   155   86-11573
ISBN 0-444-70042-0 (U.S.)

PRINTED IN THE NETHERLANDS

Preface

The present book is the result of a symposium "Theory Building in Developmental Psychology" convened by the editor. It was held at the Inaugural European Conference on Behavioural Development which took place in Groningen, 28-31 August 1984. Papers were presented by Paul Vedder (now at Curaçao), Alan Leslie (London), Peter Bryant (Oxford), and Paul van Geert (Groningen). During the Conference, contacts were made with potential contributors to the present book, namely Jan ter Laak (Leiden), Francine Orsini-Bouichou (Aix-en-Provence), Maria Tyszkowa (Poznań), and Dieter Geulen (Berlin). After the first sketches of the structure of the book had been made, further contributors have been invited, namely John Morton (London), Bea de Gelder (Tilburg), Martin Atkinson (Colchester) and Ed Elbers (Utrecht).

Since the origin of the book lies in a European Conference, only European developmental psychologists have been invited to contribute. The purpose of the book is to present a European perspective on theory building in developmental psychology. The perspective presented is probably not statistically representative, and probably also not very different from a North American or Asian perspective. Nevertheless, the editor hopes the book will be sufficiently representative to offer an informative and not too parochial expression of new, old and renewed traditions in theory building currently existing in Universities of different European countries.

The study of theory building in developmental psychology is directly related to understanding the nature and direction of empirical research and application of theoretical viewpoints and empirical findings in the field. It should not be seen as an exercise in applied philosophy of science, taking developmental psychology as its subject, instead of physics or economy. Studying theory building in developmental psychology implies that one tries to understand how implicit and explicit concepts of development and psychological change shape our views on the nature of childhood or the life span; how they direct our research methods and the selection of topics of empirical investigation.

The book addresses five questions.

The first question is about the concept of development and the structure of developmental theories. Are there various concepts of development, how are they related, and how are they expressed in existing theories? What is the relation between the underlying concept of development employed by a theory and the theory's structure and structural components?

The second question deals with the causes and conditions of actual developmental change. Theories assert that people move from one particular developmental state to another, but they should also specify a factor or mechanism that provides a causal and conditional explanation of the stage transition.

The third question deals with the social and cultural framework of development and developmental theory building. The origin of developmental psychology as an empirical science lies undoubtedly in biology. On the other hand, psychological development is characterized by a strong cultural and historical component borne by the social dimension. It is questioned how the social matrix of individual development influences or shapes the processes of theory building.

The fourth question is about the relationship between theoretical views and the building of actual theories. Three examples are provided of views on how processes of psychological change can also become processes of development.

The final question addresses a traditional issue in psychology, and developmental psychology in particular, namely the rationalism versus empiricism controversy. In view of the respectable amounts of philosophical ink and energy devoted to this issue, an exemplary approach has been chosen. One chapter discusses the "cognitive" nature of developmental theories, while two others apply the rationalism-empiricism discussion to concept-acquisition and development in infancy.

Finally, the present book would not have been possible without the help of several people, among whom Hans Hommes, Henk Camstra, Cees Tempelman, Barbara Wijnberg, and Ineke Jansen, for typing and editorial assistance.

Groningen
February, 1986   Paul van Geert.

Contents

PART 1

DEVELOPMENT: CONCEPT AND STRUCTURE

Theory Building in Developmental Psychology
P.L.C. van Geert (editor)
© Elsevier Science Publishers B.V. (North-Holland), 1986

1

The Concept of Development

Paul van Geert

Four types of analysis of the concept of development are presented. In etymological analysis, the original meaning of "unwrapping" is compared with the way in which the concept is used in current theories of development. In semantic analysis of the syntagmatic type, two basically different conceptualizations of development are found, viz. a prospective and a retrospective conceptualization. In semantic analysis of the paradigmatic type, "development" is compared with "evolution" and "learning". Finally, in the system theoretic analysis, the various conceptual components of "development" found in the previous forms of analysis are re-interpreted in system theoretic terms.

It seems obvious that theories of development have at least one thing in common, namely the fact that they deal with development. Thus, in order to find a definition of the concept of development, one should only try to isolate the common element of developmental theories. It is highly probable, however, that such a strategy will not lead us very far.

First, it is possible that, although every developmental theory shows considerable conceptual overlap with at least one other, there is no developmental theory that shows considerable conceptual overlap with all the others. That is, the concept of development might have a "Wittgensteinean" form, in that it resembles a chain of conceptual links. Each theory of development covers only a part of the chain, and is connected with other theories via several overlaps.

Second, it is possible that, although all developmental

theories claim they are theories of development, some, many, or all are not about development at all. That is, the truth of the claim that a theory is about development, depends on whether or not the word "development" as employed in the theory refers to development. At present, it is unclear whether "development" is a taxonomic term, invented and defined for the sake of book keeping, or whether it is a natural kind term, such as "water" or "Andromeda Nebula". If it is a natural kind term, it is possible that all our theories of development are basically wrong, just as all the Medieval theories about gold or mercury were wrong. Any serious progress in the theory of development would depend, then, on empirical and theoretical discoveries in the field of natural processes of change and transformation which have yet be made. For lack of such discoveries, it is possible that some existing theories of development are true, while we simply do not know and cannot know whether they are true. It is clear that, if development is a natural kind term, any attempt at discovering the properties of development by means of conceptual analysis of existing theories is futile. Why, then, proceed with our analysis? The reason is that the existing theories of development are the only "headed" knowledge of development we have, that is, they are the only sources of knowledge about which there is a certain consensus that they address the issue of development. The conceptual analysis might result in a -probably very rudimentary- sketch for a further research programme that is able to distinguish the real empirical issues from the purely conceptual or terminological ones.

In the present paper, I shall present three ways for analysing the concept of development as it is employed in theories as well as in colloquial language, namely an etymological analysis, a semantic analysis containing a syntagmatic and a paradigmatic approach, and a system theoretic analysis.

ETYMOLOGICAL ANALYSIS.

"Development" stems from the Old French "desvoloper" which means "to unwrap" (the German "Entwicklung" or the Dutch "ontwikkeling" is a literal translation of the term). The word is related to the Latin "evolutio" (to unroll) and the semantically related "explicatio" (to unfold). The words originally refered to the unfolding or unrolling of book rolls, and have found a metaphoric use in the words "development" and "explication" (Thomae, 1959; Trautner, 1979). In order to uncover some of the conceptual aspects of the unroll- unfold metaphor, let us look at the figure of a piece of paper which has been folded in the form of a triangle (figure 1).

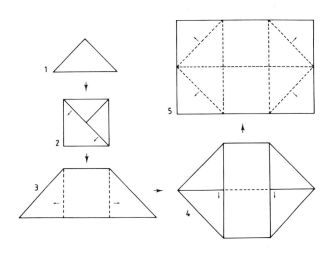

Figure 1. A paper model of the "unfolding" concept of development: finite number of states (5) and steps (4) which are qualitatively different, and preformed in the first state (the triangle).

With the first unfolding, the paper takes the form of a square, with the second it takes the form of a trapezium, then of a hexagon, and finally a rectangle.

The paper model provides a metaphorical illustration of some fundamental conceptual aspects of the traditional development concept.

First, the process consists of a finite number of steps and a finite number of states (forms of the paper).

Second, the order and nature of the transformations is determined by the initial state of the folded paper.

Third, all states are qualitatively different (triangle, square, etc.).

Fourth, the nature of the transformation is the same for all transformation steps, namely unfolding.

Finally, if only the initial state of the folding is accessible, it is impossible to tell which unfolding and which corresponding forms will follow.

The paper metaphor corresponds quite well with Nagel's classical description of the fundamental components of development, namely a system with a specific structure and specific initial capacities on the one hand, and a set of successive changes in the system leading to relatively permanent, new structural properties (Nagel, 1957, 17).

The scientific concept of development typical of nineteenth century biology, is very close to the idea of preformation present in our paper metaphor. Haeckel's Biogenetic Law or the Law of Recapitulation (Haeckel, 1866), for instance, emphasizes the notion of preformed stages of development in the individual, which reflect the biological history of the species. The concept of recapitulation was at the basis of Stanley Hall's "Genetic Psychology" and is still perceptible in Piaget's theory.

The nineteenth century idea of development as preformation is often attributed to the biological basis of developmental thinking, which found its starting point in Darwin's works on the origin of species. The reference to Darwin is somewhat remarkable, in that Darwin's view on the origin of species was exactly the opposite to a preformist, essentialist conception which had dominated evolutionary thinking before his time. Qualitative differences between species are the result of accumulating quantitative differences. Species properties are not essential charactericterics of an animal, they are properties of a population of animals. A real Darwinian developmental psychology, that is, a developmental theory which applies the basic principles of transformation discovered by Darwin, would differrentirely from the recaptulationist conceptions of Haeckel and Hall who are Darwin's alleged heirs (Van Geert, in press).

Piaget's theory fits the paper metaphor quite well, although Piaget's theory in particular applies the notion of unfolding in a very abstract sense. It is entirely incorrect to think that Piaget's theory is a maturation theory, as if the stages of cognitive development are represented in the genetic programme of the human body. It is a theory of "inevitability" rather than of preformation. That is, in view of the fact that the human mind is essentially a biological organ, that biological organs cooperate in the process of adapting the individual to the environment and the environment to the individual, and finally, in view of the basic properties of the social and physical world in which the mind has to operate, the process of development cannot follow another path than the one described by Piaget. Thus, the set of stages and transformations is finite, the distinctions between the stages are qualitative, the stages and processes are determined by the properties of the initial state as previously described, and the nature of the transformations is invariant over stages, i.e. it consists of processes of assimilation, accomodation and equilibration. Finally, from the form of the initial state it cannot be told whether or not the entire developmental path will be traversed (in various traditional cultures, for instance, the process will stop at the concrete operational stage, depending on the historical evolution of the culture).

A second classical conception of development, the concept of differentiation, which we might find in Werner's "orthogenetic principle" (Werner, 1957) as well as in modern

theories such as Bower's (Bower, 1979), is based on an idea
which is actually the reverse of the paper metaphor. The
initial state is the state of least internal differentiation,
which might be compared with the unfolded rectangular sheet of
paper. A process of differentiation, comparable with the
folding of the paper, will take place, transforming the
original structure into increasingly complex forms (e.g. a
piece of paper consisting of numerous folds and layers of
paper). Differentiation theory easily allows for partial
regression and restructuring.

It should also be noted that the original biological
conceptions of preformed "unfolding" were accompanied by a
conception of differentiation, i.e. the notion that
development proceeds from the simple to the complex,
notwithstanding the fact that the simple contains the complex
in some form or other. These problems are reminiscent of
classical philosphical discussions, associated with Plato and
Aristotle, on how something can come forth that was not
present from the beginning (e.g. Olshewski, 1974; Weimer,
1973). In developmental psychology, the Platonic version of
preformationism has been revived in the theories of Chomsky
and Fodor (see Atkinson, in this volume, for a discussion). It
is probable -although we may hope it is untrue- that issues
like the potential-actual discussion reflect problems that are
unsolvable due to inherent weaknesses in our thinking about
fundamental properties of the world such as development and
change.

SEMANTIC ANALYSIS: THE SYNTAGMATIC TYPE.

By syntagmatic analysis I understand the analysis of the
linguistic contexts in which the term "development" may occur.
That is, we shall try to discover the semantic extension of
the set of nouns occupying the "..." slot in the syntagm "the
development of ...". The underlying idea is that the semantic
extension of the second noun-slot in the "development of ..."
is entirely determined by the noun "development" to which it

stands in an agentive-intransitive relationship. The "..."-
slot can be occupied by a variety of nominal phrases: "the
child", "a child", "a photograph", "photography", "an idea",
"a prototype", "an animal species", etc.

Two Types of Development.

In order to illustrate the conceptual analysis, I shall
use a non-psychological development-noun, namely "Volkswagen".
Let us start with some history. The National-Socialists wanted
every good German - a species whose definition has fortunately
changed since then- to possess a cheap car, whereafter they
ordered dr. Porsche to invent one (the car, that is). The
conception of the Volkswagen officially took place on the 17th
January 1934 with Porsche's presentation of an "Exposé
concerning the construction of a German people's car". In
1938, a prototype was ready, appropriate for mass production.
On the 26th of May 1938 the building of a Volkswagen factory
started. Many good Germans made weekly savings of five
Reichsmark which should have allowed them to buy the desired
vehicle, if it would not have been for the intervention of an
unsuccessful architect. As historians of cars, we might call
the period between the first conception of a people's car to
the first real Volkswagen "the development of the Volkswagen".
We know that none of the saving Germans got their car, becaus-
e the war interfered. After the war, the Volkswagen was
produced in massive numbers, the model was improved and became
one of the most popular cars of the century, a true testimony
of the post-war Wirtschaftswunder. We might call the period
starting with the first or "Ur-Volkswagen" until the model was
no longer produced, at least in Europe, "the development of
the Volkswagen".
It is clear that the two uses of "development" have a
different meaning: the first one takes the first Volkswagen
and looks back, so to say, whereas the second one takes the
first Volkswagen and looks ahead. We shall call the first
variant the retrospective definition of development, the

second will be called the prospective definition of development. In order to find the rules which govern the semantically correct use of either variant, we might compare a great number of contexts in which each one might appear. In order to shortcut this long process, I shall present those rules by way of hypothesis, and then check whether or not these rules cover the actual use of the retrospective and the prospective variants of development.

The rules that govern the retrospective use of "development" are as follows.

A process P is adequately called "the development of X_1" if

1) X_1 is the name given to the final point or final state of P

2) the states of P are ordered, given the properties of X_1

3) it is possible to define a non-trivial initial state of P, given the properties of X_1.

In order to fulfill the first rule, it is necessary that P is finite, that is, we need a criterion to decide which state, in an infinite stream of time, is conceived of as the final state. In principle, every state in a process marks a final state, namely the final state of the sub-process consisting of every preceding step. The latter criterion, however, is cognitively trivial. A more acceptable criterion is succesful name giving. That is, as soon as it was accepted that a certain prototype got the name "Volkswagen", the final state of the designing process had been achieved. A still better criterion is that the final state is the state which fulfills certain preliminary requirements, e.g. a certain cost-benifit relation, maximal speed, number of passengers allowed, etc. If no such requirements are available, the final state might be defined as the state which is optimally stable, i.e. which undergoes minimal change in the future.

The second and third rule can be exemplified as follows. The rule of ordered states implies that if one is presented with all the preliminary models and steps in the designing process of the Volkswagen, for instance, then it should be possible to reconstruct the real order of development, given the properties of the final "Volkswagen" prototype. The "initial-state"-rule implies that, given the Volkswagen prototype as the final state, it should be possible to determine an initial state as the first step towards the Volkswagen. Neither the ordering nor the determination of an initial state are trivial issues. They both require that the final state, the Volkswagen prototype, has some essential properties, essential not in the Platonic but in the developmental sense of the word. If the designers would have made a number of arbitrary different models, one after the other, and then would have decided to conceive of the last one as the Volkswagen prototype, there would not have been a structured developmental process. Looking ahead, the structure may be imperceptible, that is, it might have been unclear to the designers whether they were making progress or not. The structure becomes perceptible, or even logically necessary, in view of the model conceived of as the final state, the Volkswagen prototype. The determination of the initial state also depends on the properties of the final Volkswagen prototype. History is a quasi-infinite series of events with bifurcations and dead ends at many successive points. The question as to which bifurcation marks the initial state of the Volkswagen, depends on the set exemplified by the term "Volkswagen". In the present case, we are lucky to have Porsche's "Exposé" as an offically marked starting point, which described the properties any future possible car should have in order to be called "Volkswagen". However, if by Volkswagen we should understand any cheap, mass produced car the general public can buy, which is also the original meaning of the German word, the historical starting point of the people's car would be very difficult to determine exactly.

The prospective definition of development obeys the following rules:

A process P is adequately called the development of X_2 if

      1) X_2 is the name given to all the states of P

      2) the states of P are ordered, given the properties of X_2

      3) it is possible to define a non-trivial final state of P, given the properties of X_2.

The prospective developmental series starts at the moment a
prototype is considered the first Volkswagen, and ends at the
moment the Volkswagen is no longer manufactured, or when so
many alterations of the original model have been made that the
result is no longer considered a Volkswagen. The latter
example suggests that the determination of the final state as
a well defined breaking point may be very difficult. This is
not unlike the difficulties that may arise with the
determination of the initial state in the retrospective
models. Either type of developmental series may take the form
of a "one-tailed" fuzzy set, so to speak. Applying the principle of developmental order may provide comparable
difficulties. Some alterations to the original model may occur
in a completely arbitrary order (e.g. alterations of the motor
or of the windscreen). Other alterations may take a nested
form, e.g. a general improvement of some mechanical principle,
which is then further improved, or allows for the improvement
of some other detail). Only the latter type of changes will
obey the ordering principle.

The Retrospective Conception of Development.

It can now be questioned whether the developmental conceptions which held for the Volkswagen, are also applicable to
the psychological dimension of the human life span. The human
life span consists of a series of events which are ordered
along the temporal dimension. The question is whether the
temporal ordering reflects either a prospective or a retrospective developmental ordering, or both.
There is no doubt that most of the classical developmental
theories are of the retrospective type or at least have a
strong retrospective component. These theories explain how and
why a specific final state is achieved starting from an
initial state in which the distinctive properties of the final
state are absent.
Take for instance Piaget's theory. Basically, Piaget was
not a developmental psychologist, but a genetic epistemo-

logist. That is, his main interest was in the nature of knowledge, a question which he wanted to solve by investigating the development of knowledge. Moreover, Piaget was not so much interested in knowledge in general, as in a very particular type of knowledge, namely scientific knowledge, and formal operational thinking. This kind of knowledge is not a general property of mankind, but something which issued from a particular historical, cultural and economic process. This kind of knowledge and its associated forms of thought is acquired by most children in the West, and as such, Piaget's Genetic Epistemology became a sort of developmental psychology.

If one wants to capture the nature of a specific form of knowledge or thought by studying its development, one should seek for a starting point where this specific form of knowledge or thought is lacking. This starting point might be found with the early Greeks, or even further back in history, or with the beginning of the life of the individual child, e.g. between birth and eightteen months. In Piaget's case, such a starting point was found both in historically anterior times and in the beginning of the human life span. The fact that one starts with the "nil-state" of a developmental outcome is based on a conceptual decision which issues from one's choice for a retrospective developmental model. The fact that the "nil-state" can be found with the neonate, or with the physics of Aristotle, is an entirely empirical matter.

It is not surprising that Piaget has often been criticised for his narrow perspective on human identity, that is, an identity which is defined by a specific form of cognitive activity. Every relevant property earlier in life is viewed in the light of this particular outcome. Maybe this is not entirely unforgivable as far as children growing up in the West are concerned, but serious problems will arise as soon as different cultures, that is, cultures with a different culmination of development, are taken into consideration. Although the culmination of development is highly culture specific, many transitional stages are not, for instance the sensori-motor thinking of the baby, or the understanding of

practical problems achieved during childhood. Therefore, it
might be a grave theoretical error to understand and define
these more or less universal properties of thinking in the
narrow light of a culturally specific product, namely
scientific thinking (see for instance Buck-Morss, 1975;
Mangan, 1978; Van Geert, 1983). It may be questioned, however,
whether "specific" means "arbitrary". Scientific, formal
thinking is clearly the product of Western culture, but this
should not necessarily imply that this thinking is arbitrary,
that is, that there is as much truth in it as in mytho-magical
thinking , for instance. If thinking is defined as a means for
achieving true knowledge, then every form of thinking,
wherever and whenever it occurs, can be evaluated against the
standards of truth. These standards are, to the best of our
knowledge, maximally incorporated in the scientific thinking
which arose in the West. Thus, it is implied that scientific
thinking does form the matrix in which every other form of
thinking, anterior and posterior, may be understood. The
previous discussion reflects some of the conceptual and
philosophical problems that may arise with the choice of a
final state of development: the actual choice reflects a
specific view on the nature of man and cannot be decided on
mere empirical grounds.
Besides the choice of a final state and the consequent
definition of an initial state, the retrospective nature of
Piaget's developmental theory requires that the states -or
stages as Piaget has called them- reflect an intrinsic order
which is not merely temporal. Piaget's stages are defined by
structural properties with conditional relationships. For
instance, it is a matter of (Piagetian) definition that formal
thinking requires operational thinking. Therefore, the
emergence of operational thinking takes place on a level
anterior to formal thinking, which, again by (Piagetian)
definition, is concrete thinking. Thus, the order of the
concrete operational and the formal operational stages is
conceptually fixed (in the next chapter, I shall discuss the
details of developmental state-orders). The latter does not
mean, however, that all instances of concrete operational

thinking necessarily precede all instances of formal operational thinking. This problem has clearly been noted by Piaget, and endowed with a theoretical status in the form of the concept of "décalage". On the other hand, it is a matter of conceptual necessity that, if there is a particular instance of formal operational thinking, it should have been preceded by a particular instance of concrete operational thinking, although it is not conceptually determined which actual precedent is necessary. The necessity of developmental order is further illustrated by the parallellism between ontogenetic and historical processes. The cognitive development of the individual recapitulates the history of logic and scientific thinking to a certain degree, not because there has been some transformation of the historical process into the genes of the individual, but because both processes are based on the same abstract mechanisms. Nevertheless, there are some notable structural asynchronies between the history of science and individual development, for instance the order in which topological and Euclidean theories of space emerge.

Psychoanalytic theory provides another example of a classical approach to development which is basically retrospective in nature. There are differences, however, between the original Freudean model based on the erogeneous zones, and the later ego-psychological versions of the theory. Viewed from the perspective of a genital stage as the final state of development, the preceding stages are characterized in the form of investments of libidinal energy in different zones, that is the anal, the phallic or the oral. There is no intrinsic developmental order among these zones, however. There is nothing in the definition of the genital that conceptually requires the oral zone to be the initial state. There is a temporal order that might be explained on the basis of the biology of the human body.

The ego-psychological aspect of the theory, shows the retrospectively ordered succession of the developmental states much more clearly. The final state to be explained is the genitally productive ego, an autonomous and self conscious source of action which has solved the conflict between the instinctual drives and the requirements of reality. In view of this final state, the initial state should be a non-ego state, lacking the differentiation between the subject and the object. The place where the differentiation between the subject and the object can be discovered is where the objective (the world) intermingles with the subjective (the person), namely the mouth, hence the oral mode as the initial state of development. The fact that the mouth is the place of subject-object discovery is a matter of biological - construction of the human body, it is not a logically necessary consequence of how the subject-object differentiation is defined. The discovery of the subject-object differentiation precedes the discovery of the subject as a self, that is, an autonomous being with a free will. The developmental steps further proceed in a logical order, leading to the properties of the final state.

The Prospective Conception of Development.

The second group of theories is characterized by a prospectively defined concept of development. These theories divide the set of processes characterizing the human life span into sets of subprocesses that each represent a specific phenomenon. Wohlwill (1973) has named these subprocesses "developmental dimensions". Examples of such dimensions are "perceptual constancy", "thinking", "object knowledge", etc. Each state in the dimension of "perceptual constancy", for instance, is an instance of perceptual constancy, however primitive it may be. The theory then tries to define the transformations that occur with this perceptual constancy, until transformations no longer occur, or until the nature of the phenomenon changes, e.g. when perceptual constancy develops into something conceptual. The developmental order within the perceptual dimension is simply a matter of quantitative increase, e.g. in the relation between correct and erroneous judgments of size or form constancy, in the distance within which constancy is still operative, etc.

Werner's theory of differentiation (Werner, 1948, 1957) provides another example of a prospectively defined developmental concept. Development is conceived of as a process of differentiation. The first state of the process is the least differentiated. The final state is simply the most differentiated state available. Differentiation theory is currently revived in Bower's general developmental theory (Bower, 1979) and Spelke's theory of the development of object knowledge (Spelke, 1985). According to Spelke, there is sufficient empirical evidence that the first state of object knowledge in the infant is a true instance of object knowledge, that is, the infant perceives objects as soon as perception begins. Objects are defined as spatiotemporal entities with elementary characteristics of permanence and unity. Development consists of a further elaboration, i.e. differentiation, of this initial object definition. Spelke's view on object development stands in sharp contrast with Piaget's, for instance. In Piaget's retrospective view, the initial state of object knowledge consists of the lack of object definition, represented by subject-object diffusion (Piaget, 1937). There is nothing intrinsically wrong in adopting a retrospective view on the development of the object concept. The empirical question, however, is whether or not the beginning of human life coincides with the theoretically inferred initial state, i.e. the state of lacking elementary object knowledge. According to Piaget, there is evidence of that coincidence, according to Spelke, there is not. With regard to object knowledge, the theoretically inferred initial state of object knowledge is supposed to lie far away in phylogenetic history.

In differentiation theory, the final state may be very hard to define, in that differentiation may proceed infinitely and stop only with the contingent fact of death. On the other hand, it is probable that many units of differentiation, e.g. the initial state of object knowledge, or the initial state of perceptual constancy, put some intrinsically defined constraints upon the level of differentiability. The concept of object, for instance, may be differentiated and refined until a level of understanding of the object is achieved which shows that the object concept is not the right way of physically categorizing nature. Such a level is clearly achieved with the development of modern physics. That is, the concept of object can be differentiated within the limits of practical understanding of reality, but stops being a concept of object as soon as the boundary between sophisticated practical understanding and modern physics is crossed.

An Additional Type: Topological Theories Sensu Stricto.

At several places in the discussion, we have seen that the requirements of order and of non-trivial initial or final states may be too strong for some of the theories. In Freud's theory, we have seen that there is no intrinsic developmental order in the erogeneous zone-defined stages. The order arises from the properties of the human body.
A comparable ordering problem might be noticed in Bruner's theory on the development of representation (Bruner, 1964). The theory explains how the final state of representation, the state of symbolic representation, develops on the basis of an initial form of representation which is enactive in nature. Enactive means that knowledge is represented in the form of action patterns. The transition from enactive to symbolic takes place via the iconic stage, when knowledge is represented in image-like form. Unless "symbolic" would be trivially defined as "emerging-from-an-enactive- basis-via-an-iconic-interval", there is no logical necessity in the developmental order. Computers, for instance, historically started with an entirely symbolic representation and then proceeded to an enactive representation in the form of "scripts" and iconic representations in the form of computer vision.
Another example of a theory which lacks firm logical order is Havighurst's theory of developmental tasks, i.e. tasks which have to be fulfilled at various ages (Havighurst, 1953).
It may be questioned whether these topological theories

are developmental in the true sense of the word. What they call "development" is a process of transitions between unordered states. Any state can be the initial one, any state can be the final one, and any state may precede or succeed any other. Such a process should be called a process of change, not of development. The fact that the developmental process distinguished by these theories takes the form of an ordered set of states, depends on the empirical conditions under which the process takes place. Enactive representation, for instance, is a part of the human genetic endowment, while symbolic representation is a cultural invention. Since people cannot progress other than from "biology" to "culture", the enactive stage should precede the symbolic. Developmental tasks are milestones in the process of socialization and enculturation. Since (most) children have to progress according to the paths set by society, there is a fixed order in the succession of developmental tasks.

In addition, what also makes these theories developmental is the fact that the order of developmental states corresponds with a hierarchy of values, e.g. that symbolic representation is more valuable than enactive, and the fact that the order of developmental states is (empirically) irreversible.

Although all developmental theories discussed thus far are topological in the broad sense of the word (they consist of states or "topoi" connected with specific paths), the theories which lack specific logical order will be called "topological" sensu stricto.

In summary, a syntagmatic analysis, based on the extension of the second nominal phrase in "the development of ...", revealed three types of developmental conceptions: a retrospective type starting from the final state and looking back, a prospective type starting from an initial state and looking ahead, and a type which is topological sensu stricto and borrows its internal order from criteria which are not inherent to the developmental states.

SEMANTIC ANALYSIS: PARADIGMATIC TYPE.

In paradigmatic analysis, we shall follow a "Saussurean" path: We start from a specific semantic field, namely the set of meanings related to the concept of change, and investigate how the field is separated into subfields by various terms, such as "development", "change", "evolution", etc. The idea behind this particular type of semantic analysis is that the meaning of a term is neither represented by a prototypical referent alone, nor by the complete set of possible referents, but by the contrast between the set of referents and contexts of use of the term or the one hand, and semantically adjacent fields on the other hand.

Development and Evolution.

In the previous analyses, we have already noted some etymological similarities and distinctions with other terms, such as "unfolding", "unrolling" and "evolution". In view of the evolution-theoretical roots of early developmental psychology, it might be worthwhile to pursue the analysis.
Let us start with some lexical contexts of "evolution", for instance "the evolution of the Darwin finches", "the evolution of the French social system in the eighteenth century", or "the evolution of Matiss's art". It may be noticed that there is no sharp terminological boundary between "evolution" and "development": particularly in the second and third context, "evolution" and "development" are interchangeable terms. In the first context, i: is the accepted technical use of evolution in the biological sense of the word that prevents us from using the term "development". Let us therefore proceed with "evolution" confined to its biological definition.
Some similarities between "evolution" and "development" are striking. First, both can be defined in a prospective as well as in a retrospective sense. For instance, it is possible to regard a species as a conceptually determined final state of an evolutionary process, and then regress along the

evolutionary line until one crosses the boundary of the genus,
for instance. Such an evolutionary line is, by definition,
unbranched. It is also possible to investigate the evolution
of a biological form or function, for instance the principle
of paddle function or fin form. The evolutionary path may be
branched, but it is, by definition, convergent (e.g. paddle
functions in fish or in sea mammals that emerged from totally
different starting points, but converge in largely identical
functional adaptation, namely motion through water by means of
paddle-like organs). A prospectively defined evolutionary line
starts with some point of bifurcation in the evolutionary
tree, and then reconstructs the form of the branching that
followed until extinction or until the present day. Like
development, evolution is an ordered process (see figure 2).

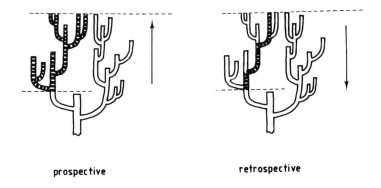

prospective   **retrospective**

Figure 2. An imaginary evolutionary tree, showing the effect of
prospective (left) and retrospective (right) reconstruction of an
evolutionary process.

Any change in the properties of a population or a species is determined by the actual properties of the population or species. Species are not deliberately changed by a creator, who can change any part or aspect he or she wants. This is not to say that evolution is predetermined, though there exists something one might call a "geometry of evolution" (e.g. Thom, 1975) or a "principle of irreversibility" (e.g. Prigogine and Stengers, 1979).

One might get the impression that "evolution" and "development" differ only with regard to the subject of the process - i.e. biological species versus psychological properties- while being similar regarding the abstract form of the process. There is one distinction, however, which might be more like a difference of emphasis than of essence. In principle, evolution processes are open-ended, that is, no state in the process is more stable or better than any other on mere grounds of principle. The stability of a species is based on stability of environment and gene pool, which may be a function of the properties of the species itself. The present state of evolutionary diversification is as transient as any preceding one, although some people like to think that evolution has been created in order to enable man to evolve and become the crown of history's work. The concept of development, however, and the retrospective version in particular, is often associated with a state of development which is more stable than the preceding ones, and is generally associated with a state of maturity. The fact that a concept of maturity is important in development and not in evolution is a direct consequence of the time span and the subject to which both processes respectively refer. Development deals with the individual and its ontogenesis, while evolution deals with a series of individuals related in phylogenesis. Development, interpreted in the sense of ontogenesis, forms the expression of a specific state of phylogenesis or evolution, and, as such, development is confined to the limits set by the form of evolution at a specific moment. For instance, in times of rapid environmental change, some forms of maturity may be more probable than others, viz. those forms of maturity that are optimally adapted to the new environmental conditions. This relationship is not limited to the biological realm, but holds also for the mental and the cognitive, although at those levels the relation becomes extremely complicated.

Development and Learning.

In developmental psychology, one of the classical problems has been the relation between development and learning. Developmentalists, such as Piaget, have emphasized the primacy of the developmental process, defining learning as a function of development, while learning theorists of various convictions have defined development as a terminological convention necessary to keep hold of the accumulating effects of learning (e.g. Inhelder et al., 1974; Gagné, 1966). It is beyond the goal of the present discussion to solve this controversy. Let us investigate whether or not we can discover some conceptual distinctions between both terms which might enable us to get to a better understanding of the boundaries of the aforementioned empirical discussion.

In order to delineate the conceptual distinction between "development" and "learning", that is, in order to determine which part of the semantic field of psychological change the terms are covering, we may compare their respective syntagmatic contexts. The question is: What properties do X_1 and S_1 and X_2 and S_2 take in the expressions "the learning of X_1 by S_1" and "the development of X_2 in S_2".

The first striking distinction lies in the prepositions. They suggest that learning is an activity of S_1, that is, that the relationship between "learning" and S_1 is agentive, while "development" is something that occurs to S_2. That is, the relationship between "development" and S_2 is passive or locative, so to speak. This is not to say that development cannot be the result of an activity carried out by S, such as learning or practicing. But whatever development is the result of, it is not the subject who does the developing. It should

be noted, however, that prepositions might have very limited
value in determining conceptual distinctions between terms,
take for instance the considerable differences between
languages as regards the prepositions used with semantically
identical terms.

Thus, let us turn to some lexical specifications of X and S.
"Logical thinking", for instance, can be used in both
contexts, while "the names of the capitals of Europe" or
"personality" cannot. If logical thinking is used in both
contexts, a difference of emphasis results. The distinction
between developing and learning logical thinking is that, in
the first case the acquisition of the thinking is viewed as
the goal of intentional acts carried out by the learner, such
as paying attention to instructions, doing exercises,
practising, rehearsing, etc. In the second case, the
acquisition is the non-intentional result either of something
that occurs to the subject, such as biological maturation, or
of intentional activities of the subject himself.

Piaget has always very explicitly noticed the apparent
ambiguity of "development" versus "learning" in the context of
logical or formal thinking. Piaget made a distinction between
learning "sensu lato" and learning "sensu stricto", "...the
former embracing cognitive development as a whole and
including the latter, which is always subordinate" (Inhelder
et al., 1974, 1). Piaget has tried to further clarify the
issue by introducing a distinction between simple and
reflective abstraction, which are both forms of cognitive
activity of the subject. Simple abstraction is the extraction
of information from an object, while reflective abstraction
implies that the subject derives the information from a
coordination of the mental actions that he carries out on the
object (Inhelder et al., 1974, 7). The effect of reflective
abstraction is entirely based on the operatory structures of
the child's thought at that very moment. The operatory structures should be viewed as explanative entities located at a
conceptual level beyond the level of intentional action talk.
It is a conceptual error, therefore, to state that the child
infers his or hers abstraction from the operatory structures,

or changes his or hers operatory structures in the same way as
the child intentionally infers information from an object.
The question of whether something that can be learned can
therefore be taught is not easy to answer. Often, the relation
goes the other way round. That is, if something is taught,
that is, if somebody tries to bring about some cognitive
result by deliberate action, and if as apparent result this
something is acquired by the subject of the teaching, then we
say that this something has been learned. Probably, Piaget
would have said that something acquired is more often
apparently the result of teaching than not.
In summary, however, we may state that the first property of a
"learnable" X is that the X is the intentional result of
specific activities carried out on the X by the subject, a
tutor or both.
      Let us now take some further examples, such as "the
learning of the names of the capitals of Europe by my son",
"the development of personality", "the learning of the alfabet
by Ernie from Sesame Street", "the development of the alphabet
in the Etruscans", and, finally, "the development of the
alphabet by the Etruscans". The hypothesis we may test is that
"learnable" X's are X's that are present, in one form or
another, at the beginning of the learning process, and that
the process is directed by form or properties of the X's.
X can be present in the form of examples, a tutor, a book, a
definite image of X in the mind of the learner, etc. If one
speaks about "the learning of the alphabet by Ernie", it is
implied that there is an alphabet and that there is somebody
or something who or which teaches the alphabet, e.g. by
showing one letter after the other and letting Ernie rehearse
the series. It would be quite awkward to speak about "the
development of the alphabet in Ernie", unless one would mean
by "alphabet" something with an autodynamic structure, that
is able to establish itself without deliberately consulting or
following a model. Likewise, it is possible to speak about
"the learning of the names of the capitals by Ernie", but not
about "the development of the names of the capitals in Ernie".
There is no intrinsic structure in the list of names of the

capitals that would enable the list to emerge in a subject as a result of an autonomous mental constructive activity, independent of any model. On the other hand, it is perfectly appropriate to speak about "the development of the alphabet in the Etruscans". That is, it is understood that there has been an Etruscan culture, for instance at 700 BC, which showed a gradual growth of a primitive alphabet toward something which is considered the predecessor of our Latin alphabet.

The term development implies that the increase in the number of letters and the gradual emergence of letter-phoneme relationships is to be considered a process with an internal logic and direction, that there are rational or pragmatic connections between a former and a later stage of the alphabet. It is also possible to speak about "the development of the alphabet by the Etruscans", thereby crediting the Etruscans with the active invention and elaboration of the letter system. In general, it is possible to employ the preposition "by" in development-contexts in order to emphasize that the development would not have occurred without intentional activity of the subject. Unlike learning, however, the developmental event itself is not the activity of the subject. The conceptual break between the activity level and the development level may be compared with the break between the physico-chemical level of activity of the brain, and the level of conscious information processing. It would be a conceptual mistake to say, for instance, that the physical processes are engaged in moving items of knowledge around in the brain.

The reason why "personality" occurs in a developmental but not in a learning context is that, in view of its definition, personality can neither be subject to intentional action, nor can it exist in the form of some external model. Certainly, much of the personality of others is expressed in the form of public behaviour, but then the model is not the personality, but the behaviour, which can be imitated and learned.

Finally, there is also an important point of similarity between learning and development, namely the ordered nature of the process. Learning implies that there is a certain progress in the acquisition of the content or skill to be learned. This progress can be very complicated, e.g. take the form of an inverted U-curve, but nevertheless, the content to be learned must be acquired in a finite amount of time.

The order of the process can be inferred from the definition of the content to be learned. For instance, in the learning of series, as the names of capitals, it does not matter which item is learned first, as long as the number of known items steadily increases, whereas the learning of hierarchically ordered knowledge, such as knowledge consisting of general principles and applications proceeds according to the structure of the knowledge to be learned. This does not imply that the order in which the contents can be presented in a teaching process is fixed. The teacher may begin with the examples, and then go on with the general principle, or he might work the other way round. However, the pupil cannot have learned that some event is an application of a general principle unless the general principle as such is known. The preliminary presentation of examples and applications may facilitate the learning of the general principle, but knowledge of the general principle is required in order to recognize the given examples as applications of the principle. The order of the learning process is reminiscent of the order in retrospective developmental processes: the progress is understood in light of the final state, the learned content. We have seen, however, that, unlike development, learning is characterized by the presence of the final state, in one form or another, from the beginning of the learning process (e.g. in the form of a teacher or a trainer). For instance, when a member of the species Columba Skinneria accidentally turns its head some degrees to the left at the beginning of a training session, the trainer may view this training as a first approximation to a counterclockwise turning of the entire animal, and reinforce the turning. It may also be viewed as a first approximation to a swinging movement of the head, and also be reinforced. Thus, the animal's behaviour does not define its meaning by itself, but is defined in function of its distance from a desired, operantly conditionable final state behaviour.

In conclusion, we might state that at least some of the discussion on the contribution of learning to development and vice versa, rests on conceptual distinctions that must be clarified before the empirical discussion can take place.

A SYSTEM THEORETIC APPROACH.

In the previous paragraphs, we have conceived of development as a temporally and logically ordered set of states. That is, we have implicitly adopted system theory as the most general model for dealing with developmental processes (Van den Daele, 1976). A system can be defined as a collection of variables. When we deal with psychological changes, we use a system consisting of variables that specify psychological properties. Psychological properties are not implicitly mental properties. Some aspects of the environment when they are directly associated with mental and submental events such as books, schools or cars may be considered psychological in the sense of "belonging to a psychological system". A system, viewed as a structure of variables, is embodied in an organism (or a mechanism or anything else a system theorist wants to describe).

In principle, any organism can be described in the form of an infinite number of variables (as in the extreme of defining it in terms of its position to any of the stars in the Cosmos). Such a description is cognitively nonsensical. In order to characterize a system, we have to select a finite number of variables we consider sufficient to distinguish the system from other systems and make it similar to any system of the same class. The selection of variables embodies a specific view of the nature of the system, namely that the chosen variables are necessary and sufficient for characterizing the system. The chosen set of variables, for instance embodied in the form of a specific child, constitutes the set of all possible states of the system. A state of the system is the set of values of all variables at a specific moment t_i. The variables can take various forms, e.g. the form of a nominal scale, describing a property as either present or absent, or an interval scale, as with intelligence.

The Principle of Developmental Order.

Suppose that we define a psychological system in the form of two variables. The first variable is the average number of different words spoken every five minutes, while the second variable is the total time spent at looking in a picture book every five minutes. Although these variables seem rather ridiculous, they can be used to specify the behavioural state of every possible subject, for instance children between two and four years of age. For instance, if the child sleeps, both variables take the value zero. We may now agree on a measuring interval, i.e. the amount of time between two successive determinations of the value of the variables. The interval may equal five minutes, one week, one month or a year. The ordered set of measuring points constitutes the so-called "line of behaviour" of the system (see Ashby, 1952/1970 for further details). It is obvious that development must be a line of behaviour, but it is also obvious that not every line of behaviour will suffice(learning too, must be a line of behaviour, but it is clearly a different one). The only order we have in a line of behaviour is a temporal order, but that is not enough. We want to know whether there is also an "intrinsic" or logical order in the line, which is a requirement if the line should represent a developmental process. Finding the logical order of such a line encompasses nothing more than providing an explanation for the direction of the line.

If we would measure the value of the variables every five minutes, it is highly probable that we would not find a series with a cognitively penetrable sort of order. Put differently, given a state S_p at t_i, the probability for any of the available states in the system to occur at t_{i+1} or t_{i+2} is equal. We might explain the behaviour of the system by stating that the relationship between the value of both variables on

the one hand, and two successive measuring points on the other
hand is random. If we would take a one month interval, that
is, if the value of the variable would be the average value
over a period of one month, we would very probably observe a
more systematic connection. That is, we will probably see a
more or less parallel increase in the value of both variables,
which in plain language means that children who spend much
time looking in books use many different words and vice versa,
and use more different words and look longer in books as they
grow older.

Put differently, given a state S_p at t_i, the probability that
a specific state S_q will occur at t_{i+1} is much higher than the
probability that any other of the states available in the
system will occur. That is, order is defined in statistical
terms. In order to arrive at something which resembles a more
or less stable line of behaviour, with only some points of
bifurcation, the conditional probability that a specific state
will follow given the occurrence of another should be 100 %
for the absolute majority of states in the system, unless the
number of measuring points, i.e. possible points of state
transition, is extremely small. For instance, if any possible
state would be followed by either of two possible successors,
after 10 state transitions there are 1024 different possible
states. Thus, in order to arrive at a set of transitions
characterized by cognitively satisfactory order, we should
either select extremely stable variables, or define the
distance between the measuring points. The distance can thus
be so defined as to cancel the effect of "noise" by making the
interval over which a possible state transition is defined
sufficiently large. A third possibility is that the variables
used show a minimum number of values. The least possible
number is two, i.e. the values associated with a nominal
variable. A nominal variable defines a property as either
present or absent. The effect of long measuring intervals or
binary variables is the same, namely a considerable decrease
in the number of states available in the system.

The existing developmental theories employ any of the previous
methods. The theory may be based on a sort of growth

principle, which implies very high conditional probabilities for a specific S_q to succeed a predecessor S_p. S_q characterizes a state in which the magnitude of a certain property is higher than in S_p. Learning theories are typical examples of models based on such growth models. It may be questioned, however, whether we would still call them developmental theories. Second, a theory may separate its measuring points far enough to cancel the effect of unpredictable transitions, which are often typical of periods of transition following relative stability. For instance, children might have made a choice for a specific profession or religion at a very early age. In early adolescence, however, they start to actively experiment with these choices, resulting in unstable commitments and unpredictable choices. Only in late adolescence does the commitment again become stabilized. In such a case, one should compare commitments in childhood with those in late adolescence, and not compare two successive moments in early adolescence. The prolongation of the measuring interval often coincides with a reduction of a variable to two values. For instance, in the commitments case, there is a variable "active exploration", which has a negative value in childhood (no active exploration of one's social commitments has taken place) and a positive value in early and late adolescence. In order to arrive at a three stage model covering commitment in childhood, early adolescence and late adolescence, one should add a second binary variable, namely commitment, which has a positive value in childhood and late adolescence, and a negative value in early adolescence (see for instance Bosma, 1985).

In summary, we have seen that one of the main distinctive features of the concept of development - order - is a statistical property of a system. A developmental system, therefore, is either a system with very high transition probabilities, or a system defined over state transition intervals which are sufficiently long as to cancel the effects of noise, or finally, a system defined in terms of a very limited number of possible states.

In the artificial system we started with as an example, we

shall probably find that the system arrives at a sort of
equilibrium state, that is a state which does not change
significantly over time, and, if change occurs, the system
will drift back to the equilibrium state. The equilibrium
state is achieved when the increase in the vocabulary is nil
or stable, as is the increase in interest in picture books.
However, if our system would be defined with the variable
"factual knowledge" and the variable "interest in books in
general", we will probably find that there is no such
empirical equilibrium point. As long as the system exists, it
continues changing. The former type, with a relatively stable
final state, may provide the basis for a retrospective theory
of development, while the second, lacking a stable final
state, corresponds with a prospective theory. However, since a
system is not a given of nature, but a deliberate selection of
defining variables, one is free to search for a group of
variables characterized by equilibrium, or a group of
variables where no such equilibrium occurs.
Differentiation theories, which are particular instances of
prospectively defined theories, can be specified by employing
a separate binary variable for any differentiation step. For
instance, a particular theory might describe development as a
process starting with a differentiation between subject and
object during the first month of life, then proceeding with a
differentiation between social and non-social objects at three
months, a differentiation between familiar and unfamiliar
social objects at eight months, and so on. Up to this point,
the theory needs three binary variables, namely (+/- subject
object differentiation), (+/- social), (+/- familiar). In the
present theory, the order of the state transitions is
conceptually determined, that is, it is conceptually
impossible, for instance, to distinguish a familiar from an
unfamilar social object, unless one has learnt to distinguish
a social object from a non-social one (see also Morton, in
this volume). It is not conceptually necessary, however, that
a differentiation occurs at a specific age, for instance that
familiar from non-familiar persons are distinguished at the
age of eight months. In view of the conceptual necessity of

the developmental order, differentiation theories have a very important property in common with retrospective theories, namely the fact that it is possible to reconstruct the preceding developmental process starting from the definition of a succeeding state. The difference with the retrospective theory, however, is that in a differentiation theory no state can be conceived of as the final one, in the sense of being the state that will no longer change.

The concept of development has two important connotations which are directly related to the problem of developmental order, namely irreversibility, and increasing complexity. Irreversibility implies that there is no way back in development, although there are some theories, such as the Freudean theory or differentiation theories, that permit regression or partial reversibility. In principle, learning theories subscribe to the possibility of reversibility: what can be learned, can be unlearned. However, learning theories are not theories of development. The concept of increasing - complexity implies that development is not mere change, but progressive change, change towards a state of higher complexity of whatever property that is under development. It may be questioned how both properties can be accounted for in a system theoretic framework, describing a developmental state as a set of values of variables defining the developing system. Since order has been defined as probability, irreversibility and increasing complexity too must be defined in similar terms. In a simple graph consisting of only a few nodes, e.g. a graph consisting of four or five nodes, reversibility is not improbable, and it is the less improbable the fewer the number of states following the initial state. It is highly unlikely, however, that a developmental system might consist of so few states as four or five (i.e. two variables with two or three values). Developmental systems consist of a very large number of variables, although most developmental theories may lack a clear definition of the kind of variables required. In general, they are confined to only a few variables, for instance, a few developmental stages, which summarize the values of numerous subordinate variables.

Theories of skill learning are more explicit about the number,
nature and structure of the variables defining a specific
state of skill controll, e.g. the various motor chains,
concepts, relations, rules etc. In a system consisting of many
variables, it is a matter of simple statistics that the exact
-or even approximate- reversion of the developmental path is
extremely improbable. That is, there is no information in
available the system on the path, the line of behaviour, taken
in the past. However, this simple statistical explanation is
rather trivial. Developmental systems are highly ordered, they
are not just loose collections of variables which may take any
random value. The concept of increasing complexity in
development implies that developing systems proceed from less
to more order. Reversibility, then, would mean that the system
is able to regress from more to less order. Thus, the
explanation of irreversibility and of increasing order in
development are linked. Let us first try to provide a simple
statistical definition of order in a system of n binary
variables. In such a system, it should be possible to
characterize the conditional probability of each logically
possible state, i.e of each logically possible combination of
values of each variable, given a specific value of a variable
v_i. If all logically possible states are equally probable,
then the system is as far from (statistical) order as
possible. Put differently, we might say that the "entropy" of
the system is maximal (note that the present concept of
entropy resembles the "entropy" of physics and mathematical
information theory only at the intuitive level). If we define
our idiosyncratic entropy as

$$E = 1 - \frac{1}{\Sigma(p_i^2) \cdot n}$$

then maximal entropy (or equilibrium) equals 0, while minimal
entropy (or order), i.e. when one possible state has a
probability of occurence of 1., approaches 1. It is very
probable that natural systems that are characterized by a high
amount of order in the present sense, are highly structured.
That is, the variables from the system form nested groups,

sub- and superstructures which emerged by virtue of a highly temporally ordered process, plainly, a developmental process. In nature, all highly ordered systems are under the constant threat of entropy increase (a wooden barn which is not well maintained decays and finally collapses). In the system, the following may happen: either the system maintains its level of order, or increases it, or shifts to less order, either by the reverse of the path it took to arrive at its present level of order, or by any other path. Since the path which led to its present level of order is extremely specific, it is also extremely unlikely that the system would be able to follow the reverse path (a principle which is nicely illustrated in a labyrinth). Thus, if regression to lower order is allowed, then it will very probably follow a path which bypassess the original developmental path and which very quickly leads to a very low level of order (e.g. it takes much more energy to construct a barn than it takes to destroy it). Thus, if systems of a very high order are possible anyhow, then they should be structured so that they do not allow increasing entropy (i.e. decreasing order) to occur. Thus, the system should undo the ever present activity of entropy increase by changing its state, which, by definition, equals either an increasing or an equal level of order. If the system is highly structured, it is highly probable that any change which is not a regression towards less order, is a step towards more order (simply because the number of alternative states of the system which are characterized by an equal amount of statistical order is much smaller than the number of states with higher or lower amount of order, and because states of lower order are not allowed). Put differently, it requires much more energy to maintain the same level of order than to change it. The very fact that systems with a high amount of statistical order exist, implies that they are obliged to do only one thing, namely increase their level of order, i.e. become always more complex (these ideas will sound rather familiar to readers acquainted with Prigogine's work; see figure 3).

In summary, psychological systems, such as knowledge about the structure of the world, or personality, are multi-variable

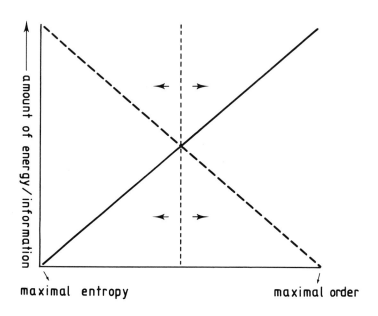

Figure 3. A diagram showing the amount of energy and/or information
required to increase amount of order (dashed fat line) or to increase
the amount of entropy (continuous fat line). Systems above a specific
level of order tend to increase order, systems below this level tend
to increase entropy. The relations between the variables are highly
simplified.

systems which are very far from statistical entropy or
equilibrium. Like all such systems, they are obliged to follow
a centrifugal path away from equilibrium, i.e. to
continually increase in degree of complexity. However, like
every system in nature, there will be a time when the second
law of thermodynamics finally wins, and they very quickly
reverse to a low level of order (simply stated, every complex
system increases its complexity untill the powers of decay
finally win and it dies).

The Principle of Developmental Explanation.

In the preceding section, we discussed the principle of order in a system. In general, we found that, if the system changes its state, the principle of order implies that the successive state should be predictable. Whe have not questioned why the system should change its present state, or why the predictable successor state, if any, should occur. That is, we have not asked the question of developmental explanation. The definition of "explanation" I shall propose is the following: to explain a developmental process implies that one has a rule or principle that automatically generates the successive developmental state, given a set of properties of the preceding state. By successive developmental state is understood the state that occurs at t_{i+1}, giving that the preceding state has occured at t_i. The latter constraint is important in that we should also be able to explain why the system eventually does not change its state, i.e. why the system, being in state S_p at t_i remains in that state at t_{i+1}. What we are currently aiming at is the explanation of developmental succession, that is, the actual occurrence of state change or stability, not of developmental order as such, that is, the order in which states will occur, given that a state change has taken place.

Explanations of the latter sort may be quite trivial. For instance, in the example of the number of words/time spent on looking in picture books, we might explain development by the rule that the magnitude of both variables increases with a certain amount every month. Such an explanation is not cognitively satisfying, since we use the variable that should be explained as the explaining factor itself. This is against the general principle that the number of explaining variables in the universe of possible systems of any sort should be as small as possible. Thus, in order to explain the process in the two variable system, we shall have to extend the number of variables specifying the system. It is only by doing so that we might be able to cover a subset of explanative factors that are common to a very extensive set of variables, e.g.

variables including book reading, number of words, knowledge
of facts, personality, moral judgement, etc. The reason behind
this principle is a simple rule of class inclusion
probability, stating that in a universe consisting of n
elements and m classes, the probability that any two classes
have an element in common increases as the number of elements
in each class increases. In system theory, there is a distinction between variables defining the system sensu stricto,
and variables defining the environment of the system. The
environment is a source of input to the system, and thus, of
possible system change. The environment is also a receptor of
outputs of the system.

Making a distinction between system and environment
implies, among others, that the set of variables definining
the system is subdivided according to their respective
distances to the environment.
At least, there has to be a set of transducer variables, that
is variables that covary with certain changes in the
environment. The sensory systems, such as vision and audition,
are examples of transducer variables: the state of the opened
eye, for instance, covaries within certain limits with the
structure of light projected onto the retina. If we define
development as a process of state change in a system, the
transducer variables are clearly not implied, given their
contingency on the state of the environment.
On the other hand, the system will contain some variables that
are maximally remote from the environment, that will not be
affected by any state of the environment except via physical
destruction of the system itself. Let us call these the core
variables.
Finally, there is a set of variables that will change
according to the aforementioned principles of logical and
empirical order. Those are the variables that constitute the
developmental process. The state of the developmental variables might be affected by the state of the transducer
variables, providing information from the environment, on the
one hand, and the by state of the central, "encapsulated" core
variables on the other hand. Developmental systems can differ

as to the amount of influence exerted by either of these variable types. In general, the stronger the effect of the transducer variables, the lesser the effect of the core variables, and vice versa.

In order to explain developmental processes, we should make a distinction between two kinds of properties of developmental states.

First, a developmental state can either be open or closed: the state, defined as a specific set of variables, is either sensitive or not to properties of variables from outside the system, more precisely to properties of the environment. By definition, the states of the transducers are open, while the states of the central core of the system are closed.

Second, a developmental state can be either internally stable or unstable. If internally unstable it changes as a mere consequence of passing time. If internally stable, it can only change if affected by an external source. These properties of the developmental system also apply to the environment. That is, the environment may be open or closed to influences exerted by the system, and it may be internally stable or unstable.

If we combine the dimensions "environment-developmental system", "open-closed" and "internally stable-unstable", we obtain a 2x2x2 matrix in which we can locate all possible developmental theories, according to the principles of explanation they employ (figure 4).

Let us first discuss developmental theories according to their views on the nature of subject-variables (i.e. the non-environmental variables). Although I suggested that theories can be located in the matrix, it is more correct to say that it is the theory's conception of a specific topic, for instance the acquisition of concepts, or of grammar, for which the matrix offers a framework. We have seen that every theory discerns open states (the transducer states) as well as closed states (the core states). It has also been stated that development happens to states of an intermediary position, i.e. neither to transducer states nor to core states. Thus, the question is how much of the concept of development as

P. van Geert

	states are open	states are closed
states are unstable	*Piaget 's theory*	*Nativist theory (Fodor)*
states are stable	*Learning theory*	–

SUBJECT

	states are open	states are closed
states are unstable	*Cultural Historical School (Wygotsky)* *Transactional th.*	–
states are stable	*Piaget 's theory*	*Nativist theory (Fodor)*

ENVIRONMENT

Figure 4. A 2x2x2 matrix representing the position of various theories with regard to the open-vs.-closed and instable-vs.-stable nature of states of the subject-vs.-environment system.

described by a specific theory, is based either on core or on transducer state properties (or, stated in plain language how much is innate, how much is learned). As an example, let us take the development of concepts according to various theories.

In Fodor's view (see Atkinson, this volume), all of the

concepts that can possibly be acquired should be represented in the form of core variables, i.e. they should be innate or subject to maturation. That is, the variable "potentially acquired concepts" is closed, and, to the degree it is subject to maturation, internally unstable (an example of a concept which is subject to maturation might be the concept of "sexual partner" which might evolve around the onset of adolescence). The variable "actually acquired concepts" is semi-closed. It is heavily constrained by the potential concepts residing in the core. These centrally stored concepts determine which transduceable instance of information will act as a "trigger" to the actualization of a potential concept. Thus, from all the information available through the transducers, it is only an extremely limited part that has actual developmental effect. Moreover, the potential triggering value of information is determined by the order in which the potential concepts are made available by the central core (e.g. the concept-of-dog-triggering-information is made available before the concept-of-poodle-triggering-information). Although the appearance of a triggering experience might be necessary for the actualization of a potential concept, the concept itself is under-determined by the bare content of the experience. The fact that seeing a dog causes the concept of "dog" to become manifest, is in no way determined by the properties of the dog seen. In another species, the dog might have caused the concept of "food" to appear, or the concept of "motion". In this specific sense, the state of the variable "actually acquired concepts" is internally unstable, i.e. the change is caused by an internal mechanism which needs only a triggering mechanism to be set in motion. The state of the variable becomes internally stable if all potential concepts have been actualized, which, if there is only a very limited number of potential concepts, can occur very soon. If a theory would exist claiming that all concepts are innate and actually present at the beginning of life, such a theory would describe the states of the variable "acquired concepts" as internally stable and closed. Let us compare the previous conception with Piaget's.

In Piaget's theory, the core contains very general biological adaptation principles, such as accomodation and assimilation (both the sides of the adaptation process), and strong principles of internal structuration and equilibration of the future cognitive system. In addition, the core contains the species-specific outfit of the initial state, for instance, a number of reflex-like uncoordinated activities. These initial activities exert a specific influence upon the environment, which brings about specific information made available through the transducers. It is this specific information, born from an interaction between the environment and the subject, that will change the contents (the initial reflexlike activities) upon which these activities were based. These new mental contents bring about new actions in the environment, which causes new events to occur, again changing the contents, and so forth. The variable "acquired concepts" stands in an intermediary position between open and closed. It is clearly open to environmental influence. The nature of the influence, the information on which change is based, however, depends on the present state of mental development, because the information is brought about by the subject's actions and only by these actions. Mental activity, however, is not limited to actions in the environment. There is also very important internal activity going on, namely the activity of internal structuring and restructuring of contents. In this sense, the states of the variable "acquired concepts" is internally unstable. It should be noted, however, that the instability depends on the point in development actually reached. The cognitive system strives for equilibrium, that is, internal stability. This stability is achieved at the end of each developmental stage. However, before the final stage of development is reached, the stage of formal operations, the stability at the end of each stage is a form of meta-instability: as soon as a stage-specific type of cognitive system is in equilibrium, a fundamental restructuring of the system takes place, starting with a state of maximal desequilibrium, that is, internal instability. The nature of the instability lies in the interaction between the state of the system, and the properties of the environment created by that system. As far as the basic structural properties of concepts are concerned, there is a state of development which is internally stable, namely the final state of formal operations (see also the chapter "The structure of developmental theories", in this volume).

Let us finally discuss a learning theoretical approach of concept development, for instance Klausmeier's theory of concept learning (Klausmeier, 1976). Learning a concept is a matter of following a fixed path. It starts with the recognition of identical appearances of an object, then proceeds with the recognition of different appearances of an object as one single object. Next, common properties of different objects are used as a basis for classification, and finally, the common property is explicitly recognized and named. The core of the mental system should possess some general operative principles, such as the ability to recognize similarity. The state of the variable "acquired concepts" is open. There is no intrinsic limitation to the nature and number of the concepts that can be acquired. The only limitations are caused by the learning process required. For instance, if the learner is at the first stage, he or she is not sensitive to information typical of the third or fourth stage. Naturally, if some concepts logically require others, the logical order will determine the possible effect of information associated with the various concept levels. The order of the developmental state transitions is not determined by internal principles - except for the principles of the learning process itself - but only by the properties of the world, instantiated in the logical or empirical order of the concepts. The state of the variable "acquired concepts" is also internally stable. If no information from the environment is transduced, no concepts will emerge by themselves, or no change in the set of acquired concepts will occur, except maybe for the process of forgetting.

The open-closed and stable-unstable dichotomies may also be applied to the environment, that is, a set of world variables specified by the set of subject variables (the environment can be defined as the set of variables affected by and affecting the subject).

If we take concept development as an example once more, we may observe that the influence of the subject on the environment is not an explicit developmental factor neither in nativist theories, such as Fodor's, nor in learning theories. New learning opportunities are only provided if the environment changes by itself, i.e. if it is internally unstable.

In Piaget's theory, the concept of activity of the subject plays a crucial role. Activity implies that the subject can change the environment, i.e. that the environment is open. The environment is internally stable -from a developmental point of view- in that the properties of the environment to which cognitive development is sensitive are stable over generations and cultures. Probably, there is one exception to this general principle, namely the properties necessary for the construction of formal operations, which do not occur in all cultures and times.

Sameroff's transactional theory of development employs the concept of an open, internally unstable local environment (e.g. Sameroff, 1975). By local environment I mean the child's family and peers, i.e. the people with whom there is developmentally relevant face-to-face interaction. The basic idea of the theory is that the child changes the caretaker as much as the caretaker changes the child.

Finally, the Cultural Historical School of Soviet psychology provides a conception of an environment which is open and internally unstable in a very fundamental sense. The activities of generations of subjects change the cultural environment, cultural environments determine the course of development of new generations (see for instance Vedder, in this volume). This cultural environment is internally unstable, not in the sense of labile, but in the sense of pos-sessing its own dynamics of change and construction.

It is easy to see that there is a certain connection between the nature of the environmental state properties, and the retrospective or prospective nature of the developmental theory. Theories with a conception of the environment as a fundamentally open and unstable structure are incompatible with a retrospective view. Since the environment determines the course of development, and since the environment itself is subject to fundamental change, there can be no fixed final state of development. Development must be an open-ended process. It is only the universal, i.e culture independent aspect of development, if any, that can be understood in the form of a retrospective theory.

SUMMARY.

What everybody seems to know about development is that it is a process taking place over a considerably long time, for instance the life span, or the period between birth and adulthood; that it is concerned with qualitative changes; that it is different from learning, although learning cannot be missed; and that it contains a certain maturational component. In the present chapter, some forms of analysis have been tried, in order to conceptually clarify the common notion, which is not very remote from the concept of development as it is, often implicitly, employed in developmental theories. The present analyses drew heavily upon types of ordinary language analysis, which is only acceptible in view of the non-formal character of the concept of development in current theories.

To begin with, we have seen that the etymological meaning of development, unrolling, was optimally compatible with traditional preformationist theories of qualitative change. The first form of semantic analysis, the syntagmatic type, showed that there is a conception of development as a looking back, starting from a point which is conceived of as a final state, and reconstructing the preceding process from this particular point of view (the retrospective conception). There is a second conception which views development in the form of a looking ahead, starting from an initial state, and following the changes that may occur. In both conceptions, two aspects were of central importance, namely the nature of the developing entity, and the logical order of developmental steps. It was found that both aspects stood in an close relationship. The aspects of length of time span, and the qualitative nature of the developmental changes, were not found to be of serious importance.

In the second type of semantic analysis, the paradigmatic form, "development" was compared with "evolution" and "learning". It is especially the comparison with learning that is of theoretical importance. It was found that, apart from the empirical discussion on the relation between learning and development, some conceptual distinctions between both terms could be discerned, which enabled us to separate empirically decidable issues from mere semantic confusion.

In the system theoretic analysis, we separated the question of developmental order from that of developmental explanation. In a system defined by a set of variables, order was defined in statistical terms, translating order, among which the irreversibility of developmental processes, in terms of probabilities of state transition between 1 and 0. We have seen that qualitative changes reflect specific definitory choices, for instance the choice for binary instead of modal variables. The choice for a variable of a specific nature is less a matter of nature than of man: in order to arrive at cognitively satisfactory orders of state transition, developmental psychologists have to reduce the internal differentiation of their variables to a very high degree. The same holds for the time span covered by a developmental process. Developmental order that is perceptible to our feeble minds will emerge only after we have separated developmental transitions by sufficiently large temporal gaps. There is no logical necessity, therefore, for the fact that development is of life span size. Short, ordered mental processes that show the defining characteristics are developmental in the true sense of the word (these short term developmental processes have been termed "Aktualgenese" in the German litterature since Sander's introduction in 1928, or "microgenesis", according to Heinz Werner; Koops, 1981). The time span occupied by a developmental process is determined by its subject, and by the requirement that a developmental process should be ordered in the defined sense.

Finally, we have discussed the principle of explanation in developmental psychology in system theoretic terms. Explanation was conceived of as the search for generative rules, i.e. rules for generating correct predictions of state transitions. These rules drew upon three properties of developmental states, namely their open versus closed character, their internal instability versus stability, and their subject- versus environmental nature. Several theories dealing with concept development, have been located according to the explanative principles they apply.

Although specific theories have been employed in order to illustrate specific developmental concepts, e.g. the retrospective and the prospective one, it should be noted that most theories are probably more than the representatives of a single type of developmental concept. In Freud's theory, for instance, we observed a topological component sensu stricto, and a retrospective component. Differentiation theories in particular, are often difficult to localize on the prospective-retrospective scale. This is not to say, however, that it is impossible to catch the essence of a theory in the form of a specific developmental conception.

Finally, what does an analysis of the concept of development contribute to the issue of theory building in developmental psychology? Although it is very difficult to predict what such an analysis will actually contribute, let me try to say what it might contribute. Ideally, a conceptual analysis might show that some of the discussion among developmental theorists is a matter of different conceptualization of development. It should show in how far different conceptualizations are allowed without touching the boundary of empirical test. It should also show whether and how different conceptualizations of development can be transformed into each other, and which empirical domains are more naturally related to one conception than to another. Finally, the conceptual analysis might show that some, if not the majority, of the differences and distinctions between current developmental theories are more the reflection of the many-sided and complex nature of the developing mind itself, than of the alleged scientific weakness of developmental psychology.

REFERENCES.

Ashby, W.R. (1952/1970). Design for a brain. The origin of adaptive behaviour. London: Chapman and Hall.

Atkinson, M. (1986). Learning and models of development. In P. van Geert (ed.), Theory building in developmental psychology. Amsterdam: North Holland.

Bosma, H.A. (1985). Identity development in adolescence: Coping with commitments. Unpublished doctoral dissertation. State University of Groningen.

Bower, T.G.R. (1979). Human Development. San Francisco: Freeman.

Bruner, J.S. (1964). The course of cognitive growth. American Psychologist, 19, 1-15.

Buck-Morss, S. (1975). Socio-economic bias in Piaget's theory and its implications for cross-cultural studies. Human development, 18, 35-49.

Gagné, R.M. (1977). The conditions of learning (3rd ed.). New York: Holt, Rinehart and Winston.

Haeckel, E. (1866) Generelle Morphologie der Organismen. (2 volumes). Berlin.

Havighurst, R.J. (1953). Human development and education. New York: Longmans, Green & Co.

Inhelder, B., Sinclair, H. & Bovet, M. (1974). Learning and the development of cognition. London: Routledge and Kegan Paul.

Klausmeier, H.J. (1976). Conceptual development during the school years. In J.T. Levin and V.L. Allen (Eds.), Cognitive learning in children: Theories and strategies. New York: Academic Press.

Mangan, J. (1978). Piaget's theory and cultural differences. The case for value-based models of cognition. Human Development, 21, 170-189.

Morton, J (1986). Developmental contingency modelling. In P.

van Geert (Ed.), Theory building in develomental psychology. Amsterdam: North Holland.

Nagel, E. (1957). Determinism and development. In D. B. Harris (Ed.), The concept of develoment. Minneapolis, University of Minnesota Press.

Olshewsky. T.M. (1974). On competence and performance. Linguistics, 122, 47-62.

Piaget, J. (1937). La construction du réèl chez l'enfant. Neuchatel: Delachaux et Niestle.

Prigogine, I. & Stengers, I. (1979). La nouvelle alliance: Metamorphose de la science. Paris: Gallimard.

Sameroff, A. (1975). Transactional models in early social relations. Human Development, 18, 65-79.

Spelke. E.S. (1985). Perception of unity, persistence and identity: Thoughts on infants' conceptions of objects. In J. Mehler and R. Fox (Eds.), Neonate cognition: Beyond the blooming buzzing confusion (pp. 89-113). Hillsdale (NJ): Lawrence Erlbaum.

Thom, R. (1975). Structural stability and morphogenesis: An outline of a general theory of models. Reading (Mass.): Benjamin.

Thomae, H. (1959). Entwicklungsbegriff und Entwicklungstheorie. In H. Thomae (Ed.), Handbuch der Psychology, Band 3: Entwicklungspsychologie. Gottingen: Hogrefe.

Trautner, H.M. (1978). Lehrbuch der Entwicklungspsychologie (band 1). Gottingen: Hogrefe.

Van den Daele, L.D. (1976) Formal models of development. In K.F. Riegel and J.A. Meacham (Eds.), The developing individual in a changing world: volume 1. The Hague: Mouton.

Van Geert, P. (1983). The development of perception, cognition and language. A theoretical approach. London: Routledge and Kegan Paul.

Van Geert, P. (1986). The steucture of developmental theories. In P. van Geert (Ed.), Theory building in developmental psychology. Amsterdam: North Holland.

Van Geert, P (in press). Sociocultural reproduction and individual mental development. Cognitive Systems.

Vedder, P. (1986). Development and social expectations. In P. van Geert (Ed.), Theory building in developmental psychology. Amsterdam: North Holland.

Weimer, W.B. (1973). Psycholinguistics and Plato's paradoxes of the Meno. American Psychologist, 15-33.

Werner, H. (1948). Comparative psychology of mental development. New York: International Universities Press.

Werner, H. (1957). The concept of development from a comparative and organismic point of view. In D.B. Harris (Ed.), The concept of development. Minneapolis: University of Minnesota Press.

Wohlwill, J.E. (1973). The study of behavioral development. New York: Academic Press.

Theory Building in Developmental Psychology
P.L.C. van Geert (editor)
© Elsevier Science Publishers B.V. (North-Holland), 1986

2

The Structure of Developmental Theories

Paul van Geert

First, a brief review of three methods for analysing the structure of developmental theories is presented. A fourth method, describing structure in terms of an underlying "grammar", is introduced. The two main components of the grammar are, first, rules that generate ordered sets of developmental state successions, and, second, rules that specify the conditions and forms of state transitions. A few examples of the analysis of the underlying grammars in prospective and retrospective developmental theories are discussed. It is demonstrated, that the analysis of structure may lead to the building of new theories, or the completion of existing ones.

As a starting point for an analysis of the structure of developmental theories, we might take a look at the various models of the structure of scientific theories in general (Suppe, 1973). In the traditional "Received View" analysis, theories are divided into three components. First, a theory contains a theoretical-logical language, consisting of strictly theoretical terms and logical operators. Second, the theory contains an observational language used to describe observed events and facts. Finally, a finite set of correspondence rules is defined, connecting theoretical statements and observed states of affairs. The main disadvantage of the Received View-analysis is that it requires theories to possess maximal coherence and logical form. Few, if any, theories in the social sciences, including developmental theories, can meet these strict requirements.

The alternative "semantic" forms of analysis (including the "Weltanschauungen"-analysis) conceive of theories as ways

to construct specific images of a reality domain. The image
should conform to requirements of optimal conceptual
coherence, meaningfulness, etc. Because semantic analysis
deals with logically "weak" structures, it is particularly
appropriate for analyzing psychological (and developmental)
theories.

Both the "Received View" and the Semantic Analysis view
conceive of theories as structures of statements. A theory can
be conceived of also as a reserach programme (e.g. Lakatos) or
a programme for social action (e.g. Holzkamp). In the present
article, I shall follow the more traditional view of the
theory as a structure of statements, or a speech and discourse
form.

The aims one tries to achieve with an analysis of the
structure of developmental theories are the following. First,
the analysis should define the the concept of (mental,
behavioural) development employed in the theory at hand.
Second, the analysis should make clear what the nature of the
differences between developmental theories is, i.e. what are
the basic elements that distinguish developmental theories
frome one another. Third, the analysis should reveal the
underlying "architecture" of the theory, that is the set of
underlying rules and principles on which the construction and
form of the theory is based.

The present article will be devoted mainly to an approach
that tries to discover the underlying architecture, or, more
precisely, the "grammar" of the theories of development, i.e.
the set of rules and rule-like methods necessary for
generating theory-specific statements, either existing in the
actual form of a specific theory or not. By way of
introduction to this specific approach, I shall discuss three
existing methods of analysis, namely the analysis of
arguments, of underlying world-views, and of underlying
logical state networks.

DEVELOPMENTAL THEORIES AS NETWORKS OF ARGUMENTS.

According to Toulmin (1958), a scientific theory consists of a network of arguments. Arguments are structures consisting of interlocking statements with distinct functions. The basic functional element is the "claim" (C) made in the argument. In principle, each structural element of an argument, such as the "backing" or "data", can be viewed as a claim on a lower level, which, in its turn, is the basic functional unit of a (subordinate) argument.

Bromley (1970) has applied the analysis of arguments to "disengagement theory". In order to provide a sketch of the analysis of arguments, I shall present Bromley's analysis of the most general argument contained in this theory. The basic "claim" (C) of the theory is that "society and most individuals are preparing in advance for the consequences of changes which occur later in life" (Bromley, 1970, p. 96). Since the truth of this claim has not been sufficiently empirically supported, we must add the "qualifier" (Q) "apparently" (p. 96). The basic "data" (D) that support this claim consist of the fact that "society and most individuals engage in various activities which have age-related consequences in late life" (p. 96). The "warrant" (W), i.e. the statement that refers to a license to infer Q(C) from D, states that (by preparing for the consequences of changes in late life) "society tries to provide for the systematic replacement of individuals, and individuals try to maintain good living standards" (p. 96). The "backing" (B) that provides support for the previous warrant is that W will occur "on account of the self-maintaining mechanisms that operate in large, complex human communities" (p. 96). The final element of the argument consists of a "rebuttal" (R), which, in the present case, might take the following form: (disengagement in the present form will not occur) in societies with a strong gerontocratic structure. Each element of the basic argument of disengagement theory can be transformed into a set of statements at lower levels of generality. Furthermore, each statement can be taken as a claim, which on its turn is based on specific data, warrants, etc. As a result, the analysis of the argumentational structure of a developmental theory will lead to a complex, heterarchical structure of interlocking arguments.

The complexity of the resulting analysis is the main disadvantage of the method. A second disadvantage of the analysis of arguments is that it will not reveal the structural distinctions between theories. Irrespective of whether the theory deals with development, pathology, physics, biology, or whatever remaining subject one might think of, the basic structure of the argument remains identical. The method does not reveal the basic structural difference between developmental and non-developmental theories. That is, the first aim of theory analysis cannot be achieved.

By revealing the basic, underlying argument of a theory, the analysis of arguments conforms to the second aim of theory analysis, i.e. to make explicit what distinguishes one theory from another.

Whether or not the analysis of arguments has achieved the third aim, i.e. revealing the underlying architecture of the theory at issue, depends on one's definition of "underlying architecture". If we state, as Toulmin and Bromley do, that all scientific theories have the same underlying structure, i.e. the structure of arguments, then the present form of analysis has (tautologically) achieved the third aim. If, however, by "underlying structure" we mean the content-specific structure of the theory, i.e. the underlying structural principles that make a developmental theory a theory on development, the analysis of argument is clearly not appropriate for our present purposes.

Finally, the basic advantage of the analysis of arguments is that it shows how and to which degree the basic claim of the theory is supported either by fact or by faith.

DEVELOPMENTAL THEORIES AS EXPRESSIONS
OF DISTINCT WORLD VIEWS.

The idea that world views are mutually incompatible
models of reality, based on specific "basic metaphors" has
been advanced by Pepper (1942). Although Pepper has
distinguished four world views ("world hypotheses"), only two
have been applied to developmental psychology, namely the
organismic and the mechanistic world view, based on the
metaphor of the organism and the metaphor of the machine (cf.
Langer, 1969; Reese and Overton, 1970; Sameroff, 1972; Overton
and Reese, 1973; Reese, 1973; Baltes et al., 1977; Kuhn, 1978;
Lerner, 1978; Kitchener, 1982; Overton, 1984).

Reese and Overton (Reese and Overton, 1970; Overton and
Reese, 1973) define mechanistic versus organismic
developmental theories, first, on the basis of four conceptual
oppositions which form the hard conceptual core of either
family of theories; and second, on the basis of the models of
causality employed by the theories. According to Overton
(1984), the mechanistic and organismic families of theories
form two different "research programmes" in the sense of
Lakatos and Laudan. The hard conceptual core and the
conception of causality are associated with a specific
heuristics, i.e. a set of questions, types of question
formation and methods of investigation, which constitute the
pragmatic, research programme aspect of the respective world
views applied to psychological development.

Mechanistic models, such as the learning theoretical
model, are characterized by elementarism, the primacy of
antecedent-consequent relations (e.g. antecedent reinforcement
causes consequent changes in the frequency of behaviour), the
fact that development is defined as behavioural change, and
finally, a conception of development as a continuous process.
The organismic model, illustrated by Piaget's theory, for
instance, is characterized by opposite properties, namely
holism, the primacy of structure and function relationships,
the fact that development is defined as the reorganization of
mental structure, and finally, the conception of development

as a discontinuous, stepwise process.

As to the conception of the causal processes involved in development, the mechanistic approach is confined to material cause-effect and condition-effect models. The causal relations are viewed as unidirectional and linear. The organismic approach adds a teleological form to the previous forms of causality. The organism evolves towards a goal, a final state contained in the process of development itself. Moreover, causal relations are reciprocal and connected in an organized whole.

As to the first aim of theory analysis, we might state that the world view analysis is only suited to the purpose of making clear the differences between theories clear (the second aim).

However, if the organismic metaphor is made conditional to the concept of development, then world view analysis has also attained its first goal, i.e. to provide a definition of the property that distinguishes theories that describe development from those that do not. Finally, it is unclear whether world view analysis provides an appropriate model of the underlying structure of developmental theories, since the concept of the organism upon which developmental theories would be based, is left largely undefined.

In summary, the main advantages of the present form of analysis are, first, that it provides insight into the underlying differences between developmental theories; second, that it might provide a definition of the concept of development in terms of an underlying basic metaphor. Finally, by referring to the concept of a world view, the present method of analysis might explain the tenacity with which (some) developmental psychologists stick to their theory, irrespective of the critical empirical data and conceptual analyses that might have been raised against it. Since theories are ways of perceiving and conceiving of the world, they are insensitive to findings and arguments based on other world views.

Nevertheless, the incompatibility of distinct world views should not be exaggerated. First, theories based on distinct

world views sometimes raise largely identical empirical
predictions (Merlino, 1974). Second, world views can be
located in spaces consisting of relatively "elastic"
explanatory dimensions. These dimensions can be mapped upon
each other, thus converting a theory of one world view into a
largely identical theory based on a different world view (Van
Geert, 1983).

DEVELOPMENTAL THEORIES AS DESCRIPTIONS
OF LOGICAL NETWORKS OR GRAPHS.

While the previous forms of theory analysis exemplify the
"Weltanschauungen-approach", the present and next form of
analysis illustrate semantic analysis in Suppe's sense (Suppe,
1973).

The analysis of developmental transition and
infrastructure in terms of logical networks or graphs, based
on the logic of sets, has been elaborated by van den Daele
(1968, 1974, 1976; see also Riegel, 1972; Reese, 1973;
Meacham, 1980).

In contrast with conventional quantitative approaches,
which deal with quantitative changes in invariant traits,
developmental theories start from the primacy of qualitative
change. The processes of qualitative change can be analysed in
set theoretical terms. Three problems have to be dealt with:
first, the form of the transitions between developmental
states (the diachronical aspect), second, the composition of
each developmental state in terms of subordinate components
(the synchronical or infrastructural aspect), third, the
relationship between synchronic (transitional) and diachronic
(infrastructural) aspects. For the sake of simplicity, I shall
confine the present discussion to the synchronical aspect (for
a discussion of the second and third aspect, see van den
Daele, 1974).

According to van den Daele (1968), there are three
independent dimensions according to which the state
transitions between and within individual subjects can be

described.
The first dimension specifies the number of possible state
differences between subjects, and the associated transition
networks. A distinction is made between unitary and multiple
progression. Multiple progressions can take a divergent,
convergent, and parallel form (see figure 1).

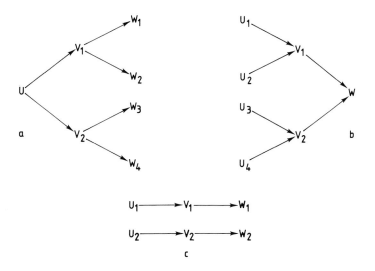

Figure 1. Three forms of multiple simple progressions (according to Van
den Daele, 1969); a: divergent, b: convergent, c: parallel.

The second dimension specifies the number of possible state
predicates applicable to one subject at one specific point in
a developmental progression. If one subject is characterized
by one and only one state predicate (at one single level of
analysis) at a time, the progression is called "simple". If
the subject can be ascribed more than one state predicate at a
time, the progression is called "cumulative".

The third dimension specifies whether or not successive states contain common elements. If the succeeding state integrates properties of the preceding state, the progression is called conjunctive. If there are no common elements, the progression is called disjunctive.

The three dimensions can be employed to describe the nature of the state transitions and transition networks in various developmental theories. I shall discuss some examples based on the first and second dimension.

Piaget's theory, more particularly the theory in its prototypical metamorphosis form (Flavell, 1971) is a good example of a unitary-simple progression. All subjects pass through the same developmental sequence. No subject is characterized by more than one developmental state at a time. If "décalages" are (conceptually) allowed, Piaget's theory turns into a unitary-cumulative form. Take for instance a six-year-old who solves a number of problems at the pre-operational level, and a number of different problems at the concrete operational level. At this particular moment, the child is characterized by two state predicates, namely "preoperational" and "cognitive operational". That is, the ascription of state predicates occurs in a cumulative manner.

An example of a multiple-simple theory of development is provided by Erikson's theory of identity development. The developmental progression is simple because the subject is characterized by one and only one state predicate at a time. The progression is multiple, because at each point of state transition, the subject has a choice among two state predicates, one specifies the solving of the identity problem at issue, while the other specifies the lack of success in solving the problem (e.g. the choice among initiative versus guilt during the age of early childhood).

Finally, the multiple-cumulative progression is illustrated in Gagné's learning theoretical approach of skill development (Gagné, 1968, 1970). Gagné describes the development of a skill as an ordered acquisition of subskills. The subskills are hierarchically ordered, but, since at each hierarchical level there are several hierarchically equivalent subskills, subjects may choose which one they will acquire first when making the step towards this particular hierarchical level. That is, the theory describes a multiple progression. The progression is cumulative since the acquisition of a skill consists of an accumulation of subskills.

Finally, let us look at the advantages and disadvantages of the logical network analysis in light of the aims set at the beginning of this paper.

The first advantage of the present method is that it describes the concept of development in the form of structured progressions in time.

Second, by employing a system of logical dimensions, the method gives a clear view of the differences between developmental theories. Each possible developmental theory occupies one and only one cell in the system. Cells that are empty at present may provide guidelines for the development of new theories, which might provide better explanations than the existing ones. That is, the method of logical network analysis may have a heuristic function.

Third, by distinguishing the logical properties of the progressions, the present method clearly reveals the underlying transitional and infrastructural architecture of developmental theories.

The main disadvantage of the method of logical network analysis is precisely its purely logical form. The states as well as the transitions are conceptually empty. What matters is the structure of the state transitions that make up the skeleton of the theory. Structural distinctions concerned with the nature and definition of the states and transitions, and with the nature of the rules that describe the cause of the transitions cannot be accounted for by logical network analysis.

In the next section, I shall present a method of analysis that tries to reveal the conceptual and definitorial distinctions between developmental theories, while preserving the advantages of a logical network analysis.

DEVELOPMENTAL THEORIES AS GRAMMARS THAT GENERATE
DEVELOPMENTAL PSYCHOLOGICAL STATEMENTS.

The present method of theory analysis has been inspired by the conceptions of the transformational-generative theory of language (e.g. van Geert, 1983). According to this approach, a set of linguistic statements, e.g. a description of a theory on cognitive development, forms the expression of an underlying system of rules. We may also say that, in an abstract sense, the rules have generated the set of statements. In principle, an existing theory of development, for instance all the writings of Piaget and those of his followers, can be conceived of as a coherent set of statements, experimental actions, educational applications, etc., in that they form the expression of a specific underlying set of rules. These rules form the "grammar" of Piagetian theory. Ideally, if we would know this grammar, we would be able to reconstruct Piaget's theory without knowing it in advance, we would be able to add new chapters to Piaget's theory, etc.

For clearness' sake, it should be noted that the actual corpus of - for instance - Piagetian statements, which may be found in books, articles and lectures, must not necessarily express all of the rules of the underlying Piagetian grammar (in practice, however, the actual corpus should express most of the rules; otherwise, the Piagetian grammar would be underdetermined by the corpus, and consequently, it would be impossible to make the grammar explicit).

Second, the actual corpus of Piagetian statements may be incoherent as far as the underlying grammar is concerned. That is, some of the statements may express ideas or notions that are not truly Piagetian. In that case, an analysis of the underlying grammar may be used to trace the incoherent elements in the existing Piagetian writings.

Finally, the grammar does not range beyond the purely conceptual domain. Empirical statements, e.g. statements concerning the ages at which developmental transitions are made, must be made on the basis of empirical research, within

the conceptual framework generated by the grammar.
If understanding the structure of a developmental theory
means understanding its underlying grammar, there should be a
test for deciding whether or not a given set of rules is
indeed the grammar underlying the theory at issue. Following
the test for generative grammars in language, we may state
that, if a set of rules is the underlying grammar of a
developmental theory, then, it should be possible to generate,
first, all possible states discerned by the theory, second,
all possible state transitions and state orders, and third,
the conditions of actual state transition. The first and
second criterion concern the developmental process as an
ordered set of states, the third criterion concerns the
transition rules. I shall first discuss the states and state
orders in prospective and retrospective theories, and then go
on with the transition rules.

The Grammar of States and State Succession
in Prospective Theories.

In the chapter on the concept of development, prospective
theories have been defined as theories that look ahead, i.e.
they define an initial state and investigate the ordered set
of changes that may start with this initial state, within the
boundaries of a definition of what it is that actually
develops. In principle, a grammar of a prospective theory
should consist of

    1. a specification of all the developmentally relevant
       properties of an initial state
    2. a specification of a set of transformation rules
       that operate upon the initial state and upon all
       possible states within the theory
    3. a specification of a space within which the set of
       operations is applicable.

It should be noted that the set of operations from the second
requirement are abstract generative operations: given a state
from the developmental space, they will define the state that

succeeds and the state that precedes. These generative rules should not be confused with the transition rules, i.e. rules that determine whether or not an existing developmental system in a specific state, will proceed to another one. The transition rules describe actual transition mechanisms, while the conceptual transformation rules describe ways for defining states of a developmental system.

Although the nature of the transformational operations depends on the states upon which they have to operate, it is possible to demonstrate some general types of operations. If the developmental states can be described in numerical terms, i.e. as a specific amount of something, for instance reaction time, it is possible to apply numerical operations, such as addition and subtraction (e.g. an increase in reaction time, an increase in the amount of processable information, etc.).

If the developmental state can be described in geometrical terms, e.g. concepts in terms of their position with regard to a prototype, or unstructured wholes, it is possible to apply geometrical operations, such as rotation, translation, or differentiation. Differentiation is an operation dividing a space into subspaces characterized by respective positions and distances.

A Theory of Face and Voice Recognition.

The reconstruction of theories working with numerically describable states is rather trivial. Take for instance a theory on the development of the recognition of faces or voices of nonfamiliar people (e.g. Carey and Diamond, 1977; Diamond and Carey, 1977; Mann, Diamond and Carey, 1979). The theory can be divided into two subtheories, i.e. a theory describing the relative amount of unfamiliar faces or voices recognized after one presentation, and a theory describing the mechanism of face or voice recognition after single presentation. The first theory is the one we shall try to reconstruct. As stated before, a distinction should be made between the conceptual aspect of the theory, containing all of the theoretically possible states and state orders, and the empirical aspect of the theory, containing only the empirically verified states and state orders. Understanding the structure of the theory is confined to the conceptual aspect. The initial state of development is a state of recognition on chance level, i.e. the amount of faces recognized is 0. The set of possible developmental states consists of all recognition levels described by all possible natural numbers between 0 and an arbitrary defined maximum level, e.g. 100 if percentages are employed. The set of all possible developmental state orders consists of all numerically ordered sets. It is clear that the present conceptual reconstruction of the theory is extremely trivial, simply because the conceptual framework of the theory itself is extremely trivial. According to the aforementioned authors, the empirically verified developmental process consists of a gradual increase between the sixth and the tenth year, a partial decrease between ten and fourteen, and a final increase between fourteen and sixteen when the adult level is achieved. It is clear that there is nothing in the basic conceptual structure of the theory that enables to automatically reconstruct empirical findings or predictions.

Jakobson's Theory of Phonological Development.

    In 1941, Roman Jakobson published a small book on phonological development, its regression in aphasia and the relation with the phological structure of languages, which became a classic in the field of phonological development. According to Atkinson (1982), who analysed the structure of the theory, Jakobson states that phonological development "..consists in part, of the acquisition of a set of distinctive oppositions. These oppositions are selected from a small set of oppositions which account for all possible phonological oppositions in the world's language " (page 27). There are thirteen of those distinctive oppositions, some of them are universal, others are associated with specific languages. The initial state of development consists of an undifferentiated set of sounds based on a language specific subset of the thirteen oppositions (e.g. the sounds of Eastern Flemish, or the sounds of Lingala). The sounds of a language, based on its proper subset of oppositions, constitutes the space within which the developmental operations are applicable.

The main developmental operation is differentiation, i.e. a successive division of the set of sounds which corresponds with simple logical operations on the set of thirteen oppositions. Although Jakobson is quite obscure about the nature of the differentiation operation, as Atkinson rightly remarks, he states that the differentiation follows a principle of maximization of contrast. The amount of contrast is defined by the mechanism of sound perception,but particularly by the mechanism of sound formation, i.e. articulation.

The first contrast is the maximal contrast within the set of oppositions, namely between consonants,liquids and glides on the one hand and vowels on the other hand, expressed by the opposition pairs "consonantal/non-vocalic" and "non-consonantal/vocalic". Within the set of vowels, the maximal distinction is between wide and narrow vowels. The differentiation proceeds according to the maximal contrast principle, until all the oppositions present in the mother tongue are acquired by the child.

In order to really reconstruct the theory, it would be necessary to provide a detailed account of the thirteen oppositions which together constitute the space within which phonological development may take place, and of the perceptual or articulatory mechanism on which the saliency of phonological contrasts is based.

In Jakobson's theory, there is some confusion with regard to the distinction between the conceptual rule generating possible developmental states and state orders, and the actual state transition rule. Both rules are called "differentiation according to maximal contrast". The conceptual rule belongs to the conceptual repertory of the linguist. It is a rule the linguist may use in order to infer the possible developmental states, but also the possible sets of phonological oppositions which may characterize languages. The transition rule describes a mechanism of information processing and system change, which actually takes place in the developing subject, and which causally explains why a specific transtion in the phonological development of a particular child has occurred.

Bower's and Spelke's Theories of Development.

Bower (1979) describes a general theory of development based on a differentiation principle starting from the general, more abstract, and proceeding to the specific, more concrete. The theory does not provide a complete description of human development. Rather, it defines a general principle -the differentiation from abstract to specific- for generating developmental states in a variety of fields. In order to construct a developmental theory, one should specify a space in which the principle is applicable and define an initial state onto which the differentiation principle may be first applied.
Noble (1985) has proposed the construction of a theory of personality development along these lines. As developmental space, he employs Kelly's system of personal constructs, i.e. the system of personal cognitive models of social facts, other persons, ourselves. As initial state, a nondifferentiation between the human/non-human category is proposed. The first differentiation, between human and non-human defines the most abstract characterizing of the social world possible. Further discriminations will take place according to the principle of increasing specificity. In principle, there is no intrinsic constraint on the level of specificity which might be achieved, although there are very specific constraints on the directions of the differentiations.
    Spelke's theory provides a second example of a partially elaborated differentiation theory (Spelke, 1982, 1985). She

has defined a developmental space, the space of object knowledge, and an initial state, namely the earliest form of object knowledge in life. Spelke's empirical and theoretical work focuses on the properties of the initial state. The implicit theory of development is prospective, in that the earliest state of object knowledge is already characterized by genuine object knowledge. The earliest object knowledge, the understanding of an object as spatiotemporal unity of a bounded volume in space, remains the core of object knowledge throughout life. The nature of the developmental transformation, however, is unclear. Spelke has made the suggestion that new elements of the object definition may be added, for instance the element "unity of colour and texture". It is unclear however, whether progression in object knowledge is based on such simple addition of properties, on a form of differentiation (e.g. between social and material objects), on restructuring of the initial knowledge, or on a combination of operations. Thus, in order to arrive at a theory of object knowledge development, an essential element of prospective theory, the state transformation rule, should be added.

Bower's and Spelke's theory slightly obscure the distinction between the conceptual principle of generating possible states, and the transitional principle of actual state change in a subject. For instance, it is clear that the psychologist may apply the principle of maximal concept differentiation to a given state description, in order to arrive at a description of another possible state in Bower's theory. It is less clear, however, whether and how the process of conceptual differentiation functions in a child, bringing the child from the current state of development to a new one.

Erikson's Theory of Identity Development: Prospective or Retrospective?

Erikson's theory of ego development, published in his book "Childhood and Society" (1950), is probably the most influential psychoanalytic theory of development, mainly for two reasons. First, it provides a theory of ego development, which makes it more suitable as a model for the normal healthy personality, second, it is a theory that encompasses the entire life span.

Erikson discerns eight pairs of opposed ego feelings or functions, for instance basic trust versus mistrust, or industry versus inferiority. Each pair is present at each stage of development. For instance, during the oral sensory stage, there is an oral sensory trust and mistrust, oral sensory industry and inferiority, and so forth. What distinguishes the stages is the dominance of one of the eight oppositions. For instance, in the first or oral sensory stage, it is the basic trust versus mistrust pair which is dominant, during puberty and adolescence, it is identity versus role confusion.

The operation which generates a new state of development is called "crisis" (or conflict, exploration). Its function is twofold. First, it has the effect of placing one of the oppositions in the foreground, i.e. of making it the dominant oppositions of that particular state. Second, it should effect a specific ratio of one element of the pair over the other, e.g. a favorable ratio of basic trust over mistrust. It depends on which element of the pair becomes dominant basic trust over mistrust. It depends on which element of the pair becomes dominant whether or not the effect of the crisis is a step forward in psychosocial adaptation (e.g. if as a result of the first crisis trust dominates over mistrust, a positive step in psychosocial adaptation has taken place).

Erikson's model of development represents an epigenetic chart, that is, "the human personality in principle develops according to steps predetermined in the growing person's readiness to be driven toward, to be aware of, and to interact with, a widening social radius" (Erikson, 1963, p. 260). Therefore, culture and society provide the epigenetic landscape, the set of possibilities, while the process of healthy personality development, i.e. of psychosocial adaptation, follows one specific path through this landscape. Thus, the specific social and cultural nature of being a baby,

foreground, is the presence of a specified ratio. Further, the explanation of developmental order based on the structure of society is begging the question, since society and the human life span are conceived of as being structurally similar (to a developmentally relevant degree, that is).

In summary, it is likely that the formal reconstruction of Erikson's theory in the form of a prospective differentiation theory is not the most appropriate one, in spite of some explicit hints made by Erikson himself. In the next paragraph, I shall discuss the grammar of retrospective theories, and investigate whether a retrospectively oriented reconstruction of Erikson's theory is possible.

The Grammar of States and State Succession in Retrospective Theories.

In the chapter on the concept of development (Van Geert, this volume), we have seen that retrospective theories aim at understanding how a specific configuration of properties have come about. This configuration of properties is conceived of as a description of a final state of development. All preceding states are viewed in light of the final result. A retrospective theory, therefore, has an explicit finalist flavour. The finalism, however, is not a causal or natural finalism which is clearly not compatible with what we know about change and transformation in nature, but a conceptual form of finalism. That is, all preceding states are conceptually interpreted according to their similarities and differences with regard to the final state (just as the length of persons may be interpreted in relation to the standard meter length or the size of the foot of Apollo; the interpretation says nothing about the intrinsic biological relationship between the growth of persons and the standard meter or Apollo's foot).

In principle, the grammar of retrospective theories consists of the following rules

1. all developmental states should be described as a

finite set of binary variables, that is variables
of the form "A, non-A"

2. the set of variables required is determined by the
   final state description; e.g. if the final state is
   described as the set of properties (A, B, C), the
   set of variables required is (A, -A), (B, -B),
   (C,-C).

3. the maximal distinction between states consists of
   different values on all variables; if the final
   state is defined as (A, B, C, ..) then the
   maximally different state is defined as (-A, -B,
   -C, ...), which, by definition, is the initial
   state.

4. the minimal distinction between states consists of
   a distinction on one variable; since two
   developmentally adjacent states are minimally
   different, the developmental state transition which
   relates them should consist of the substitution of
   one and only one variable value; e.g. (A, -B, -C,
   ...) is transformed into (A, B, -C, ..) or (A, -B,
   C, ...)

5. a transformation of a negative into a positive
   variable value is irreversible.

   It should be noted that the rule of state transformation
is a conceptual rule, i.e. it is a rule for transforming a
state desription into the description of the successor state.
It should be clearly distinguished from the transition rule,
which is a rule explaining why and when an actual
developmental system in a specific state proceeds to a
following state. It is clear, however, that the effect of the
transition rule should be within the limits determined by the
conceptual transformation rule, unless one of the rules is
incorrectly determined (see also the grammar of prospective
states, where the same distinction was met).

   In principle, there is no logical reason for employing
the final state as the conceptually primordial one. That is,
we could as well define a set of negative properties
specifying an initial state, and then reconstruct the process

until one or several logically possible final states are achieved. There would be no fundamental difference with a prospective theory. Nevertheless, there is a clear cognitive reason for putting the final state at the beginning of the reconstruction process. Cognitively, a set of negative properties is defined by its contrast with a set of positive properties. There is no boundary to the set of psychological properties that are absent in a baby, or in an adult, for that matter. However, cognitively, there is a boundary to the set of properties which are present in a baby or an adult if this set is employed as a definition of being a baby or being an adult. If a baby is viewed as something which is the starting point of a process which will lead to adulthood, then the set of properties ascribed to the baby is the negation of the set of properties used to define the adult. It is not stated that babies should be defined as non-adults by logical or conceptual necessity. It is only stated that many theories of development do conceive of babies as negative instances of a mature form the emergence of which the theory tries to explain. Various authors have emphasized the conceptual primacy of the final state definition in developmental theories thereby expressing a specific, i.e. retrospective view on development (e.g. Kessen, 1962, 1966; Flavell and Wohlwill, 1969; Bart and Smith, 1974; van den Daele, 1974; Wexler, 1974). In the present section, I shall present the following: an example of simple theory reconstruction, namely Piaget's theory of the main stages of cognitive development; a re-analysis of Erikson's theory of stages in the form of a retrospective theory; an example of how a theory of identity statuses may be transformed into a developmental theory; and finally, a reconstruction and partial elaboration of two educational-developmental theories, namely Gal'perin's theory of the formation of mental acts, and Klausmeier's theory of concept acquisition.

Piaget's Theory of the Main Stages of Cognitive Development.

Piaget discerns four main, structurally distinct stages in cognitve development, namely the sensorimotor, the preoperational, the concrete operational and the formal operational stage. These stages are believed to occur universally and in a fixed order. In the following discussion, I shall not deal with the question of whether the stages are psychologically real or just a matter of developmental book keeping (see Brainerd, 1978b; Baldwin et al., 1978, for a discussion). Whatever the ontological status of the stages, at present we are only interested in the conceptual rules upon which the stage model has been grounded.

Assuming that the Piagetian stages are consistently defined, we may infer the number of defining variables on the basis of the grammatical rule 4. If each developmental step consists of changing one value of one variable, a theory with three steps between initial and final state should employ only three defining variables.

It is possible to characterize the final state, the formal operational stage of cognitive development, by three properties.
First, the subject is able to think with formal (abstract) contents (F). Second, the subject's thinking is of an operational nature (O), that is, thinking takes place in the form of "representational act(s) which (are) an integral part of an organized network of related acts" (Flavell, 1963, 166). Finally, the thinking process of the subject occurs internally (I) (e.g. in the "mental space").
Starting from the definitions of the above mentioned properties, the negations of the properties are: first, thinking is about non-abstract, that is concrete contents (C); second, it is non-operational, i.e. actional (A); and, finally, thinking is a non-internal, that is, external process (E) (i.e. it takes the form of observable, bodily movements, actions with objects, etc.). These properties define the theoretical initial state of development. The properties coincide with Piaget's first stage of development, i.e. the

sensorimotor stage (since Piaget's stage theory is conceptually coherent, we could expect nothing else but a complete coincidence between Piaget's definition and the present reconstruction).

Figure 2 represents the set of possible state transitions.

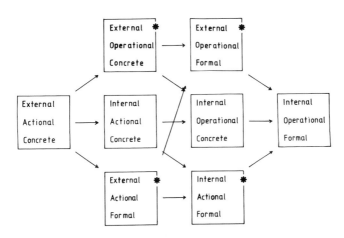

Figure 2. A reconstruction of possible states and state transitions in Piaget's theory. States marked by an asterisk violate conceptual constraints.

Some of the intermediary states we have found, i.e. the states EOC^*, EAF^*, EOF^* and IAF^*, violate the conditional relationships between the variables. According to the definition, "formality" cannot be a property of actional thinking, i.e. the processing of formal contents requires an organized network of internal acts (operations). According to the definition of "operationality", operational thinking cannot take place in the form of overt, external acts. If we delete the four conceptually impossible states, a structure remains which is exactly similar to Piaget's four stages. The

second stage, characterized by internalized actions with
concrete (i.e. imagined) objects equals the preoperational
stage. The third stage, internalized operations with concrete
contents, equals the concrete operational stage.
The previous reconstruction of Piaget's stage theory has no
other purpose than to illustrate process of reconstructing
developmental order on the basis of a final state definition.
It adds nothing to our insight into the theory.

Erikson's Model of Eight Stages of Psychosocial Adaptation.

    In the paragraph on prospective theories, we have seen
that Erikson's theory, in spite of several explicit
statements, is probably not a prospectively defined
differentiation theory. Let us now conceive of the theory as a
retrospectively defined theory of mature psychosocial
adaptation, described as the stage of ego integrity versus
despair.
The number of defining variables is obvious, namely eight,
adopted from the eight oppositional ego feelings or functions.
It is very appealing to treat the positive element of each
opposition as the positive value (e.g. ego integrity) of the
required binary variable, and the negative feeling (e.g.
despair) as the negative value. This solution is entirely
wrong, however. The effect of a crisis, the basic mechanism of
transition, is that the person finds a specific ratio between
the components of the opposition. The oppositional feelings
themselves remain present, and were present during any of the
previous stages. If we call the variables by their ordinal
numbers, we may define a transition of the negative to the
positive value, for instance,

$$-1 \longrightarrow 1$$
$$-8 \longrightarrow 8$$

as follows, according to the formalism adopted in the
paragraph on prospective theories

(trust, mistrust) $\longrightarrow$ trust/mistrust or mistrust/trust

(ego integrity, despair) $\longrightarrow$ ego integrity/despair or despair/ego integrity

and not

mistrust $\longrightarrow$ trust

despair $\longrightarrow$ ego integrity

The reconstruction of the developmental states and state orders is now a trivial matter. If we apply the rules, we find a great number of possible states and developmental paths, which have not been described by Erikson (see figure 3).

Erikson has defined a strict conceptual order between the types of crisis that may occur. The "ego integrity versus despair"-crisis cannot occur if it has not been preceded by a "generativity versus stagnation"-crisis, which requires that an "intimacy versus isolation"-crisis has taken place, and so on. We need not be concerned here with the justification behind all this. We may suffice with the statement of the conceptual implications rule as follows

$$8 \longrightarrow 7 \longrightarrow 6 \longrightarrow 5 \longrightarrow 4 \longrightarrow 3 \longrightarrow 2 \longrightarrow 1$$

For instance, if a state has a positive value on variable 3, i.e. a definite initiative versus guilt ratio, it should also show a definite ratio between autonomy versus shame, and between trust and mistrust. If we apply this rule to the diagram in figure 3, we end up with a set of simple unitary progressions of crises, one of which has been described by Erikson. The theoretically interesting thing, however, is to try to find out where the conceptual implications come from. As stated above, we do not need to concern us with these justifications if we only aim at finding the grammar of state succession. Having found this grammar, we would not be theorists of development if we were not curious about the grounds upon which the grammar rests. This question, however interesting, falls beyond the scope of the present paper.

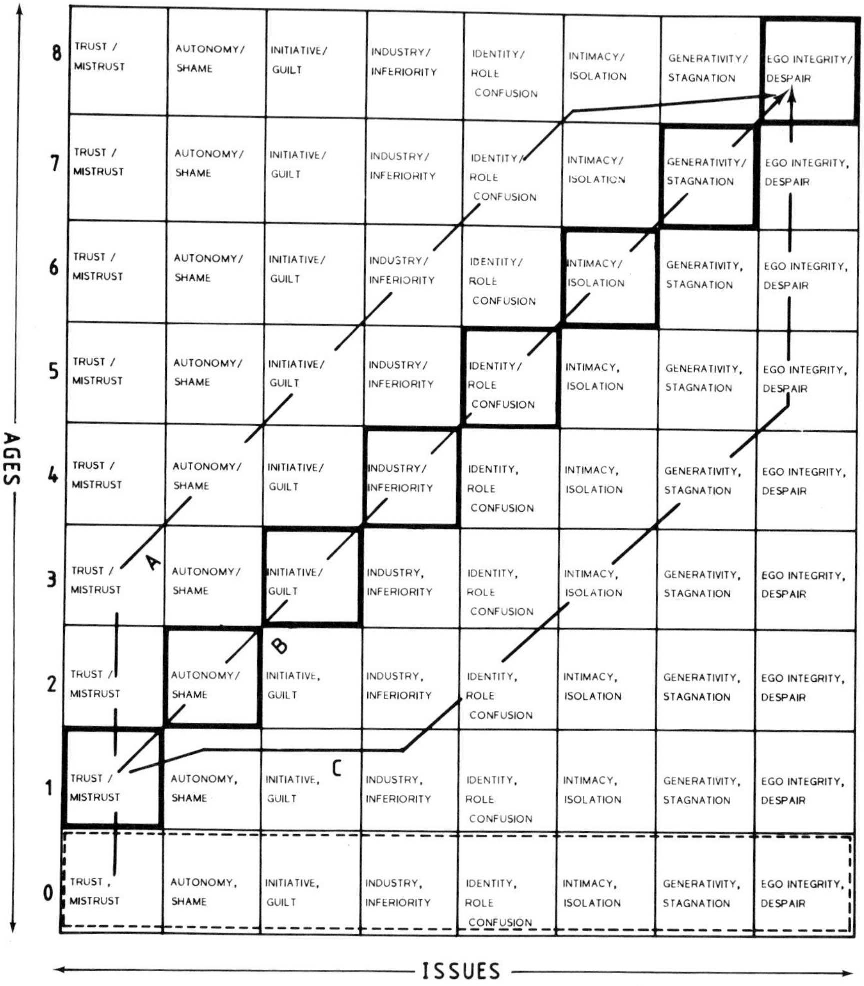

Figure 3. An extended Eriksonian model of development. The "0-state" is not explicitly distinguished by Erikson. The straight diagonal line represents ideal "epigenetic" developmental progression. The line above the diagonal represents the process in a "slow starter", the line under the diagonal represents a process which moves too fast in the beginning phase.

Marcia's Theory of Identity Statuses in Adolescence.

In principle, an analysis of the underlying grammar of a developmental theory might show that the theory at issue is conceptually incomplete. That is, it is possible that there are more conceptually allowed developmental progressions than the theory itself has made explicit.
There are two cases in which incompleteness is a natural consequence of the purpose of the theory in question. First, a theory might aim at a differential typology of a set of psychological states, without taking into account the possible developmental relationships between those states. Second, a developmental theory might present only the educationally desirable progression, without mentioning additional, i.e. deviant, progressions.
An example of the first kind of theory is Marcia's theory of identity states (Marcia, 1966, 1976; Matteson, 1977; Waterman & Waterman, 1971; Waterman, 1982). Marcia's theory is an elaboration of one of the developmental states of Erikson's life span theory, namely the stage "Identity versus Identity Diffusion" which occurs during adolescence. In Marcia's approach, identity implies a choice or commitment of the subject with regard to a profession, ideology, etc. Making such a commitment implies that one has made a personal choice, i.e. that one has thought about possible alternatives, that there has been a period of doubt, etc. The period during which such a "real" choice has been made is called a "crisis". By means of these binary variables (i.e. either commitment or not, either as a consequence of a crisis or not), Marcia is able to make a distinction between four (instead of two, as in Erikson's theory) identity states (see figure 4).
Starting from this grammar of identity states, we can theoretically infer the possible state progressions.
Let us start by making a distinction between a crisis which is actually occuring (CR_a) and a crisis which is finished (CR_f). The most mature identity state (i.e. the final state of the progression) is characterized by a finished crisis CR_f and commitment CO.

	commitment	no commitment
crisis (finished/ actual)	IDENTITY ACHIEVEMENT	MORATORIUM
no crisis	FORECLOSURE	IDENTITY DIFFUSION

Figure 4. Marcia's two-dimensional model of identity statuses during adolescence.

The initial state must be characterized by opposite properties, i.e. the lack of crisis (either actual or finished) "-CR" and the lack of commitment "-CO". Taking the necessary progressions into account, namely

$$-CR \rightarrow CR_a \rightarrow CR_f$$

and

$$-CO \rightarrow CO$$

we may infer a developmental progression sketched in figure 5. States 2 and 3 correspond with Marcia's moratorium and foreclosure states. At first sight, state 1 corresponds with the Identity Diffusion state (no crisis, no commitment). We may assume, however, that "diffusion" implies that the subject has had the chance to make a choice among alternative commitments, that is, the subject should have passed through a period of crisis. State 1 is simply the initial state of identity development. It should correspond with Erikson's fourth stage, i.e. "Industry versus Inferiority", occuring during middle childhood. This stage does not require a commitment with regard to profession, religion, etc. Stage 4 - the subject has gone through a crisis but has not succeeded in making a choice - corresponds with the actual state of Identity Diffusion. State 5 clearly corresponds with Identity

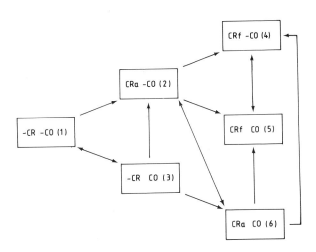

Figure 5. A model of possible states and state transitions in the development of identity statuses during adolescence.

Achievement. State 6 has not been distinguished by Marcia, yet it follows from the conceptual framework upon which the original identity states have been based. In state 6, a subject has made a specific commitment, but is still in a period of crisis. That is, the subject keeps feeling uncertain about the choice made, the subject may even reject the choice but is unable to renounce it. Such a "schizophrenic" or double-bind situation may occur sufficiently frequently to give it a distinct place in a developmental theory.

The interpretation of the crisis variable as a nested binary variable, that is $(-CR, (-CR_f$ or CR_a, $CR_f))$ was natural. It is also possible to define the commitment variable in the same way, i.e. $((-CO, +/-CO), CO)$. That is, the state of non-commitment is a binary variable in itself, either there is no commitment at all, or the commitment is loose, the person does not care very much about the commitment made. This interpretation is psychologically realistic, in that there are adolescents who, after having explored a possible commitment,

either did not succeed in solving the issue and gave up, or
did not succeed and have adopted a commitment for which they
do not care very much (Marcia, personal communication). In
that case, we see a model of identity achievement in
adolescence which is still more complicated than the model
from figure 5, but which is probably also more psychologically
real (the drawing and interpretation of the model is left to
the interested reader).

Marcia's theory of identity statuses during adolescence
enabled us to show how a model consisting of independent
descriptive dimensions, can be transformed into a
developmental theory. It will be clear that such a theory is a
purely theoretical, conceptual construct which has to be
validated in the course of further empirical investigation. In
the next sections I shall try to show that "missing"
developmental states and progressions may be found by an
analysis of the underlying "grammar" of developmental states.

The theories that will be discussed -Gal'perin's theory
of the formation of mental acts and Klausmeier's theory of
concept learning - are not typical developmental theories.
They do not describe the varieties of developmental
progression in a population. Rather, they describe directed
processes, i.e. processes of acquiring a skill on the basis of
directed teaching. The questions I want to discuss are, first,
which is the set of possible developmental progressions out of
which the learning theory has made a particular selection,
and, second, are there theoretical reasons for explaining why
this particular selection is made instead of another one?

Gal'perin's Theory of the Formation of Mental Acts.

Gal'perin's theory on the stepwise formation of mental
acts describes a number of steps a child should make in order
to achieve a final stage, i.e. the stage of mental acts
(Talyzina, 1969/1980). The final level is characterized by the
following properties. First, the act carried out by the child
is a mental act. Second, no irrelevant, accidental properties

are involved. Third, there is a minimum of separately performed sub-acts. Finally, the act is carried out with a maximum of automatization. The first property, the mental nature of the act, is of particular importance. "Mental" means that the act is taking place internally ("in the mind"), and that it takes the form of a symbolic process (i.e. in the form of inner speech). For the sake of simplicity, we may summarize the second, third and fourth property of the final state by the term "maximal economy" (that is, the act is carried out with a minimum of circumstantiality). Thus, we have a final state characterized by three properties, i.e. "internally occuring", "symbolical" and "with maximal economy".

The acquisition of the final state is not a matter of spontaneous development. If children are left to themselves, they will either acquire the final state very slowly and after much trial and error, or they will remain in some inadequate intermediary stage. Children must be taught the art of mental action in a carefully controlled process consisting of determined intermediary steps.
The first step consists of the orientation stage. The children are presented with the act they will have to carry out. During the second stage, children perform the act in a material or materialized form, with a maximum of circumstantiality (i.e. the properties or sub-acts are minutely performed, controlled, etc.). In the third stage, the act takes an external verbal form, i.e. the child gives a minute oral or written description of the act and sub-acts. During the fourth stage, the children speak to themselves, i.e. the act is now taking place in an internal, verbal form. Although, the verbal form makes the act more condensed and generalized, it is still not automatized (i.e. maximally economical). In the last stage, the internal, verbal act is finally automatized, condensed and generalized.

Let us now reconstruct the developmental progression, starting from the final state. Since the final state is characterized by the properties "internal", "symbolic" and "maximal economy", the theoretical initial state must have the opposite properties. In the framework of Gal'perin's theory,

84 P. van Geert

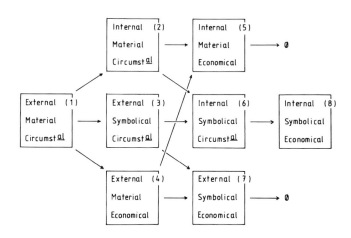

Figure 6. A reconstruction of the state transition model underlying
Gal'perin's model of the stepwise formation of mental acts. States 5
and 7 are developmental dead ends. They are not contained in
Gal'perin's educationally oriented theory.

these opposite properties are "external", "material" and
"circumstantial". By changing one property at a time, we
obtain the set of possible developmental progressions
presented in figure 6.

States 2, 4, 5 and 7 are conceptually and empirically possible
states, yet they are not contained in Gal'perin's model. In
state 2, for instance, the child has interiorized the
circumstantial material act it has been performing in the
previous stage. In stage 4, the child has automatized his
external, material act (e.g. automatized adding and
subtracting on the fingers). It is easy to see why states 2,
4, 5 and 7 are not contained in Gal'perin's model: each of
these represents a developmental dead end. Neither automatized
nor interiorized acts are amenable to directions by the
teacher. Automatized acts are no longer penetrable, since they
occur in the form of a single unit. Changing only one fragment

often results in the breakdown of the total act. Interiorized acts are impenetrable because they are not observable, they occur in the "private" mental domains. Consequently, if we want to achieve an adequate command of mental acting in our pupils, we should not allow them to automatize or interiorize an act, until the act has been acquired in a correct, verbal form. A theory that describes how children achieve the final, mental state, does not specify states that lead to developmental dead ends. It may be questioned, however, whether or not the description of possible unsuccessful progressions might be suitable for clinical reasons, i.e. for the diagnosis of learning problems in children.

Klausmeier's theory of concept acquisition.

An analysis of Klausmeier's (1976) theory of concept acquisition shows that theories with a simple surface structure may hide very complex "deep structures". Klausmeier describes the acquisition of a concept (e.g. "animal" in terms of four stages or "levels". At the first, i.e. concrete level, the subject may recognize a specific appearance of an object (and only that specific appearance), and is able to learn and remember a name associated with the appearance. At the second, i.e. identity level, the subject recognizes various appearances as the appearances of one single object, and is able to learn and remember the name of the object. At the third, i.e. concrete level, the subject is able to recognize objects as members of a class. Although the subject may learn and remember the name of the class, he or she has not yet acquired the principle underlying the classification. At the fourth, i.e. formal level, the child has acquired the underlying principle of classification, and is able to generalize it to potential members of the class.

The final state of development, i.e. the formal level, may be defined as the ability to form sets (S) of objects (O), to learn to remember the name (N) of the set, and to distinguish the relevant features (F) of the objects, and finally, to know and apply the classification criterion (C).

Hence, the initial state is defined by the following opposite properties: the subject is directed towards appearances (A) instead of objects, he does not operate with sets but with single, elementary appearances (E), the subject perceives the appearance in terms of a global "Gestalt" (G) instead of distinct features, and finally, the subject is ignorant of any name (-N) or classification criterion (-C).

The first main step in the developmental process should consist of the acquisition of an object concept (that is, the substitution of the predicate A by O). The object concept may be defined, among others, as the ability to form a set of appearances, characterized by common features, in addition to knowledge of the classification criterion (i.e. the ability to generalize to new appearances of the same object). Knowledge of the name of appearances or objects is an optional property. Put differently, the first constraint to the progression (A)⊢→(O) is that (O) implies (A, S, F, C). Since knowledge of a classification criterion implies, first, that there exists a class or set S, and, second, that the set is characterized by common features (F), we may describe a second constraint, namely (C) > (S > F). If we take the two constraints into consideration, the conceptually allowed developmental progression (A) → (O) will take the following form (see figure 7).

The analysis of the first developmental step in Klausmeier's theory shows that the structure is much more complicated than a four stage process.

We have now reconstructed the first step of concept acquisition in the form of the acquisition of an object concept. That is, the child should first learn that several different appearances of a dog are appearances of one and the same dog. According to the present theory, the child has defined the dog as a set of features of different appearances of the dog. Such an interpretation of an object concept may be extremely unrealistic. However, we are not concerned here with the empirical value of theories, only with their structure.

We may now proceed with the reconstruction and claim that, in order to make the next step in the development of a

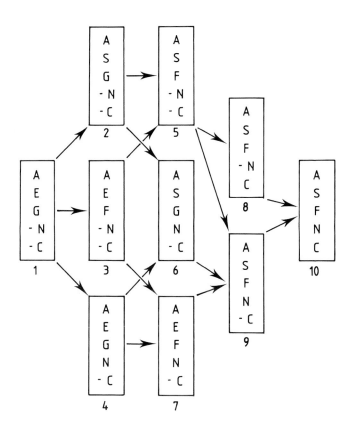

Figure 7. Possible states and state transitions between Klausmeier's first and second stage of concept development. Only conceptually allowed states are presented.

concept, the child should have knowledge of single objects. This requirement is described by any state characterized by the features, A, S, and F, i.e. by states 5, 8, 9 and 10. Any of these states may be the starting point for further concept development. According to the theory, the object known by the child is a single element, it does not belong to a class (E), it has a global Gestalt form (G), it might have a name but it does not have a class name (-N), and, obviously, no classification criterion is known since there is simply no classification (-C). Given the similarity of defining features, the structure of further steps in concept development equals the steps leading from appearance to object as depicted in figure 7, with the exception that "A" should be replaced by "O" in each state description.

At present, it is unclear to which level of detail a theoretical description should push through in order to achieve practical and theoretical validity. Since a further discussion of this problem would exceed the scope of the present paper, I shall confine it to the present demonstration of the possible complexity of a seemingly simple developmental progression as described in Klausmeier's theory of concept acquisition.

THE GRAMMAR OF TRANSITIONS.

In the previous paragraphs, we have discussed the grammar of developmental state construction and order. The questions we have tried to answer were: which developmental states are conceptually allowed in a specific theory, and how can we construct them, and second, which possible developmental orders are conceptually allowed, and how can they be reconstructed. The latter question led to the description of conceptual transformation rules, i.e. rules for rewriting a developmental state description in the description of its successor or predecessor. We did not explain why and when a specific system currently in a state S_i, for instance, changed to a state S_{i+1}.

The rules dealing with actual state transition have been called the stability rules (see the chapter on the "Concept of Development", Van Geert, this volume). Two principles for explaining whether or not state changes occured were discerned, namely the open or closed nature of the states on the one hand, and the internal stability or instability on the other hand. The domains and ranges of the conceptual transformation rules and of the stability rules should be equal. For instance, if the application of a stability rule would lead to a state which is not allowed conceptually, something is wrong either with the stability rule or with the conceptual rule.

The reconstruction of the way in which the stability rules actually operate on the properties of developmental states requires a much more detailed discussion of the theory than the reconstruction of mere developmental order. In general, developmental theories are much more specific about the number of states and the allowed state orders they employ than they are about the exact nature of the transition mechanisms. Therefore, I shall limit the present discussion to three examples, namely Erikson, Piaget's and learning theory.

Stability and Change in Erikson's Theory.

We have already discussed the principle of transition in Erikson's theory, and found that the principle of crisis (or conflict, or exploration) in addition to the structure of society or social groups, played a central role in it. We also noted that the theory is quite obscure on the exact nature of the change process. For instance, why does the first crisis result in putting the trust-mistrust pair at the foreground, why is the order of crises described by Erikson actually occurring? In the previous paragraphs, a purely conceptual answer was given. The stability rule, however, should account for the causality, the actual occurrence of the process. At this point, the theory is insufficiently explicit. As we already noted, explaining the order by referring to the structure of society is begging the question, since the structure of society is conceived of as being similar to the structure of the life cycle. Still, even if we would rely on the structure of society, at present we would not be able to explain developmental change. The concept of crisis does not allow us to construct a generative procedure which is able to automatically select the relevant properties of society and environment, given a specific set of properties of the

developmental state.
In the sense of explanation as earlier defined, the automaticity of the procedure is extremely important. Understanding the reason why a state change takes place implies that one has a algorithm - the stability rule - which, applied to a state description, exactly specifies whether the necessary and sufficient conditions for state change are present or not. This algorithmic level is certainly not achieved in Erikson's theory.

Piaget's Theory of Qualitative Cognitive Change.

In the previous description of developmental order in Piaget's theory, we employed the principle of replacing one value by its opposite. It is very clear that this operation is purely conceptual, i.e. it cannot be confused with the activities or events that make a child proceed to a higher level of cognitive development.
According to Brainerd, "Piaget's cognitive structures are said to grow and change as a function of two immutable laws of development: organization and adaptation", while the "actual process whereby structural change takes place is called equilibration" (Brainerd, 1978a, 20). Brainerd describes equilibrium as consisting of four steps. The process starts with a limited range of situations that the present cognitive structure can handle. Second, the subject encounters situations whose demands lie beyond the scope of its cognitive structure. Third, these situations cause a state of "disequilibrium" in the cognitive structure. Finally, the cognitive structure reorganizes itself and is now able to deal with the new situations. That is, the structure has reached a new, more complex level of equilibrium.
I shall now try to give a more systematic account of the process. The basic variables consist of a cognitive structure in a specific state on the one hand, and an environment on the other hand. The state is open to properties of the environment that emerge on the basis of state-environment interaction

(hence, the state is closed with regard to non-emergent properties). For instance, during the sensorimotor stage, the child shows "circular reactions", i.e. reactions that produce stimulation that causes repetition of the action. Hence, the environment of the child consists merely of particular forms of stimulation. All other forms of stimulation, i.e. those that do not lead to repetition of the action, are neither understood nor perceived. The stimulation is called "emergent" because it would not exist as such if the child would not display the required action.

We can now state the following rules.

1. a state is either in equilibrium or in non-equilibrium
2. the transition from equilibrium to non-equilibrium is a state transition, the transition from non-equilibrium to equilibrium is a state consolidation
3. properties of the cognitive state call forth properties of the environment, that is, emergent properties
4. emergent properties of the environment are either in conflict with cognitive state properties or not
5. if in conflict, emergent properties cause a change of equilibrium state. If emergent properties are not in conflict with properties of the cognitive state, then the state remains in its equilibrium state, that is, state transitions will no longer occur.

These rules can be summarized in the form of the following flow chart (figure 8).

The fifth rule is especially important, since it determines the causal condition according to which the process of state transitions will stop. In the chapter on the concept of development (this volume), we have seen that a developmental process can be deductively inferred on the basis of a final state definition. Thus, acoording to this basically conceptual approach, it is tautologically true that the process ends with the final state. According to the transition rule approach, however, the Piagetian state transitions may continue until there is no longer a conflict between emergent

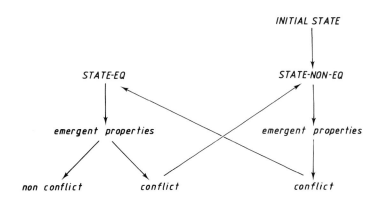

Figure 8. A flow chart of state changes in Piaget's theory.

properties and cognitive properties.

It must be questioned, then, why the conceptual and transition approach coincide as far as the final state is concerned. Why, for instance, are the emergent properties of the environment no longer disequilibrating, as soon as the formal operational equilibrium is achieved?

After all, the reason for this coincidence is quite simple. The environment, described by the developmental psychologist, is not the world "as such", it is the world as conceptualized, understood and perceived by the psychologist. If our developmental theory states that the formal operational understanding of the physical world is the highest form of understanding we can get, the description of the environment in which development takes place necessarily follows the rules of formal operational understanding. That is, the properties of the described world are emergent with regard to this particular understanding. Thus, as soon as people have achieved the formal operational stage, the properties emergent on their and the psychologist's understanding of the world coincide. Put differently, there is no longer a friction between the structures of cognition and the structures of the world "as it really is" (that is, as it is conceived of by the scientist). The emergent properties of the world are no longer able to cause disequilibrium. As soon as one conceives of the world in different terms, the developmental process, as well as the final state in which one would be interested, will change in accordance with this altered understanding. Riegel's fifth state of cognitive development, i.e. the state of dialectic operations, which succeeds Piaget's stage of formal operational thinking, is based on a dialectic understanding of the world (Riegel, 1973). In a world conceived of in dialectic terms, formal operational understanding is a necessary condition for discovering that the world is structured according to dialectic principles. That is, a disequilibrium will occur, which will lead to the final equilibrium state, i.e. the state of dialectic operations.

Transition Rules in Learning Theories.

In learning theories, such as Gagné's cumulative theory, a developmental state is defined as a specific internal response disposition. In principle, the state is internally stable (at least, it will remain stable as long as its normal conditions of existence are fulfilled; one of these conditions may be that the response is regularly exercised). The developmental state is open to the environmental effects of the response. The internal state, e.g. the disposition towards a specific frequency of utterance of the response, will change in accordance with the subjective value of the effects. The changes of developmental states are incremental, i.e. by small steps, cumulative and specific (Rohwer et al., 1974, 57). The internal instability of the states, however, is not absolute. There are three internal mechanisms, generalizations, horizontal, and vertical transfer, that will alter the range of the response. Since the change does not occur at the level of the response itself, we may still stick to the idea that learning theoretical developmental states are internally stable.

Not all state transitions of the described kind are of a developmental nature. For development to occur, the state transition must contribute to the acquisition of "complex rules" (Gagné, 1968). Complex rules consist of "simple rules", which in their turn consist of "concepts", "concepts" are based upon "multiple discriminations", etc. Thus, learning theory also describes development as a function of a preconceived final state (the state of "complex rules", for instance; in operant conditioning, the initial and intermediary states may be interpreted in light of the desired behaviour). On the other hand, the theory may describe an infinite number of possible final states, that is, there is an infinite number of distinct "complex rules" that might provide the final state of a developmental process.

OPEN VERSUS CLOSED DEVELOPMENTAL PROCESSES.

In accordance with our analysis of the concept of development, two types of developmental theories have been distinguished, namely prospective theories, and retrospective theories. Both types have been conceived of as possible conceptual viewpoints in their own right, or as two complementary views on the nature of psychological development. If one refrains from empirical claims, there is no possibility of considering one theory to be more adequate than the other. We have also seen that the retrospective point of view is the most powerful generator of elaborated developmental theories. Thus, on purely heuristic grounds, the retrospective view seems the most adequate.

Retrospective theories, however, describe development in the form of closed processes, consisting of a finite set of states. The grammar underlying the developmental theory is unable to generate new developmental states, once the finite set of states has been enumerated. It may be questioned whether finite, closed models are descriptively adequate tools for understanding the nature of human development. If the final state of human development is an immanent property of the human species, the use of finite models is perfectly appropriate. It is quite improbable, however, that such an immanent final state exists. In light of long term historical processes, individual development may be defined as a single link in the process of reproduction and production of the social and cultural system. Skills, knowledge, cognitive system are transmitted from generation to generation. In complex societies, the process of cultural reproduction is subject to a division of labour. During the process of reproduction, society and culture undergo changes which, in their turn, must be reproduced by future generations. Thus, the final state of development is nothing but a specific point in the history of a culture (cf. Lerner and Busch-Rossnagel, 1981; Tobach, 1981; Van Geert, in press; the submission of individual development to the process of social and cultural history is also one of the main tenets in the Cultural Historical School in Soviet Psychology).

The prospective type of developmental theory is able to explain the emergence of new final states of development, on the basis of its own underlying grammar. That is, the grammar generates an infinite set of possible final states in a rule-governed fashion. Unfortunately, most of the existing prospective theories are considerably less elaborated than the retrospective theories. Their way of dealing with the human life span is less systematic and often limited to a few examples of possible developmental processes.

In the future, theories of psychological development should try to obtain an explanative power which equals that of the present theories of biological development and evolution. Biological theories are able to explain how biological species reproduce (and co-reproduce), but they are also able to explain how new species emerge. Their explanations are built, first, on knowledge of the material basis of reproduction of genetic complexes, and, second, on knowledge of the conditions of co-reproduction in ecological systems.

Theories may stick to the closed character of the retrospectively defined developmental process by setting themselves some specific limitations.

First, theories may explicitly be confined to the purely individual aspect and abstract the intergenerational (i.e. teaching or tutorial) part from the developmental process. Piaget's theory may exemplify this approach. It does not imply that the intergenerational aspect (e.g. adult-infant- or tutor-pupil-interaction) is unimportant or unnecessary in development. Rather, it is just that the theory wishes to direct its attention solely to that part of the developmental process that takes place in the developing individual. Nevertheless, there is ample evidence for the thesis that the intergenerational aspect is of fundamental importance at the very beginning of human development (Trevarthen, 1978), and that early parent-baby interactions have a definite developmental value, in spite of their seemingly simple, spontaneous, and unstructured character (e.g. Snow and Ferguson, 1977; Bruner and Sherwood, 1976; Ratner and Bruner, 1978). There is also evidence, however, showing that the style and content of early parent-infant interaction has undergone considerable historical changes (e.g. Ariès, 1962; Shorter, 1975; compare with Kroll, 1977; Pollock, 1983). Differences in the treatment of young children may relate to the nature of the entire course of development the subject has to pass through. Differences in the rearing of young children may also be self-explaining. That is, the function of the affectionate, careful intercourse between parents and young children, may be that the children on their turn will become affectionate, careful parents.

Second, developmental theories may confine to socially and culturally stable periods of psychological reproduction. If the world of the parents is similar to the world of the children, there is no need for an evolutionary viewpoint on development. The age of scientific developmental psychology, however, coincides with fast, fundamental changes in the structure of society and culture. These changes have set new developmental goals to people. Certainly, it is possible to define developmental goals in terms so abstract that they are insensitive to the kind of historical changes that have taken place during the past century. It may be questioned, however, whether this is the right thing to do if we want to achieve better understanding of the processes of development and education that take place in our time (see Vedder, this volume). Developmental theories should obtain an open character, that is, they should be able to explain how new developmental goals emerge from existing developmental processes. At present, however, it is not quite clear which structural and empirical consequences the change from a closed to a fundamentally open world view will have for developmental psychology. A synthesis should be sought between the two viewpoints - the prospective and the retrospective - that presently make the course of theory building divergent.

REFERENCES.

Ariès, P. (1962). Centuries of childhood. A social history of family life. New York: Vintage Books.

Ashby, W.R. (1952). Design for a brain. London: Chapman and Hall (revised edition 1960).

Atkinson, M. (1982). Explanations in the study of child language development. Cambridge: Cambridge University Press.

Baldwin, J.D. and others (1978). Open Peer Commentary on Ch.J. Brainerd's The stage question in cognitive-developmental theory. The Behavioral and Brain Sciences, 2, 182-206.

Bart, W.M. & Smith, M.B. (1974). An interpretive framework of cognitive structures. Human Development, 17, 161-175.

Brainerd, Ch.J. (1978a). Piaget's theory of intelligence. Englewood Cliffs N.J.: Prentice Hall.

Brainerd, Ch.J. (1978b). The stage question in cognitive-developmental theory. The Behavioral and Brain Sciences, 2, 173-213.

Bromley, D.B. (1970). An approach to theory construction in the psychology of development and aging. In L.R. Goulet &

P.B. Baltes (Eds.), Life span developmental psychology: Research and theory. New York: Academic Press.

Bruner, J.S. & Sherwood, V. (1976). Peekaboo and the learning of rule structures. In J.S. Bruner, A. Jolly & K. Silva (Eds.), Play: Its role in evolution and development (pp. 277-285). Harmondsworth: Penguin.

Carey, S. & Diamond, R. (1977). From piecemeal to configurational representation of faces. Science, 195, 312-314.

Chomsky, N. (1972). Language and Mind. New York: Harcourt Brace Jovanovich (enlarged edition).

Diamond, R., & Carey, S. (1977). Developmental changes in the representation of faces. Journal of experimental child psychology, 23, 1-22.

Erikson, E.H. (1950/1963). Childhood and Society (2nd ed. rev.; originally published 1950). New York: Norton.

Flavell, J.H. (1963). The developmental psychology of Jean Piaget. London: van Nostrand.

Flavell, J.H. (1971). Stage-related properties of cognitive development. Cognitive Psychology, 2, 421-453.

Flavell, J.H. & Wohlwill, J.F. (1969). Formal and functional aspects of cognitive development. In D. Elkind & J.H. Flavell (Eds.), Studies in cognitive development (pp. 67-120). Oxford: Oxford University Press.

Fodor, J.A. (1983). The modularity of mind. Cambridge (Mass): MIT Press.

Gagné, R.M. (1968). Contributions of learning to human development. Psychological Review, 75, 177-191.

Gagné, R.M. (1970). The conditions of learning. New York: Holt, Rinehart & Winston.

Jakobson, R. (194). Kindersprache, Aphasie, und allgemeine lautgesetze. Stockholm:Almqvist and Wiksell.

Johnston, T.D. (1981). Contrasting approaches to a theory of learning. The Behavioral and Brain Sciences, 4, 125-173.

Kessen, W. (1962). Stage and structure in the study of children. Monographs of the Society for Research in Child Development, 27, 65-81.

Kessen, W. (1966). Questions for a theory of cognitive

development. Monographs of the Society of Research in Child Development, 31, 55-70.

Kitchener, R.F. (1982). Holism and the organismic model in developmental psychology. Human Development, 25, 233-249.

Klausmeier, H.J. (1976). Conceptual development during the school years. In J.T. Levin & V.L. Allen (Eds.), Cognitive learning in children. Theories and strategies (pp. 5-29). New York: Academic Press.

Kroll, J. (1977). The concept of childhood in the middle ages. Journal of the History of the Behavioral Sciences, 13, 384-393.

Kuhn, D. (1978). Mechanisms of cognitive and social development: one psychology or two? Human Development, 21, 92-118.

Langer, J. (1969). Theories of development. New York: Holt, Rinehart & Winston.

Lerner, R.M. (1978). Nature, nurture and dynamic interactionism. Human Development, 21, 1-20.

Lerner, R.M. & Busch-Rossnagel, N.A. (1981). Individuals as producers of their development: conceptual and empirical bases. In R.M. Lerner & N.A. Busch-Rossnagel (Eds.), Individuals as producers of their development (pp. 1-36). New York: Academic Press.

Mann, V.A., Diamond, R. & Carey, S. (1979). Development of voice recognition: parallels with face recognition. Journal of experimental child psychology, 27, 153-165.

Marcia, J.E. (1966). Development and validation of ego identity status. Journal of Personality and Social Psychology, 1, 551-558.

Matteson, D.R. (1977). Exploration and commitment: sex differences and methodological problems in the use of identity status categories. Journal of Youth and Adolescence, 6, 353-374.

Meacham, J.A. (1980). Formal aspects of theories of development. Experimental Aging Research, 6, 475-487.

Merlino, F.J. (1975). Metatheoretical isolationism reconsidered: its impact for developmental theories. Human Development, 18, 391-395.

Noble, R. (1985). Towards a theory of life span development. Paper presented at the Founding Conference of the International Society for Theoretical Psychology, Plymouth.

Overton, W.F. (1984). World views and their influence on psychological theory and research: Kuhn, Lakatos, Laudan. In H.W. Reese (Ed.), Advances in Child Development and Behavior: vol. 18. New York: Academic Press.

Overton, W.F. & Reese, H.W. (1973). Models of development: methodological implications. In J.R. Nesselroade & H.W. Reese (Eds.), Life-span developmental psychology: Methodological issues (pp. 65-86). New York: Academic Press.

Pepper, S.C. (1942). Worldhypotheses. A study in evidence. Berkeley: University of California Press (1970 edition).

Pollock, L.A. (1983). Forgotten children. Parent-child relations from 1500 to 1900. Cambridge: Cambridge University Press.

Ratner, N.K. & Bruner, J.S. (1978). Games, social exchanges and the acquisition of language. Journal of Child Language, 5, 391-401.

Reese, H.W. (1973). Models of memory and models of development. Human Development, 16, 397-416.

Reese, H.W. & Overton, W.F. (1970). Models of development and theories of development. In L.R. Goulet & P.B. Baltes (Eds.), Life-span developmental psychology. Research and theory (pp. 115-145). New York: Academic Press.

Riegel, K.F. (1972). Time and change in the development of the individual and society. In H.W. Reese (Ed.), Advances in Child Development and Behavior: Vol. 7 (pp. 81-113). New York: Academic Press.

Riegel, K.F. (1973). Dialectic operations: the final period of cognitive development. Human Development, 16, 346-370.

Rohwer, W.D. Jr., Ammon, P.R. & Cramer, P. (1974). Understanding intellectual development. Three approaches to theory and practice. Hinsdale (Ill.): Dryden Press.

Sameroff, A.J. (1972). Learning and adaptation in infancy: a comparison of models. In H.W. Reese (Ed.), Advances in

Child Development and Behavior: Vol. 7 (pp. 169-214). New York: Academic Press.

Shorter, E. (1975). The making of the modern family. New York: Basic Books.

Spelke, E.S. (1982). Perceptual knowledge of objects in infancy. In J. Mehler, E. Walker en M. Garrett (Eds.), Perspectives on mental represenation. Hillsdale (N.J.): Lawrence Erlbaum.

Spelke, E.S. (1985). Perception of unity, persistence and identity: thoughts on infants' conceptions of objects. p.89-113 in J. Mehler en R. Fox (Eds.), Neonate Cognition: Beyond the blooming buzzing confusion. Hillsdale (NJ.): Lawrence Erlbaum.

Suppe, F. (1974). The search for philosophic understanding of scientific theories. In F. Suppe (Ed.), The structure of scientific theories Urbana: University of Illinois Press.

Talyzina, N.F. (1969). Teoreticeskie problemy programmirovannogo obucenija. Izd-vo, Moscow (Dutch translation by J. Haenen). In A.G. Vroon & S.E. Everwijn (Eds.) (1980), Handboek voor de onderwijspraktijk. Deventer: Van Loghum Slaterus.

Tobach, E. (1981). Evolutionary aspects of the activity of the organism and its development. In R.M. Lerner & N.A. Busch-Rossnagel (Eds.), Individuals as producers of their development. New York: Academic Press.

Toulmin, S. (1958). The uses of argument. Cambridge: Cambridge University Press.

Trevarthen, C. (1978). Modes of perceiving and modes of acting. In H.L. Pick & E. Saltzman (Eds.), Modes of perceiving and processing information. Hillsdale (NJ): Erlbaum.

Van den Daele, L.D. (1968). Qualitative models in developmental analysis. Developmental Psychology, 1, 303-310.

Van den Daele, L.D. (1974). Infrastructure and transition in developmental analysis. Human Development, 17, 1-23.

Van den Daele, L.D. (1976). Formal models of development. In

K.F. Riegel and J.A. Meacham (Eds.), The developing individual in a changing world: vol. 1. The Hague: Mouton.

Van Geert, P. (1986). The Concept of Development. In P. van Geert (Ed.), Theory Building in developmental Psychology. Amsterdam: North Holland.

Van Geert, P. (1983). The development of perception, cognition and language. A theoretical approach. London: Routledge & Kegan Paul.

Van Geert, P. (in press). Sociocultural reproduction and individual development. Cognitive systems.

Vedder, P. (1986). Development and Social expectations. In P. van Geert (Ed.), Theory Building in developmental Psychology. Amsterdam: North Holland.

Waterman, A.S. (1982). Identity development from adolescence to adulthood. An extension of theory and a review of research. Developmental Psychology, 18, 341-358.

Waterman, A.S. & Waterman, C.K. (1971). A longitudinal study of changes in ego identity during the freshman year at college. Developmental Psychology, 5, 167-173.

Wexler, K. (1982). A principle theory for language acquisition. In E. Wanner & L.R. Gleitman (Eds.), Language Acquisition: The state of art. Cambridge: Cambridge University Press.

Wohlwill, J.F. (1973). The study of behavioral development. New York: Academic Press.

PART 2

CAUSES AND CONDITIONS OF DEVELOPMENTAL CHANGE

Theory Building in Developmental Psychology
P.L.C. van Geert (editor)
© Elsevier Science Publishers B.V. (North-Holland), 1986

3

Learning and Models of Development

Martin Atkinson

This paper argues that adequate theories of development must contain a specification of a mechanism which explains how, in interaction with its environment, the organism moves from one developmental stage to the next. Recent work in language development, while having little to say in detail on the nature of such mechanisms, has usually subscribed to hypothesis formulation and testing and the general characteristics of this approach are outlined. It is maintained that linguists and cognitive scientists have advanced interesting views on developmental mechanism and it is shown how the work of linguists such as Chomsky is geared towards circumscribing the set of hypotheses available in a hypothesis formulation and testing model. This remains true of Chomsky's more recent work on parametersetting and the paper argues for an important contrast between such an approach and that advocated by Fodor to the acquisition of concepts, where hypothesis formulation and confirmation is rejected in favour of triggering.

In this paper I shall discuss some ideas on the role of learning in adequate theories of development, with particular reference to the development of aspects of human language and systems of concepts. For the most part, the ideas in question have not emerged from the work of developmental psychologists, but from work in Linguistics and Cognitive Science. Because of this, the form of the arguments I shall consider is somewhat unusual from the perspective of developmental psychology, paying no attention to how children behave in relevant respects at certain stages of their development. The question as to how far one can proceed with such a methodology is itself an interesting one, which can be seen as having an optimistic answer to the extent that the arguments reviewed below have substance. I feel that the conclusions we shall meet merit the serious attention of anyone interested in developmental phenomena and that they deserve to be taken into account in the context of more traditional forms of enquiry. In the discussion that follows, I begin by briefly reiterating the conditions for the explanatory adequacy of developmental theories that I put forward in Atkinson (1982). I go on to consider ideas on the development of language, associated most notably with the work of Chomsky and his associates (Chomsky, 1975, 1980, 1981a; Hornstein and Lightfoot, 1981; Hornstein, 1984), and speculations on the origins of concepts due to Fodor (1975, 1981). Since much of this work is likely to be unfamiliar to developmental psychologists, I shall largely restrict myself to uncritical presentation of the arguments. However, I shall occasionally express reservations where these seem to be particularly pertinent.

CRITERIA FOR ADEQUACY.

The need for criteria for evaluating the explanatory status of theoretical proposals in developmental psychology is self-evident. In Atkinson (1982) I proposed that an adequate theory of development in some cognitive domain should satisfy a number of conditions. Briefly, such theories were viewed as $(n + 1)$-tuples $(T_1, T_2, \ldots, T_n, M)$, where each T_i $(1 \leq i \leq n)$ was itself a (non-developmental) theory constructed to account for the relevant data at sampling point t_i $(1 \leq i \leq n)$ and M was a mechanism which constituted an adequate account of the transition from T_i to T_{i+1} $(1 \leq i \leq n - 1)$. Construing developmental theories in this way suggested a set of five conditions which were offered as necessary conditions on theory adequacy.

First, each T_i $(1 \leq i \leq n)$ should provide an adequate explanation for the relevant data at t_i $(1 \leq i \leq n)$. What qualifies as an "adequate explanation" in this context is going to be a consequence of how we view the problem of explanation in non-developmental psychology, and this latter problem will, to some extent, have its character determined by what we are prepared to accept as "relevant data". In particular, it is clear that such a problem might change its complexion in fundamental ways if we restrict the class of relevant data to samples of quantifiable behaviour collected in controlled experimental environments (e.g. reaction times), as opposed to adopting a more liberal stance where, for example, naturalistic observations or introspective reports are legitimised. Different views on these complex issues have been associated with the major trends in psychology since the mid-nineteenth century, and it is certainly not the case that a consensus has emerged. The answerability of psychological theories to experimentally controlled behavioural data, so dominant in the behaviourist period and in much modern cognitive psychology, has recently been challenged by Chomsky (1980) in terms which are strikingly reminiscent of the pluralist methodology advocated by Wundt in his pioneering work in the foundations of psychology. Recognition of the complex aetiology of any behaviour involving the comprehension and use of language suggests that it is too simplistic to regard the psychological plausibility of a linguistic theory, interpreted as a theory of mental representation, as seriously challenged by behavioural investigation, and for instructive discussion of some of the difficulties involved, the reader is referred to Berwick and Weinberg (1984) and Hamburger and Crain (1984).[1] For the purposes of this paper, it is sufficient to note that the status of explanation in non-developmental psychology is controversial, and to be clear that any discussion of explanatory developmental theories will inherit this controversy. Later sections of the paper will be concerned with ideas which have emerged outside the experimental study of behaviour, and I submit that currently we have no methodological reason for believing that they are any the worse for that.

My second condition was that each T_i ($1 \leq i \leq n$) should be constructed with reference to some general conception of what a theory in the domain in question should look like. In other words, each of the theories in the sequence $(T_1, T_2, \ldots, T_n)$ should be instances of a particular general theory. Obviously, the nature of the general theory will depend crucially on taking a certain stand on my first condition, as it might be anticipated that theories accounting for behavioural data will be rather different to theories responding to other classes of phenomena. I maintain that only if this condition is satisfied, is it possible to compare theories in the sequence in a meaningful way and make sense of the transition from one stage to the next as a developmental process. Furthermore, a failure to refer particular theories to a general theory leaves open the possibility, in my view frequently exploited in studies of language development, for the introduction of ad hoc concepts and notational devices to deal with recalcitrant phenomena at individual sampling points.

An attempt to capture the robust intuition that cognitive systems become more complex as the organism develops led to the formulation of my third condition. Originally, I believed that this would provide a particularly powerful tool for examining developmental theories. However, it is important to be prudent for a variety of reasons. Most importantly, one should not impose a condition which excludes the possibility of a more or less fundamental reorganisation in some cognitive domain, whereby certain capacities, previously organised in terms of one type of structure and/or process, begin to partake of a different form of organisation.[2] In such cases, it is quite likely that complexity will not be easily defined between the two systems of organisation, and there may be no clear sense in which a later system can be regarded as more complex than its predecessor. Despite this reservation and others which I shall not raise here, increasing complexity remains a feature of many developmental processes. In particular, the idea that the developing organism builds up more complex systems of cognitive representation by adding to what it already has is an appealing one, and a statement of such a desideratum with various riders constituted my third condition.

These first three conditions can be seen as generally concerned with the conceptual coherence of developmental proposals. Satisfaction of them requires the theorist to display some metatheoretical awareness and to subscribe to standards of explicitness which ought to be a characteristic of any rational enquiry. Seen in this light, I believe that they are quite uncontroversial. Equally, however, it can be maintained that they do not engage the more substantive questions that the developmentalist must face, and recognition of this indicates the need for further conditions.

To approach what is required here, we can consider a situation in which a theorist has offered a sequence of theories $(T_1, T_2, \ldots, T_n)$ which satisfies the three conditions I have outlined above. More specifically, and in order to keep the exposition simple, assume that the sequence satisfies a version of the third condition whereby each T_{i+1} is more complex than each T_i ($1 \leq i \leq n$) by virtue of the addition of new items.[3] The obvious question such a situation leads to is that of why items enter the sequence in the order in which they do, and there appear to be at least three types of answer that we can consider to this question. First, it could be the case that the organism's environment is temporally structured in such a way that the information necessary for the emergence of later items is available only after the information necessary for the emergence of earlier items. To take a simple example, it seems plausible to suggest that a child's lexical development is to some extent determined by the availability of lexical forms in the linguistic environment and that mothers and others, when speaking to small children, do not employ arbitrary samples from the lexicon of the language being acquired. In short, we can tell an environmental story as to why "dog" is acquired before "rationalism" and such a story would amount to a first step in producing an environmental explanation for the sequence in question.[4] Second, it may be that the structure of the general theory of which the T_i ($1 \leq i \leq n$) are instances is such as to make sequences other than the postulated one unintelligible. Here simple examples are not so easy to find, but one which is reasonably approachable and will concern us later is to do with the development of concepts. Suppose that we adopt a position that the concepts available to a mature organism can be partitioned, according to some explicit criterion, into two sets, a primitive set and a complex set, members of the latter being definable by applying a specified set of operations to members of the former. Thus, to ascribe to the view that the concept BACHELOR is definable as the logical conjunction of the concepts HUMAN, MALE and UNMARRIED and to have some criterion for recognising these latter three concepts as primitive would be a species of the position with which I am concerned. From this simple view of what a system of concepts can look like (i.e. a general theory of possible conceptual systems for the organism in question), it follows that the logically complex concepts cannot appear before their primitive components. Therefore, aspects of the sequence we might be considering will be necessary consequences of the structure of the general theory we are using. To the extent that the general theory provides an acceptable characterisation of the organism's mature state in the relevant domain, we are likely to be particularly attracted by such proposals: if the organism ends up in such and such a state, then it could only have got there by this route. In Atkinson (1982) I referred to such explanations as teleological explanations.

Thirdly, it may be possible to systematically relate a developmental sequence in one cognitive domain to a similar sequence in another in such a way as to defend the view that development in the domain under study is causally dependent on development in this second domain. Many students of language development have been attracted by the propositions that aspects of this process are causally dependent on aspects of non-linguistic cognitive development and that to flesh out this dependence is to explain the former. Piaget and his followers have also fairly consistently subscribed to this position (see contributions to Piattelli-Palmarini 1980). Such a strategy gives rise to many complications which it would be inappropriate to pursue here (see Atkinson 1982 for some discussion). If such a dependence can be convincingly defended, then we have a reductive explanation for the developmental phenomena with which we started.[5] My fourth condition is simply a catalogue of the three possibilities mentioned here, with successful theories offering one type of explanation or a mixture of explanation types, there being no reason to believe that all aspects of development, even within one domain, are going to succumb to the same sort of analysis. It is not claimed that the catalogue is complete.

So far there has been no mention of the mechanism which I suggest is a necessary part of any explanatory account of an organism's development in any cognitive domain. The requirement that the theory contain a specification of such a mechanism constitutes the fifth and final condition from my earlier work, and it is this aspect of developmental models to which I shall be giving most attention in the remainder of this paper. It is important to be clear that the call for a mechanism is in response to a different, though related, question to that leading to the previous condition. There we were concerned with getting a hold on why development proceeds in the way it does, but here we are interested in how the process takes place. Thus, even if we are in a position to provide an environmental account of a certain developmental sequence, this will not tell us how the organism recruits the information supplied by the environment in developing its cognitive systems. Similar considerations apply to the two other types of explanation mentioned above.

These five conditions, then, constitute some kind of framework against which we can evaluate specific developmental proposals. In my 1982 book, I conducted this exercise for a large number of theoretical positions in different areas of first language acquisition, finding most of these positions inadequate in serious respects, and it is not my intention to rehearse these arguments here. Instead, I wish to take as a starting point the claim that satisfaction of my final condition - specification of a mechanism - is virtually non-existent in such work and use this as an excuse to

introduce the considerations mentioned in my opening
paragraph.

Insofar as any attention at all has been paid to the
nature of developmental mechanisms in first language
acquisition work conducted on the basis of collecting data
from children, most writers appear to subscribe to a variety
of hypothesis formulation and testing model. Such a model
assumes that the child comes to acquisition equipped with a
set of hypotheses. These hypotheses constitute a hypothesis
space through which the child must search for the correct
hypothesis as he is exposed to data from the relevant domain.
Standardly, the hypothesis space will be viewed as part of the
child's innate endowment. However, there is usually scant
regard for the problem of specifying the hypothesis space
which provides the hypotheses nor for the question of how
hypotheses are selected and rejected.[6] Some attempt to remedy
these defects appears in the proposals we shall be considering
below.

Before turning to the questions which are going to
directly concern me, it will be useful to justify the
identification of hypothesis formulation and testing with
learning. Fodor (1977) construes learning as a change in
epistemic state occasioned by an external event where there is
a relation of content between the organism's representation of
the external event and the consequent change in epistemic
state. Such a construal allows us to distinguish between
learning and the arbitrary fixation of belief, where the
latter does not require the aforementioned relation of
content. Accordingly, coming to believe that it rains a lot in
Edinburgh by being hit over the head, swallowing a pill or
being told that 2 + 2 = 4 do not constitute instances of
learning (although they are externally occasioned changes in
epistemic state), whereas coming to believe this proposition
by virtue of living in Edinburgh and opening the curtains
every morning or having someone tell you that it rains a lot
in Edinburgh look like paradigmatic instances of learning.
Given this distinction, any sensible hypothesis formulation
and testing mechanism is going to be a learning mechanism. The

qualifier "sensible" here is intended to rule out a device which selects and rejects hypotheses at random which would not be plausibly regarded as a learning mechanism. In practice, of course, though the considerations are not usually explicit, purveyors of hypothesis formulation and testing mechanisms regard the testing of hypotheses as taking place in conjunction with new data and the rejection and adoption of hypotheses as taking account of these data. From now on, therefore, I shall assume that any developmental account which includes such a mechanism has a significant learning component.

I shall now proceed to discuss the following issues. In the second section, I shall explain why some linguists insist that the range of hypotheses available to the learner should be restricted, and give some examples of the sort of restriction which might be necessary.

In the third section, I shall outline Chomsky's recent views (1980, 1981a) on language acquisition in the context of parameter-setting as a developmental mechanism and consider whether these views constitute a significant shift from his earlier discussions (1965) which fairly consistently adopted a hypothesis formulation and testing framework. The fourth section will examine the motivation for Fodor's (1981) attack on hypothesis formulation and testing as a suitable mechanism for understanding the acquisition of concepts and the alternative he offers to this traditional approach, concluding with an analysis of the relationship between Fodor's views on concept acquisition and Chomsky's stance on the development of language. Here we shall be concerned with whether there is a "Chomsky-Fodor position", as the alliance these two figures present in Piattelli-Palmarini (1980) would seem to suggest.

RESTRICTING THE HYPOTHESIS SPACE.

The arguments I shall present in this section are concerned exclusively with the syntax of natural languages. There are probably two major reasons why such arguments are

fairly easy to find. First, syntax is the most extensively
researched area of language structure within modern
linguistics. Thus, analyses and hypotheses are more readily
available in this area than in phonology or semantics. Second,
linguists working within the Chomskian framework usually
subscribe to the view that if language has certain properties
which distinguish it from other cognitive systems - if there
is a language module (Fodor, 1983), these properties are
likely to be related to syntax, as both phonology and
semantics are probably going to interact extensively with
non-linguistic cognitive systems, the former with aspects of
general auditory perception and articulatory programming, and
the latter with the general conceptual system (for relevant
work in phonology, see Dresher 1981, McCarthy 1981, and in
semantics, Hornstein 1984).

Let us begin by considering a simple example which
Chomsky himself has used on numerous occasions (1975, 1980).
Linguists concerned with the syntax of natural languages
assume that the system consists of a set of rules of various
formal types which determine the legitimate combinations of
words in the language. It is further assumed that a hypothesis
as to the nature of these rules constitutes a hypothesis about
the mental representation of a language in the minds of its
speakers, i.e. it is assumed that the rules are
"psychologically real". However, it is not assumed that the
rules are utilised in any straightforward way in the
production and comprehension of speech, one reason for this
being that these activities standardly involve complex
interactions between the language system and other
non-linguistic capacities, and it follows that experimentally
testable predictions about the dynamics of speech production
and perception are not going to be readily formulable on the
basis of the linguist's hypotheses. It also follows that it is
going to be extremely difficult to refute or confirm a
linguist's claims on the basis of behavioural data, since from
the present perspective such data have no privileged status in
evaluating psychological theories. What we have, then, is the
methodological pluralism referred to above, where behavioural

data constitute one type among several which may be relevant in evaluating a hypothesis about the mental representation of language (for an alternative view from within linguistics, see Bresnan 1978, Bresnan and Kaplan 1982).

It is clear that it is unnecessary to perform experiments to show that native speakers of English, given a declarative sentence, can form the corresponding yes-no interrogative. So, presented with the declaratives in (1), no native speaker of English will have any trouble in supplying the corresponding interrogatives of (2):

(1) a. The man is here
    b. The man has left
    c. The tall man has left
    d. The man who is outside is impatient

(2) a. Is the man here?
    b. Has the man left?
    c. Has the tall man left?
    d. Is the man who is outside impatient?

The nature of the rule which underlies this correspondence is not difficult to see. In each of these examples, we are forming the yes-no interrogative by inverting the order of the subject of the sentence and the first verbal element following the subject, and, while this is not sufficiently precise for the full range of English yes-no interrogatives, it will serve for our purposes here. Assuming, then, that mature native speakers of English have this rule as part of their mental representation of the language, we can now consider the question of how they got it.

Consider a learner of English who has been exposed to (1a), (1b), (2a) and (2b) and to no other declarative-interrogative pairs. Of course, the correct rule is consistent with this restricted set of data but so are other rules which might be viewed as simpler than the correct alternative. In particular, a rule which says that in forming yes-no interrogatives in English from their corresponding declaratives, you should move the third word to the front works equally well for these data, and, as it does not require recognition of the abstract linguistic construct of subject,

it might be thought to be more readily available to the
learner than the subject-inversion rule. Of course, if the
learner were to adopt such a rule, it would go wrong on (1c),
yielding (3):

(3)*Man the tall has left?

Now, there are two possibilities to consider. Some learners of
English produce errors such as that in (3), are corrected and
formulate a new hypothesis. Alternatively, no learners of
English produce errors such as that in (3). Chomsky maintains
that the latter is the case, and, if this is so, it seems to
demand that no learner of English ever considers the
hypothesis which refers merely to the linear position of words
in the sentence, even though such a hypothesis consists of a
perfectly good rule which accounts for the learner's data up
to the point in question.

The argument can be extended by now granting the learner
exposure to (3a) and (3b) along with the earlier
declarative-interrogative pairs. Now the learner will not be
tempted by the simple linear hypothesis, but a rule which
requires movement of the first verb in the sentence to the
front will still work, and again it may be possible to
construct an argument that the category of verbs is somehow
more available to the learner than the notion of subject and
that this rule will be preferred to the correct one. However,
this rule comes unstuck on (1d) where it yields the
ungrammatical (4):

(4)*Is the man who outside is impatient?

Again Chomsky maintains that children learning English do not
commit this sort of error and that therefore they must never
consider the incorrect hypothesis. Accordingly, the hypothesis
space through which the learner must search in acquiring the
syntax of English is restricted so as not to permit hypotheses
which embrace rules which are perfectly easy to formulate and
completely explicit but which have the wrong sort of formal
properties.

Before going on to consider a less well-known example, it
will be useful to locate Chomsky's argument within a more
general context. The above discussion of yes-no interrogatives

is an instance of a "poverty of the stimulus argument" and the nature of such arguments is systematically discussed in Hornstein and Lightfoot (1981) and Hornstein (1984). These authors suggest that there are three ways in which the child learner's linguistic environment can be viewed as impoverished from the point of view of learning syntax.

First, they rehearse a point, often stressed by Chomsky himself in the 1960s, that the child's linguistic environment is populated by false starts, hesitations and various forms of speech error along with well-formed grammatical strings. If this is so, the induction of a syntactic system which characterises all and only the well-formed strings of the language being acquired is going to be impossible, unless the hypothesis space available to the child is severely restricted. However, research on the speech addressed by mothers and others to small children has shown that it contains a remarkably small number of syntactically ill-formed strings (papers in Snow and Ferguson 1977), so it is difficult to assess the force of this argument.[7]

Second, Hornstein and Lightfoot note that the syntactic system that the learner acquires must comprehend an infinite class of data, since it has been accepted since the beginnings of modern linguistics that the number of well-formed strings in any human language is not finite. The data to which the learner is exposed are, of course, finite in number. Now, while it may be difficult in practice to formulate a procedure that will come up with the correct system characterising an infinite set of data on the basis of exposure to only a finite number of instances, Hornstein and Lightfoot recognise that there is no clear problem of principle here. However, this does not affect their overall position which they believe to be completely vindicated by their third argument.

Mature native speakers of English have a range of knowledge concerning English expressions which extends beyond knowing that certain strings of words are well-formed. They know that (5) is ambiguous, that (6) and (7) are paraphrases and that (8) is ill-formed:

(5) John likes linguistiscs more than Mary

(6) It is obvious that the mind is modular

(7) That the mind is modular is obvious

(8)*The men said that Mary kissed each other

Hornstein and Lightfoot ask how it is possible for mature native speakers to have such knowledge. In considering their answer to this question, let us focus on ill-formedness, as it is here that the issues are clearest. Thinking of (8), one might contemplate the possibility that all native-speakers of English have, at some point in their development, been explicitly told that such strings are ungrammatical, but, while activity such as this may occasionally go on in the second language learning classroom, it is evidently not a feature of first language acquisition. As an alternative, it might be maintained that information about the status of (8) is supplied indirectly and there are various possibilities that might be considered here. For example, one could suppose that adults respond negatively or do not respond at all to children's ill-formed strings, thereby providing the child with information which enables him to deduce that the string he has just uttered is ill-formed. Suffice it to say that any such story would require some fairly sophisticated processing by the child and, more importantly, that the available evidence on the status of adults' responses to children's ill-formed strings does not encourage belief in the story (see Brown and Hanlon (1970) for the classic study and Hirsh-Pasek, Treiman and Schneiderman (1984) for some recent interesting findings). The upshot of all this is that linguists working within this framework have embraced the assumption that the child receives no information about ill-formed strings as he learns a language. Therefore, the fact that the child grows into an adult who knows about ill-formed strings and can make this knowledge explicit becomes remarkable.[8]

We can see now how Chomsky's argument, that the child must never consider hypotheses containing rules which refer merely to the linear position of words in sentences fits into this general pattern. We would expect some learners of English to accept (3) and (4) as well-formed at some stage in their development. However, there is nothing to suggest that this is ever the case. So, in the absence of explicit and implicit information about the status of (3) and (4), how do we know never to try them? The answer is that we are forbidden from trying them by constraints on the hypothesis space to which we have access, and the belief is that similar considerations could be brought to bear on the phenomena illustrated by (5)-(8) and countless other examples.

An interesting and clear case of the sort of argument I am concerned with here is presented by Baker (1979). He considers sentences such as those in (9) and (10):

(9) a. John gave a book to Mary

     b. John told a story to Mary

(10) a. John gave Mary a book

     b. John told Mary a story

Clearly, there is a syntactic and semantic relation between (9a) and (10a) and between (9b) and (10b) and we might try to formulate a rule encoding this relation along the lines of (11):[9]

(11) whenever we have an English sentence of the form:

     Noun Phrase$_1$ - Verb - Noun Phrase$_2$ - to - Noun Phrase$_3$

     then we have a synonymous English sentence of the form:

     Noun Phrase$_1$ - Verb - Noun Phrase$_3$ - Noun Phrase$_2$

The problem with this rule is that it is too general, as the data in (12) and (13) indicate:[10]

(12) a. John donated a book to the library

     b. John said something flattering to Mary

(13) a.*John donated the library a book

     b.*John said Mary something flattering

But if we adopt the assumption that the child is not provided with information about ill-formed strings, we would seem forced to expect children to make errors like those in (13a) and (13b) at some point in their development. Positive data - the only data to which the child has access - suggest the generalisation of (11), so the child should make the generalisation and produce the errors. Baker maintains that children do not produce such errors (but see Mazurkewich and White, 1984) and if he is correct, there is a profound puzzle

here. Baker's solution to the puzzle is, of course, easy to
anticipate: he proposes to constrain the hypothesis space
available to the child in such a way that the generalisation
of (11) cannot be part of a legitimate hypothesis. The details
of how he does this need not concern us here, nor would it be
appropriate to pursue how he captures the relationship between
(9) and (10) within an alternative framework. The important
point for our purposes is that the hypothesis space must be
constrained.

I hope that these rather simple examples are sufficient
to give the non-linguist reader some insight into the thinking
that lies behind the linguist's preoccupation with
constraints. The picture of the acquisition of syntax which
emerges from such considerations is a straightforward one. The
child has available a set of hypotheses, the form of which is
constrained by his genetic endowment. Furthermore, although
this has not been discussed here, the constraints on the
hypotheses are specific to language and are not derivable from
constructs in any non-linguistic domain. At some point in the
child's development, it will be appropriate to credit him with
a syntactic system and this will be modified, while continuing
to honour the constraints, by a process of rejecting
inadequate hypotheses and selecting new ones in the light of
new data as the child gets older.[11] In his own work from the
1960s Chomsky was never very explicit on the details of this
mechanism of hypothesis formulation and confirmation and it
was left to Wexler and Culicover (1980) to formulate an
explicit learning theory for syntactic systems of the type
Chomsky had been working with some years earlier.[12]
Interestingly, their work showed that in order to achieve
learnability in the sense of selection of the correct
syntactic system after a finite amount of exposure to positive
data, it was necessary to constrain the hypothesis space
available to the learner. Furthermore, several of the
constraints they found it necessary to formulate were
strikingly similar to those arising in more traditional
linguistic analyses.

Summarising this section, then, we can see why the

linguist wishes to maintain that the learner of a language is not confronted with myriad hypotheses of every conceivable form. The hypotheses which the learner will entertain are constrained in non-trivial ways; this much is Chomsky's rationalism and constitutes a sophisticated attempt to satisfy my second condition. However, insofar as explicit ideas on mechanisms of development appear within this approach, these ideas appear to come down to hypothesis formulation and testing, i.e. a learning mechanism.

It might strike some as odd that in his more recent work Chomsky has not been very enthousiastic about Wexler and Culicover's results (1981a). After all, the convergence on abstract constraints might be seen as encouraging for all. Significantly, Chomsky's vocabulary for discussing language development has shifted in this recent period, and now one finds references to parameter-setting rather than to hypothesis testing. It is not clear whether Chomsky himself sees this shift in vocabulary as having much substance, but certainly one commentator who ought to know presents hypothesis testing and parameter-setting in a way that makes them look like alternatives. Fodor (1983, 5) says:

> "The child is viewed as using his primary linguistic data either to decide among the candidate grammars that an innately represented "General Linguistic Theory" enumerates .... or to "calibrate" endogenous rule schemas by fixing parameter values that the innate endowment leaves unspecified".

It is the purpose of the next section to try to exemplify what is involved in parameter-setting and to get clear what differences there are, if any, between this notion and that of hypothesis formulation and testing.

PARAMETER-SETTING.

One thing that immediately distinguishes recent work by Chomsky and his associates from earlier proposals is an explicit emphasis on the deductive structure of syntactic

theories. Chomsky (1981a, 6) has this to say:
"We will see that there are certain complexes of
properties typical of particular types of language;
such collections of properties should be explained
in terms of the choice of parameters in one or
another subsystem. In a tightly integrated theory
with fairly rich internal structure change in a
single parameter may have complex effects, with
proliferating consequences in various parts of the
grammar."
It is my contention that this emphasis on deductive structure
contains the clue to the major differences between the later
and earlier approaches and also to the reasons for Chomsky's
rather lukewarm attitude towards Wexler and Culicover's work.
Furthermore, as the above passage makes clear, there is a
close relationship between the notion of setting a parameter
and understanding what is involved in a deductively rich
theory.

Unfortunately, most of the examples that might be chosen to
illustrate these ideas are deeply embedded in the concepts and
terminology of Chomsky's linguistics and it would not be
possible to give a short exposition of them in this context.
However, the problem of learning the basic word-order
properties of a language has been approached from this
perspective and can be appreciated without developing too much
technical machinery.

    Greenberg   (1963)   is   responsible   for   examining
correlations between different aspects of word-order across a
variety of languages. One of his discoveries was that
word-order properties tended to cluster as indicated in the
groupings of (14) where we could view each of the columns as
representing "complexes of properties" in the passage from
Chomsky cited above (see next page).

Thus, in a language like Japanese, the basic word order in a
simple sentence has the subject preceding the object and the
verb in final position; modifiers, such as adjectives,
genitives and relative clauses, precede the noun they modify;
adverbs precede the verb or adjective they modify; and, rather

(14)

than there being prepositions which precede their noun phrase as in English, there are postpositions which follow their noun phrase (i.e. as if in English we had expressions like "the table on").[13] A language such as Welsh has the mirror-image properties appearing in the right-hand column of (14).
Now, of course, Greenberg did not claim that all languages fall into one or other of these patterns - English is an immediate exception in several respects - but he was convinced that these clusterings were significant and he attempted to capture them by formulating a number of descriptive statements of the general form in (15):

(15)   If a language has X, then with (overwhelmingly) greater than chance frequency it has Y

In this schema, X and Y range over properties of languages which include the word-order properties of (14). Instances of (15) are known as statistical implicational universals.

Huang (1982), working within a modern Chomskian framework, has two criticisms of Greenberg's approach. First, it does nothing to explain why the clusterings of (14) are the ones we find rather than any of the large number of conceivable alternatives. There is nothing logically incoherent about an SOV language with prepositions, so why are such languages uncommon. Further, had Greenberg discovered a positive correlation between SOV and prepositions rather than between SOV and postpositions, he could have encoded this correlation equally well using the schema of (15) and there would be nothing in such a treatment to indicate that such a correlation was unexpected. Second, Greenberg merely notes exceptions - the statistical nature of (15) acknowledges that exceptions exist - but does nothing to explain them. Huang goes on to explore an alternative approach which, he believes, meets both of these criticisms. Here I shall consider only the first problem, as discussion of the second would raise too many complexities of terminology.

Returning to the clusters of (14), there is an obvious generalisation to be made about them in terms of where the head of syntactic phrasal categories occurs. Thus, to say that modifiers, such as adjectives, genitives and relative clauses, precede the noun in Japanese is to say that Japanese noun phrases are head final, the noun being the head of the noun phrase. Similarly, to say that abverbs precede the adjectives they modify is to say that Japanese adjectival phrases are head final, and so on for other entries in the left-hand column of (14). Finally, some linguists have argued that the verb is appropriately regarded as the head of the sentence and if this is so, we can say that the SOV order of simple Japanese sentences shows that the sentence too is head final in this language. By similar considerations, Welsh is head initial across a variety of syntactic categories.

Now, Huang proposes that what is involved in learning the basic phrasal organisation of a language is the setting of various parameters. One such parameter is that of (16):

(16) head initial vs head final

The idea is that a child comes to language learning with this parameter unset and linguistic experience in the form of perception of a head initial or head final construction serves to fix the value of the parameter. Furthermore, once the value of the parameter has been fixed, certain deductive consequences flow. For example, if the child is exposed to and perceives a head final noun phrase and if this is sufficient to fix the value of the parameter as head final, then the child will "expect" the language being learned to have SOV word-order, postpositions, etc., and to the extent that subsequent experience confirms these expectations, the child has nothing else to learn in this area of syntax. Of course, if subsequent experience does not confirm these expectations, as would be the case for a child learning English, something will have to be done, and, while the details of what this is

would take us into the complexities I am anxious to avoid, it
is clear that the rejection of the global setting for the
parameter of (16) would be involved (see Atkinson 1985a for
more detailed discussion of this).[14]

Armed with this fairly straightforward example, we can
attempt to assess the status of parameter-setting as a
developmental mechanism. One thing that seems obvious to me is
that there is no reason why we should not treat the two values
of the parameter in (16) as constituting a pair of hypotheses.
Further, the selection of one or the other hypothesis is
contingent on the occurrence of an external event, the
representation of which is related in content to the selected
hypothesis: if I perceive a head final construction in my
linguistic environment, then I choose the hypothesis that says
that all major phrasal constructions are head final. This does
not look different in kind from a process whereby perception
of white swans leads to the belief that all swans are white.
Finally, a global setting of the parameter as head final will
be rejected on the basis of encounters with head initial
constructions. In short, this looks like a paradigmatic
instance of a learning mechanism. It is, therefore, somewhat
puzzling to repeatedly come across statements from Chomsky and
his supporters such as the following from Lightfoot (1982,
19):

> "It is probably inappropriate .... to speak of
> language "learning" .... but rather we should think
> in terms of language emergence, development, or
> growth, analogously to the growth of a physical
> organ."

What distinguishes Chomsky's recent work form that of Wexler
and Culicover is not the fact that the latter includes a
significant learning theory while the former does not. Both
confront the learner with sets of hypotheses which have to be
selectively eliminated in the light of new experience.
However, because of the rich deductive structure of the theory
favoured by Chomsky, it follows that the role of learning in
his approach is relatively attenuated. What the rich deductive
structure of the theory amounts to is that learning about some

aspect of the language - having the value of a parameter fixed
- may have profound consequences for other aspects of the
language, so that no learning is necessary in these areas. In
our simple illustrative example, learning about noun phrase
structure had implications for adjectival phrase structure,
etc. Furthermore, there will be far fewer hypotheses for the
learner to consider than in the Wexler and Culicover approach.
This is because possible loci of variation are no longer
viewed as independent, but as clustering on certain values in
a way determined by the deductive structure of the theory.[15]
We can conclude, then, that while Chomsky's rationalism is
perhaps taken a step further with the parameter-setting model,
learning continues to play a fundamental role. Talk of growth
and analogies with bodily organs is really quite out of place
in this context. As Fodor points out, what distinguishes the
development of language from that of bodily organs is that the
former involves the emergence of representations which have to
be the objects of propositional attitudes and, as such, are
related in content to the representations of external events
(1983, 5):

> "So Chomsky's account of language learning is the
> story of how innate endowment and perceptual
> experience interact in virtue of their respective
> contents." (emphasis in original).

The innate endowment is the set of open parameters along with
a specification of their deductive consequences; the
interaction with perceptual experience is a learning process.

Finally, it seems likely that articulation of the
deductive structure of the theory will provide a framework for
studying a variety of phenomena in first language acquisition.
In particular, we might anticipate that forms of teleological
explanation for aspects of syntactic development would emerge
from this theoretical perspective.

THE ACQUISITION OF CONCEPTS.

There are two main strands to Fodor's arguments

concerning the status of what he takes to be traditional
empiricist accounts of concept acquisition. The first,
presented in detail in Fodor (1975) and in his contributions
to Piattelli-Palmarini (1980), is that such theories, whatever
their virtues in other respects, cannot be interpreted as
theories of concept acquisition. The second, appearing in
Fodor (1981), is that such theories are flawed in crucial
respects however they are construed, and this indicates the
need for an alternative which Fodor goes on to outline. It is
the relationship between this alternative and Chomsky's views
on the acquisition of syntax which will ultimately concern us.

Let us begin by considering the argument that a certain
view on the acquisition of concepts does not in fact address
that phenomenon. This view is that concepts are acquired on
the basis of the formulation and testing of hypotheses, i.e.
learning. The way in which it is intended to work is seen most
clearly in the context of the "concept learning" experiment,
but Fodor maintains that subscribers to the view would
normally expect it to be applicable to more naturalistic
situations.

In the typical concept learning experiment, the subject is
presented with stimuli which vary along a number of dimensions
(e.g. shape, colour, number) and has to learn to sort them
into two sets on the basis of some experimenter-determined
criterial attribute(s). The sorting may involve putting
stimuli into two piles, producing a specified nonsense
syllable to the appropriate stimuli, etc. and the experimenter
provides feedback on the correctness of the subject's
responses. After a number of runs through the stimuli, the
subject will sort them correctly and will then be said to have
learned the concept.

Fodor insists that only one remotely plausible story has ever
been told about what is going on in this situation. This is
that the subject proceeds by formulating and testing
hypotheses. Thus, if the experimenter has decided that the
concept to be acquired is RED CIRCLES with number being an
irrelevant cue, the subject may begin with the hypothesis that
the concept is BLUE with both number and shape being

irrelevant. Presented with three blue triangles, the subject
offers a positive response and gets the feedback that this is
wrong. This immediately serves to refute the hypothesis and
the subject formulates another hypothesis for the next trial,
say RED. Three red circles leads to a positive response which
is reinforced so the hypothesis is retained, but then one red
square also leads to a positive response which is not
reinforced and this requires a further modification in the
hypothesis. Continuing in this way, the subject eventually
comes up with the correct hypothesis from which point on no
further errors occur.

Now, if something like this story is approximately correct,
there are many interesting questions one can formulate to do
with the manner of selection of hypotheses, the nature of the
confirmation measure for hypotheses, etc., and the enormous
literature devoted to this paradigm can be seen as an extended
investigation of such questions. However, it is readily
apparent that a story along these lines cannot be a story
about the learning of concepts. The reason for this is that,
in order to be in a position to produce the appropriate
behaviour, the subject must first formulate the hypothesis
which, of course, includes the relevant concept. It follows
that what the subject learns in such an experiment is not a
new concept - common sense suggests anyway that RED CIRCLES is
not going to be a new concept for such subjects - but the fact
that the experimenter wants a particular sort of behaviour to
be produced to instances of a concept with which the subject
is already familiar, i.e. what we have is a case of fixation
of belief and not concept learning.[16]

The generalisation of this is that if learning is construed as
hypothesis formulation and testing, and if a developing
organism exhibits increasingly powerful systems of
representation in a given domain as it matures, then the
mechanism mediating the development cannot be learning. This
is because such a mechanism requires the formulation of
hypotheses within the less powerful system which express the
notions of the more powerful system and this is not possible.
Note further that this generalisation applies to the notions

of syntactic development I have considered above, since I have argued at some length that hypothesis formulation and testing is crucially involved in these processes. So here again what we would have would be a process of fixation of belief - the belief that the current hypothesis is the correct representation of the syntactic system of the linguistic environment.

Turning now to the second aspect of Fodor's deliberations, in Fodor (1981) he contrasts what he takes to be traditional empiricist and rationalist accounts of the acquisition of concepts. For the empiricist, says Fodor, there is a set of primitive concepts which is relatively small and standardly defined with reference to some epistemological criterion. Such a criterion usually involves sensory properties, so, according to this position, RED; STRAIGHT and SWEET would be candidates for membership in the primitive set. Alongside the primitive concepts, there is a larger set of complex concepts and these can be defined in terms of members of the primitive set using some sort of combinatorial apparatus. The nature of this apparatus may be association, as in many traditional accounts, or something more modern such as a set of Boolean operations. Whatever its nature, it is assumed to apply iteratively to the complex concepts, yielding concepts which can only be expressed using a phrase in English, e.g. LIKES LINGUISTICS.
The distinctions between primitive, complex and phrasal concepts provides a schematisation of the possible conceptual repertoire for an organism, this consisting of the set of primitive concepts and those concepts which result from the application of the presumed combinatorial apparatus to the primitive concepts; sometimes such results will be complex non-phrasal concepts and sometimes they will be phrasal. The question then arises as to how the different types of concept are acquired within this schematisation. For the complex concepts and the phrasal concepts, we have already met the answer: they are acquired via hypothesis formulation and testing, and, because of the considerations above, it is not clear that we have a serious model for the acquisition of

concepts here. What of the primitive concepts? Here talk of
hypothesis formulation and testing is out of place, as the
primitive concepts are not decomposable into more primitive
components, some combination of which could constitute the
substance of a hypothesis. Traditional empiricists such as
Hume were well aware of this and Fodor's construal of their
views is that they assumed that the mechanism responsible for
the acquisition of primitive concepts was a non-learning
mechanism, triggering. What distinguishes triggering from
hypothesis formulation and testing is that, whereas the latter
depends on there being a rational relation of content between
the organism's representation of an occasioning instance of a
concept and the concept acquired, the former requires only a
"brute-causal" relation. Thus, learning is a rational-causal
process and triggering is brute-causal, and, according to the
empiricist position, primitive concepts are acquired by
brute-causal triggering by the environment whereas complex and
phrasal concepts are acquired via rational-causal learning
involving the formulation and testing of hypotheses defined on
the primitive basis.

Turning to the rationalist position, it agrees entirely with
that of the empiricist for phrasal concepts. However, it
maintains that many (or perhaps all) non-phrasal concepts are
triggered via brute-causal processes.

Fodor feels that there are overwhelming arguments in favour of
the rationalist position and it would take too long to review
these arguments here. Probably the most compelling concerns
the failure of what Fodor calls the Definition Hypothesis (see
also Fodor, Garett, Walker and Parkes 1980). If the empiricist
view were correct and if we interpret it linguistically, it
ought to follow that the vast majority of lexical items in a
language is definable in terms of a relatively small number of
words referring to sensory properties. But, Fodor claims, not
only is the vast majority of lexical items in any language not
definable in this way, it is not definable tout court. Several
centuries of trying have failed to provide adequate
definitions for anything other than a tiny fraction of the
vocabulary of any natural language, and restricting terms in

the definition to those which refer to sensory properties makes this situation even worse.

If we are convinced by such arguments and others like them, a serious problem arises. According to the rationalist view, the acquisition of non-phrasal concepts appears to depend upon chance encounters with environmental triggers. But, unless we are to assume that such encounters have a mysterious temporal structure, this would entail that there are no constraints on the order in which we acquire concepts. But this sits uncomfortably with the observation that there are important commonalities across children with regard to this order. Fodor must face up to this and his response, while very programmatic, leads to an interesting comparison with the views of Chomsky we have examined earlier.

Fodor proposes that the human mind is organised in terms of a "triggering hierarchy" into a number of layers. The most accessible layer in this hierarchy consists of concepts which can be directly triggered by events in the environment; more remote layers are distinguished by containing concepts which have previously acquired concepts as causal antecedents for their acquisition. The emphasis on "causal" here is extremely important for Fodor. The empiricist can explain why two concepts A and B must precede a third C in development in terms of C being logically composed from A and B, this, of course, being a teleological explanation in my terms.[17] But such a view also leads to the conclusion that C will be definable in terms of A and B and Fodor feels that this conclusion must be resisted. He therefore replaces the logical relation by a causal one, suggesting that A and B are causally necessary for the acquisition of C, and from this nothing follows about the logical status of the relationship between A, B and C.

We can see now that there are important differences between Chomsky's views on the acquisition of syntax and Fodor's on the development of concepts. Both believe that an understanding of the innate structure of the mind is vital to comprehending the processes in which they are interested, and this is probably the substance of the "Chomsky-Fodor position"

alluded to earlier. Beyond this, they can both be seen as
subscribing to a two-stage view of developmental mechanisms,
but the assumed mechanisms at each stage are quite distinct.
For Chomsky, the first stage is that of parameter-setting and
I have argued that this is a rational-causal process of
hypothesis formulation and testing. Fodor's environmental
triggering of the most accessible layer of the triggering
hierarchy is a brute-causal, non-learning process. A parameter
having been set, the rich deductive structure of the theory
takes over and far-reaching consequences for the language
being acquired will emerge. But what emerge will be logical
consequences and this contrasts sharply with Fodor's higher
level triggering where, again, there need be no logical
relation between the causal antecedents for the concept being
acquired and the concept itself.

Everything I have said in this paper is, of course, consistent
with both Chomsky and Fodor being correct (or incorrect) for
their different domains of interest. It would be quite wrong
to conclude that there is a fundamental disagreement between
them. However, I feel that it is important for the
developmentalist to be aware of the differences to which I
have drawn attention, as I believe that both perspectives open
up new possibilities for the study of developmental
mechanisms, possibilities which I see as being extensively
explored in the next generation of research.

NOTES

1. Chomsky's own position on the use of traditional
   methodology in the study of language acquisition is
   apparent from the following statement (1981b, 35):
       "... the explosive growth of language in the child
       makes it impossible to investigate the cognitive
       state attained by the methods of data collection and
       analysis characteristic of developmental psychology,
       requiring modes of analysis of the sort appropriate
       for the investigation of adult knowledge, with the

added difficulty that the system is in transition and that it is generally impossible to elicit judgements with any confidence."

2. Note that such a possibility is not necessarily incompatible with satisfaction of the second condition, although it will require a more abstract general theory to accommodate two individual theories which embrace different principles of organisation. Obviously, one would be suspicious if this more "abstract" theory were simply a disjunction of the two systems, and I suspect that there are complex problems here about what we are prepared to tolerate in the general particular relation.

3. Here I follow Flavell (1972) in using "items" as a superordinate term for any of the constructs we might contemplate appearing in our developmental theories, e.g. habits, categories, concepts, schemas, rules. A more general discussion of what is required here, taking account of the possibility of reorganisation, appears in Atkinson (1982).

4. One should not be misled here by the simplicity of the example. While it is apparent that the existence of lexical forms in the child's linguistic environment is a necessary condition for their acquisition, it is not at all clear that it is a sufficient condition. Even in a case such as this, the environmental account is unlikely to be the whole story.

5. The reduction of some aspect of language development to non-linguistic cognition is, of course, only one of the possibilities that might be considered. Thus, one also finds attempts to explicate aspects of language development in terms of certain views of social structure (Halliday 1975). The issue of modularity is vital here (see below and Fodor 1983). Note further that to successfully effect a reduction in this way would leave

the question of order of development in the reducing domain unanswered.

6. Note that the specification of such a hypothesis space can be seen as satisfying my second condition. To this extent, it is impossible to consider the nature of developmental mechanisms without addressing my second condition.

7. It is worth pointing out, however, that even small amounts of "noisy" data could have very serious implications for a language learning device. See Osherson, Stob and Weinstein (1984) for discussion of this within a formal framework.

8. For more systematic discussion of the assumption about negative data, see Atkinson (1983, 1986). Those familiar with the work of Gold (1967) will recognise the distinction between the assumption that the learner does or does not get exposure to negative data as his distinction between two different modes of data presentation, informant presentation vs text presentation.

9. Readers familiar with the linguistics of the 1960s will recognise this as an informal statement of the transformational rule of Dative Movement.

10. Note that these examples are carefully chosen to suggest that no semantic account of the phenomena is readily available. Thus, we have a physical transaction verb "give" entering into both structures and a similar verb "donate" entering into only one. And we have a verbal transaction verb "tell" appearing in both structures and a similar verb "say" only legitimate in one. The most obvious semantic parameter is orthogonal to the formal variation. See Mazurkewich and White (1984) for much more extensive discussion of these structures and their development.

11. The point at which it becomes appropriate to credit the

child with a syntactic system is itself contentious and is further confused by the difficulty of assessing the import of behavioural data for the nature of the child's representational system (see above). For discussion of some of the issues here, see Gleitman (1981), Atkinson (1985b). The relationship between linguistic theory and the grammatical systems of the child is discussed extensively in White (1981) where account is taken of various possibilities not raised here.

12. Insofar as there was discussion of hypothesis selection in Chomsky's earlier work, it was embedded in considerations of an evaluation measure which could be seen as providing a ranking of hypotheses.

13. To make non-linguists a little more comfortable with this, we can note that the basic word-order in English is SVO; English adjectives precede the noun they modify, relative clauses follow the noun, and there are two genitive constructions, one of which "the man's" precedes the noun and the other of which "of the man" follows the noun; adverbs can precede or follow the verb, "slowly walk", "walk slowly", but they only precede adjectives, "very slow"; English, of course has prepositions and not post-positions. This is not intended to be a comprehensive catalogue of the word-order facts of English.

14. Huang's discussion is principally concerned with the structure of Mandarin Chinese. Interesting experimental work within the parameter-setting approach which is closely related to Huang's ideas has been published by Lust and Chien (1984).

15. Chomsky is happy to speculate in his recent work that the number of core grammatical systems available to the learner is finite. This contrasts with the Wexler and Culicover theory where the learner is confronted by an infinite number of hypotheses.

16. Fodor (1975) considers whether a learning account of this
    type can be saved from complete vacuity by suggesting that
    while the relevant concepts must be available to the
    organism for the formulation of hypotheses before the
    organism has gone through the learning process, the
    concept cannot at this stage be deployed in a range of
    other cognitive tasks. There might be a sense in which the
    organism does not have the concept until after it has
    "learned" it according to the outlined procedures. Fodor
    himself is sufficiently struck by the paradoxical nature
    of his conclusions to say in Piattelli-Palmarini (1980,
    269):

    ".... there must be some notion of learning that is
    so incredibely different from the one we have
    imagined that we don't even know what it would be
    like as things now stand."

17. Of course, equating primitive concepts with sensory
    concepts leads to the prediction that sensory concepts
    will be acquired first on the empiricist position.
    Certainly, lexical development is not consistent with such
    a prediction.

REFERENCES

Atkinson, M. (1982). Explanations in the study of Child
    Language Development. Cambridge: Cambridge University
    Press.
Atkinson, M. (1983). "FLATs and SHARPs: the role of the child
    in language acquisition research." In J. Durand (Ed.), A
    Festchrift for Peter Wexler. University of Essex
    Occasional Papers in Linguistics, No 27.
Atkinson, M. (1985a). "Mechanisms for language development."
    In P. Fletcher & M. Garman (Eds.), Child Language Seminar
    Papers. University of Reading.
Atkinson, M. (1985b). "How linguistic is the one-word stage?"
    In M. Barrett (Ed.), Children's One-word Utterances.

Chichester: Wiley.

Atkinson, M. (1986). "Learnability." In P. Fletcher & M. Garman (Eds.), Language Acquisition (2nd ed.). Cambridge: Cambridge University Press.

Baker, C.L. (1979). "Syntactic theory and the projection problem." Linguistic Inquiry, 10, 533-581.

Berwick, R.C. & Weinberg, A.S. (1984). The Grammatical Basis of Linguistic Performance: Language Use and Acquisition. Cambridge, Mass.: MIT Press.

Bresnan, J. (1978). "A realistic transformational grammar." In M. Halle, J. Bresnan & G. Miller (Eds.), Linguistic Theory and Psychological Reality. Cambridge, Mass.: MIT Press.

Bresnan, J. & Kaplan, R. (1982). "Introduction: grammars as mental representations of language." In J. Bresnan (Ed.), The Mental Representation of Grammatical Relations. Cambridge, Mass.: MIT Press.

Brown, R. & Hanlon, C. (1970). "Derivational complexity and the order of acquisition in child speech." In J.R. Hayes (Ed.), Cognition and the Development of Language. New York: Wiley.

Chomsky, N. (1965). Aspects of the Theory of Syntax. Cambridge, Mass.: MIT Press.

Chomsky, N. (1975). Reflections on Language. New York: Pantheon.

Chomsky, N. (1980). Rules and Representations. Oxford: Blackwell.

Chomsky, N. (1981a). Lectures on Government and Binding. Dordrecht: Foris.

Chomsky, N. (1981b). "Principles and parameters in syntactic theory." In N. Hornstein & D. Lightfoot (Eds.), Explanation in Linguistics: The Logical Problem of Language Acquisition. London: Longman.

Dresher, B.E. (1981). "On the learnability of abstract phonology." In C.L. Baker & J.J. McCarthy (Eds.), The Logical Problem of Language Acquisition. Cambridge, Mass.: MIT Press.

Flavell, J. (1972). "An analysis of cognitive-developmental

sequences." Genetic Psychology Monographs, 86, 279-350.

Fodor, J.A. (1975). The Language of Thought. Hassocks: Harvester.

Fodor, J.A. (1978). "Computation and reduction." In. C.W. Savage (Ed.), Perception and Cognition: Issues in the Foundations of Psychology. Minnesota Studies in the Philosophy of Science: 9. Minneapolis: University of Minnesota Press.

Fodor, J.A. (1981). "The present status of the innateness controversy." In J.A. Fodor, Representations. Hassocks: Harvester.

Fodor, J.A. (1983). The Modularity of Mind. Cambridge, Mass.: MIT Press.

Fodor, J.A., Garrett, M.F., Walker, E.C. & Parkes, C.H. (1980). "Against definitions." Cognition, 8, 263-367.

Gleitman, L.R. (1981). "Maturational determinants of language growth." Cognition, 10, 103-114.

Gold, E.M. (1967). "Language identification in the limit." Information and Control, 10, 447-474.

Greenberg, J. (1963). "Some universals of grammar with particular reference to the order of meaningful elements." In J. Greenberg (Ed.), Universals of Language. Cambridge, Mass.: MIT Press.

Halliday, M.A.K. (1975). Learning How to Mean. London: Arnold.

Hamburger, H. & Crain, S. (1984). "Acquisition of cognitive compiling." Cognition, 17, 85-136.

Hirsh-Pasek, K., Treiman, R. & Schneiderman, M. (1984). "Brown and Hanlon revisited: mothers' sensitivity to ungrammatical forms." Journal of Child Language, 11, 81-88.

Hornstein, N. (1984). Logic as Grammar. Cambridge, Mass.: MIT Press.

Hornstein, N. & Lightfoot, D. (1981). "Introduction." In N. Hornstein & D. Lightfoot (Eds.), Explanation in Linguistics: The Logical Problem of Language Acquisition. London: Longman.

Huang, J. C.-T. (1982). "Logical relations in Chinese and the theory of grammar." Unpublished MIT dissertation.

Lightfoot, D. (1982). The Language Lottery: Towards a Biology of Grammars. Cambridge, Mass.: MIT Press.

Lust, B. & Chien, Y.-C. (1984). "The structure of coordination in first language acquisition of Mandarin Chinese: evidence for a universal. Cognition, 17, 49-83.

McCarthy, J.J. (1981). "The role of the evaluation metric in the acquisition of phonology." In C.L. Baker & J.J. McCarthy (Eds.), The Logical Problem of Language Acquisition. Cambridge, Mass.: MIT Press.

Mazurkewich, I. & White, L. (1984). "The acquisition of the dative alternation: unlearning overgeneralizations." Cognition, 16, 261-283.

Osherson, D.A., Stob, M. & Weinstein, S. (1984). "Learning theory and natural language." Cognition, 17, 1-28.

Piattelli-Palmarini, M. (Ed.) (1980). Language and Learning: The Debate Between Jean Piaget and Noam Chomsky. London: Routledge & Kegan Paul.

Snow, C. & Ferguson, C. (Eds.) (1977). Talking to Children. Cambridge: Cambridge University Press.

Wexler, K. & Culicover, P.W. (1980). Formal Principles of Language Acquisition. Cambridge, Mass.: MIT Press.

White, L. (1981). "The responsibility of grammatical theory to acquisitional data.". In N. Hornstein & D. Lightfoot (Eds.), Explanation in Linguistics: The Logical Problem of Language Acquisition. London: Longman.

Theory Building in Developmental Psychology
P.L.C. van Geert (editor)
© Elsevier Science Publishers B.V. (North-Holland), 1986

4

Developmental Contingency Modelling

A framework for discussing the processes of change and the consequence of deficiency

John Morton

This paper introduces a notation for discussing
development. A Developmental Contingency Model
(DCM) focusses on the representations and
processes that are necessary for a particular
piece of behaviour to emerge. The idea is to
trace the contingencies (mostly internal) for
the presence of such representations back in the
developmental history of the child until we
reach something that seems unlearnable. In this
way we build up a list of likely candidates for
innate "primitive" functions or structures.
Absence of the behaviour that provided the
starting point for the analysis could then be
due to absence of one of the primitives.
A DCM analysis is provided of some recent work
on the nature of autism. The methodology is
further illustrated by considering what a child
must possess in order to exhibit the "stranger
reaction". The properties of the framework are
discussed.

Change can arise for a number of reasons and in a number
of ways. It is often helpful to draw sharp divisions between
different types of change even though all individual examples
of change are mixed in their origins. Thus we find it useful
to contrast the innate and acquired components of knowledge,
even though every act of acquisition has an innate aspect,
howsoever small, and every piece of knowledge that is
postulated as innate will require some learning to take place
if the innate structures are to exert an influence on
behaviour.

Change can also be examined at different magnifications
in terms of the time scale, the domain size and the level of
generality. At one extreme we can look at the microdevelopment
of a particular skill in individuals. At the other extreme we

can try to set up a framework within which all change can be located and, so, contrasted. Neither of these approaches will answer all the questions we might wish to put. Clearly there is no one approach that could answer all such questions. Any particular notational device that one uses in theorising will be best suited to a particular type of question.

The specific question to be addressed here concerns contingencies in development. We commonly ask what mental elements (processes, structures, etc.) are necessary before a particular piece of behaviour will develop. Less commonly, we ask about the conditions under which the elements themselves will develop. What is missing completely is a diagrammatic representation of such questions. For people who operate as scientists in a purely verbal mode, the latter stage may seem unnecessary or even confusing. For visualisers, like the author, it is a prerequisite for constructive thought. It is the only way I can keep the complexities in simultaneous view.

The impetus for talking about and depicting developmental contingencies came from attempts to analyse the preconditions for autism. Inevitably it proved to be more general.

A STORY ABOUT AUTISM.

One day in November, 1982, Alan Leslie was talking to our in-house seminar about pretend play. The special thing about pretend play is that it cannot involve normal use of normal representations (i.e. knowledge of objects and their properties). When a 15 month old infant pretends that a banana is a telephone, the memory of that episode has to be kept separate from (or very clearly distinguished from) the representations relating to normal use of bananas and normal use of telephones. Otherwise, the properties of the banana would get mixed up with the properties of telephones and the baby could end up trying to eat the telephone, which could be confusing.

Overall, the properties of pretend play resemble the properties of mental state terms like "believe". Thus, the following two sentences are similar in a number of repects:

1. Bill believes there is a king of France.

2. I pretend that banana is a telephone.

While asserting these two statements we can simultaneously assert:

3. There is no king of France.

4. That object is really a banana.

where "that banana" in 2 and "that object" in 4 have the same referent. The predicates in sentences 1 and 2 are protected from reality. Thus, whether or not sentence 1 is true is unaffected by the truth of sentence 3. Equally, given that we first say "I pretend", we can go on to complete the sentence with anything at all without actually coming into conflict with what we believe. On the other hand, bits of knowledge like sentence 3, facts about the Queen of England, the taste of butterscotch or the way to Burnham Market can be directly confronted by perceptual experience or by factual knowledge gained by other means. They can, that is, be falsified. Such bits of knowledge are stored in the brain in what Leslie (1986) calls first order representations.

As we have seen, the predicates of sentences 1 and 2 cannot be falsified. Now, these sentences could be descriptions of the beliefs of an individual, and what is true for the sentences is also true for the mental events that would be described by those sentences. That is to say, when we are actually pretending, we have to protect the contents of our pretence from reality. Otherwise they might be falsified and that would be the end of the pretend. Equally, we do not confuse as a matter of course what we know of other people's beliefs with what we "know" to be the case. It follows, then, that if we want to represent in our brains the belief structures of another person, we cannot use first order representations. If we did, they would be susceptible to normal confirmation procedures. We have, then, to use another form of representation that is not susceptible to confrontation perceptually or by other means. In Leslie's terminology this would be a second order representation. For such representations to be created we need some process over

and above that used for first order representations. Leslie
has termed this device an "expression raiser". Its exact form
is not of any concern for the current argument. What we do
want to be able to do is to refer to its function of being
able to create representations, or parts of representations,
that are protected from the normal verification processes.

In the course of the discussion of Alan Leslie's ideas,
Uta Frith remarked that autistic children were supposed not to
pretend play (Sigman & Ungerer, 1981; Wing & Gould, 1979).
Now, we know that one of the defining characteristics of
autism is an abnormal view of other people (Frith, 1982;
Kanner, 1943; Rutter, 1983). It is as if the autistic child
misses something rather fundamental about humanity (Hermelin &
O'Connor, 1985; Hobson, 1983, in press). Suppose, then, (the
discussion continued), the problem is that autistic children
lack an expression raiser and so cannot form second order
representations. This would, by definition, explain their
inability to pretend play. What consequences would it have for
the way they view other minds? The clearest prediction was
that they would be unable to attribute to anyone else a belief
that was different from their own beliefs. So, they would be
unable to represent the fact that Bill believed there was a
King of France was bald, given that they actually knew there
was no King of France.

The proposal, then, is that autistic children are unable
to form second order representations. The prediction that
follows, concerning the attribution of beliefs, was later
tested by means of a little puppet show (derived from Wimmer &
Perner, 1983) acted out in front of autistic children, normal
children and children with Down's syndrome. In the story, one
doll, Sally, has a marble and puts it in a basket. She then
leaves. Another doll, Ann, takes the marble out of the basket
and hides it in a box. Sally then comes back. At this point
the child is asked, "Where will Sally look for the marble?"
Normal children, aged 4, and Down's children with mental age
of 6 had no trouble with the task. On the other hand, 16 out
of 20 autistic children, with average mental age of about 9,
were unable to do that task, responding as if Sally had the

same knowledge as themselves (Baron-Cohen et al, 1985).

WHO NEEDS A MODEL?

The theoretical task was to represent all the relevant claims in an interesting way; in a way, that is, that would help us to relate the underlying facts to other facts, in an unexpected way. The claims of interest are as follows:

c1. Pretend play requires second order representations

c2. MENTALISING - i.e. Understanding the mental states of others -
    requires second order representations

c3. The creation of second order representations requires an expression raiser that acts upon first order representations

c4. Autistic children lack an expression raiser

c5. Autistic children cannot pretend play as a consequence of c1 and c4,

c6. As a consequence of c2 and c4, autistic children cannot mentalise.

Of these claims, c5 is an empirical observation, c1, 2 & 3 are theoretical claims, c4 is an interpretation of c5 in the light of c1-3, and c6 is an empirical prediction from the others. Note there are a number of optional views, in particular that there are different expression raisers for representations referred to in c1 and c2. That would be a different interpretation of c3.

The main point that we wished to express in the model is that of the contingent relationship between the existence of an expression raiser and the ability to understand the mental states of others. More specifically, we want to express our hypothesis that the absence of pretend play in the autistic infant is caused by the absence of an expression raiser and we also want to express the consequent prediction that autistic children would not be able to mentalise. This was the reason for performing the Sally/Ann experiment described above. The point that we wished to make in addition was that of a

developmental relationship. An expression raiser would have to
have been present for mentalising to develop. At this instant
it is irrelevant whether expression raising is learned or
innate, though we cannot imagine how it might be learned. In
either case it would have to exist before any pretend playing
or mentalising could take place.

Autism, by the account given above, is a developmental
disorder caused by the lack of an expression raiser. Since it
is likely that such a statement still strikes the reader as
peculiar, let me remind you that it was this hypothesis that
led to the triumphant Sally/Ann experiment. However, we know
that there are a lot of other things the matter with autistic
people (Frith, 1982; Hermelin & O'Connor, 1970; Prior, 1979;
Rutter, 1983), and many of these need to be accounted for in
the model. What we need to be able to explore is whether the
lack of an expression raiser would lead to such symptoms. As
an example we could take a defining characteristic of autistic
children, that their language development is retarded. How
could this possibly be accounted for by the absence of an
expression raiser? One possibility is that the key deficit is
in speech production. Consider that a large proportion of
early utterences on the part of children have to do with
communicating to another mind reflections on the contents of
their mind. Early naming, for example, seems to have this
property. A child without second order representations and,
so, without a concept of mind, would have far less to say than
a normal child.

The form of the model also encourages us to identify the
prerequisites for an expression raiser and see if the absence
of one of those could lead to the other symptoms associated
with autism. We must, of course, also allow for the
possibility of more than one kind of autism (Coleman, 1976;
Fein et al, 1985; Waterhouse et al, in press) and that
autistic people, particularly subnormal ones, have other
processing problems that interact with the lack of an expression raiser. We must also allow for the possibility of a
redefinition which would exclude some people who would, at the
moment, be classified as autistics.

In this article we will not approach the goals just outlined very closely. However, the first step along the road is shown in Figure 1. This is a developmental contingency model and not a flow chart or an information processing model. The symbol on the lines in Figure 1 is to be read as "(normally) requires the (pre-) existence of". Thus, pairs of connected elements are related developmentally. Each such pair of elements in the figure effectively represents a hypothesis about developmental contingencies. We have choice of which elements to represent and in their relationship.

The particular form of Figure 1 was driven as follows. We (and Uta Frith in particular) wanted to separate pretend playing from mentalising. We did so by dividing representations into two kinds, one to do with things and one to do with people. Provisionally, I will call these representations Material and Individual, or MAT and IND. IND constitutes those representations that have to do with individual people. MAT is made up of all other representations. Note that this is a content division. I am not postulating the existence of two different memory stores and it would be a grave error to imagine that Figure 1 represents two or, indeed, any memory stores. In Figure 1 IND is to be understood as the ability to create representations with respect to individual people rather than as those representations. If we did produce an information processing model or an information flow diagram, we would then want to depict IND (and MAT) representations. However, Figure 1 is not, repeat not, an information processing model and it is illegitimate to read anything into the notation that has not been put there explicitly.

I will, in fact, in the text, from time to time, refer to MAT and IND as representations. When I do so I will be refering to their functions in some as yet unspecified (except Leslie, unpublished) processing model[1].

MAT and IND are first order representations. The equivalent second order representations are created by the action of the expression raiser on first order representations.

figure 1

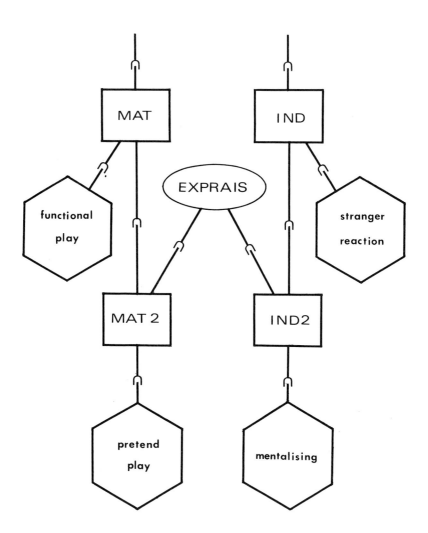

1. A D.C.M. (Developmental Contingency Model) relating to autism. There
   are three kinds of elements used: representations (rectangles),
   behaviour (hexagons) and processes (ellipse). The relation between
   linked pairs of elements is that of contingency or implication. Thus,
   the development of pretend play is contingent on the development of a
   MAT2 representation which, in turn requires EXPRAIS (see the text for
   further explanation).

We call the resulting second order representations MAT2 and
IND2. Again, it would be a grave error to imagine that we
propose to divide our knowledge into four stores, two for
first and two for second order representations. A single
knowledge fragment, or "thinks", could include all four kinds
of representation:

> Daddy is on his brown chair (which I am pretending
> is my space machine) and he believes I'm human.

In this fragment, the four kinds of representation are as
follows:

> MAT: The chair is brown
> MAT2: the chair is a space machine (alien)
> IND: Daddy is on the chair
> IND2: Daddy believes I'm human

We maintain the separation between these four classes of
knowledge because we believe that some people cannot create
some of them and because they do not appear to develop at the
same time. In Figure 1, the relationship between MAT and MAT2
should be understood as: the development of the ability to
form MAT2 representations is contingent on having previously
developed the ability to form MAT representations.

In Figure 1, we find the six claims made above, in a more
specific form. Thus pretend play is linked to MAT2
representations and mentalising (the ability to attribute
mental states) is linked to IND2 representations. The contrast
is made on the one hand with ordinary play, which only
requires first order MAT representations, and on the other
hand with the stranger reaction which only requires first
order IND representations (this will be discussed at length in
the next section). If someone cannot mentalise, as with the
majority of the autistic children in the Sally/Ann experiment,
it is because they cannot form IND2 representations. The
diagram makes it obvious that such an inability could arise
for two reasons. In the first place, if the expression raiser
(EXPRAIS) was missing there could be no IND2. This was our
original supposition for autism. The resulting inability to
mentalise would be accompanied by a lack of pretend play.

The second possibility, that we have not yet considered,

is that there could be someone with no IND representations. Such a deficit would also lead to a lack of IND2 representations. A person with this deficit would fail the Sally/Ann experiment but would be able to pretend play, so long, that is, as the expression raiser existed. This person would have other problems associated with the absence of IND representations and we would want to be able to spell these out. In such a case, the figure would also encourage us to think in terms of the prerequisites for the establishment of IND and to consider which of them might be missing in someone who lacked IND.

At this point, however, we will leave the topic of autism for a while in order to explore the properties of the methodology depicted in Figure 1. We will call the method of theorising Developmental Contingency Modelling.

DEVELOPMENTAL CONTINGENCY MODELS - THE PROPERTIES OF THE FORMALISM.

There are always hidden presuppositions or biases when one begins to theorise. Some are surprising, some are not; some have consequences, others are incidental.

The first presupposition in the DCM shown in Figure 1 is that the causes of major deficits are traceable to the absence, actual or operational, of some biological givens. Thus, the theoretical method itself would encourage one to think in terms of a biological cause for autism rather than, say, a social cause (e.g. "refrigerator mothers"). It is not that the need for a particular kind of social interaction as a prerequisite cannot be represented in a DCM, it is just that there is a bias against it.

The second presupposition is that such biological givens will be buried deep with respect to behaviour. Each one will be implicated in a wide range of activities and the absence of any one would have far-ranging consequences.

A third presupposition is that no special environmental conditions are required for the normal fruition of the givens.

That is not to say that there is no learning, simply that the learning is effort-free. The child learns about language, objects, family, causality, number and so on in an effort-free way because what is happening in the course of such learning is that the givens are being used. There is almost a teleological element about this. The processing machinery and the innate structures are constructed in the way they are in order that the goals shall always be reached. This is the achievement of evolution. The child has no choice in the matter; its "learning" is under the control of its processes. A child can choose not to speak but it cannot choose not to learn its native language. The biological givens which subsume language learning make sure of that. However, effort-free learning has its natural borders. If you get a group of children to use LOGO there are no biological guarantees of anything. Hence the need for some externally imposed structure rather than relying entirely on the hazards of discovery in the classroom.

The DCM framework is one in which the focus is on the prerequisites for the emergence of a particular process or structure. Such properties of the infant brain form "elements" in a DCM model. Note that while our direct evidence for the existence of such an element will be behavioural, our primary focus will be on the elements and not on the behaviour. There are two main reasons for this.

Firstly, an element may be present without being visible in behaviour. Thus, if one takes a profoundly deaf infant who is not signed to, we would want to say that the innate component of the language learning apparatus was present but not able to exert any significant influence on behaviour.

The second reason for focussing on the underlying elements rather than behaviour is that a particular piece of behaviour could be mediated by a variety of means. For example, autistic children may learn to have exchanges of utterances with adults. However, in the majority of cases, such exchanges would not, on close analysis, be confusable with the conversations that normal children have. Normally, conversations are driven by IND2 representations (among other

things) and are intrinsically "reinforcing" for normal
children. The autistic child would have to learn that they
were appropriate modes of behaviour. Even if they did happen
to match a normal conversation in form and content, they would
never have other than a utilitarian function.

In the preceding paragraphs I indicated why the focus of
the DCM method is on the elements of the child's cognitive
apparatus rather than on behaviour. We should now look at
elements more closely. To start with, we can make the point
that elements are either primitive or not. By "primitive" I
mean innate and irreducible. Trivially, it must be the case
either that a particular element E can only emerge given that
an element D has already emerged (to some level of
specification) or that E is a primitive. The development of
non-primitives depends upon the prior functioning of
particular primitives plus exposure to specific kinds of
stimuli. Primitives require at most a minimal environment.
Note that primitives need not be present from birth but could
arise in the course of maturation.

In practice there will be a variety of patterns of
contingencies. Thus, one can imagine a skill whose emergence
is a function of a late maturing structure but which also
depends upon the prior existence of other processes or
knowledge. We would want to be able to represent all such
contingencies. The general form of the contingency model is
that of elements connected in a directed graph. The elements
can be of a variety of kinds - processes, structures,
knowledge, perceptual or other experiences, or biological
elements. The symbols on the connecting lines have
temporal/causal implications. Roughly speaking, a dyad of the
form

$$P \longrightarrow\!\!\!\!\Big(\!\!\!\!\longrightarrow Q$$

can be read weakly as "P emerges before Q". Where theoretical
statements are being made, a stronger reading of the dyad
would be required such as "P is a precondition for Q" and the
strongest reading would be "P causes Q". In the case that P is
a set of elements, the dyad might be interpreted as "some of P

(which ones to be specified) are a precondition for Q" or "the elements in P will influence the way in which Q emerges". Which one of these interpretations is to be applied to a particular dyad will have to be understood from the context. This is a very useful property for a framework. Note that the default implication is that P is necessary for Q. There may be cases in which P is sufficient for Q but this would have to be spelled out.

The elements that can enter into a DCM have certain restrictions as to where they are allowed to occur. The most obvious ones are that a specified behaviour will rarely (if ever) be found as a precondition, equivalent to P in the diagram, that is. Thus, we will not want to say in our theories that the emergence of any particular behaviour A is a precondition for the emergence of some other behaviour B. Nor would we wish to specify in a DCM that a particular behaviour A is to be found developmentally before or after any other behaviour B. Statements of this kind will, rather, represent an important source of data that enter into the formation of a model fragment. The resulting DCM statement could take one of two forms. The first would be "a theoretical element A' is a precondition for the emergence of behaviour B", where A' is an element also underlying behaviour A. An alternative claim might be that "A' is a precondition for B'" where A' and B' are the processes, etc. underlying behaviours A and B respectively. Note that if one found a child where B was found before A, such a discovery would constitute a challenge to claims concerning the order of emergence of the behaviours, but would not by itself consitute a challenge to a theoretical claim of the form:

$$A' \longrightarrow\!\!\!\!\!\subset\!\!\!\!\!\longrightarrow B'$$

The defence would be that the emergence of A required another process or structure, X, to be present and it was this that was delayed. The full model would, in this case, look like Figure 2. In this DCM fragment we can see that the absence of X would hold up or prevent the emergence of behaviour A but would not affect B.

figure 2

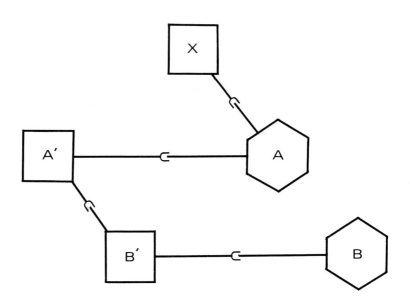

2. Behaviours A and B are contingent on representations A' and B'
respectively. B' is contingent on A' and A normally appears before B
in development. If X were delayed then B could occur before A.

(While we are here we might as well remind ourselves that
the presence of a behaviour B in an individual child does not
necessarily require that we infer the presence of the normal
underlying representation, B', in that child. There may be
other data indicating the absence of B'. In such cases, the
general principle of compensatory mechanisms allows us to
postulate that this child performs B by different means than
normal. The example of the way in which autistic children
might come to carry on conversations, referred to above, is

one such case.)

The other element type we can think of as restricted is the biological type. Thus, we would not normally expect to find a biological element being dependent on the emergence of either a behaviour or a process, etc. A statement of the form "One cannot pass puberty until the twelve times table has been learned" would have a distinctly peculiar ring to it.

A DCM ANALYSIS OF THE STRANGER REACTION.

Having outlined some properties of a DCM we can explore the notation further. Let us take a standard piece of behaviour and look at the DCM that results. Most children, at 7 or 8 months, will, under the appropriate conditions show a fear or distress reaction to a stranger, a reaction not found prior to that age. To the caretaker, C, there will be a different response. There are many possible patterns of behaviour depending on circumstances, including the finding that the fear reaction is stronger if the caretaker is present but about four feet away than when she is absent (Bowlby, 1969; Morgan & Ricciuti, 1969). A complete discussion of the stranger reaction would include considerations of smell and touch, movement and affect. For the moment let us consider simply the situation of a child left on its own briefly and compare the reactions when either the caretaker returns or a stranger enters.

The question to be asked is what inferences can be drawn from the behaviour with respect to the representations and processes possessed by the child at that time. The first thing we can do is simplify the observation for the moment by removing from consideration the nature of the infant's response. We can bring this back later. Secondly, we will assume that the differential reactions can be found simply to faces and that the faces do not need to be attached to bodies or voices, etc. If the data turn out to be otherwise, then the inferences will have to be changed accordingly. On this basis, then, we have evidence of discrimination, from memory, of C's

face from other faces. This means that there must be a
representation of C's face at some level of detail. In the DCM
we turn such an inference into the claim that a prerequisite
for the stranger reaction is a representation of C's face. We
would diagram this, trivially, as in Figure 3. We can
immediately go further.

figure 3

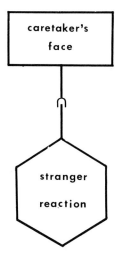

3. A DCM fragment representing the fact that the stranger reaction is
contingent on the baby having a representation of its caretaker's
face.

Since there is also a particular response to C, this response
must be accessible from the representation of the face. The
response is, however, only elicited under the appropriate
circumstances (C having been away and currently at a distance,
for example). The response cannot be directly connected to the
representation of the face. Rather, (and obviously, if one
were not attempting to proceed painful step at a time), the
face must be connected to some individual, affect-laden,
specification of C. It is natural, here, (well, for me,

anyway!) to think in terms of a Headed Record, where one part of a memory serves as the means of access to another part (c.f. Morton et al, 1985). In this case there would be a representation of C's face in the Heading and the specification of C in the Record. Questions about the content of this Record and how it may come to be set up will be left, as will those questions relating to the nature of the infant's reaction and how this reaction follows from the content of the Record. We merely note at the moment that such questions can be posed in the context of the current framework. For the moment we are pursuing other hares.

To recap, the infant establishes a differential response to C's face with respect to other human faces. I assume that the stranger reaction would not be elicited by the face of a previously unknown stuffed animal. If this is the case, then we can advance the DCM to include a generalised representation of the human face. This is shown in Figure 4.

In effect, in this figure, we now have the hypothesis that there cannot be a representation of C's face unless there is a generalised representation of the human face. Note that this is not implied by the data we have assumed. It would be perfectly possible for a representation of C's face to be set up without there being a generalised representation of the human face but that the Stranger Reaction be dependent upon the existence of both. This would be indicated by the DCM in Figure 5. Figures 4 and 5 constitute competing theories.

We should note here that a number of obvious things have been left out. For example, as I have already indicated, the specification of C that is found in the Record has presumably been set up previously and is also accessible by smell, and so on. There will have been a lot of experience of C by the infant in order to make such a specification possible. This experience will have been of a special kind, including feeding and other pleasurable activities. I also want to postulate that there is another element that is required.

figure 4

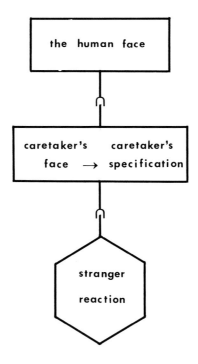

4. A DCM fragment representing the hypothesis that the infant must have
a generalised representation of the Human Face before the crucial
representation of the caretaker can be set up.

figure 5

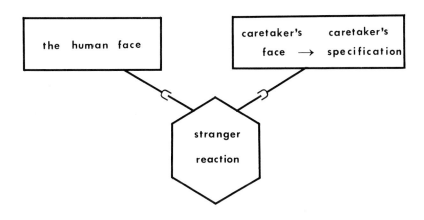

5. The DCM representation of an alternative hypothesis to that in Figure 4. In this case the proposal is that the crucial representation of the caretaker can be set up independently of that for the Human Face.

This element I will call ATTACH. It corresponds to the factors in other kinds of theories that lead to "attachment" or "bonding".

The assumption I am making at this point is that the interaction between C and the infant, while necessary, is insufficient by itself to give rise to the observed phenomena. For example, it seems to be the case that some autistic children who have had exactly the same exposure as normal children will nonetheless fail to respond in the same way, will fail to set up the special relationship with C and will not show a differential Stranger Reaction at the usual age. This shows that the "experience" is insufficient, and that some other factor is required. In Figure 6, then, ATTACH is shown as a prerequisite for the formation of a specification

figure 6

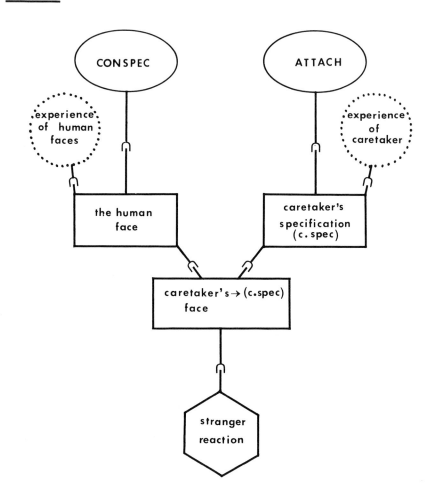

6. An expansion of the theory in Figure 4. This introduces a fourth type of element, interaction with the environment, which is indicated by the dotted circle.

of the caretaker.

This representation will be unique by virtue of the participation of ATTACH. In the model in Figure 6, there is no reason why the infant should not simultaneously set up representations containing specifications of other people.

These would not, by definition, involve ATTACH and, from the model, would be an insufficient precondition for the stranger reaction to occur. The model, then, expresses the hypothesis that the Stranger Reaction is only made once the infant has set up a specification of an individual, C, with the participation of ATTACH. Note that while it is possible that ATTACH is learned, I assume that it is a biological given, a primitive.

One of the elements of Figure 4 is the generalised representation of the human face. I assume that this is in large part learned and that a human infant who had not seen any human faces would not show a unique reaction if presented with one for the first time at the age of, say, twelve months. It is natural, in the context of a DCM, to ask whether there are any other prerequisites for learning about the human face. Certainly, it would make biological sense if human (or, in general, mammalian) young were predisposed to learn the nature of the faces of the species into which they have been born. This seems to be the case for chicks (Bolhuis et al, 1985; Johnson et al, 1985; Johnson & Horn, in press). The fact that chicks are precocial might be crucial, but we can speculate that mammals also have special ways of learning about faces. We may hypothesise that the innate contribution to this consists of a rough specification of what kind of thing a face is together with some size and distance constraints. Such a specification, possibly together with some specialised learning processes, could constitute a universal mammalian package. Be that as it may, I will term the relevant element CONSPEC and will assume that it is a primitive. This constitutes a further (falsifiable) hypothesis.

The DCM in Figure 6 summarises the discussion in this section. Some, but not all, of the prerequisites for the Stranger Reaction have been spelled out and some ancillary hypotheses have been postulated. In the course of doing this we have seen the way in which a DCM is structured and have used four kinds of elements: behaviour, experience, representations and primitives. In addition we have been able to see the need for specification of certain kinds of processes. A number of things have still been left out, notably any account as to why fear should be expressed to a stranger and why there are individual differences in the reaction. Such considerations would involve extending the formalism and will have to await another occasion.

SOME PLAYBACK.

Developmental Contingency Modelling is an attempt to tighten and enrich our normal scientific practice. Basically, I have taken a hypothesis concerning autism that was formulated on the basis of a theory by Alan Leslie concerning the relation between pretend play and mental state terms (Leslie, in press). On this theory, both pretend play and mental state terms require the use of an "expression raiser". From the observation that autistic children are incapable of pretend play, the hypothesis was formulated that such children lack an expression raiser. If this were the case, it would follow that autistic children would also be incapable of mentalising - i.e. attributing beliefs to others. This prediction was upheld with the Sally/Ann experiment (Baron-Cohen et al., 1985).

A diagramatic representation of the above reasoning has led us in certain directions. We have been led to differentiate between two kinds of representations, one, MAT, to do with things, and the other, IND, to do with individual people. Use of an expression raiser allowed the formulation of second order representations. The hypothesis concerning autism was that autistic people, lacking an expression raiser, also lacked the ability to form second order representations. The Sally/Ann experiment was designed to test for a lack of IND2 representations. The DCM made it clear that a lack of IND2 representations could also arise in the absence of IND representations. Some possible preconditions for the formation of IND representations have been proposed following a DCM analysis of the stranger reaction. In particular, I have suggested the involvement of a primitive termed ATTACH. We have noted the feature of DCM's that they encourage the theorist to focus on the biological givens. The implications of some of these ideas for autism have been sketched by Frith (1985).

The representations that concern things, MAT, are fundamental for any degree of learning. The equivalent second order representations, MAT2, are implicated in pretend play. One can also note that a well developed MAT2 ability is essential for the creation of DCM's. Their refinement, however, will require hypothesis testing, and this resides at the MAT level only.

NOTES

1. I have dwelt on the difference between a DCM and an information processing model at length and anticipate doing so at greater length in future. This is a consequence of the need readers have to impose their own view of the notation.

DEBTS

I am grateful to Alan Leslie and Uta Frith for the ideas I first represented in a DCM. Uta Frith has also spent a lot of time discussing the form of the model for autism, particularly on the separation of MAT and IND. I have talked about DCM's a number of times to the internal seminar of the Cognitive Development Unit. The free and frank criticism I received has helped to make the ideas and their exposition clearer. Jean Mandler, Annette Karmiloff-Smith, Mark Johnson, Amanda Sharkey and Paul van Geert have also devoted time to various drafts of this manuscript. Peter Taylor drew the figures.

REFERENCES

Baron-Cohen, S., Leslie, A.M. & Frith, U. (1985). Does the
autistic child have a "theory of mind"? Cognition, 21,
37-46.

Bolhuis, J.J., Johnson, M.H., & Horn, G. (1985). Effects of
early experience on the development of filial preferences
in the domestic chick. Developmental Psychology, 18,
299-308.

Bowlby, J. (1969). Attachment and Loss: Attachment: Vol. 1.
London: Hogarth Press.

Coleman, M. (1976). The Autistic Syndrome. Amsterdam: North
Holland Publication Co.

Fein, D., Waterhouse, L., Lucci, D. & Snyder, D. (1985).
Cognitive subtypes in developmentally disabled children:
A pilot study. Journal of Autism and Developmental
Disorders, 15, 77-95.

Frith, U. (1982). Psychological abnormalities in early
childhood psychoses. In L. Wing & J.K. Wing (Eds.),
Handbook of Psychiatry: Vol. 1. Cambridge: Cambridge
University Press.

Frith, U. (1985). A developmental model for autism.
Proceedings of Colloque International sur d'Autisme.
INSERM, Paris.

Hermelin, B. & O'Connor, N. (1970). Psychological experiments
with autistic children. Oxford: Pergamon Press.

Hermelin, B. & O'Connor, N. (1985). Logico-Affective states
and Nonverbal language. In E. Schopler & G.B. Mesibov
(Eds.), Communication Problems in Autism. New York:
Plenum Press.

Hobson, R.P. (1983). The autistic child's recognition of
age-related features of people, animals and things.
British Journal of Developmental Psychology, 1, 343-52.

Hobson, R.P. (in press). On people and things: The engima of
autism. Journal of Child Psychology and Psychiatry.

Johnson, M.H., Bolhuis, J.J. & Horn, G. (1985). Interaction
between acquired preferences and developing
predispositions during imprinting. Animal Behaviour, 33,

1000-1006.

Johnson, M.H. & Horn, G. (in press). An analysis of a predisposition in the domestic chick. Behavioural Brain Research.

Kanner, L. (1943). Autistic disturbances of affective contact. Nervous Child, 2, 217-250.

Leslie, A.M. (1986). Pretence and Representation in Infancy (submitted for publication).

Morton, J., Hammersley, R.H. & Bekerian, D.A. (1985). Headed Records: A model for memory and its failures. Cognition, 20, 1-23.

Morgan, G.A. & Ricciuti, H.N. (1969). Infants' responses to strangers during the first year. In B.M. Foss (Ed.), Determinants of Infant Behaviour: Vol. 4. New York: Wiley.

Prior, M.R. (1979). Cognitive abilities and disabilities in infantile autism: a review. Journal of Abnormal Child Psychology, 7, 357-80.

Rutter, M. (1983). Cognitive deficits in the pathogenesis of autism. Journal of Child Psychology and Psychiatry, 24, 513-531.

Sigman, M. & Ungerer, J. (1981). Sensorimotor skill and language comprehension in autistic children. Journal of Abnormal Child Psychology, 9, 149-165.

Waterhouse, L., Fein, D., Nath, J. & Snyder, D. (in press). Pervasive developmental disorders and schizophrenia occurring in childhood: A review of critical commentary. In G. Tischler (Ed.), DSM-III: An interim appraisal. Washington, D.C.: APA.

Wimmer, H. & Perner, J. (1983). Beliefs about beliefs: representation and constraining function of wrong beliefs in young childrens's understanding of deception. Cognition, 13, 103-128.

Wing, L. & Gould, J. (1979). Severe Impairments of social interaction and associated abnormalities in children: Epidemology and classification. Journal of Autism and Developmental Disorders, 9, 11-29.

Theory Building in Developmental Psychology
P.L.C. van Geert (editor)
© Elsevier Science Publishers B.V. (North-Holland), 1986

5

Theories about the Causes of Cognitive Development

Peter Bryant

Two major hypotheses have dominated discussions about the causes of cognitive development. One is that children develop cognitive skills largely as the result of cultural, and particularly of linguistic, experiences; the other that these skills are the product mainly of internal intellectual conflict and of the consequent disequilibrium which stems from the conflict. I argue that both hypotheses have weaknesses: the first hypothesis because it does not explain the obvious constraints in intellectual development and the second because it cannot account for the process by which the child solves the hypothesised inner conflict. There is an alternative hypothesis - the "agreement" hypothesis - which is that children advance as a result of understanding the connections between different intellectual strategies. I review the evidence for this hypothesis and I end by discussing the best way to test ideas about it.

As children grow older their behaviour changes radically again and again, and in a rather predictable fashion. Theories about these developmental changes have to deal with two different and quite separable questions.

WHAT CHANGES?

One is the question what actually changes? We have to know why it is that, for example, three year old children do things in one way and five year olds in another. The

theoretical question here is about the differences in the
underlying mechanisms which govern the behaviour of the
different age groups. So, when Piaget claims that an eight
year old child possesses the quality of reversibility which
completely eluded her when she was younger by a year or so, he
is in effect producing a theoretical explanation for the
reasons why children set about problems like the conversation
task very differently at one age then at another. It is easy
to think of other examples. Every developmental theory and
practically every piece of empirical research on children of
different ages contains some statement about the underlying
structure which determines how children respond, and about the
changes in the structure which go with age. No proper theory
of development could ignore the question. We cannot possibly
explain children's development unless we know what it is that
changes in them, and that must involve our finding out about
changes in the underlying psychological mechanisms. In fact a
great deal has been found out about these mechanisms and it
seems to me that this side of developmental psychology is
going very well. It is not the side with which I shall be
dealing in this chapter.

WHAT CAUSES THE CHANGES?

The chapter is about the second question faced by any
developmental theory, which is about the causes of these
developmental changes. Simply to say that children behave
differently because there has been a change in psychological
mechanisms is not on its own enough. You also have to say what
makes the changes happen. Reversibility, for example, is not
and was not meant to be a causal explanation. In fact it is a
postulate which naturally raises a causal question. If
children do go from a state of non-reversibility to one of
reversibility, what has led them to change in this way? How
did they manage to acquire the new capacity?
The distinction between these two questions has not
always been made as clearly as it should have been, in my

view, but it is vitally important. One reason for making it is to be able to assess the evidence for theories of development properly. It is in principle possible for a developmental theory to be right about the underlying changes and yet quite wrong about the causes of these changes, or vice versa. It is also possible that all the evidence for a particular theory may be about one of the two aspects and not at all about the other. Indeed this is more than just a possibility. It has happened quite frequently that developmental theories come equipped with statements about the psychological mechanisms and also about the causes of the changes and yet provide evidence only about the first of these things and not about the second.

Piaget's theory is the most prominent example of this sort of imbalance. Though it has much to say on the causal side hardly any of Piaget's work and very little of his colleagues' deals directly with his causal ideas. The notions of equilibration and the importance of intellectual conflicts as a cause of intellectual progress in childhood have had a widespread influence in the world of education as well as in developmental psychology. Yet the actual evidence for them is desperately small and unimpressive too. This is not an isolated example. If one turns to theories, like Vygotsky's, that a child's linguistic experiences underly much of his intellectual growth or to more recent developmental theories couched in information processing terms it is easy to show that, though there are plenty of causal statements in these theories, the actual causal evidence for them is sparse indeed.

The contrast between the huge amount of evidence about the form of intellectual development and the considerably smaller accumulation of data about causal hypotheses needs to be noted. There are several reasons for it. One is simply that it is much harder to get evidence about causes of development. It is easy enough to show what the developmental changes are by putting children of different ages through some experiment and establishing that different age groups respond in different ways. But the changes which you are illustrating take place outside the laboratory, and that is where the causes are to be found. But how do you find them? It really is not so easy. Another reason for the dearth of good evidence about the causes of intellectual development is that the causal postulates are often too general to pin down easily in any empirical piece of work. If you think, as Piaget for example thought, that the same factor causes developmental change right through childhood you are likely to produce, as Piaget indeed did, an idea that is so broad that it is hard to reify in particular instances.

On top of all this the major theories of intellectual development are afflicted by another serious difficulty. Even when one forgets the awkward question of evidence, these theories suffer from inherent implausibility on purely internal grounds. They offer us a machine which could not work. I shall describe this problem first and shall go on to offer a solution in the form of a causal machine that might get off the ground, and then at the end of the chapter I shall try to find a way of solving the empirical problem of how to prove or disprove such a theory.

TWO MAJOR THEORIES.

Over the last few decades two possibilities have dominated people's ideas about the causes of intellectual development. One is Piaget's theory (1978) about equilibration. The other is the idea, which dates back to Vygotsky (1962), that children grow intellectually largely as a result of linguistic experiences and linguistic changes. The contrast between these two ideas - the hammer and anvil of theories of intellectual development - is stark.

Piaget's Equilibration Theory.

The equilibration idea is of a child who has her own ideas about her environment and who is forced to change these ideas every now and then when she finds that some of them are in conflict with others. The child finds herself in the uncomfortable position, described as disequilibrium, of having two mutually irreconcilable beliefs about the same thing and her only solution is to change the ideas themselves:

> "disequilibria at the beginning are a fact and since the search for coherence is another ... an explanation is owing of the transition from the first of these to the second, which is the proper concern of a theory of equilibration" (Piaget, 1978, p. 15).

The resolution of the conflict and the consequent return to equilibrium are in fact the stuff of intellectual development. The child is forced to acquire a new set of ideas which cope much better with events around her and are more sophisticated than those which preceded them.

Note two things about the intellectual turmoil which, according to Piaget, lies at the heart of every major intellectual development. One is Piaget's idea that the child has to notice the contradiction for it to have any effect. It is perfectly possible, for the child to hold two opposing beliefs without being aware of it, and indeed Piaget (1974) went to some lengths to show that there are many contradictions which children do not recognise as such until quite late in childhood. The other thing to note is that the conflict is usually an internal one. Piaget's claim about logic mirrors W.B. Yeats' about poetry: "We make out of our quarrels with others, rhetoric; but out of our quarrels with ourselves, poetry". The child's dialectic, according to Piaget, is with herself: she produces the thesis and antithesis which cause the trouble and she comes up with her own synthesis. Piaget did allow other people, peers and even adults, an occasional role in these cognitive dramas, but it was never more than the role of a small part actor. The child is the prima donna, and the producer and director too.

Vygotsky's Linguistic Theory.

Theories which insist on the importance of language in intellectual development tell a very different story. There are many versions of this kind of theory of course, but I shall stick mainly with Vygotsky's. Vygotsky (1962) was in many ways a cautious theorist. Though he thought of language, and of linguistic experience, as crucial determinants of intellectual change, he was quite happy to agree that children could solve quite difficult problems in a totally non-verbal way. He never claimed (as his colleague and successor Luria claimed) that all human thought is internalised language. But he did argue that the acquisition of inner speech at the end of the pre-school years does lead to some formidable cognitive changes. He thought that as a result children become vastly more flexible, efficient and abstract in the way they set about intellectual questions.

Such an idea leads inexorably to an emphasis on the significance of other people and usually of older people in children's development. Whether or not there are innate mechanisms for acquiring language is something that makes no difference here. The actual language, and the network of ideas and associations embodied in it, are provided for the child by others around him - by brothers and sisters, and by parents. Though Vygotsky's original ideas about the significance of inner speech deal with the child on his own, and talking to himself, so to speak, the influence of other people who provided the basis for the speech in the first place is quite plainly to be seen in Vygotsky's account of this part of childhood. And of course when Vygotsky (1978) produced the idea of the zone of proximal development - the idea that what an adult helps a child do today the child will be able to do on his own tomorrow - he came down firmly and explicitly on the side of the importance of communication in children's development. The importance of this social experience as the first of two steps that have to be taken in every intellectual development is to be seen in this oft-quoted passage:

"Any function in the child's cultural development appears twice, or on two planes. First it appears on the social plane, and then on the psychological plane. First it appears between people as an interpsychological category and then within the child as an intrapsychological category. This is equally true with regard to voluntary attention, logical memory, the formation of concepts, and the development of volition." (Vygotsky, 1981, p. 163).

PLAUSIBILITIES AND IMPLAUSIBILITIES.

So, one model treats the child as the main arbiter of her intellectual fate, and the other dwells on the importance of other people. One has little to do with language, the other has a great deal. We might count ourselves lucky to be given such a strong and explicit contrast. In cases like this the truth often lies some way between the two extreme models and tests of each of them can show where that middle position lies. But in this case that happy solution does not seem to me to be possible. Both theories have strengths and weaknesses, but the strengths of each do not make up for the weaknesses of the other.

Plausibilities and Implausibilities of the Equilibration Model.

Let us consider the equilibration model first. It certainly has one great strength and that is to provide a reasonable account of the constraints in cognitive development. It is not always recognised that a causal theory of cognitive development must explain not only what causes children to change and progress, but also what stops them changing and progressing any faster than they do. We need to know why the whole of intellectual development cannot be polished off in a one hour tutorial. Why does it take sixteen or more years? Piaget understood this requirement very well, and the equilibration model gives us two good reasons for development taking such ages. One is that children will not abandon their existing intellectual strategies until they have proved to themselves that these are mutually contradictory. Telling them that there are better strategies will not help: nor will providing them with a model to copy. The children have to work it out for themselves and they will only do that after an internal conflict which often takes a long time to happen. I have already mentioned the other reason. It is that the conflict per se is not enough to cause disequilibrium. The child has to see the contradiction as one for it to disturb her.

However, this considerable success on the part of Piaget's causal theory is considerably diminished by an inherent weakness in the theory's central argument. The trouble is that the theory accounts for the constraints but not for the eventual successes of intellectual development. Conflicts tell you that something is wrong, but they do not show you what to do about it. They may warn you about the existence of a problem, but they do not provide the solution to it. I can illustrate this with a mundane every day sort of conflict which adults experience as well as children. If I add up a column of numbers from top to bottom, and then do the same from bottom to top, and I arrive at two different answers each time, I am immediately in a quandary. Evidently something has gone wrong, but I have no inkling about the right answer. One of my two different answers may be right (but which one?), or they may both be wrong. It is just the same with the conflicts which, Piaget claims, lead to fundamental intellectual changes.

Suppose that, as Piaget suggests, the child suddenly finds herself thinking two mutually contradictory things about the same topic. That will certainly tell her that something is wrong with her intellectual processes. She knows now that both views cannot be right: therefore something is wrong: therefore somehow, somewhere the child has taken a false intellectual step. That much the child will glean from the internal

conflict which Piaget attributes to him. That much, but no
more. The existence of the conflict could alert the child to
the fact that either one or both of her beliefs is wrong. But
it will not even tell her whether both are wrong or, if only
one is wrong, which one, and it certainly will not tell her
what the solution is.

To resort to the Hegelian analysis which originally
prompted Piaget's idea of intellectual conflict, the child has
a thesis and anti-thesis alright, but no way through to the
synthesis. I think that it was Neil Miller who said of
Tolman's cognitive theory about learning that it left the rat
at the choice point of a maze "lost in thought". Piaget's
theory, it seems to me, is just as incomplete. It abandons the
child stuck at a hopeless intellectual impasse. The theory
does not and indeed cannot explain how she breaks through.

Plausibilities and Implausibilities of the Linguistic Model.

No such difficulty afflicts theories that language
provokes intellectual development, particularly if those
theories deal with the effects of verbal communication. After
all the child must spend a large proportion of her time
hearing parents, teachers and elder siblings, to name but a
few, telling her how to do things properly. So if this
communication is going to have an effect (what the adult and
child do together today, the child will be able to do on her
own tomorrow) we have a plausible explanation of the successes
of intellectual development. Here is a possible source of
information for the child about the right things to do, the
proper way to think. But what about the constraints of
development?

The weakness of linguistic theories is that they have
nothing coherent to tell us about these constraints. They do
not explain why the child does not develop at breakneck speed.
After all a great deal of verbal information can be packed
into that one hour tutorial, but tutorials do not get the
child to solve the conservation problem, to use perspective in

drawings or even to know what on earth is going on in a simple multiplication sum. It is not so easy. These achievements depend on a great deal more than the mere acquisition of the appropriate language or the mere transmission of the correct information. On reflection Piaget's idea of the child having slowly and often erroneously to construct things for herself begins to look rather attractive. It is a pity that it might not work.

A POSSIBLE SOLUTION - THE "AGREEMENT" HYPOTHESIS.

It seems to me that there is an alternative approach which includes the advantages of the two that I have just discussed and yet is entirely different from them. It is in fact the opposite of Piaget's conflict theory. It is that children progress when they realise that two ways of approaching the same problem produce the same result. When they see that, they realise that both strategies work. The children validate one intellectual strategy against the other. That is the way that they find out whether to and when to adopt a particular strategy.

The Agreement Hypothesis.

I can find in work on cognitive psychology very little about the cognitive effects of what I shall now call "agreement", and yet these seem to me to be very powerful. Let us revert to the mundane example of the column of numbers. I add these up both ways, top to bottom and bottom to top, in order to be able to check one answer against another. If I do arrive at the same figure both times, I am usually strongly convinced (not always correctly) that I have the right answer. My argument is that children check one thing against another in much the same way to find the right circumstances to employ particular strategies.

The obvious difficulty for the agreement hypothesis is

that it does not account for the existence in the first place of these strategies which I claim children check against each other. How does the child acquire them? This, in the light of recent work on cognitive development, is quite an easy question to answer. It is now clear that young children do possess many of the strategies which earlier experiments by Piaget and several others had suggested they would only acquire many years later. This work seems to show that the major intellectual developments involve finding out when and where to employ intellectual strategies.

I shall not go into the work which shows this. The research has often been reviewed (Bryant, 1974; Gelman and Gallistel, 1978; Donaldson, 1978; Kail and Pellegrino, 1985), and it is enough to say that it seems to show that many of the failures in traditional experiments like conservation, transitivity, perspective-taking and the like, are due to the child not realising at the time what is the appropriate intellectual move to make. It seems to be more a question of a failure to apply the strategy rather than of its absence in the intellectual repertoire of the pre-school child. So where do they come from, these intellectual strategies? We cannot say at the moment. Some may be innate, but we shall need a lot more work on infants to be sure of that. Some may come through linguistic experience: again we do not know. In a way it does not seem to matter much. The important question posed by the children's failures and successes in the traditional cognitive tasks like conservation is now about how they realise when it is appropriate to use a strategy which they already possess.

If one takes this view, it is easy to see how the hypothesis about agreement could account for intellectual development. There are usually more ways than one of solving a problem correctly. Let us say that a particular problem X can be solved by intellectual moves A and B. Let us also say that the child is not at all sure about this: he is capable in principle of both moves but is uncertain whether one, or perhaps, both of them are the right ones. But he tries both out and finds, both being correct, that they come up with the same answer. Now he has convincing evidence that both A and B will work in the future.

Three Examples.

We can take three concrete examples, about which we
already do have some evidence. One is to be found in the
interesting recent work by Lawler (1985). He made detailed
observations of hiw own daughter's developing understanding of
various mathematical operations and particularly of addition.
Lawler argued that she built up "microworlds" and by that he
meant that she learned the facts, say, of addition in highly
specific circumstances and that at first this learning was
confined to these particular circumstances. One microworld was
the experience that she was getting at the time with the
computing language LOGO, another involved the way she spent
her pocket money and the price of particular sweets that she
bought regularly. Lawler's main argument is that she made
developmental progress when these different microworlds came
together - when, that is, she began to realise that she was
actually making the same calculations with the same results in
very different circumstances.

My second example concerns measurement. Children can
measure: they are able to use an intervening measure to
compare two discrete quantities (Bryant and Kopytynska, 1976).
But they often do not do so when they should. They resort
instead to inappropriate direct comparisons between the two
quantities even when the circumstances are quite unpropitious
for such direct comparisons. So instead of measuring they will
make direct comparisons between two towers or two blocks of
wood placed at different levels and at some distance from each
other. They only seem to measure properly when direct
comparisons are completely impossible. In other words they do
not realise when this particular move, measuring, is
appropriate.

According to the agreement hypothesis children should begin to
measure when they have had the chance to check the results of
measuring with the results of some other strategy. We looked

at this some time ago in a training experiment (Bryant, 1982).
The task was to compare the heights of two blocks of wood. The
child had to say whether these were the same or not: half the
time they were the same and the other half not. In the pre-
and post-test one block was on a table and the other on the
floor, and this made a direct comparison a very risky one
since the difference between the lengths of the two blocks was
quite small. There was however a stick, which happened to be
the same length as one of the blocks, lying conspicuously
around and the question was whether the child would use this
stick as a measure. In the pre-test the children hardly ever
did; they resorted instead to direct, and often erroneous,
comparisons.

After the pre-test the experimental group was given training
in "agreement". In every trial the child was encouraged both
to use the stick as a measure and to lift the lower block up
and put it beside the other one to make a (correct) direct
comparison. Thus the child had the experience of agreement:
his measuring judgements (which were almost always correct)
agreed with the correct direct comparisons. The children in
the control group were given twice as many trials as the
experimental group, but they only did one thing on each trial.
On half of them they were encouraged to measure, and on the
other half to lift the lower block and to make a direct
comparison. Thus they got exactly the same experiences as the
children in the experimental group, except that they were not
shown how the strategies agreed with one another. We predicted
that the experimental group would end up measuring more in the
post-test, and that is what happened. Measuring was fostered
by agreement, and not at all, as we showed in later
experiments, by conflict.

Another example is some work that we have done on
subtraction (Bryant, 1985). We had found that many young
children could do simple subtractions, but did not use their
knowledge of subtraction to solve many simple concrete
subtraction problems. If these children were given, say, a row
of nine counters which they counted as nine and then saw us
subtract two of them and were then asked how many were left,

they would again count all the counters from scratch, despite the fact that they knew that 9-2 equals 7. They did not use their knowledge of subtraction and resorted instead to another way of solving the problem - a perfectly good, though lengthy, way.

Our experiment on this was rather similar to our measuring experiment. We showed children in an experimental group that subtraction and counting from scratch lead to exactly the same answer in situations of the sort that I have just described. We did this by encouraging them to subtract and to count from scratch in the same trials. Again we gave the control group twice the number of training trials, in half of which they did one thing (subtracting) and in the other half the other (counting from scratch). Thus the two groups had exactly the same treatment, but for the fact that the children from the experimental group experience agreement between the results of the two strategies while the control group did not. We found once again that the experimental group changed in a subsequent post-test much more than the control group did. The children in the experimental group were much more likely to use their knowledge of subtraction and less likely to just to count from scratch in the post-test. So there are good reasons for taking the agreement hypothesis seriously. It offers a plausible account of the reasons for children's intellectual progress, and there is now some empirical evidence for this account.

Explaining the Constraints in Development.

What about the other requirement of a causal theory - that it should explain the constraints in children's development as well? Here the agreement hypothesis does reasonably well. There are good grounds for thinking that development which depends on the child checking out one intellectual strategy against another will take some time. For one thing the child may be content enough with an existing strategy (such as counting from scratch in our subtraction example) to take some time before he makes any connection between it and a relatively new strategy (subtraction in the same example). For another it may take the child some time to realise that there is any possibility of a connection to be made.

Better still the theory also gives an entirely adequate account of the effects of simple verbal communication. Let us restate the problem about verbal communication. As we have already noted it is usually not enough just to tell a child the best way to solve a problem. Theories based on linguistic communication have no good solution to this problem. Piaget's solution was his argument that verbal communication is not particularly important. This could be right, but given the enormous time and effort that we devote to explaining to children how to do things it does not seem unlikely that this communication plays a peripheral role in their development. So, neither approach gives a convincing account of the effects of verbal communication.

The theory about agreement takes a different tack. It is that verbal communication does have a significant effect, but that it does so as the first part (shades of Vygotsky) of a two-stage process. In that first stage the child may acquire a skill such as subtraction. She may learn by being taught the mechanics of it, and she knows that it is something one does in arithmetic. But she is not at all clear when one should do it. The strategy is part of her intellectual repertoire as a direct product of verbal communication, but it is not deployed to any great effect. The child has learned, has probably been taught, to subtract, but is not sure when she ought to do so. The next stage is the checking stage and this is something that the child usually does for herself. She begins to realise that this new strategy fits in with other existing strategies like counting. The strategy then becomes a working part of the child's system for solving problems and she begins to use the strategy spontaneously and at the appropriate time.

I should make two things clear about the relationship between this two stage scheme and the question of the effects of verbal communication. One is that the first stage - the original acquisition of the strategy - is sometimes based on verbal communication, and sometimes not. If one takes mathematical skills as an example, it is clear enough that a skill such as multiplication depends very heavily on the child being taught. On the other hand the basic understanding of some, though not all, aspects of addition and subtraction could be innate (Starkey and Gelman, 1982). The second point is that in principle verbal communication could play a role in the second stage as well. I have painted a picture of the child on her own, verifying one thing against another for herself without any help from any adult. However I can see no reason why an adult should not help a child to see these connections, and it seems to me that this is exactly what many sensitive teachers spend a lot of time doing.

This means that the theory about agreement deals equally with skills which are innate, those which the child learns on her own and those which she is taught by other people. It is a theory which has a better internal logic than the two more traditional approaches that I reviewed earlier: it works and they do not. It is also a theory for which there is now some evidence. But is that evidence good enough? In fact it is not. We must turn to the question of how to prove and disprove theories about the causes of development.

EMPIRICAL EVIDENCE AND CAUSAL THEORIES.

So far my arguments have been entirely about the internal plausibility of various models. But simply to show, as I have tried to show, that one model is more plausible than another is not enough. One has to be able to establish empirically whether a theory is right or not. One of the main difficulties about finding out about the causes of development has always been that we lack an accepted framework for deciding what is sufficient evidence for a cause. Certainly it is difficult to find any sign of such a framework in research on the causes of intellectual development. There is, however, one highly specific topic where a great deal of progress has been made towards getting together a system for establishing causes.

This is the study of how children learn to read.

Children's reading poses much the same problems as children's overall intellectual development to anyone trying to find out about causes. The basic difficulty is that in both areas there are two ways only of getting evidence about these causes and both are faulty. One is correlational; the other involves intervention.

The Correlational Method.

Correlations are of course notoriously tricky things, but let us concentrate on the least tricky form of correlational evidence, the longitudinal prediction. You think that A determines a particular development, B, and so you measure A in a large group of children a year or so before B does develop and then follow the same children through in order to see whether the strength of A is related to the speed with which B develops. In theories about reading there are, for example, hypotheses that a child's awareness of the sounds in words ("cat" can be divided into c-a-t) is major determinant of the speed with which she eventually learns to read. There is ample positive evidence that measures of this phonological awareness taken before children begin to read do predict how well they do learn to read later, even when the proper steps are taken to rule out the effects of other related variables such as intelligence.

This longitudinal information has one major strength and one major weakness. Its strength is that, so long as the measures are suitably sensitive, you can establish a genuine relationship between your variables A and B. To use the example of reading, it is now well established that there is a connection between young children's awareness of sounds and their progress in learning to read several years later (Bryant and Bradley, 1985). The difficulty is that you cannot say what sort of connection this really is. It may be a causal one: A may be determining B. But there is another possibility which is the tertium quid. Both may be influenced by C, an unknown and therefore unmeasured variable. However many variables you control for, however sophisticated your multiple regressions and your path analyses, you can never be completely confident that the relationship you are plotting is a genuinely causal one.

The Intervention Method.

We can turn now to intervention, and here we encounter the opposite problem. The method does not establish causes, but the causal connection may be an entirely artificial one. Intervention experiments can establish causal connections, because that is what experiments do. If you want to find out whether A provokes the development, B, you simply give an experimental group large doses of A and a control group exactly the same attention, experiences, material and so on, except for A itself, and you predict that the experimental group will develop B sooner than the control group. If that happens you can be sure that you have established a causal connection, but there is still a problem. The connection may be an artificial one, something that is entirely confined to your laboratory. You have no check that the connection exists in real life. One obvious example is conservation training experiments. So many, using so many different methods, have been successful that it is impossible to believe that they all reflect causal connections in real life. Some of them must have established a causal connection in the laboratory which have no bearing at all on anything that happens outside it.

Combining Correlation and Intervention in One Study.

So, one has two faulty methods but that is not a reason for despair, for by good fortune the strengths and weaknesses of the two methods are complementary. The strengths of each cancel out the weaknesses of the other. Intervention studies establish causal connections (which longitudinal correlations cannot do) and longitudinal predictions show that such connections do genuinely exist out there in the real world (which training studies never do). The obvious but rarely tried solution is to combine the two methods in one study, and that is what has happened now in studies of reading. We ourselves have pursued the question of awareness of sounds with the help of this combined design and have shown in one study (Bradley and Bryant, 1983) that measures of this awareness taken before children read do predict how quickly they eventually learn to do so, and also that training children on this skill does help them to learn to read and write. The combination of these two results establishes a causal connection.

There is no good reason why the same solution should not be tried in work on the causes of intellectual development, and until it is tried nothing definite will ever be established about these causes. Of the three approaches that I have described two at least are amenable to this sort of research. There is no difficulty at all in applying the design that I advocate to hypotheses about linguistic experience. Measure this experience and see how well it predicts later development, and intervene as well in the children's linguistic environment. The agreement hypothesis can also be studied quite easily with this two-barrelled sort of design. It should be quite easy (by adopting for example the kinds of observations that Lawler (1985) made) to measure how young children make connections between different kinds of experience and then see how well this predicts later development, and as we have seen there is no difficulty at all about teaching children these connections. The conflict theory poses greater problems because it is quite hard to pin down when an internal intellectual conflict is actually taking place or even what form it might take: Piaget did not give us many concrete examples. So predictive studies might be difficult. But someone should be able to find a reliable way of detecting disequilibrium when (or if) it happens.

Surely the next and the most urgent task is to get the evidence right. We have been given causal statements about

children's intellectual development, causal theories and
causal claims galore, but never a proper attempt to test them
effectively. Every empirical study of the causes of
intellectual development that I know of (including my own on
measuring and subtraction) involves either just correlations
or just intervention. No serious attempt has been made yet to
link the two methods and until that link is forged we can only
speculate about causes. Of course one should do one's best to
make sure that these speculations are as plausible as
possible. But we really must find out now whether they are
true or not as well, and for that we need the right kind of
evidence.

REFERENCES.

Bradley, L. & Bryant, P.E. (1983). Categorising sounds and
    learning to read: a causal connexion. Nature, 301, 419-
    420.
Bryant, P.E. (1974). Perception and Understanding in Young
    Children. London: Methuen.
Bryant, P.E. (1982). The role of conflict and agreement
    between intellectual strategies in children's ideas about
    measurement. British Journal of Psychology, 73, 242-251.
Bryant, P.E. (1985). The distinction between knowing when to
    do a sum and knowing how to do it. Educational
    Psychology, 5, 207-215.
Bryant, P.E. & Bradley, L. (1985). Children's reading
    problems. Oxford: Blackwells.
Bryant, P.E. & Kopytynska, H. (1976). Spontaneous measurement
    by young children. Nature, 260, 773.
Donaldson, M. (1978). Children's minds. London: Fontana.
Gelman, R. & Gallistel, C.R. (1978). The child's understanding
    of number. Cambridge: Harvard University Press.
Kail, R. & Pellegrino, J.W. (1985). Human intelligence:
    Perspectives and prospects. New York: W.H. Freeman and
    Co.

Lawler, R.W. (1985). Computer experience and cognitive development: a child's learning in a computer culture. Chichester: Ellis Horwood Ltd.

Piaget, J. (1978). The development of thought: equilibration of cognitive structures. Oxford: Blackwells.

Piaget, J. (1980). Experiments in contradiction. Chicago: The University of Chicago Press.

Starkey, P. & Gelman, R. (1982). The development of addition and subtraction strategies prior to formal schooling in arithmetic. In T.P. Carpenter, J.M. Moser & T.A. Romberg (Eds.), Addition and subtraction: a cognitive perspective. Hillsdale, N.J.: Lawrence Erlbaum Ass.

Vygotsky, L.S. (1962). Thought and language. Cambridge, Mass.: M.I.T. Press.

Vygotsky, L.S. (1978). Mind in society. Cambridge: Harvard University Press.

Vygotsky, L.S. (1981). The genesis of higher mental functions. In J.V. Wertsch (Ed.), The concept of activity in Soviet Psychology. Armonk N.Y.: Sharpe.

PART 3

THE SOCIAL DIMENSION OF DEVELOPMENT

Theory Building in Developmental Psychology
P.L.C. van Geert (editor)
© Elsevier Science Publishers B.V. (North-Holland), 1986

6

The Conditions of Human Development

Implications of socialization research for developmental theory

Dieter Geulen

Many theories of human development tend to underestimate the role of environmental conditions in determining qualitatively different life paths and, consequently, resulting personality structures. On the ·other hand it is widely acknowledged that external conditions are necessary and that personality development is the result of the interaction between internal and external conditions. Empirical research on socialization has convincingly demonstrated that (1) there are many external factors which determine human development, (2) these factors qualitatively and decisively influence the direction and course of development, (3) they affect all aspects of personality, (4) they are in effect throughout the entire life span, and (5) they are contingent, that is they depend upon parameters of the social system and are subject to historical change.

After a critical discussion of the theories of Werner, Piaget, Freud, and Erikson it is argued that the implicit assumptions of developmental theories which focus on universal courses, stages and/or goals of human development systematically lead to an underestimation of external conditions. Thus the metatheoretical postulate is formulated that a theory of human development must be kept open with regard to assumptions about paths and ends of development. Some concepts and models are presented which may serve as logical elements of a developmental theory that fully takes into account external conditions. This includes an analysis of (a) the subject-environment interaction, (b) the role of critical life decisions in a "switch points model", (c) the intertemporal interaction of different effects within human subjects, and (d) the effects of historical conditions and events upon individuals of different birth cohorts.

Developmental psychology has produced a number of theories and models dealing with the psychological characteristics of humans from infancy through adolescence and later adulthood, and presented various hypotheses about how subsequent stages "develop" from earlier stages. It seems fair to say, however, that most developmental theories are descriptive and analytical rather than explanatory. Much less of the literature has been devoted to causes and conditions of development, particularly external factors, than to development itself.

No modern writer would express any serious doubt that external factors are necessary for human development. This is true even for writers aligned with a nativistic (Gesell, 1946) or biological (Waddington, 1957; Dobzhansky, 1962; Vale, 1980) position. There is also a broad consensus on the view that the relationship between internal (especially inherited) factors and environmental factors has to be regarded as interactive (Riegel, 1975; 1976; Lerner, 1976; 1978; Datan & Reese, 1977; Endler & Magnuson, 1978; Oerter & Montada, 1982). This is a clear indication that the aims of theory formation in developmental psychology extend beyond pure description and are directed ultimately at explanation.

The interactionistic approach as such is apparently not controversial. Since it represents a very general version of the causality principle, it may be accepted as a logical starting point and shall be stated here as a first metatheoretical postulate for a theory of human development.

The realization and elaboration of this general concept, whose beginnings can be traced back to William Stern's (1914) formulation of the "convergence principle", seems to be much less advanced in empirical research and in the construction of related theoretical models. The closest we can get is recent research in life-span development (Baltes & Brim, 1979; Baltes & Lipsitt, 1980; Lerner & Busch-Rossnagel, 1981). The question of external conditions is addressed in the most prominent theories (e.g. Piaget) at best in such a way that external factors are regarded as stimulating or accelerating agents for precisely the kind of development that is already described in the theory. It is often assumed that they are historically constant and, therefore, that they affect the development of all individuals in the same way. In other theories external conditions are either scarcely mentioned, are implicit, or are even implicitly denied.

If we begin with the premise that a theory of human development should also be explanatory and that causal relationships can be regarded within the framework of a multiconditional interactionistic approach, it follows that, in principle, all relevant internal and external factors, as well as all mechanisms of their interaction, should be revealed. Obviously, the interaction cannot be analyzed until all of the external factors have been taken completely into account. We can then expect that the analysis will lead to many complex mediating variables so that even the general terms "interaction" or "dialectic relationship" will ascend beyond their programmatic function and attain a more precise and differentiated meaning.

SOCIALIZATION AND DEVELOPMENT.

Empirical research on socialization (for reviews see: Stevenson, 1963; Hoffman & Hoffman, 1964; 1966; Goslin, 1969; Mussen, 1970; Caldwell & Ricciuti, 1973; Hetherington, 1975; Horowitz, 1975; Hartup, 1982; Wolman, 1982) has provided a large body of data which convincingly demonstrate that: (1) There are many different external factors that can determine human development, in a manner that no current theory of development has predicted. (2) These factors include catalysts (i.e. excitatory, acceleratory or inhibitory factors) as well as conditions which qualitatively and decisively influence the direction and course of development. This is particularly true under the assumption of the subject's interactive role.

The many variables which have been shown to have effects on development, particularly during early and middle childhood, can be summarized as follows:

- deprivation of physical, social, emotional, verbal and

cultural stimuli, e.g., in a poverty-stricken milieu, due
to absence of the mother or being raised in an orphanage
(Yarrow, 1964; Sinha, 1982);
- family structure, siblings (Clausen, 1966; Herzog &
  Studia, 1973);
- relationships and interactions within the family, style
  of child-rearing, kinds of sanctions, etc. (Caldwell,
  1964; Becker, 1964; Ainsworth, 1973; Martin, 1975; Joffe
  & Vaughn, 1982);
- Ecological factors (Gump, 1975);
- mass media, especially television (Maccoby, 1964);
- various institutions outside the family, e.g.
  kindergarten and school (Swift, 1964; Glidewell et al.,
  1966; Busch-Rossnagel & Vance, 1982; Weinert & Treiber,
  1982);
- peer groups (Campbell, 1964).
(3) External socialization factors affect all aspects of
personality. The following variables are those that have been
most extensively studied:
- psychosexual development (Kagan, 1964; Maccoby, 1966;
  Mischel, 1970; Shepherd-Look, 1982);
- moral development (Kohlberg, 1963, 1964; Hoffman, 1970;
  Carroll & Rest, 1982);
- cognitive development and creativity (Gallagher, 1964;
  Sigel, 1964; Bayley, 1970; Wallach, 1970; Sinha, 1982);
- language development (Ervin & Miller, 1963; Ervin-Tripp,
  1966; Cazden, 1966; Molfese et al., 1982);
- social and sociocognitive development (Bryan, 1975;
  Glucksberg et al., 1975; Shantz, 1975);
- occupational motives and roles (Borow, 1966; Moore,
  1969);
- retarded and pathological development (Zigler , 1966;
  Robinson & Robinson, 1970);
as well as some other specific variables for instance,
dependency (Hartup, 1963; Maccoby & Masters, 1970),
achievement motivation (Crandall, 1963; Trudewind, 1982), and
aggressivity (Bandura & Walters, 1963; Feshbach, 1970).
(4) Socializing factors are in effect throughout the entire

life span, from early childhood to old age, although the kinds
of factors, their interaction and their effects may differ. In
addition to studies on early and middle childhood, a large
number of results is available on older age groups and their
problems:

- adolescence (Campbell, 1969; Lerner & Shea, 1982; Newman,
  1982);
- middle and later years (Riley et al., 1969; B. Newman,
  1982);
- professional role and the work place (Moore, 1969;
  Havighurst, 1982; Vondracek et al., 1982);
- partners and family (Hill & Aldous, 1969; Biller, 1982;
  Doherty & Jacobson, 1982).

(5) The factors are mostly contingent; that is, they depend
upon social parameters of the society's system, are subject to
historical change and differ from one system to another.
This has been demonstrated in studies which have shown the
historical changes in parents' child-rearing methods
(Bronfenbrenner, 1958; Miller & Swanson, 1958) but also in
studies which reveal that socialization within a particular
social system depends on sociostructural conditions, e.g. SES
(Clausen, 1963; Hess, 1970; Deutsch, 1973).
Comparisons of cultures which differ in many conditions
simultaneously make this very clear indeed (Levine, 1970;
Ember, 1977).

These facts may have wide-reaching consequences for the
construction of models of human development. One of these is
that personality development can no longer be conceived of as
a passage through a predetermined sequence of stages, because
different individuals follow different developmental paths,
depending upon which contingent socialization conditions they
encounter.

Although modern textbooks of developmental psychology
have incorporated many findings from socialization research,
the most prominent theoretical designs of human development
have largely ignored them. There are several reasons for this.
Theories of human development have their origins in psychology
and were formulated in the 1920's-1940's, with traditions

extending back to the 19th century. Socialization research, on the other hand, began in the late 1920's and blossomed out in the 1940's and 1950's (Geulen, 1980). Its origins were in cultural anthropology and it was taken up later by sociologists, family therapists and others who were less interested in abstract theories than in solutions to specific political, educational and clinical problems.

Since both approaches deal with the problem of human development and the conditions which determine it,from different perspectives, it should prove fruitful for both of them to enter into a discussion. This is particularly true since their perspectives complement each other: Developmental theories focus on the course over time but neglect, to a certain extent, contingent external conditions. Socialization research, on the other hand, focuses on the effects of external conditions; it analyzes them in general but only at one specific time and not in the diachronic context of personality development. Each of the two approaches is one part of the whole story; it would therefore be desirable to look for possibilities of integration. This is the aim of the present paper. It deals with the question which theoretical implications follow from the results of socialization research for the construction of models of human development.

The next section is devoted to a critical discussion of some representative theories of development. In the third section some postulates are formulated and a conceptual framework is sketched for a development model which may better incorporate the external conditions of human development.

THE CONDITIONS OF DEVELOPMENT IN SOME REPRESENTATIVE THEORIES.

Werner's Orthogenetic Theory.

One influential theory about development was presented by Heinz Werner (1948; 1957). He begins with the dialectic statement that the concept "development" implies change in an organism which retains its identity during the change. More precisely, development - Werner's examples deal mainly with cognitive processes - is described, in analogy to organic development at phylogenetic and ontogenetic levels, as "orthogenesis". It consists of two interrelated tendencies: increasing differentiation (i.e. specialization, multiplicity and specificity of the parts) and corresponding increasing centralization (i.e. subordination of all disparate parts under one hierarchical order). Development is a universal succession of stages, each of which is in itself coherent and qualitatively different from the preceding stage. In fact, development can be regarded both as discontinuous (qualitative) and as continuous (quantative) change. Werner also expresses interest in interindividual differences, which he regards as variations in degree of differentiation and thus in stages of development.

As a descriptive model of human development this theory has a certain plausibility but perhaps less relevance for adulthood and beyond, where a rather one-sided specialization or de-differentiation can be observed. As to the question of conditions, however, there is no concrete mention of internal or external factors in either of Werner's main writings. A "mechanistic" explanation - apparently an explanation based on external causes - is explicitly denied; instead he proposes an "organic" (analogous to biological) view.

> "Originally the concept of development was assumed to be of a mechanistic order. Today it is oriented according to an organic point of view. This means that each level is conceived organically and that the relationship between levels is organic in nature" (Werner, 1948; p.5).

Thus, Werner seems to attribute immanent grounds for development to the organism itself; his recourse to Goethe and Hegel supports this interpretation.

One may ask whether this development model is fundamentally incompatible with the assumption of external factors. This does not appear to be the case. On the contrary, the assumption of specific stimulating and supportive environmental conditions for the developing organism appears essential. Werner suggests it might be possible that there are different courses of development, e.g. bifurcations (1957; p.137). This would necessarily imply that external conditions also determine the direction of development. But even here their influence would be limited, since the theory is bound to the concept of differentiation which is only one of many possible ways of viewing development. In the end, however, Werner seems to give preference to the thesis of a universal developmental pattern.

Piaget's Theory of Intellectual Development.

The theory of Jean Piaget (1970a; Flavell, 1963) is the one most often discussed today. In the basic postulates of this theory explicit mention is made of the environment's role in development. For the most part, development is viewed as the development of intelligence, which enables the organism to adapt to his surroundings. The individual is a subject who interacts and comes to terms with his or her environment. As a result, the actions and their real components are internalized and thus form cognitive operations or schemata. Experiences and objects which do not adequately conform to or fit in with existing schemata make a new adaptation necessary: (1) through assimilation of the object into existing schemata and (2) through accommodation of existing schemata to the object. Intelligence develops, therefore, as a result of accommodation.

The speed with which this development takes place depends upon whether the subject encounters those objects in his environment with which he can just about deal in his present developmental stage so that the next stage will be stimulated. In the course of development the schemata become increasingly generalized and coordinated with each other; in this way the subject constructs a system of logical operations that is increasingly better adapted to reality and internally consistent. According to Piaget, this is explained by the organism's inherent tendency toward equilibration. Piaget goes on to say that, for all human subjects, development follows a specific, universal sequence of stages. The sequence cannot be altered, nor are other, different stages possible since one stage is always a prerequisite for the next. Piaget describes a sensorimotor stage, a stage of representational (but not yet logical) intelligence, a stage of concrete operations, and finally the stage of formal logical operations. In this last case, which is reached at about the age of 11-13 years, the form of abstract, propositional and hypothetical thinking is attained which is typically represented in mathematics and natural science. There are interindividual differences in the time taken to progress through the stages and in the final level reached. This is primarily dependent upon the given external stimulating conditions.

Piaget's work is by far the most detailed genetic theory of intelligence. For purposes of our present discussion, however, two interrelated limitations have to be pointed out.

Our first criticism is aimed at the claim that there is only one possible path of development which is the same for all individuals and leads to the same goal for everyone, namely, being capable of logical, fully-developed scientific thinking which, for Piaget, is almost normative.
The related assumption that the formal stage is a consistent whole seems to be untenable (Flavell, 1977; 1982; Dasen & Heron, 1981). In one of his later writings Piaget himself remarks that the development of formal operations can be subject-specific and thus create interindividual differences (Piaget, 1970b; Neimark, 1975).
Another serious limitation is that the theory does not account for the fact that development continues after adolescence. Several authors have pointed out that there are even certain logical operations and structures beyond formal intelligence - for example, dialectic thought (Riegel, 1975; Labouvie-Vief, 1980; Kramer, 1983). It seems obvious also on a common sense level that thought processes and personality structure of adults and even adolescents are much more complex and cannot adequately be described solely in terms of "formal operations" as conceived by Piaget.

The reason for these problems apparently lies in the fact that Piaget's theory only deals with one section of what the average person psychological theories call "personality" and "human development". Even if we accept that every human being is capable of developing formal intelligence, we would have to assume that "personality" is defined in a much broader sense and by very different variables (Geulen, 1977). The weight attached to intelligence is only relative. It depends first upon its place in the total personality structure (the psychological context). Second, it depends upon the kind of demands which the social reality places on the individual (the sociological context). Formal intelligence is not equally important in all societies, and cross-cultural research has convincingly shown that different cultural preconditions really do lead to qualitatively different forms of intelligence (Price-Williams, 1969; Cole & Scribner, 1974; Berry, 1976, Ember, 1977; Lloyd, 1983). Thirdly, it is dependent upon the cultural values implicit in the work of the scientist himself. Several authors have argued that Piaget's theory reflects a definite Western bias which even we find to be increasingly problematic (Preiswerk, 1976; Berthoud, 1976).

Our second objection refers to Piaget's view of external conditions. He regards external factors, in the form of material for the active interaction between subject and environment, as a necessary prerequisite for development. However, these conditions function only as stimulators for the next step in the developmental sequence; they cannot influence the direction of development. Indeed, this possibility is logically excluded, since Piaget assumes only one possible course of development.

> "The stages we mentioned are accelerated or retarded in their average chronological ages according to the child's cultural and educational environment. But the very fact that the stages follow the same sequential order in any environment is enough to show that the social environment cannot account for everything. This constant order of succession cannot be ascribed to the environment" (Piaget, 1970a;

p.721).

Although Piaget makes hardly any precise statements about conditions, it is clear that he sees them primarily in the subject's experiences with material objects (Piaget, 1970a; p.720). In his early work on moral development (1932) Piaget placed an even greater importance on social experiences with other people, but dropped this in later writings, speaking only about the cultural and educational milieu in general (Piaget, 1970a; p.721).

A consequence of this narrow view of conditions is a second limitation: that the relevant conditions are regarded as being historically invariant and thus universal. This assumption is necessary in order for Piaget to establish a universal developmental sequence for his theory. Empirically, however, the assumption is false. Results from socialization research have demonstrated that a great many of the conditions which Piaget assumed (at least in their particular constellation) but also many conditions not mentioned by Piaget are dependent on contingent conditions in the social system and historically variable.

Piaget's theory, therefore, is really a grandiose contribution on the genesis of one particular kind of intelligence. For a comprehensive model of human development, however, it is far too limited.

The Psychoanalytic Theories of Freud and Erikson.

Although less interest has been shown in the psychoanalytic theory of development (Freud, 1940; Fenichel, 1945; Noam et al., 1982) in recent years, it does offer some interesting views on our problem. In Freud's original version, human development and personality are the result of a conflict between powerful, inborn drives, that are primarily sexual (libidinal) but also aggressive. These drives develop in early childhood where the libido is organized in a specific, predetermined sequence of stages related to different body zones and objects. These "polymorphous perverse" drives are opposed by reality (in the form of personal figures representing social norms), which seeks to threaten and constrain them. The resulting conflict can be resolved either by the formation of an autonomous ego or by defense mechanisms and personality structures (depending upon the set of conditions) which are unconscious and not subject to the ego's control (e.g., fixation on certain objects, introjection or identification, countercathexis and reaction formation). In the latter case they are expressed later as uncomprehended peculiarities of character, or neurotic symptoms. Freud assumed that the (male) child typically goes through the Oedipus conflict and resolves this by identifying with his father. As a result, the superego comes into being as a moral judge and representative of social norms.

We see that in psychoanalytic theory a major role has been assigned to external conditions in interaction with inherited factors. Furthermore, the theory provides for different individual (if also "pathological") paths of development; indeed, this is the usual case, if we recall the clinical interest which was the reason behind the theory's original conception. It should be noted, however, that the Oedipus situation and superego formation is intertwined with the historical form of upper-class families in Central Europe at the turn of the century, and cannot therefore be a universal characteristic of development (Malinowski, 1927). Another criticism is that Freudian theory is limited to early childhood and says nothing about later development.

Erik H. Erikson (1959; 1963) took up the theory at this point. He too regards development in a specific sequence of "crises" that have to be worked through. He does not, however, view this at the level of drive organization but at the level of ego or identity development over the entire life span. Each crisis arises from a specific, dichotomously formulated problem which is either solved so that it becomes integrated into the ego (progression) or not (retardation or fixation). Eight developmental stages are distinguished and presented in an epigenetic table: in early childhood, Basic trust vs. Mistrust, Autonomy vs. Shame and Doubt, Initiative vs. Guilt;

in latency, Industry vs. Inferiority; in adolescence, Identity
vs. Role Diffusion; and in adulthood, Intimacy vs. Isolation,
Generativity vs. Stagnation and Integrity vs. Despair
(Erikson, 1963; Ch.7).
An important point is the assumption that the way in which the
ego resolves a particular crisis depends upon the previous
history of conflict resolution. This determines the further
course of development; thus, at each stage of development two
alternative routes for further development are available. In
contrast to Piaget's theory, Erikson provides for different
courses of development with different consequences. In
addition, decisions about the future course are possible at
any period, even in later years. The general model of
development implicit in this theory seems to be very
important. Erikson's concrete definition of crises, their
number and sequence are, however, less evident and should
perhaps be kept open.
As for the conditions, Erikson speaks of endogenous and
external conditions which he explicitely labels "social" (he
has investigated these himself in his cultural anthropological
studies of Indian tribes, 1963). However, the precise role
these conditions play and how they are related to each other
remains unclear.
> "The underlying assumptions are (1) that the human
> personality in principle develops according to steps
> predetermined in the growing person's readiness to
> be driven toward, to be aware of, and to interact
> with, a widening social radius; and (2) that
> society, in principle, tends to be so constituted as
> to meet and invite this succession of potentialities
> for interaction and attempts to safeguard and to
> encourage the proper rate and the proper sequence of
> their enfolding" (Erikson, 1963; p.270).

As this quotation shows, Erikson gives endogenous conditions
the decisive, leading role and the social conditions only a
supporting, catalytic role. The kind and sequence of the
crises is, in his opinion, endogenous and preprogrammed. In
this Erikson remains an orthodox Freudian. In his case this

assumption is untenable, however. In contrast to Freudian theory, in which the developmental phases are based in a genetically-fixed drive development, it obviously makes no sense to talk about inborn "drives" in Erikson's later stages. On the contrary, his concepts (e.g., trust, autonomy, guilt, industry, role etc.) clearly indicate an essentially social origin of the conflicts. Thus, it would appear that Erikson's assumptions about conditions of development need to be revised so as to allow external, social conditions to play a decisive role in determining an individual's developmental path, i.e. in the decision choices at the various critical points in human life.

External Conditions and Theoretical Level of Detail.

It might be argued that the omission of conditions for development in current developmental theories is only accidental, that there would be no great difficulty in supplementing an existing theory with appropriate empirical research. And for some theories this would be partially true. It would appear, however, that for a specific developmental theory there are also logical limits set which preclude the question of external conditions in any consistent manner. In other words, a developmental theory in which the course and final goal of development is determined a priori by normative assumptions is wholly or partially incompatible with the postulate of external developmental conditions.
Assigning the question of conditions only a peripheral importance could be interpreted as an immunizing strategy. For, if all real conditions were taken into account, it might turn out that the development of individuals would show a very different pattern. Not only would this disprove the theory: even worse, perhaps, it would reveal the underlying normative assumptions to be unrealistic.
My thesis is that there is a systematic relationship between the amount of detail with which a theory describes human development and its assumptions on external conditions: the

more definite, i.e. unambiguous and specific, the statements
dealing with the course of development are, through specific
stages to a specific end goal, the less attention the theory
is able to direct to the external, especially historically
contingent, conditions.

If external factors are explicitly denied or dismissed as
irrelevant, this would have to be called explicit nativism.
Such a position seems hardly tenable today. There are
versions, however, in which the same kind of deficit is more
or less latent.
In a first case the theory specifies certain conditions which
could actually apply to the development of some individuals
but overlook other conditions that would produce a different
developmental course in other individuals.
A second way in which conditions for development are neglected
occurs in the case where the theory specifies only those
conditions which seem to be relevant to the dependent
variables stated in its descriptive part. Thus conditions
which may actually be effective as well as conditions which
pertain to other aspects of personality are excluded. In both
cases the limitation of the search for conditions is a
consequence of the limitation of the theory itself to one of
several possible development paths or dependent variables. The
theory may then be valid for some variables in certain
individuals in specific circumstances, but must renounce its
claim to be a general, universal theory.
A third case arises when external factors are specified but
are falsely claimed or implied to be historically invariant.
In this instance the error is that, while the theory appears
to be universal it is in fact valid only under very specific
historical and social conditions, e.g. in the highly civilized
Western societies of the first third of the 20th century.
Even more important is the fact that conditions assumed to be
historically invariant can no longer be considered as a source
of variance for different courses of development in different
individuals. Development then appears to be the same for all
individuals at all times. Given the false assumption of
invariance, therefore, the question of external causes for

different courses of development is logically excluded. An
implicit nativism is evident here, which serves as an
immunizing argument for the claim of a universal and unidirectional development, or vice versa.

For purposes of subsequent discussion, our position can
now be summarized and positively formulated as a second
metatheoretical postulate: The more a theory of development
takes external conditions - which we have to assume are
largely historically contingent - into account the more unre-
stricted and open its presuppositions about developmental
courses and goals must be.

We have derived this postulate from the first, that external
conditions should be incorporated into the theory within the
framework of an interactionist model. Several other postulates
and hypotheses for a developmental model can also be derived.

SOME POSTULATES AND HYPOTHESES FOR A GENERAL MODEL OF
DEVELOPMENT.

Subject-environment Interaction.

As mentioned previously, most of today's authors view the
relationship between internal and external factors of
personality development as interaction. This means not only
that both kind of factors contribute to the result but also
that the way in which one factor works is dependent on one or
more other factors.

It would seem that in the general interaction formula at
least four different mechanisms (and, accordingly, different
consequences for development) have to be distinguished.

The first mechanism is that the environment and the
events occurring in it are perceived by the individual and
processed internally. Although the environment appears here to
be given and the individual to be a passive recipient, an
interactive process does exist. The way in which events are
perceived and processed depends upon specific internal
motivational and cognitive conditions on the part of the

individual, who is therefore an active participant. It is well established in psychology that the same event is processed differently by different individuals, and that different consequences for their development will result. This type of interaction is exemplified in psychoanalytic theory.

The second mechanism is that the individual is mobile and therefore selects certain situations. He seeks out certain areas and conditions and avoids others. Developmental effects result both from experiences in the selected situations and from the acts of searching and selecting. This type of interaction is implied in the behaviouristic reinforcement paradigm. The specific interaction effect is seen in the fact that the strategies and criteria of the search and selection process, and consequently of the actual situation attained, are dependent upon internal conditions. In addition there is also an interaction process of the first type, i.e. an internal processing. It seems that we could analyze the relevance of biographical decisions (e.g., choice of education, occupation, job location, partner) for development in this way.

These examples show, however, that yet another mechanism is implied. The individual is also selected by reality, i.e. he or she experiences selectively either acceptance or rejection, and the result of this then determines conditions for his or her future development. This is particularly evident in the case of selecting a partner or choosing a job location. This, too, is a particular interaction effect; it plays a decisive role in the theory of evolution but is also relevant for developmental psychology (cf. Anastasi, 1958). The condition on the individuals' side is how they present themselves to others, or the corresponding personality attributes. On reality's side the conditions are, for example, the number of places to choose from, requirements, number of competing applicants, and how the people in charge perceive and evaluate the individual and his or her behaviour.

The fourth interaction mechanism is that the individuals' actions change reality and consequently the external conditions of their future development. This process is

different from that of the search and selection of particular
areas of reality in that, first, completely new conditions can
be created which then have new consequences for his and
others' psychological development. This is especially evident
in the example of technological development in advanced
societies. Second, the active, purposeful modification of
parts of the physical and social reality implies different and
more complex learning processes than exist in a simple
selection. For example, it requires a thorough analysis of the
features of the object and its relationships, processing of
feedback, accurate judgement of one's abilities, competence
etc. In Piaget's theory and in materialistic psychology
(Piaget, 1970a; Leontiev, 1964) this mechanism is regarded as
essential for personality development.

From the diversity of the interaction mechanisms it
becomes evident that many, if not all, areas of personality
may be involved. Indeed, the spectrum of personality variables
that have been studied in socialization research with positive
results is rather impressive (see introduction). Thus the
postulate can be stated that any theory of human development
which claims to be comprehensive must not fixate a priori on
one single, narrow group of personality variables, since any
such choice would be arbitrary and necessarily exclude other
areas. The theory has to encompass all areas of personality.
This argument is particularly forceful if one assumes
intrapsychic interaction effects, so that the personality
variables included in the theory (e.g. cognitive variables)
are dependent upon variables excluded by the theory (e.g.
motivational variables) and upon their external conditions for
which the theory has no explanation.

The Switch Points Model.

We can now ask what consequences this kind of interaction
between individual and environment has for an analysis of
psychological development. In general it can be said that the
type and result of this interaction at a particular time t_1

determine which internal and external conditions will be present at a later time, t_2. This is illustrated by a model we
have called the "Switch Points Model". There is some formal
analogy to Waddington's "Epigenetic Landscape" (1957), a model
of genetic canalization by the environment. Although it is
already simplified, some interesting properties of courses of
development can be derived from it, under the premises we have
set up to now.

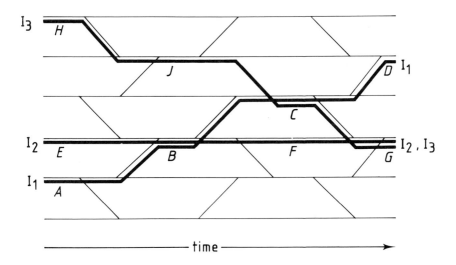

Figure 1. The switch point model. Thick lines represent three possible
    courses of development of individuals I_1, I_2, and I_3. Thin lines
    represent a lattice of possible switch points.

The starting-point for the model is the fact that in the
course of their life individuals encounter certain decision
alternatives presented by society and that each decision then
determines their future course, which is different from other
alternatives, is often irreversible and has far-reaching
consequences. Some typical decision points are choice of type
of education and occupation, selection of a partner,
parenthood, joining an organization, changing jobs, moving
house, etc.
Relevant structural characteristics, as illustrated in Figure
1, are:
(1) There are several different starting points and end
points.
(2) The number of decision points and the number of
alternatives at each point is limited. (For the sake of
simplification, only two alternatives are shown.)
(3) The decision points have a temporal, logical or
institutionalized relationship to each other. One of the
consequences is that with regard to the course of an
individual's career or psychological development no decision
is reversible, but that with regard to certain end points,
some decisions can later be corrected.
(4) From a specific starting point not every end point can be
reached, although there is a certain range of leeway, first
with regard to the end points attained from a specific
starting point, second with regard to the starting points
leading to a specific end point. This kind of structure offers
a certain (but always finite) number of possibilities for an
individual career, and thus for an individual developmental
history.
        If the external conditions upon which development depends
are contingent, as we must assume, it follows that the course
of development in different individuals varies to the extent
that the kind and constellation of their external conditions
differ. We know that this is even the case for brothers and
sisters living together in the same family (Toman, 1969). So
one individual I_1 may encounter the events A, B, C, D, while
another individual I_2 encounters the conditions E, B, F, G,

and a third individual I_3 encounters H, J, C, G (see Fig.1). It is fair to assume that this is true for all people - i.e. that each individual has a unique developmental history (Block, 1971; Mumford & Owens, 1984). Thus development corresponds to what Lerner (1980), following Gottlieb (1970), calls "probabilistic epigenesis".
This fact is obviously relevant for the origin and explanation of human individuality, i.e. for interindividual differences (Brim & Kagan, 1980). There is no good reason why a theory of human development should concentrate solely on common interindividual phenomena and ignore interindividual differences. Differential developmental psychology might even be the more interesting side of the business.
Individualization in development does not mean that individuals are totally different, however. It should be kept in mind that individuals living in society must share some understanding, values, norms, and skills to be able to interact with each other. Society would not function without some consensus of this kind. This point has been made clear by sociological theory (cf. Parsons, 1937) and is one reason for the sociologist's interest in socialization. But the individual personality is much more complex and goes far beyond such common elements (Geulen, 1977).

Intertemporal Interaction Effects.

    The preceding discussion shows, as does empirical socialization research, that the influence of external conditions is not limited to a particular age or stage of development, but extends throughout the entire life span, from early childhood on. Very different conditions can, of course, be in effect at different developmental stages. Here again any limitation of the theory to one particular stage would be arbitrary and processes would be overlooked that contribute to the final result.
This argument too weighs more heavily when we assume that there are intrapsychic interaction effects between earlier and

later events. A relationship of this kind - I suggest it be called "intertemporal interaction effects" - can be seen, for example, when the result of earlier socialization processes come into play as internal conditions in later interactions with external conditions. In this case, focusing on one particular segment of the total development would leave the proportions in the result that came from earlier segments unexplained.

The assumption of intertemporal effects is not arbitrary. It follows logically from two assumptions which can be regarded as being completely safe, or even trivial, first, that earlier developmental events are "stored" over time in the personality, and second, that the personality, and consequently the manifestation of earlier events, play a part in the processing of later events in the sense mentioned in our first postulate. If one assumes an organismic model of personality (Reese & Overton, 1970; Looft, 1973) these effects are probably more complex and include different levels and self-reflecting processes (e.g., the conscious reconstruction and working-through of events that occurred in early childhood). But the assumption of intertemporal effects would also be compatible with a mechanistic model (for example, in the Skinnerian model of learning, the previous history of reinforcements is a factor in current learning). In fact, each of the developmental models we have described contains this assumption, at least in the form that subsequent stages of development can only be reached when certain conditions in previous stages have been met.

Earlier (see the section on "External Conditions and Theoretical Level of Detail") it was noted that a theory of development that takes external conditions into account should be kept open as far as possible. This does not mean, however, that it actually be completely open, i.e. can make no more general statements whatsoever about paths of development. If the assumption of intertemporal, internal interaction effects is true, i.e. that the processing of later events is influenced by the results of processing former events, then the actual contingency of external events is reduced on the subjective side. The development of the personality is not simply a gradual accumulation of external events; it has a structure of its own which follows certain laws. For example, after a certain event, A, has occurred and been processed, the effects of a subsequent event, B, are no longer unlimited. The effects of a third event, C, are determined by event A, event B and the internal interaction AB. In the processing of a fourth event there are already seven complexes taking part: A, B, AB, C, AC, BC, ABC. Several models have been proposed to deal with these problems (Van den Daele, 1969; 1976; Flavell, 1972; Fischer, 1980).

It is apparent that, in contrast to actual contingencies, the number of ways in which a subsequent event is processed, or a corresponding developmental step is completed, increases with the number of previous events. This relationship is not linear but, because of the various internal interaction effects between all events, exponential. This is why, at least theoretically, the number of possible developmental paths increases with continued development. In common sense this corresponds to increasing individuation with age.

Now we see again - as compared to the randomness of external events - specific diachronic processes and structures within the individual which classical theories of development have favoured. At this stage of analysis, however, it is not necessary to impute to the subject any kind of inherent entelechy or hypothetical constructs such as innate competence, consistent stages, or a tendency toward equilibration.

Effects of Historical Conditions upon Different Cohorts.

Another dimension which should be introduced into a general model of development is the dimension of historical change over time. This is a consequence of the fact that - as we have seen - external conditions of personality development are subject to historical change. Moreover, our critical discussion of the various developmental theories showed that

ignoring the historical dimension can lead to false
conclusions about the degree to which a developmental theory
can be generalized. The most decisive reason, however, is
again the rather banal observation that the development of
individuals is different in different eras (Ariès, 1960;
Peeters, 1966; Elias, 1969; Pinchbeck & Hewitt, 1969; deMause,
1974; LeGoff, 1978).
It seems somewhat difficult to incorporate the full
implications of this fact into a general model of ontogenetic
development. One could, for example, assume that in the Switch
Points Model described above the decision points and possible
paths change during an individual's lifetime, that is the
chances of certain decisions increase or decrease. It is also
possible that certain possibilities disappear altogether
and/or new ones arise. Because the variance of external conditions is made larger by historical change, it follows that, in
the long term, the number of theoretically possible
developmental paths also increases. As far as a single
individual is concerned, however, the consequences are less
clear. On the one hand, more and different experiences can be
made within the life span. On the other hand, historical
change causes a larger discrepancy to arise between the
subjective developmental conditions laid down in the
individual and the changing external conditions, so that the
range of possibilities of interaction and hence of the
individual's future development is narrowed down.
    I would like to point out one interesting effect which
results from the interaction of historical change with
internal conditions - or, more precisely, with internal
intertemporal relationships. This effect is well illustrated
in a cohort analysis (Ryder, 1965; Schaie, 1965; Baltes,
Cornelius & Nesselroade, 1977; Baltes, Reese & Lipsitt, 1980).
A cohort is an aggregate of individuals who experienced one
particular event in their life, usually their birth, at the
same historical time. The basic idea behind a cohort-
analytical socialization model is, first, that individuals in
different cohorts are confronted with different events and
have different experiences (namely, those that take place

during the particular historical period of time in which they
live). Secondly, and more importantly, different cohorts
experience the same event at different points in their
biographical development; some experience it in old age,
others find themselves at this point in their middle years,
and still others encounter it at adolescence or in childhood.
A well-known study (Elder, 1974) showed for example, how the
economic crisis in 1929 affected different cohorts.

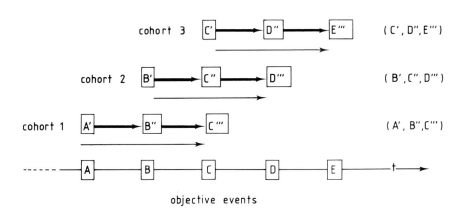

Figure 2. The cohort model and intertemporal relationships.

Two distinct kinds of effects follow from this. First, each
cohort experiences the event in a social context or in a role
in which it finds itself because of its age. Its experience of
this event is therefore specific and selective. Secondly, each
cohort experiences the event against a different biographical
background which is determined by previous socialization
processes or events and is specific to each cohort. This is

based on the intertemporal interaction of socialization
experiences during a particular time interval.

Both effects together lead to a consequence which seems to me
to be especially important: that even in neighbouring cohorts,
despite the objective events they have in common due to the
partial overlapping, the life course and socialization of each
and every cohort is unique, qualitatively different from the
next cohort. Each cohort has its own stratification of
experiences.

As shown in Figure 2, the objective events A, B, C etc. are
processed subjectively; since the previous events of each
cohort also take part in the processing of each subsequent
event (represented by the narrows) the subjective
representation alters accordingly (shown in the dashes). Not
only does each cohort experience a specific set of events, it
also processes objectively identical events differently (see
the characteristics listed in the right-hand column).

SUMMARY AND CONCLUSIONS.

It has become clear that there are considerable
consequences for the construction of theoretical models of
personality development when the external conditions of human
development are fully taken into account. Empirical socialization research has demonstrated that external and
contingent conditions are relevant - often crucial - for
practically all personality characteristics and ages, and this
must be regarded as a fact. The assumption that the course of
personality development follows more or less the same pattern
and has the same goal for all individuals can no longer be
considered tenable. Our critical review of the theories of
Werner, Piaget, Freud and Erikson showed that such assumptions
systematically lead to neglect or restriction of the view of
external development conditions. This violates, at least in
part, the postulate that personality development is the result
of the interaction between internal and external conditions -
a postulate with which almost all contemporary authors agree.

It therefore seems necessary to begin with the assumption that paths of human development can be very different, or that a theory must be kept open with regard to assumptions about developmental paths. The number of possibilities is not infinite, however, it is limited by internal intertemporal interaction effects and structures. The ontogenetic effects of historical change may best be analyzed within the framework of a cohort approach.

This presents a new situation for theoretical and empirical research. If it no longer seems sufficient to investigate one specific, theoretically-conceived course of development because this is at best one segment out of the development of a few individuals under very specific historical conditions, one might ask which problems should be posed, then, for scientific work? It would seem realistic to first investigate a fairly modest question: Which external events, under which internal conditions, lead to which results? The long-term goal will certainly remain the same: to construct models for the course of development over the entire life span, which will incorporate the postulates developed here. A first step might be to identify various kinds of developmental paths (cf. Mumford & Owens, 1984) and to analyze the different underlying conditions. Next, new concepts and hypotheses could be formulated in increasing levels of abstraction which could then be used to construct a theory of human development. Analyses similar to those we sketched above might prove useful.

This type of developmental theory will differ somewhat from the traditional approaches. Nevertheless, I believe that the humanistic intentions which inspired the great classics can still be realized.

REFERENCES.

Ainsworth, M.D.S. (1973). The development of infant-mother attachment. In B.M. Caldwell & H.N. Ricciuti (Eds.), Review of child development research: Vol.3. Chicago: The

University of Chicago Press.

Aries, Ph. (1960). L'enfant et la vie familiale sous l'ancien régime. Paris: Plon.

Baltes, P.B. (Ed.) (1978). Life-span development and behaviour: Vol.1. New York: Academic Press.

Baltes, P.B. & Brim, O.G. (Eds.) (1979). Life-span development and behavior: Vol.2. New York: Academic Press.

Baltes, P.B., Cornelius, S.W. & Nesselroade, J.R. (1977). Cohort effects in behavioural development: Theoretical and methodological perspectives. In W.A. Collins (Ed.), Minnesota symposia on child psychology: Vol.2. New York: Thomas Crowell.

Baltes, P.B., Reese, H.W. & Lipsitt, L.P. (1980). Life-span developmental psychology. Annual Review of Psychology, 31, 65-110.

Bandura, A. & Walters, R.H. (1963). Aggression. In H.W. Stevenson (Ed.), Child psychology. Chicago: University of Chicago Press.

Bayley, N. (1970). Development fo mental abilities. In P.H. Mussen (Ed.), Manual of child psychology: Vol.1. New York: Wiley.

Becker, W.C. (1964). Consequences of different kinds of parental discipline. In M.L. Hoffman & L.W. Hoffman (Eds.), Review of child development research: Vol.1. New York: Russell Sage.

Berry, J.W. (1976). Human ecology and cognitive style. New York.

Berthoud, G. (1976). L'identité et l'alterité. Pour une confrontation de l'épistémologie génétique et de l'anthropologie critique. Revue Européenne des Sciences Sociales, 14, 471-494.

Biller, H.B. (1982). Fatherhood: Implications for child and adult development. In B. Wolman (Ed.), Handbook of developmental psychology, Englewood Cliffs: Prentice Hall.

Block, J. (1971). Lives through time. Berkeley: Bancroft.

Borow, H. (1966). Development of occupational motives and roles. In L.W. Hoffman & M.L. Hoffman (Eds.), Review of

child development research: Vol.2. New York: Russell
Sage.

Bronfenbrenner, U. (1958). Socialization and social class
though time and space. In E.E. Maccoby, Th.M. Newcomb &
E.L. Hartley (Eds.), Readings in social psychology. New
York: Holt, Rinehart and Winston.

Bryan, J.H. (1975). Children's cooperation and helping
behaviours. In E.M. Hetherington (Ed.), Review of child
development research: Vol.5, Chicago: University of
Chicago Press.

Busch-Rossnagel, N.A. & Vance, A.K. (1982). The impact of the
schools on social and emotional development. In B. Wolman
(Eds.), Handbook of developmental psychology. Englewood
Cliffs: Prentice Hall.

Caldwell, B.M. (1964). The effects of infant care. In M.L.
Hoffman & L.W. Hoffman (Eds.), Review of child
development research: Vol.1. New York: Russell Sage.

Caldwell, B.M. & Ricciuti, H.N. (Eds.) (1973). Review of
child development research: Vol.3. Chicago: The
University of Chicago Press.

Campbell, J.D. (1964). Peer relations in childhood. In M.L.
Hoffman & L.W. Hoffman (Eds.), Review of child
development research: Vol.1. New York: Russell Sage.

Campbell, E.Q. (1969). Adolescent socialization. In D.A.
Goslin (Ed.), Handbook of socialization theory and
research. Chicago: Rand Mc.Nally.

Carroll, J.L. & Rest, J.R. (1982). Moral development. In B.
Wolman (Ed.), Handbook of developmental psychology.
Englewood Cliffs: Prentice Hall.

Cazden, C. (1966). Subcultural differences in child language:
an interdisciplinary review. Merril-Palmer Quarterly, 12,
185-219.

Clausen, J.A. (1966). Family structure, socialization, and
personality. In L.W. Hoffman & M.L. Hoffman (Eds.),
Review of child development research: Vol.2. New York:
Russell Sage.

Cole, M. & Scribner, S. (1974). Culture and thought: A
psychological introduction. New York: Wiley.

Crandall, V.J. (1963). Achievement. In H.W. Stevenson (Ed.), Child psychology. Chicago: The University of Chicago Press.

Dasen, P.R. & Heron, A. (1981). Cross-cultural tests of Piaget's theory. In H.C. Triandis (Ed.), Handbook of cross-cultural psychology: Vol.4. Developmental psychology. Boston.

Datan, N. & Reese, H.W. (Eds.). (1977). Life-span developmental psychology: Dialectic perspectives on experimental psychology. New York: Academic Press.

deMause, L. (1974). The history of childhood. New York: The Psychohistory Press.

Deutsch, C.P. (1973). Social class and child development. In B.M. Caldwell & H.N. Ricciuti (Eds.), Review of child development research: Vol.3. Chicago: University of Chicago Press.

Dobzhansky, Th. (1962). Mankind evolving. New Haven: Yale University Press.

Doherty, W.J. & Jacobson, N.S. (1982). Marriage and the family. In B. Wolman (Ed.), Handbook of developmental psychology. Englewood Cliffs: Prentice Hall.

Elder, G.H.Jr. (1974). Children of the Great Depression. Chicago: University of Chicago Press.

Elias, N. (1969). Über den Prozess der Zivilisation (2nd ed.). Bern: Francke.

Ember, C.R. (1977). Cross-cultural cognitive studies. Annual Review of Anthropology, 6, 33-56.

Endler, N.S. & Magnuson, D. (1976). Toward an interactional theory of personality. Psychological Bulletin. 83, 956-974.

Erikson, E.H. (1950). Growth and crises of the healthy personality. In M.J.E. Senn (Ed.), Symposium on the healthy personality. New York: Macey Foundation.

Erikson, E.H. (1963). Childhood and society (rev. ed.). New York: Norton.

Ervin, S.M. & Miller, W.R. (1963). Language development. In H.W. Stevenson (Ed.), Child psychology. Chicago: University of Chicago Press.

Ervin-Tripp, S. (1966). Language development. In L.W. Hoffman & M.L. Hoffman (Eds.). Review of child development research: Vol.2. New York: Russell Sage.

Fenichel, O. (1945). The psychoanalytic theory of neurosis. New York: Norton.

Feshbach, S. (1970). Aggression. In Mussen, P.H. (Ed.), Manual of child psychology: Vol. 2. New York: Wiley.

Fischer, K.W. (1980). A theory of cognitive development: The cognitive control of hierarchy of skills. Psychological Review, 87, 477-531.

Flavell, J.H. (1963). The developmental psychology of Jean Piaget. New York: Van Nostrand.

Flavell, J.H. (1972). An analysis of cognitive-developmental sequences. Genetic psychology Monographs, 86, 279-350.

Flavell, J.H. (1977). Cognitive development. Englewood Cliffs: Prentice Hall.

Flavell, J.H. (1982). Structures, stages, and sequences in cognitive development. In W.A. Collins (Ed.), The concept of development. Hillsdale (N.J.): Lawrence Erlbaum.

Freud, S. (1940ff). Gesammelte Werke, 18 Vols. London: Imago.

Gallagher, J.J. (1964). Productive thinking. In M.L. Hoffman & L.W. Hoffman (Eds.), Review of child development research: Vol.1. New York: Russell Sage.

Gesell, A. (1946). The ontogenesis of infant behaviour. In L. Carmichael (Ed.), Manual of child psychology. New York: Wiley.

Geulen D. (1977). Das vergesellschaftete Subjekt. Zur Grundlegung der Sozialisationstheorie. Frankfurt/M.: Suhrkamp.

Geulen, D. (1980). Die historische Entwicklung sozialisationstheoretischer Paradigmen. In K. Hurrelmann & D. Ulich (Eds.), Handbuch der Sozialisationsforschung. Weinheim: Beltz.

Glidewell, J.C. et al. (1966). Socialization and social structure in the classroom. In L.W. Hoffman & M.L. Hoffman (Eds.), Review of child development research: Vol.2. New York: Russell Sage.

Glucksberg S., Krauss, R. & Tory Higgins, E. (1975). The

development of referential communication skills. In F.D.
Horowitz (Ed.), Review of child development research:
Vol.4. Chicago: University of Chicago Press.

Goslin, D.A. (Ed.). (1969). Handbook of socialization theory
and research. Chicago: Rand Mc.Nally.

Gottlieb, G. (1970). Conceptions of prenatal behaviour. In
L.R. Aronson, E. Tobach, D.S. Lehrman & J.S. Rosenblatt
(Eds.), Development and evolution of behaviour: Essays in
honor of T.C. Schneirla. San Francisco: Freeman.

Gump, P.V. (1975). Ecological psychology and children. In
E.M. Hetherington (Ed.), Review of child development:
Vol.5. New York: Russell Sage.

Hartup, W.W. (1963). Dependence and independence. In H.W.
Stevenson (Ed.), Child psychology. Chicago: University of
Chicago Press.

Hartup, W.W. (Ed.) (1982). Review of child development
research: Vol.6. Chicago: University of Chicago Press.

Havighurst, R.J. (1982) The world of work. In B. Wolman
(Eds.), Handbook of developmental psychology. Englewood
Cliffs: Prentice Hall.

Herzog, E. & Studia, C.E. (1973). Children in fatherless
families. In B.M. Caldwell & H.N. Ricciuti (Eds.), Review
of child development research: Vol.3. Chicago: University
of Chicago Press.

Hill, R. & Aldous, J. (1969). Socialization for marriage and
parenthood. In D.A. Goslin (Ed.), Handbook of
socialization theory and research. Chicago: Rand
Mc.Nally.

Hoffman, L.W. & Hoffman, M.L. (Eds.) (1966). Review of child
development research: Vol.2. New York: Russell Sage.

Hoffman, M.L. & Hoffman, L.W. (Eds.) (1964). Review of child
development research: Vol.1. New York: Russell Sage.

Hoffman, M.L. (1970). Moral development. In P.H. Mussen
(Ed.), Manual of child psychology: Vol. 2. New York:
Wiley.

Joffe, L.S. & Vaughn, B.E. (1982). Infant-mother attachment:
Theory, Assessment, and implications for development. In
B.Wolman (Ed.), Handbook of developmental psychology.

Englewood Cliffs: Prentice Hall.

Kagan, J. (1964). Acquisition and significance of sex typing and sex role identity. In M.L. Hoffman & L.W. Hoffman (Eds.), Review of child development research: Vol.1. New York: Russell Sage.

Kohlberg, L. (1963). Moral development and identification. In H.W. Stevenson (Ed.), Child psychology. Chicago: University of Chicago Press.

Kohlberg, L. (1964). Development of moral character and moral ideology. In M.L. Hoffman & W.L. Hoffman (Eds.), Review of child development research: Vol.1. New York: Russell Sage.

Kramer, D.A. (1983). Post-formal operations? A need for further conceptualization. Human Development, 26, 91-105.

Labouvie-Vief, G. (1980). Beyond formal operations: Uses and limits of pure logic in life-span development. Human Development, 23, 141-161.

LeGoff, J. et al. (Eds.) (1978). La nouvelle histoire. Paris: Hachette.

Leontiev, A.N. (1965). Problems of mental development. Washington: U.S. Joint Publications Research Service.

Lerner, R.M. (1976). Concepts and theories of human development. Reading: Addison-Wesley.

Lerner, R.M. (1978). Nature, nurture, and dynamic interactionism. Human Development, 21, 1-20.

Lerner, R.M. (1980). Concepts of epigenesis: Descriptive and explanatory issues. A critique of Kitchener's comments. Human Development, 23, 63-72.

Lerner, R.M. & Busch-Rossnagel, N.A. (Eds.) (1981). Individuals as producers of their development. A life-span perspective. New York: Academic Press.

Lerner, R.M. & Shea, J.A. (1982). Social behaviour in adolescence. In B. Wolman (Ed.), Handbook of developmental psychology. Englewood Cliffs: Prentice Hall.

Looft, W.R. (1973). Socialization and personality throughout the life-span: An examination of contemporary psychological approaches. In P.B. Baltes & K.W. Schaie

(Eds.), Life-span developmental psychology: Personality and socialization. New York: Academic Press.

Lloyd, B. (1983). Cross-cultural studies of Piaget's theory. In S. Modgil, C. Modgil & G. Brown (Eds.), Jean Piaget. An Interdisciplinary critique. London: Routledge & Kegan Paul.

Maccoby, E.E. (Ed.) (1966). The development of sex differences. Stanford: Stanford University Press.

Maccoby, E.E. & Masters, J.C. (1970). Attachment and dependency. In P.H. Mussen (Ed.), Manual of child psychology: Vol. 2. New York: Wiley.

Malinowski, B. · (1927). Sex and repression in primitive society. New York: Humanities Press.

Martin, B. (1975). Parent - child relations. In F.D. Horowitz (Ed.), Review of child development research. Chicago: University of Chicago Press.

Miller, D.R. & Swanson, G.E. (1958). The changing American parent. New York: Wiley.

Mischel, W. (1970). Sex-typing and socialization. In P.H. Mussen (Ed.), Manual of child psychology: Vol. 2. New York: Wiley.

Molfese, D.L., Molfese V.J. & Carrell, P.L. (1982). Early language development. In B. Wolman (Eds.), Handbook of developmental psychology. Englewood Cliffs: Prentice Hall.

Moore, W.E. (1969). Occupational socialization. In D.A. Goslin (Ed.)., Handbook of socialization theory and research. Chicago: Rand Mc.Nally.

Mumford, M.D. & Owens, W.A. (1984). Individuality in a developmental context: Some empirical and theoretical considerations. Human Development, 27, 84-108.

Mussen, P.H. (Ed.) (1970). Manual of child development (2 vols.). New York: Wiley.

Neimark, E.D. (1975). Intellectual development during adolescence. In F.D. Horowitz (Ed.), Review of child development research: Vol.4. Chicago: University of Chicago Press.

Newman, B.M. (1982). Mid-life development. In B. Wolman

(Ed.), Handbook of developmental psychology, Englewood Cliffs: Prentice Hall.

Newman, P.R. (1982). The peer group. In B. Wolman (Eds.), Handbook of developmental psychology. Englewood Cliffs: Prentice Hall.

Noam, G.G., O'Connell Higgins, R. & Goethals, G.W. (1982). Psychoanalytic approaches to developmental psychology. In B. Wolman (Ed.), Handbook of developmental psychology. Englewood Cliffs: Prentice Hall.

Oerter, R. & Montada, L. (1982). Entwicklungspsychologie. München: Urban & Schwarzberg.

Parsons, T. (1949). The structure of social action (2nd ed.). Glencoe /III.: Free Press.

Peeters, H.F.M. (1966). Kind en jeugdige in het begin van de moderne tijd ca 1500 - ca 1650. Amsterdam.

Piaget, J. (1932). The moral judgement of the child. London: Kegan.

Piaget, J. (1970a). Piaget's theory. In P.H. Mussen (Ed.), Manual of child psychology: Vol. 1. New York: Wiley.

Piaget, J. (1970b). L'évolution intellectuelle entre adolescence et l'age adulte. In 3rd International Convention and Awarding of Foneme Prizes 1970. Milano.

Pinchbeck, I. & Hewitt, M. (1969/1973). Children in English society (2 Vols.), London.

Preiswerk, R. (1976). Jean Piaget et l'étude des relations internationales. Revue Européenne des Sciences Sociales, 14, 495-511.

Price-Williams, D.R. (Ed.) (1969). Cross-cultural studies. Harmondsworth: Penguin Books.

Reese, H.W. & Overton, W.F. (1970). Models of development and theories of development. In L.R. Goulet & P.B. Baltes (Eds.), Life-span developmental psychology: Theory and research. New York: Academic Press.

Riegel, K. (1975). Toward a dialectical theory of development. Human Development, 18, 50-64.

Riegel, K. (1976). The dialectics of human development. American Psychologist, 31, 689-700.

Riley, M.W., Foner, A., Hess, B. & Toby, M.L. (1969).

Socialization for the middle and later years. In D.A. Goslin (Ed.), Handbook of socialization theory and research. Chicago: Rand Mc.Nally.

Robinson, H.B. & Robinson, N. (1970). Mental retardation. In P.H. Mussen (Ed.), Manual of child psychology: Vol. 1. New York: Wiley.

Ryder, N.B. (1965). The cohort as a concept in the study of social change. American Sociological Review, 39, 843-861.

Schaie, K.W. (1965). A general model for the study of developmental problems. Psychological Bulletin, 64, 92-107.

Shantz, C.U. (1975). The development of social cognition. In E.M. Hetherington (Ed.), Review of child development research: Vol.5, Chicago: University of Chicago Press.

Shepherd-Look, D.L. (1982). Sex differentiation and the development of sex roles. In B. Wolman (Ed.), Handbook of developmental psychology. Englewood Cliffs: Prentice Hall.

Sigel, I. (1964). The attainment of concepts. In M.L. Hoffman & L.W. Hoffman (Eds.), Review of child development research: Vol.1. New York: Russell Sage.

Sinha, D. (1982). Sociocultural factors and the development of perceptual and cognitive skills. In W.W. Hartup (Ed.), Review of child development research: Vol.6. Chicago: University of Chicago Press.

Stern, W. (1914). Psychologie der frühen Kindheit. Leipzig: Quelle & Meier.

Stevenson, H.W. (Ed.) (1963). Child psychology, Chicago: University of Chicago Press.

Swift, J.W. (1964). Effects of early group experiences. In M.L. Hoffman & L.W. Hoffman (Eds.), Review of child development research: Vol.1, New York: Russell Sage.

Toman, W. (1969). Family constellations: Its effects on personality and social behavior (2nd ed.). New York: Springer.

Trudewind, C. (1982). The development of achievement motivation and individual differences: Ecological determinants. In W.W. Hartup (Ed.), Review of child development research: Vol.6, Chicago: University of Chicago Press.

Vale, J.R. (1980). Genes, environment, and behaviour. An interactionist approach. New York: Harper & Row.

Van den Daele, L.D. (1969). Qualitative models in developmental analysis. Developmental Psychology, 1, 303-310.

Van den Daele, L.D. (1976). Formal models of development. In K.F. Riegel & J.A. Meacham (Eds.), The developing individual in a changing world: Vol.1. The Hague: Mouton.

Vondracel, F.W. & Lerner, R.M. (1982). Vocational role development in adolescence. In B. Wolman (Ed.), Handbook of developmental psychology. Englewood Cliffs: Prentice Hall.

Waddington, C.H. (1957). The strategy of the genes. London: Allen & Unwin.

Wallach, M.A. (1970). Creativity. In P.H. Mussen (Ed.), Manual of child psychology: Vol.1. New York: Wiley.

Weinert, F.E. & Treiber, B. (1982). School socialization and cognitive development: In W.W. Hartup (Ed.), Review of child development research: Vol.6. Chicago: University of Chicago Press.

Werner, H. (1948). Comparative psychology and mental development. New York: International Universities Press.

Werner, H. (1957). The concept of development from a comparative and organismic point of view. In D.B. Harris (Ed.), The concept of development. Minneapolis: University of Minnesota Press.

Wolman, B. (Ed.) (1982). Handbook of developmental psychology. Englewood Cliffs: Prentice Hall.

Yarrow, L.J. (1964). Separation from parents during early childhood. In M.L. Hoffman & L.W. Hoffman (Eds.), Review of child development research: Vol.1. New York: Russell Sage.

Zigler, E. (1966). Mental retardation. In L.W. Hoffman & M.L. Hoffman (Eds.), Review of child development research: Vol.2. New York: Russell Sage.

Theory Building in Developmental Psychology
P.L.C. van Geert (editor)
© Elsevier Science Publishers B.V. (North-Holland), 1986

7

Development and Social Expectations

Paul Vedder

In this text the author describes a framework
for the generation of a theory on cognitive
development, which has three characteristics:
first, cognitive development is seen as a social
process, second, the present approach allows to
distinguish developmental dimensions, and
finally, it is open ended. The latter means that
the theory is history bound and should thus be
adapted to the society and to changes in the
society in which it is used. The central
descriptive category in the theory is the
concept of social expectations linked with the
concept of motive, which is a personalized
social expectation. The central explicative
category is the concept of activity which is
described as a transformation process in terms
of incorporation.

In this chapter the author presents some ideas on life
span cognitive development. The ideas concern categories and
instruments used to identify steps in development, and
categories used to explain the genesis of particular
developmental phenomena. This text might be seen as a first
step towards the development of a more detailed theory of
cognitive development, which gives a framework for the
generation of a research programme, for the interpretation of
new research findings and the re-interpretation of old
findings. The framework can also be used as a guide in
developing developmental standards for diagnostical and
advisory practices.

The ideas that will be presented are in part the result of the
author's restructuring and evaluation of ideas originally
presented by psychologists working in the cultural historical
or Vygotskian tradition in psychology.

THREE PROBLEMS IN THEORY BUILDING.

In a situation in which psychologists actually already use theories on cognitive development, as for instance the Piagetian theory, the description of a new theory should have a clear legitimation base. This legitimation base should describe the new theory's specific value compared to other already existing theories. In this section the outlines of such a legitimation base will be sketched by referring to three problems in building theories on cognitive development.

A first problem with a number of developmental theories is that they are individualistic. This fits in with the ideas of traditional Piagetians and behaviourists as well as with those of most of modern cognitive psychologists. In their theories the social is separated from the individual. In the Piagetian and in the modern cognitive theories this individualism expresses itself in a one-sided attention for person variables and intrapsychological processes. In the behaviourist tradition context (environmental) variables receive the most attention. The developing individual is seen as a passive, adaptive instance with regard to its environment. The individual is seen as an instance to be affected, not as an affecting instance. As a passive instance the individual is isolated in its physical shell (see Beilin, 1980; Davydov, 1977; Meacham, 1984; Perret-Clermont, 1980; Siegler & Klahr, 1983).
Criticizing the individualistic approach of other psychologists implies that another approach will be presented. The present author conceives of development as a social process taking place in activities.
Activity generally refers to internal as well as external aspects of a transformation process in which persons structure their material and social environment, their ideas and feelings. At the same time activity is the process in which the environment has a transforming effect on the persons' skills, knowledge and motives.
Activity is always both social and individual. By putting activity at the heart of a theory on cognitive development one

escapes from a principal problem in a social approach, viz. the problem of the transfer from the social to the individual and vice versa. The problem that presents itself thereafter is one of control and controlability of activities by either a person together with other persons or by an individual person. Vygotsky presented this as the problem of the change from interpersonal to intrapersonal activities (see Vygotsky, 1972), while Wertsch described it in terms of other-regulation and self-regulation (see Wertsch, 1979, 1980; and also Vedder, 1985a). The problem may also be conceived of as one of changing forms and contents of activity: as a problem of interiorization (see Gal'perin, 1980; Davydov & Zinchenko, 1981) or as a problem of incorporation (see Lomov, 1983; see also Vedder, 1985b). In the section on "The structure of activity" this problem will further be discussed.

The second problem of developmental theories was pointed out by Wohlwill in his book "The study of behavioral development" (1973). He showed that many psychologists pretending that they had generated a theory on human life span, actually did not generate a theory on development. Talking about development is, when taken strictly, only possible when one clearly distinguishes a developmental dimension, which would allow to determine progress, regression, or retardation in development in terms of this dimension. A developmental dimension is an abstract idea about a particular quality characterizing a person's activities during a longer period. The quality is manifested in a variety of forms and degrees of expression that change over time. These forms or degrees of expression are normally called stages. Given the variety of forms and degrees of expression, a developmental dimension may be conceived of as a reference point which gives a particular idea of constancy or durability for persons, particularly psychologists, who deal with the analysis of steadily changing activities. It is also a means for selecting specific activities for further analysis. A developmental dimension prevents psychologists from calling any change in activities a developmental one. For instance, the change from eating dinner to brushing teeth is normally

not seen as a developmental change, whereas the change from
saying that two glasses filled with the same amount of liquid
do not have the same amount, because the heights of the liquid
are different in each glass, to saying that they have the same
amount although the heights of the liquid are different, is
conceived of as development, viz. the development of logical
reasoning. Wohlwill pointed out that many so-called
developmental theorists did not employ the notion of a developmental dimension.

The third problem with developmental theories can be
deduced from a description of the formal structure of
developmental theories (see van Geert, in this volume). Van
Geert suggests that many developmental theories represent an
a-priori idea of development. They describe development as a
process with a clear end stage, or "final state", and
reconstruct the developmental process in light of this end
stage. These theories are "closed ended". Van Geert states
that these kind of theories are not compatible with the
conception of development as a flexible process which changes
with persons and social relations. He suggests that
psychologists should try to develop open ended theories. Such
theories should give opportunities for generating conceptions
of development that can be used to change our ideas about
developmental goals.

In the present paper, a theory on cognitive development
is described that deals with development as a social process,
that meets the idea of dimensionalisation, and that is open
ended. The first of these three problems, the individualistic
versus the social approach, will receive the most attention in
this paper. The work on this problem will result in a gross
framework of a theory on cognitive development. The two other
problems are mainly worked out in order to describe two
important characteristics of the present social approach in
more detail.

A DEFINITION OF COGNITIVE DEVELOPMENT.

The present author defines cognitive development as the process of restructuring a person's motive structure or his/her repertory of skills and knowledge, or both, in order to be better able to meet social task requirements. Restructuring refers to processes in which new contents are integrated into the motive structure or into the repertory of skills and knowledge, and to processes in which the activeness of the present repertory of skills and knowledge is increased. The restructuring of motives, knowledge and skills is not restricted to cognitive development. This restructuring may also be accomplished in for instance meditation. In order to qualify the restructuring as cognitive development, this restructuring should contribute to the improvement of the execution of tasks which are seen as being socially valuable. This implies that it is not always possible to determine beforehand whether or not a particular instance of restructuring knowledge and skills can be evaluated as cognitive development, because the social value of the restructuring is not clear as yet, but it might become clear for people from future generations when they discover the social function of the results of the restructuring. The following dialogue between Einstein (Bertie) and his neighbor Schmidt may clarify this position.

Einstein: Hi neighbor. You had a nice week?

Neighbor: Oh stop. This whole week I had to check register books. Just routine work. And, tell me, how was your week Bertie?

Einstein: Well, I developed a new theory on gravity. I thought about it for years, and all at once I got the inspiration this week. You want to hear more of it?

Neighbor: Oh no, thank you, spare me that. I always wonder how you stay alive with just thinking about crazy things like you do.

Einstein (anticipating the fabulous ideas presented and to be presented in this text): Well, maybe I am a bit crazy. People may indeed think that I am no-good because of the things I am doing. Still, I believe that, in a few years, many people reading this dialogue will agree that I made a big step in my cognitive development this week. They will then know the tremendous social value of my discoveries and explanations. If they then read this dialogue, they will also know that you did not actually come one step further in your cognitive development this week. You did not restructure your skills and knowledge or your motives in order to be better able to meet social tasks.

Neighbor   (getting angry, but still knowing how to behave): Bertie, listen boy, I'm sorry for you, but I think you should visit one of those new-fashioned shrinks from Vienna. Still..., have a nice weekend.

THE SOCIAL CHARACTER OF COGNITIVE DEVELOPMENT.

In section one, the author suggested that cognitive development is a social process. The adjective "social" refers to persons who are directly or indirectly involved in the developmental process. It refers, moreover, to the content of the process. The use of this adjective does not deny the fact that the developing occurs to individuals.

From the moment on a new born child becomes active and manifests his or her capabilities, other people try to take their part in the activities by stimulating, neglecting, providing opportunities, setting norms, etc. (c.f. Bruner, 1973; Il'enkov, 1977). This involvement in the child's activities in the form of face-to-face interaction continues being important for the child's development, but as the child grows older the face-to-face form is no longer strictly necessary. Other people's involvement does not decrease immediately but takes on an essentially different form. Other people take part in the child's activity in an indirect way. They teach the child to live according to norms, rules and principles, and to use shared meanings for analysing processes and situations, even when there are no direct social contacts. These other persons interact indirectly with the children by means of the tasks they present to the children in books, for instance. Moreover, the children anticipate future contacts (e.g. the control and evaluation of the pupils' work by a teacher).

Even when the children become Robinson Crusoes living on uninhabited islands, their developmental activities continue being social, because of the mediating influence of other people. They keep on using meanings they learned from and share with other people. These meanings in part will continue to structure their lives. The meanings enable them to communicate with other persons, eventually with future generations, by means of letters, books, pictures and other kinds of reifications of ideas and feelings (see Abul'khanova-Slavskaja, 1982; Lieven, 1982; Youniss, 1983).

So far, in the description of the social character of cognitive development we focused on the role social contacts play in this development, and on the different forms they may take.

Discussing the role of social relations in cognitive development however, concerns also the social nature of the contents of developmental activities. The contents are means by which continuity in social life is sustained. They have a social origin. They are skills and knowledge developed by former generations of people, and by experienced and specialized people from the present generation. By teaching children the skills and knowledge developed by these people, the children are assumed to realize a kind of reproduction of society: the bad things should be avoided and put away, the good things should be kept, and the better things should be sought (c.f. Davydov & Zinchenko, 1981; Leontiev, 1977, 1979). The social character of knowledge concerns conventions or habits, as well as what are called empirical and logical facts. Not only was the discovery and formulation of these facts dependent on human activity, but the functionality of these facts is also dependent on the way they are respected and maintained by people.

The present approach clearly differs from Piagetian one in the fact that it conceives of all knowledge and its use as a social phenomenon. The activity principle plays an important role in our approach as well as in the Piagetian theory, but its social character in form and content is denied in the central theme of the Piagetian theory, viz. the development of operational structures resulting in the control of logical or semi-logical structures (see Doise & Mugny, 1984; Perret Clermont, 1980).

THE STRUCTURE OF ACTIVITY.

In the first section it was pointed out that the author rejects the classical behaviourist assumption of the individual as a rather passive, adaptive instance. Instead, the concept of activity was introduced to refer to the process in which persons are seen as beings who change their own living conditions, and in which the persons as active entities are shaped in their contacts with persons and things surrounding them. In the first section a general definition of activity was given.
In this section the structure of activity will be the central theme.
In giving a description of the structure of activity we are actually dealing with one particular function of the present theory, viz. the presentation of a conceptual network which may be used for the analysis of the object under study. A second function of theories concerns the explanation of the genesis of phenomena. This function will be dealt with in more detail in the next section.
Activities are built up out of actions, or operations, or both. Actions are all the components of activity that a person can regulate and control. This means that a person uses either an imagined, verbalized, or otherwise represented plan to structure the actions. This plan contains the goal (the imagined end product) of the action and it describes at least one way to reach the goal. Operations are the activity parts

that a person does not regulate or control explicitly.
Some activities make partial use of the same operations or
actions. Learning to read and learning to write for instance
both make use of operations enabling the discrimination of the
orientation of signs in a 2-dimensional field. Therefore,
learning to write should be easier for a child who has already
learned to read, than for a child who cannot read.

Investigating whether indeed operations and actions used for
one particular activity have something in common with actions
and operations used for another activity is a dificult job.
The analysis of a particular activity up to the level of the
constituting elements called actions and operations is difficult in itself, but the job becomes even more difficult when
comparing activities. For most activities there is not just
one particular series of actions and operations needed to
realize them. From the study of even such a small task as the
calculation of an answer to the arithmetic problem "4 + 5 =
.." it is well known that children may use several ways to
find the answer, executing different series of actions or
operations (see Ginsburg, 1977; Radatz, 1980).

As is still to be shown, it is important in the present
approach of cognitive development to investigate the relations
between activities. Knowledge about operations and actions a
person is able to execute, together with ideas about the
relations between several activities, gives the opportunity to
speculate about the activities a person will be able to
execute in the near future.

Another concept that is important for the clarification
of the present idea about cognitive development, is the
concept of motive. The concept of motive is closely linked to
the concept of activity. A motive is a generating, stimulating, and directing framework for activites. A motive always
has a physical as well as a social side. The physical side is
normally called a state of need. Psychologists analyze this
phenomenon as it is related to representations of objects and
processes that can satisfy the need. These representations
make up the social side of motives, because they refer to
processes realized together with other people, and to

processes involving objects which have a social origin and a
social function. As a case in point we may think of feeding
babies with a feeding bottle. The act of feeding, satisfies a
physical need. The caretaker's feeding act is a motive which
is clearly a process of social contact in which an instrument
is used, the bottle, which has a social origin and a social
function. The social character of the act and the instrument
becomes clear in a particular sense when comparing the described feeding practice with other feeding practices. The
present author for instance never was fed by bottle. He
changed over from the breast to little spoons.

The development of any motive is dependent on learning.
As a learning task, motives should be seen primarily as
motives of society, not as motives of a separate individual
(c.f. Lomov, 1983). Motives of society can be described as
social expectations or as rule systems. These social
expectations concern processes which regulate all sorts of
qualities of life, e.g. esthetical qualities of appearance
(clothing, hairdress, etc...) and qualities of cognitive
functioning (learning to read, etc....). The expectations
differ from the skills and the knowledge which a person has to
use to meet the expectations. The expectations represent the
way the skills and knowledge function in a social system, how
they are handled. Questions such as why is learning to read
important, from what age on is it important and for whom is it
important, should be first answered to find out how the skill
of reading functions in a society or in parts of the society.
It has been stated already, that motives (social expectations)
have to be learned. It is possible now to point out an
important resemblance between skills, knowledge and social
expectations. As is the case with skills and knowledge
involved in learning to read, does one need to learn the
social expectations which stimulate one to read. How this
learning is accomplished, is, as stated before, the subject of
the next section. In learning social expectations, the social
expectations become motives linked with the child's physical
needs.
The physical needs linked with motives may be rather

fundamental ones which are generally human, e.g. hunger, thirst, movement and defense against danger (see Bergk, 1980, p. 73), but this is not necessarily the case. Children develop a physical need system linked with cultural experiences. They learn to feel dependent on particular social relations and activities that are specific for these relations (c.f. Leontiev, 1977, 1979). Many children in the western culture learn to need a strong accepting and stimulating attitude from their caretakers. The children feel bad when their caretakers show rejection. Often caretakers use this need to make children learn to execute activities that meet the caretakers' expectations. The children's execution of activities is then dependent on actual or anticipated reinforcement executed or to be executed by the referents to the expectations. The following is an example referring to the relationship a child has with his teacher. Recently, the present author was asked by a 12 year old boy to read two letters he had written. One was for his teacher and the other one for an aunt. It was surprising to see that the letter for the aunt had relatively many grammatical errors, whereas the teacher's letter was written very well. Knowing the boy had learned his grammatical rules quite well, he was asked to write the bad letter anew. The boy reacted in somewhat the following way: "Sure, I could do it, but it is not necessary for my aunt. This one for the teacher must be o.k.". For writing correctly the teacher appeared to be an important referent person for the boy. The child could meet the social expectation of writing correctly fairly well, as could be seen in the letter for the teacher, but still appeared to be quite dependent on the teacher as a referent person. A letter which would not be controlled by the teacher contained many errors.

Ultimately, expectations should be personalized as motives, which means that persons know how to satisfy motives and can personally evaluate the quality of the activity executed for satisfying the motives, without benefitting from the explicit evaluation of others.

THE MECHANISM OF CHANGE: INCORPORATION.

Changes in a person's repertory of skills and knowledge generally come about in a process we may call incorporation. Incorporation refers to a change process in which the changing person is seen as active and as someone who already controls particular skills and knowledge (see Lomov, 1983). It refers, moreover, in many developmental or learning situations to the exchange of control over particular activities. In accordance with these ideas, Wertsch studied development of children as a process of growing capability of self-regulation in task situations, based on activities that at first were executed together with a more experienced person (Wertsch, 1979, 1980). Wertsch analyzed interaction processes between mothers and their young children in which the mothers explained to their children how they should solve a puzzle. The children have no idea at all about the nature of the task with which they should cope. The mothers stimulated their children to manipulate the puzzle blocks. In such a situation children actually have many opportunities to execute activities in which they probably do not yet understand what their contributions are to finishing the task. The descriptions Wertsch gives of such interaction processes clearly show that the basis for children's learning processes are operations and actions which they are already able to execute. However, in this situation, progress in learning depends on the mothers' skills in linking the children's activities to the task. The way mothers give information to the children appears to be very important. They cannot simply tell the children what to do. They have to link up with what the children are doing, and by means of pointing, physical interference, and verbalizations, try to transmit information. By stimulating and restricting the children's activities within particular borders defined by the mothers' task interpretation, they let their children experience what the task and its solution are. In this type of situation it becomes very clear that learning is the shaping of activities in accordance with particular tasks (see also Bruner, 1979; Ninio & Bruner, 1978; Ratner &

Bruner, 1978; Walkerdine, 1982; Walkerdine & Sinha, 1981).

Actually, learning may also take place in a situation in which the student himself or herself has more control over the task. In such a situation direct interaction with other persons may eventually disturb a person's learning. Rubinstein (1977) describes interactions between a teacher and individual pupils. The pupils were required to solve a difficult geometry problem. Rubinstein shows that the teacher's propositions for the solution of the problem only have a facilitating effect on problem solving, when the pupils themselves have already analysed the problem to an extent and have tried to solve it. Only then are pupils willing and knowledgeable enough to fit in the information given by the teacher. Giving propositions at moments when pupils are not yet far enough in their problem analysis, and have not yet experienced difficulties in problem solving, has the effect that either a proposition is neglected or has a disturbing effect on the pupils' problem solving. Knowing the task and having already learned many skills and having acquired much knowledge, students know in what direction(s) they should search for a solution. Shaping activities is, in such situations, also necessary for learning, but the students are for the greater part capable of shaping the acitivities themselves. The borders of the activities are then set by others in a more indirect way by means of the task presentation and the eventual control of the students' problem solution afterwards.

The form in which an activity is executed is also important in learning. A particular learning object, the content, may be acted upon at a material level, a very overt level involving manipulable materials. The activity may also be realised at a verbal level, still rather overt. Other forms are more covert, involving listening, watching and thinking. Normally spoken the different forms of activity are linked with particular levels of generalizability, controlability, and shapability of activities by others. The contents of material activity, for instance, always have a restricted character. It is always an activity with one particular object or with a few objects. If pupils learn to add, they first

count and add for instance two groups of little red balls.
Counting and adding however, are not the sort of actions that
can be executed only with little balls. A child may also count
big green balls, blocks, and all kinds of objects with a
variety of qualities.
When changing an activity from material to verbal, the content
changes from a particular experience with objects to a model
for a variety of situations. Words and phrases give the
opportunity to refer to more situations at the same time (c.f.
Kol'tsova, 1978; Vygotsky, 1972).

The following addresses the controlability of activities
in relation to the levels of execution.
At the level of material activity the control and correction
of activities still takes the form of direct personal
interference in practical activity. At the level of verbal
activity it is executed as a check on logical consistency and
intersubjectivity of the meanings used in the pupils'
descriptions. Much of learning is directed towards learning
operations. Information processing by means of operations has
a considerable advantage in that it can partly be done
simultaneously, that is, not step by step but by way of
implicit reference to more processes at the same time (c.f.
Davydov, 1981; Sechter, 1972). This is possible because the
information is processed unconsciously.

Whereas in material activity and in verbal activity the
contents of learning is still dynamic and likely to change
because of reality checking and checking for logical
consistency and intersubjectivity, this is far less the case
with the content worked with in operations. The explicit
control which is characteristic for actions has changed into
mere attention as soon as activity is executed in the form of
operations (see Gal'perin, 1969; Kabylnizkaja, 1973). Many
operations were originally actions. The abbreviation of
actions into operations is a process which cannot be
controlled directly by other people. Pupils can only be
stimulated to abbreviate actions by bringing them into
situations in which they experience the importance of solving
problems quickly.

In any case, the genesis of a new skill or piece of knowledge is realized on the basis of skills and knowledge a student controls already. It has as a condition that a student is active and that this activity is shaped towards the activity that transmits the information necessary to control the new skill or knowledge.

The relation between the present repertory of skills and knowledge and the new one may be different in different learning situations. The distance between what one knows already and what one should know to be able to execute a task may vary. Psychologists introduced a variety of concepts referring to processes of bridging these gaps. These are concepts such as association, transfer, transformation and shift. It goes beyond the intention of this text to describe and evaluate all these concepts. An interesting article describing and comparing several of these concepts was written by Fischer (1980).

So far, this section only dealt with the learning of skills and knowledge. The remainder of this section deals with learning social expectations. Social expectations are learned in relation to the learning of skills and knowledge. Many social expectations a child is confronted with are not made explicit as learning contents. They concern the way to handle skills and knowledge in particular situations. As such they are often learned as a kind of byproduct of learning particular skills and knowledge. To describe social expectations explicitly and to teach them explicitly to children is a difficult job, because of the nature of the object. A rule prescribing how to handle a particular skill or concept may be told to a child, but knowing such a rule and using the rule are two quite different things. To use such a rule a child has to respect it and, moreover, he or she has to distinguish whether the use of the rule suits a particular situation or not. Yet, although social expectations may be very complex, sometimes they are made explicit in educational programmes. Then they may be learned like any skill or concept which is taught to students. But even if the social expectations are presented as implicit byproducts of skills

and concepts that a child is explicitly told to learn, there
is no fundamental difference. All of what was said about the
exchange of control from the educator to the child and about
the different forms of activity actually also fit the learning
of social expectations. The learning of social expectations
should result in motives a person should personally control
directly whenever possible.
In some instances the learning of social expectations may
imply a long period of more or less systematic gathering of
experiences. This gathering of experiences may involve many
conflicts with different educators who partially may want
children to live according to different social expectations
and who may have varying ideas about the situations in which
particular social expectations should be maintained.

SOCIAL STANDARDS FOR COGNITIVE DEVELOPMENT.

The notion of social expectations as the basis for
motives may be used as an important regulating principle for
the generation of a framework for the description of cognitive
development in a life span perspective. Two characteristics of
social expectations will play a central role in this
description.
In the first place, social expectations towards individuals
are linked with individual characteristics with a temporal
dimension.
In the second place social expectations are hierarchically
systematized in a social process, because they are linked with
the power particular social groups have in a society.
At the heart of this section is the idea that a
systematization of social expectation for persons belonging to
particular groups, taking the power of the referents to the
expectations into consideration, results in a formal hierarchy
of developmental expectations.
Let us first take a closer look at the first
characteristic. The characteristic which has a temporal
dimension most clearly is age. When confronting the person

with social expectations his or her age is taken into consideration. It is also the case that one sometimes takes the level of skills and knowledge into consideration as well. Skill and knowledge levels also have a temporal dimension. The fact that social expectations with which a person is confronted are linked with a person's age or a person's skill and knowledge levels, makes it feasible to make lists of social expectations with which children are confronted in a particular age group or in a particular knowledge or skill group. For instance, a boy of six should start learning to read, he should be able to maintain particular hygienic standards, and he should not yet be expected to start a political discussion, cook his own meal, etc. Such lists, however, should be specified to more specific groups than age groups, because within age groups not all persons are confronted with the same set of social expectations. Persons belonging to different ethnic or religious groups for instance often have to meet different social expectations, may it be expectations concerning bible study or the division of playtime and working time.

The following is a sort of valuation of social expectations. Here is were the second characteristic of social expectations enters the stage: social expectations are hierarchically systematized in a social process. In systematizing the expectations it seems inevitable that a choice is made for particular instances which are referents to expectations. This is necessary because many instances actually formulate expectations, and certainly not all instances are equally important. Some instances reach more people than others. The instances reaching more people can therefore be seen as more influential in the cognitive development of the members of a particular society.

As a case in point the government in western countries have a big impact on the cognitive development in 6- to 16-year-olds, because they formulate and maintain rules for education which almost all children of this age group have to obey. Parents may support these rules, and the fact that most parents do this is an important reason why governments are so influential. In the case that parents neglect the rules the governments have their representatives who look for possibilities to force the children to follow the rules. Referents to social expectations themselves aid in deciding which are more and which are less important. Referents to social expectations clearly have social power, and for varying social expectations the referents use varying amounts of power. This fact allows us to develop a hierarchy of social expectations. Referents to social expectations frequently try to clarify the position their expectations should have in the hierarchy. They often start quarrels about their respective power. Quite recently in the Netherlands, for instance, Islamitic groups wanted more freedom in the education of their children in the tradition of the Koran. They lost their struggle against the representatives of the government and were forced to obey the educational rules formulated by that government.

Such an example makes clear that in the domain of educational expectations the government is more influential than representatives of particular religious groups. But this influence holds only for particular expectations. These are expectations which concern all children in a particular society defined by a particular political constellation. The Dutch situation, as a case in point, also shows that there is still room left for particular groups belonging to this society to have some of their expectations (e.g. religious ones) realized through the educational system. Figure 1 presents a formalized example of a hierarchy of social expectations.

In figure 1 only the government, particular ethnic or religious groups and the teachers were described as important groups which formulate expectations. They are not always powerful instances for developmental expectations. In other developmental domains, like hygienics and ideology, parents and peers might have a substantial influence, at least in western cultures.

A list as presented in figure 1 may be seen as a model for the actual cognitive development of a particular person.

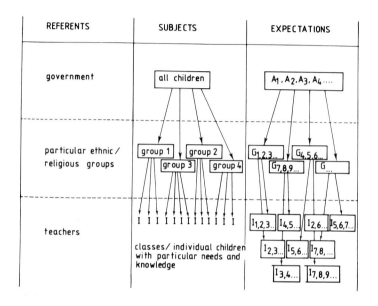

Figure 1. A scheme of a hierarchy of educational expectations, e.g. for six year old schildren living in the Netherlands.

FROM THE MODEL TO THE INDIVIDUAL.

A list of expectations as such only gives information about the probable direction particular groups in society want cognitive development to have for particular members of society. In order to be able to say something about a person's actual development one should relate the expectations to ideas about particular activities that allow people to satisfy the expectations. Comparison of a list of expectations with the results of an exploration of activities a particular person can actually execute, gives information about how far this person is in his or her development towards satisfying particular activities. Even more specific information would become available if psychologists would explore the relations between particular activities up to the level of actions and operations.

As stated before in the section about the structure of activity, this is difficult to accomplish, but it is important because it results in information about what a person still has to learn in order to satisfy particular social expectations. This information makes it feasible to speculate about possible steps a person may make in his or her near development.

One should also investigate the actual social relations in which a person is involved. These relations give indications about the motives persons presently want to realize or to satisfy, and thus give information about the activities these persons execute or are going to execute. Together with a systematization of developmental expectations (a list as presented in figure 1), the knowledge about relations between activities and the knowledge about social relations would give psychologists an alternative to their ideas of stages, and to the assessments they employ for the exploration of how far persons are in their development through the stages. An important difference with stage models is that, with this systematization, the expectations become a description of goals in development. An a-priori idea of developmental goals is no longer necessary. As described in the first section such a-priori ideas are charactistic for many current developmental theories.

The fact that the author has described cognitive development as a process in which a person satisfies expectations does not mean that he conceives of development as a process in which all persons of a particular group actually realize the activities which are necessary to satisfy the expectations. There may be circumstances that make it difficult for some persons to satisfy particular expectations. Certain skills and mastery levels of skills may be quite exceptional for a specific person in a specific group. Often these persons do meet our expectations, but not our expectations about "normal" development (see Feldman, 1980).

As a case in point, one may think of children with physical handicaps which hamper the execution of particular activities in an environment which does not offer necessary compensatory means.

THE PROBLEM OF DIMENSIONALIZATION.

The model of cognitive development described here actually does not represent the idea of development which Wohlwill wanted to become widely used in the study of human development. Meeting a variety of social expectations may be an indication for the realisation of development as the improvement of a person's abilities to execute more and more social tasks. However, the tasks may demand knowledge and skills which have hardly any relation in terms of particular dimensions, e.g. a dimension making it feasible to say to what extent a person has developed a particular geometrical capability.

The present section deals with the way the idea of dimensionalization fits in with the present idea of cognitive development. It also presents an important consequence. What one wants to accomplish with defining development in terms of developmental dimensions is to represent a particular development from its origin to its destiny. The exploration of relations between activities as proposed in the preceding section actually only shows how one activity facilitates the realization of another activity. Actually we need to know how a particular activity develops from another activity or a variety of activities. Lomov (1983) talks in this context about a genealogy of activities. Because the development of a particular activity may vary between persons, even between persons belonging to the same social group, such a genealogy can probably be realized best by studying the ontogenesis of particular persons. For doing this we need a life span approach in our methodology, tracing the paths of specific activities. An exploration, and following that, a comparison of developmental paths of specific persons concerning specific skills, may ultimately be the basis for general statements about development in terms of particular dimensions.

Approaching development from the perspective of a particular dimension, skill or ability has a particular consequence. In this approach, earlier acquired skills and knowledge play a role in future development only when they are used again in activities which are evaluated as relevant to the developmental dimension under exploration (compare also with Tyszkowa, in this volume). We can imagine, as a case in point, that primary school science studies have little developmental value for a girl who, when grown up, becomes a seamstress. The activities she has to execute as a seamstress have little or nothing in common with the things she learned in her science studies. From the perspective of the idea that development should be development in terms of a particular dimension, development is conceived of as the broadening and reactualization of a particular skill or a particular piece of knowledge.

The latter consequence of the present developmental model means that a psychologist who is employing it in his or her study of developmental processes, has chosen to restrict the domain under study to a particular part of the development of persons. We should not, however, consider the dimensionalization and the resulting restriction of the domain under study apart from what was stated earlier about the systematization of expectations and about the exploration of relations between activities linked with this systematization. The systematization of expectations tells us what activities are seen as especially important for a particular social group. These activities may be used as a reference point for the choice of developmental dimensions which will be used for the study of developmental processes. Thus, although the present approach implicates an explicit restriction of the developmental domain which is under study, the chosen developmental domain is not trivial.

THE OPEN ENDEDNESS OF THE DEVELOPMENTAL MODEL.

In the preceding sections it was stated that cognitive development is generated and regulated by the social relations in which persons participate or in which they become embedded. This may seem a mechanistic point of view. Actually it is not. Although persons are not always capable of and free to choose their social relations, these relations determine development only as far as the persons become actively involved in them. Moreover, as persons develop they are more and more capable of choosing themselves in which social relations they want to participate. In view of the fact that persons become more and more capable of choosing their own social relations, and in view of the conditional relationship between development and active involvement in social relations, the present developmental model may be conceived of as open-ended.

There is, however, still another argument for the open-endedness of the present developmental model. This argument concerns the social expectations a person of a particular social group is confronted with during a life time. Maybe the expectations do not change during one or more generations of people, but the expectations are certainly not permanent. They may change over time (see also Geulen, in this volume). People develop, until then unknown tasks. This implicates that the present developmental model is society- and time-bound. The model has to be adapted to social changes, which means that the systematization of social (developmental) expectations is a continual task for psychologists.

CONCLUDING REMARKS.

The present approach to cognitive development breaks from theoretical conceptions like the Piagetian and the psycho-analytical. This is not to say that also the research done in these traditions is of no value. Particular research outcomes, such as those concerning the development of logical thinking in the Piagetian tradition, are probably very important. They just need a re-evaluation in terms of the present model. In part such a re-evaluation is already realized in research which showed the cultural dependency of the development of logical thinking (see e.g. Donaldsen, 1978; Doise & Mugny, 1984). For a good re-evaluation, however, the present model itself has to be filled in with research findings about actual hierarchies of social expectations, and research on biographies.

The goal of this paper was to present some preliminary ideas for a theory on cognitive development which has the following characteristics: development is seen as a social process, development may be studied in terms of growth along a developmental dimension, and the theory is open-ended. In order to fill in the presented framework, one should use the categories described in the section on the structure of activity. These categories - activity, action, operation, motive, goal and social expectation - should be used for analysing social conflicts about social expectations, developmental or learning situations, and concrete activities and social relations in which a developing person is involved. Such analyses should result in a picture of the particular social character of cognitive development in a specific society, and in an overview of developmental standards in terms of lists of age- and group-bound social expectations and activities which are necessary to meet the expectations. The analyses may also result, however, in a more specific, detailed definition of the analytical categories presented and their interrelations, or eventually in skipping or adding categories.

Investigations of developmental activities should also ultimately lead to a more detailed conception of the explicative categories presented in this text. In the present text most attention was given to a general explicative category, viz. incorporation. Many problems related to the explanation of developmental processes are still waiting for their answers. How do specific motives come about to bridge a gap between what is known already and what one should know? How is, on the basis of a motive, a specific goal for actions generated which is meant to bridge the gap? How is the transformation accomplished from one form of activity to another one, e.g. from material to verbal activity, without loosing track of the contents?

In view of their theoretical and empirical importance, the previous problems deserve more attention than they currently receive.

REFERENCES.

Abul'khanova-Slavskaja, K.A. (1982). The category of activity in Soviet psychology. Soviet Psychology, 20, 3-36.

Beilin, H. (1980). Piaget's theory: refinement, revision or rejection. In R.H. Kluwe & H. Spada (Eds.), Developmental models of thinking. New York: Academic Press.

Bergk, M. (1980). Leselernprozesz und Erstlesewerke (The process of learning to read, and primary reading). Bochum: Kamp.

Bruner, J.S. (1979). The organization of action and the nature of adult-infant transaction. Paper presented at the conference on organization of action. Paris.

Davydov, V.V. (1977). Major problems in developmental and educational psychology at the present stage of development of education. Soviet Psychology, 15, 73-95.

Davydov, V.V. (1981). The category of activity and mental reflection in the theory of A.N. Leont'ev. Soviet Psychology, 19, 3-27.

Davydov, V.V. & Zinchenkov, V.P. (1981). The principle of development in psychology. Soviet Psychology, 20, 22-46.

Doise, W. & Mugny, G. (1984). The Social Development of the Intellect. Oxford: Pergamon Press.

Feldman, D.H. (1980). Beyond Universals in Cognitive Development. Norwood (New Jersey): Ablex Publishing Corporation.

Fischer, K.W. (1980). A Theory of Cognitive Development. Psychological Review, 87, 477-525.

Gal'perin, P.J. (1969). Die Entwicklung der Untersuchungen über die Bildung geistiger Handlungen (The development of investigations of the construction of mental acts). In H. Hiebsch (Ed.), Ergebnisse der Sovjetischen Psychologie (Attainments of Psychology). Stuttgart: Klett.

Gal'perin, P.J. (1980). Zu Grundfragen der Psychologie (to the basic questions of Psychology). Köln: Pahl Rugenstein.

Geulen, D. (1986). The conditions of human development: implications of socialization research for developmental psychology. In P. van Geert (Ed.), Theory Building in Developmental Psychology. Amsterdam: North Holland.

Ginsburg, H. (1977). Children's arithmetic. New York: Nostrand.

Kabylnizkaja, S.L. (1973). Die experimentelle Herausbildung der Aufmerksamkeit (The experimental formation of attention). In J. Lompscher (Ed.), Sovjetische Beiträge zur Lerntheorie (Soviet Contributions to Learning Theory). Köln: Pahl Rugenstein.

Kol'tsova, V.A. (1978). Experimental study of cognitive activity in communication. Soviet Psychology, 17, 23-28.

Leont'ev, A.N. (1979). Probleme der Entwicklung des Psychischen (Problems of the development of the mental). Frankfurt am Main, Athenäum Fischer.

Leont'ev, A.N. (1979). Tätigkeit, Bewusztsein, Persönlichkeit (Activity, Consciousness, Personality). Berlin: Volk und Wissen.

Lieven, E.V.M. (1982). Context, process and progress in young children's speech. In M. Beveridge (Ed.), Children thinking through language. London: Edward Arnold.

Lomov, B.F. (1983). The problem of activity in psychology. Soviet Psychology, 21, 55-91.(a)

Meacham, J.A. (1984). The social basis of intentional action. Human Development, 27, 119-124.

Ninio, A. & Bruner, J. (1978). The achievement and antecedents of labeling. Journal of child language, 5, 1-15.

Perret-Clermont, A.N. (1980). Social interaction and cognitive development in children. London: Academic Press.

Radatz, H. (1980). Fehleranalysen im Mathematikunterricht (Error Analysis in Mathematics Teaching). Braunschweig: Vieweg.

Ratner, N. & Bruner, J. (1978). Games, social exchanges and the acquisition of language. Journal of child language, 5, 391-401.

Rubinstein, S.L. (1977). Das Denken un die Wege seiner Erforschung (Thinking and the ways of its investigation). Berlin: D.V.W.

Sechter, M.S. (1972). Het gebruik maken van geheelkenmerken (Using properties of wholes). In C.F. van Parreren & J.A.M. Carpay (Eds.), Sovjetpsychologen aan het woord. Groningen: Tjeenk Willink.

Siegler, R.S. & Klahr, D. (1982). When do children learn? The relationship between existing knowledge and the acquisition of new knowledge. In R. Glaser (Ed.), Advances in Instructional psychology: Vol. 2. Hillsdale (New Jersey): Lawrence Erlbaum.

Tyszkowa, M. (1986). Psychic development of the individual as a process of structuring and restructuring experience. In P. van Geert (Ed.), Theory Building in Developmental Psychology. Amsterdam: North Holland.

Vedder, P. (1985a). Cooperative learning. A study on processes and effects of cooperation between primary school schildren. Den Haag: S.V.O.-report 1041.

Vedder, P. (1985b). Leren als Sociaal Proces (Learning as a Social Process). In P. Vedder & M. Bloemkolk (Eds.), Samenwerken en Probleemoplossen (Cooperation and Problem Solving). Lisse: Swets & Zeitlinger.

van Geert, P. (1986). The Structure of Developmental Theories. In P. van Geert (Ed.), Theory Building in Developmental Psychology. Amsterdam: North Holland.

Vygotsky, L.S. (1972). Denken und Sprechen (Thought and Speach). Frankfurt/M: Fischer.

Walkerdine, V. (1982). From context to text: a psychosemiotic approach to abstract thought. In M. Beveridge (Ed.), Learning through interaction. Cambridge: Cambridge University Press.

Wertsch, J. (1979). From social interaction to higher
     psychological processes. Human Development, 22, 1-22.
Wertsch, J.V. (1979). The significance of dialogue in
     Vygotsky's account of social, egocentric and inner
     speech. Contemporary Educational Psychology, 5, 150-162.
Wohlwill, J.F. (1973). The Study of Behavior Development. New
     York: Academic Press.
Youniss, J. (1983). Piaget and the self constituted through
     relations. In W.F. Overton (Ed.), The relationship
     between social and cognitive development. Hillsdale (New
     Jersey): Lawrence Erlbaum.

PART 4

THREE VIEWS ON THE NATURE OF DEVELOPMENTAL PROCESSES

Theory Building in Developmental Psychology
P.L.C. van Geert (editor)
© *Elsevier Science Publishers B.V. (North-Holland), 1986*

8

Cognitive Change and Behaviour [1]

Francine Orsini-Bouichou and Jean-Louis Paour [2]

The present paper addresses the question whether it is possible to identify changes of a developmental origin, in contrast to changes effected by situational variations, e.g. learning. The authors have chosen to give developmental status to the emergence of new behavioural classes that they have called "regularities", supported by an invariant structure.
The first part of the paper shows how the present paradigm allows one to specify developmental change observed in terms of invariance.
The second part enlarges the scope of the problem by proposing a model of a "development analyser", which allows one to take into account subject as well as environmental factors.
The third part sketches a framework for the study of developmental pasticity and of the conditions of cognitive development.

No theoretical construction concerning development can omit the more general study of change in the child. Given that childhood is the period of life the most rich in change it is important to recognize several categories of change. If we take changes which appear in the repertory of the subject into consideration (and leave aside others of an immediate or ephemeral type), then we consider two categories particularly significant for theoretical objectives: change which essentially reflects the phenomena of development and change which corresponds more to the effects of situational variations, and in particular to the effects of learning. This of course raises the question of the relationship between these two forms of change.

For a long time now this distinction has taken the form of a relative separation, the relationship between the two types of change being rarely considered or mentioned. The study of development was most often oriented, overtly or not, toward a maturationist point of view and based on a rigorously predetermined ontogenetic program (Gesell on motor behaviour, Chomsky on language ....). The study of learning, which traditionally occupied an important place in psychology, was concerned with answering the questions raised by the various problems of acquisition and discrimination in the adult (human or animal). A consultation of the principal manuals, in particular those prior to 1970, is sufficient to confirm this fact. To cite but one of the more recent French language manuals which points out this deficiency: "It is paradoxical that several important theories of learning and several important theories of development exist, but, so far, no theory of behavioural change linking development and learning has been formed" (Richelle, in Droz and Richelle, 1976, p. 383). Recently the pendulum has swung in the other direction, numerous studies have associated development and learning in the child. It was an important trend which had its apogee around the 1970's. Under the influence of the recent diffusion of neo-Piagetian ideas (Piagetian learning studies) this attempt to establish a relationship, commendable in itself, resulted too often in hasty, confused and controversial elaborations. Learning was presented as the validation or invalidation of a developmental or pedagogical theory but without the preliminary precaution of taking into account the different categories of change indicated above. We have already had occasion to denounce the bad use, in conditions of improvisation, made of learning studies (Orsini-Bouichou, Malacria-Rocco & Rohrer, 1985). Efficiently inducing controlled progression in knowledge (and situating it in relation to a developmental norm) does not of itself allow one to conclude that one has thereby accelerated cognitive development. We know that learning can result in change of a fundamental nature (comparable, subject to verification, to the effects of global or specific evolution), but it can also lead to more or less localized acquisitions or to new attitudes to the proposed tasks.

Thus we are compelled to face the following problem: is it possible to identify change of a developmental origin? The developmental nature of an observed phenomenon is never self-evident. We are abruptly confronted here with an even more fundamental problem , the delimitation of a scientific fact. In our context this delimitation, in order to be pertinent, should be able to answer this question: what are the criteria which allow us to establish that we have isolated developmental change?

Two criteria seem to us particularly pertinent in indicating the status of the emergence of developmental change.

The first criterion concerns the relationships which specify this change with regard to the developmental context. At this point we denounce a shift in meaning which may bring about confusion concerning the methodological and theoretical levels of analysis. The mere fact of constructing an experimental situation susceptible to succesfully inducing new elements of behaviour is not sufficient grounds for attaching to them the label of one's choice. The new behaviour to be studied, even if induced, should not be considered as an isolable fact to be studied as one would study an ordinary experimental variable. Far from isolating it one should, on the contrary, replace it at the very heart of the developmental context of the moment. It is here that we agree with the precautions advocated with insistence by Wallon (1941), in particular in his book "L'évolution psychologique de l'enfant":

> "L'explication d'un comportement isolé doit replacer celui-ci dans un ensemble le plus vaste qui permette de fournir, pour telle structure comportementale, des critères d'explication .... Ce n'est pas la matérialité d'un fait qui importe, c'est le système auquel il appartient, dans l'instant où il se manifeste." (The explanation of isolated behaviour should replace that behaviour in the largest context

capable of providing explanatory criteria for such a behavioural structure .... Importance should be given not to the materiality of the fact, but to the system to which it belongs at the moment of its appearance) (5th edition, 1957, p. 23).
This precaution seems indispensable, if one wishes to give to change (be it observed or induced) a significance going beyond it being the simple product of a particular acquisition and tending to liken it to a developmental fact.

The second criterion is aimed at defining change by contrasting it with non-change. It seems to us that change takes on a developmental significance if it is accompanied by the setting up of stable and regular constructions in the chronology of the evolution. Here we join with another leading figure of ontogenetic psychology, again a European: Jean Piaget. In the midst of the changing and elusive complexity of evolution he discovered stable areas, thus opening a possible way to achieve systematic exploration. Evolution will be studied from the activity of the child, who produces new behavioural schemes at each stage . The concept of scheme represents the corner-stone of his work. As early as 1936 the scheme is presented as an invariant; during development, different invariants will be constructed at different levels and at different moments. At the present time, by way of reaction, the structural aspect of the Geneva school is the subject of much polemic. But we think it is more a question of rejecting the use of a too rigid and too general concept of scheme rather than the idea itself which has certain similarities to a recent trend based on the idea of system.

In accordance with this double tradition we have chosen to give developmental status to the emergence of new behavioural classes that we have called "regularities", supported by an invariant structure and which marks the course of development according to an hierarchically stable sequential order.

In the first part of this chapter we attempt to show how this paradigm allows us to describe and specify developmental change observed in terms of invariance. We extend this descriptive analysis by introducing an explanatory hypothesis concerning the reorganizing function of these invariants. We test this hypothesis using original induction experiments.

The second part enlarges and enriches the scope of the problem. The model that we propose, freely used as a development analyser (of observed and induced changes), allows us to take into account the factors linked to the environment as well as to the individual subject. The ontogenetic approach constitutes an axis around which other methods are attached (differential, comparative and cognitive learning).

The third part sketches a framework for the study of developmental plasticity and of the conditions of cognitive development.

COGNITIVE CHANGE, EMERGENCE OF INVARIANTS.

We have thus adopted a model of cognitive development as a base which escapes the formal adultomorphic descriptions applicable to known and identifiable behaviour. We have attempted to construct, step by step, a model sufficiently flexible and evolutive to take into account spontaneous forms of cognitive activity between 3 and 8 years of age.

Knowing how closely theoretical and methodological aspects are linked we have not followed the usual practice of questioning which may appear efficient but is of little pertinence here. In order to gather these original forms we looked for rules, or in a more generic sense, regularities, practised by the child to organize his action in time, in a minimally constraining context. This research reflects a general hypothesis: the developmental organizations implicated in the course of a systematic ontogenetic program, can, in certain conditions, be discovered in activities considered to be "spontaneous" (in the sense of being not directly provoked by the situation); subsequently, these forms of organizations will be integrated (will become indiscernible) in complex wholes endowed with specific adaptive particularities, such as instrumental, social and scholastic activity. We could cite, as examples of regularities: the circular reactions of the infant and many games children play in their initial form. Considering that regularities, described in terms of structural invariants, mark out development, we have started from a comprehensive model of regularities; the dominant traits attributed to them can thus be tested and clarified in pertinent and reliable conditions.

If the concept of regularity is related to the Piagetian notion of scheme [3], it can also be likened to the terms "behavior networks" or "logical homologies" (Bates et al., 1979), terms applied to early childhood. Regularities are considered to be categories of behaviour which express rules common to a developmental period and relative to classes of situations.

The regularities are therefore based on invariants and their significance can be specified from their synchronic relationship with other contemporary behaviour and from their diachronic relationship with preceding and subsequent behaviour.

Observed Change

OPERATIONAL PROCEDURES.

The emergence of the aforementioned regularities and their specificity have been brought to light by the following characteristics of our procedures (Orsini-Bouichou, 1982).

The standard situation, subjected to few constraints, corresponds to an approach midway between free observation and experimentation. We are concerned with free combination behaviour and free covariants. It is the subjects' activity that organizes the elements of the situation. These elements consist of simple everyday objects presented at random (balls of different colours or of different sizes, small toys such as a tree, a house ...). These objects are presented as a base for relations, the subjects' task being to invent the game rules which suit them and that they will be able to reproduce afterwards in the same conditions.

The task must present temporal duration: we presume that behavioural organization obeys the particular regulatory laws of the subject at a given moment. For the same subject, in the same conditions, we ask for as many combinations as he or she is willing to produce (between 3 and 8 depending on the age and the individual).

The situation presented must be varied, both in its structure and in the nature of its elements, in order to control an eventual generalization of the regularities.

Each task and each situation must be proposed to different age groups in order to make the comparison of the different productions possible both vertically and horizontally.

Free combination and free covariant behaviour lend themselves to formal translation (in terms of mathematical functions), which facilitates the implementation of comparisons between synchronic and diachronic productions.

THE RESULTS

These results have been drawn from a series of experiments grouped into four categories according to their mode of control and the structure of the game (individual or bipartite):

- In "A", the free combination of objects (an individual game) is deprived of perceptive control (the subjects must have in mind the invented sequence of the objects, which they place, one after the other, in the "pencil box" [4], without seeing or touching the combination during the performance);

- in "B", the free combination of objects (an individual game) is accompanied by perceptual control throughout the performance (the subjects can see and touch all of the invented sequence);

- finally in "C" or "D", free covariation (a game for two: child/experimenter) is accompanied by perceptive control

("C") or is deprived of it ("D").

The subject population grouped for the totality of the experiments amounted to 850 children, mostly between 3 and 8 years of age, with a sampling of adolescents for category "A". All came from average socio-economic backgrounds.

For each of the four major categories of games, we were able to establish the types of regularities, which were identified by means of an evaluation grid. The progressive elaboration of this grid provided us with a range of sequential combinations [5] and allowed us to conveniently test (using a probability test) the proximity or the distance of each effective production in relation to the totality of rules selected. For each category the percentage of regularities in relation to the totality of response provided, increased significantly with age and tended towards 100% at 8 years.

We shall not at this point linger over the details concerning the variations within each of the categories in relation to the nature of the objects presented or the sex of the subjects. We are more concerned with clarifying the meaning of these results within the framework of our research.

THE MODEL OF SYSTEMS OF RULES OR OF OPERATORS.

These results were described in the mathematical language of functions with the collaboration of our colleagues the logicians Grize and Frey. Subsequently these rules were grouped by families, using a single formal structure, in terms of operators. This term, which implies the mathematical sense of "transformation system", is used here in a metaphorical sense.

Thus the first operator described generates repetition, the second produces local relations of couples, the third expresses correspondence rules with figural support, the fourth concerns the coordination of correspondence rules.

Let us now briefly consider a few examples of regularities adopted by the children in order to state the

rule systems which correspond to these operators.
For repetition, a uniform sequential combination (a red ball
followed by a red ball, etc. .... or a small stick followed by
a small stick, etc. ... or a pebble followed by a pebble, etc.
...).
For the couple relation: a red ball then a white ball, etc. ..
or a small stick then a big stick, etc. ... or a pebble then a
button.
For correspondence rules with figural support: symmetrical
alternance, (as many x elements as x' elements: for instance 3
red balls, then 3 white balls) or complementation, (x elements
plus x' elements to make a constant whole: for instance 3 red
balls + 2 white balls = 5 as 4 red balls + 1 white ball = 5).
For the coordination of correspondence rules: compensation
(for instance add two red balls and subtract 2 white balls).

One can recognize, in these systems of rules, features
which are also to be found in behaviour categories described
by other authors in research work of various sorts. They
represent a set of landmarks to us, when they appear for the
first time in the context of a class of given situations. At
the moment they appear they have the status of indicators
having their own hierarchical order. They correspond to levels
of development and have been evaluated and confirmed by
comparison with other cognitive indicators ("operatory",
psychometric and scholastic tests). Their generality has been
tested by other research workers in different environments and
cultures, in France (Noizet, 1965; Florés, 1979;
Desprels-Fraysse & Fraysse, 1977; Paour, 1975; Soavi, 1986),
in Brazil (Cunha de Carvalho, 1982) and in Haiti (Robeants,
work in progress).

However, these systems of rules are not comparable to
stages or mini-stages. They do not present the structural
unity characteristic of a period of development. Once they
appear, or have been installed, we consider them as
multi-purpose tools available to the subject, with varying
utility. They can thus intervene in different procedures to
select different aspects of the environment and to treat these
aspects according to the particular nature of the situation

and the temporary dispositions of the subject.

Induced Changes.

THE OPERATOR-ORGANIZER HYPOTHESIS AND RULES INDUCTIONS.

Here we are concerned with the emergence of these operators in so far as they can be inferred by means of several systems of rules during controlled observations. We first studied the emergence of these systems, during controlled observations, in ontogenetic studies of children 3 to 8 years old, (Orsini-Bouichou, 1975 and 1982). Subsequently, we studied the emergence of these systems of rules under the influence of intervention (induction by training).

We were thus led to formulate the hypothesis that the induction of such a system of rules, at a given moment, considered to be critical, can generate an important behavioural reorganization. It is for this reason that we have not spoken of "rule induction" in the sense given, for example, by Scandura (1973). We give this term a sense analogous to that employed by embryologists in describing induction experiments concerning organizing structures. These terms have also been adopted in another field of research by Spitz (1957). By analogy we thought that, during certain critical moments, the subject, given adequate conditions, can be seen to be sensitive to the proposed incentives. In these conditions we think it probable that the subject reacts and produces, via those elements of behaviour previously categorized, a new system of rules. For example the system Y which, in chronological and hierarchical order, follows the system X previously identified in the same subject. Once the new system has emerged we think that it will begin functioning and reorganise the totality of the pre-existing behaviour. What is important here, we believe, is not so much the physical characteristics of the proposed situation but rather two factors: firstly, the moment chosen for the intervention;

secondly, what one proposes to the subject. The moment chosen is evaluated with regard to the degree to which the pre-existing system of rules is implanted in the context of the situations taken into consideration. What we propose corresponds to the system of rules which follows, when the context remains constant.

More generally speaking, and to conclude this rapid outline of the theoretical framework of this research, undertaken by our team over a period of more than 20 years, we can affirm that the recorded effects attest the transition to a superior level of cognitive functioning. The emergence of a new system of rules is accompanied, often in the form of delayed effects (3, 6, 9 months, 1 year and 2 years after the intervention), by more elaborate cognitive constructions in different domains. Most of this research concerns normal school children of 6 years of age from which we excluded (after evaluating their operatory level) the few judged to have a superior cognitive level.

TOWARDS AN EXPLICATIVE ANALYSIS OF COGNITIVE DEVELOPMENT.

Change Analysis In-Vivo.

In most ontogenetic studies change is analysed after it has been brought about. Most experiments concerning learning essentially give the "pre-test/ post-test" comparison as results. One concentrates on what happens before the intervention and after it. What happens between the two is ignored. But this is precisely what is important: to study change at the very moment one observes it. Our aim is to analyse the change, during the training sessions and to trace the construction of a new system of rules. It is not simply a matter of noting what takes place but rather of carrying out a study of the dynamics of behavioural organization. What is more, we have found that this description of change during training can have a predictive value.

Desprels-Fraysse and Fraysse (1977) studied children of

four and a half years of age with this paradigm. The subjects who constructed and then generalized the new systems of rules the most rapidly during the six training sessions were precisely those who subsequently made most progress in various other tests. Similarly, in the context of collective research work with other populations (5 and 6 years of age) undertaken in the laboratory of Nice, this prediction was verified by various tests, ("operatory" and psychometric, Florès & Orsini-Bouichou, 1979).

By progressive analysis at a microscopic level and by noting even minute details, we compose an individual chronicle of the training session. These chronicles provide us with extremely important information on the behavioural plasticity of the subjects and the dynamics of their particular evolution. Fundamentally this is of considerable interest and has obvious pedagogical implications.

These training sessions offer a development analyser thanks to an indirect intervention procedure (which appears in the form of a detour).

Analysis of the Causality of Development.

We can say that the objective of our training, to a certain extent, is an intervention on the developmental causality system. We believe we are acting on the linkage of causes of diverse sorts at a given moment in the subject's history. Of course, we do not underestimate the complexity of this causality chain, which was at work before the subject reached the state described, at the chosen moment, and that obviously continues after the intervention.

The idea of an operator which, at its emergence, has a reorganizing function, invokes two aspects of genesis, continuous and discontinuous genesis. The new operator expresses a new system of rules which, nevertheless, implies the preceding one. However, as soon as it appears, different elements of behaviour (extremely heterogeneous), not previously observed will come to the fore without giving us the possibility of establishing a clear continuity in the temporal modifications of the individual repertory. We could say that this reorganizing operator has a decider function, to use a currently employed term. We think that this is a fundamental phenomenon in the cognitive development of the child. Let us consider some other more classic examples: the appearance of locomotion or of the personal pronoun "I". Locomotion is the result of continuous progress in the modification of the nervous system and the tonico-postural function. However, as soon as locomotion becomes apparent, certain aspects of behaviour and various processes will be reorganized at different levels: the perception of depth, the construction of body image and the modification of relationships with others. Similarly the appearance of the personal pronoun "I" represents far more than a lexical enlargement. We are touching on a problem crucial for genesis, the interdependence of very different terms and levels.

In the analysis of development one should be wary of the retrospective illusion. Noting the progressive character of the genesis, once it is accomplished, does not necessarily imply processes acting in a continuous and regular fashion. The examination of recognized pathological cases sometimes characterized by very large temporal and functional differences attests to the contrary and illustrates the risks continually run by genesis, whose homogeneity is never assured in advance. (Wallon, 1934, 1941; Ajuriaguerra, 1974). The different reorganizing systems are not automatically generated from the other. In this new phase of our study (which concerns the causality of development) we are led to put aside the universal aspects of developmental phenomena which concentrated on during the first phase. The study of causality processes leads us now (by means of the intervention) to take into account what occurs at an individual level. Genesis occurs only in the case history of the individual, where the various influences meet and interact; no doubt, this sort of preoccupation could seem to some not to be a scientific approach. But we think that a circumspect way to tackle the individual level consists of using several methods conjointly. Intervention allows us to act and to take into account what is effectively involved at an individual level. The differential method allows us to locate and specify the conditions corresponding to characteristics linked to different categories of subjects and environments. Proceeding by way of succesive approximations we hope to progressively delimit the individual phenomena of the genesis.

COGNITIVE CHANGE, DIFFERENTIAL ASPECTS AND INTERVENTION.

Comparing our induction experiments with children of different ages, (four, five and six years), we were able to note that these different chronological periods did not show the same sensitivity to our interventions. Thus it would seem to be more difficult to provoke the induction of the proposed systems of rules in the period five to six years than in the six to seven years period. Transitional phases and instability seem more propitious. Moreover, at the same chronological age the reaction to induction seems to depend on the duration of the exercising of the last system of rules and its degree of generalization in various situations (research in progress).

The outcome would seem to us to be of equal importance, whether it be a successful induction (the subject constructs the new system of rules) or an unsuccessful induction (the subject remains stationary). This model (the induction of systems of rules) served as the starting point for a series of studies of cognitive evolution (in particular concrete operatory structures) using varied populations. This is only a starting point and others are possible; but whichever we choose it must possess the characteristic of being a reliable developmental indicator and produce testable effects of its reorganizing function.

This model, used in the context of the experimental situations outlined above, enabled us:

- to ascertain, for various population categories, the rhythm of the accession or non accession to clearly defined ontogenetic levels;

- to favourize, indirectly, the development of new research

designed to specify the characteristics of the cognitive functioning of particular samples of population;
- to evaluate the weight of factors linked respectively to environment and to the subject;
- to describe the irreversible or modifiable nature of these characteristics under the influence of the intervention.

In order to simplify this brief presentation we shall concentrate on the developmental period corresponding to the formation of what is called "logical" or "operatory" thinking (the change from pre-operatory thinking to concrete operatory thinking). We shall evoke, by way of illustration, studies which refer to several categories of children. We shall begin by citing studies concerning retarded and precocious children (characteristics linked to the subject); subsequently we shall quickly summarize other studies concerning categories of children characterized by their socio-cultural environment.

Research on Retarded and Precocious Children.

We carried out systematic observation of 84 subjects who were examined using a longitudinal technique over periods varying from 12 to 27 months (Paour, 1975, 1979, 1981, 1985). The subjects concerned had no evident organic etiology, lived with their family (three quarters of them were from under-privileged backgrounds), and were pupils in special classes of the regular school system. They belong to the "slightly retarded" group as defined by the AAMD. The observed concordance between the classic developmental intelligence scales and the Piagetian tests led us to adopt the generally accepted diagnostic: generalized and homogeneous retarded development.

However, we were led to reject the simple conception of retardation which implies certainly a slow development, but nevertheless a continuous one (show by the curve of mental age progression). Within the temporal limits of our observation (up to 27 months), these subjects are characterized by an extended fixation at a level of development which we have located to the operator generating the relation of couple. This immobility can also be detected in their stationary behaviour in Piagetian tests and in problem solving. However, progress is possible in other tests which call on acquisition reinforced by everyday life (for example, the items of knowledge used in intelligence scales).

The retarded children of the control groups remained astonishingly fixed at the cognitive level we indicated, but this was not the case for the 140 retarded subjects of the experimental groups (rigourously matched with the former). The efficiency of these inductions is shown to be even greater than in experiments carried out with normal children (of an equivalent level of development). Out of 140 children receiving our training, 80% progressed in a radical way. This progress is evaluated according to the four following criteria:

a) the appearance of new behaviour and concepts verified by the Piagetian tasks used in the pre and post tests;

b) a phenomenon of generalization expressed by the appearance of varied logical concepts, belonging to other areas (number, classes, relations, space);

c) the extension of this phenomenon of generalization to other sorts of cognitive activity: performance in psychometric tests (important increase in mental age), linguistic tests (Paour, 1975), and scholastic tests (Meynier and Bourmault, 1978; Soavi, 1986).

d) the stability of this progress and, in addition, the appearance of new and more elaborate concepts supported by those previously induced (for example: the dissociation of weight and volume in the volume conservation test after the conservation of substance and weight in the corresponding tests).

However, to overcome that prolonged fixation at the level which was initially located, we had to introduce conditions never employed with normal children. As a pilot to the presentation of the induction situation we conducted numerous sessions designed to isolate the pertinent indices and to evoke in the subjects anticipation and control of their action. In so doing we presented them with privileged functioning conditions. These specially arranged inducing situations are conceived as a "prosthetic" environment which may help retarded subjects to treat the pertinent information and, then, to construct the new system of rules. It is in this sense that we speak of a "prosthetic" environment (Paour, Galas, Malacria-Rocco & Soavi, 1985). But let there be no misunderstanding, we do not artificially supply the appropriate answer or algorithm. We just organize the environment, sparing the subjects the preliminary exploratory phase. Furthermore, we offer them guidance in metacognitive activity (directing attention, anticipation, error correction, verbal mediation, construction of hypotheses and evaluation of them ...).

An exploratory study of the development of children of five years, considered to be precocious according to a conventional diagnosis (scholastic advance and IQ), supplies profitable information. Several small groups of precocious children, observed over two years, show an irregular evolutionary curve (Planche, 1985, and other work in progress). The moment these children attain mastery of the operator which generates correspondence relations (six chrono-logical years) they very rapidly construct the different logical notions relative to concrete operations, with little respect for the normal intervals normally observed between them. Thus it would seem that a certain symmetry can be noted between the two groups. With regard to symmetry in evolution, there is the phenomenon of acceleration in the precocious children corresponding to the immobility phase in the retarded children. With regard to symmetry in cognitive functioning, we may observe that precocious children show spontaneously and to a marked degree the same qualities and activity organization that our training attempted to intensify in retarded children. Finally, there might be symmetry in the results of our interventions: the high level of intellectual activity in the precocious children was not, apparently, significantly improved by the proposed inductions. These recent data raise the problem of the plasticity of children during development.

Studies Relative to Categories of Children Belonging to Different Socio-cultural Environments.

The research work cited in the previous paragraph seems to correspond to the influence of variables linked to the subject. The populations recruited on the criteria of retardation are also characterized by other variables. Three quarters of these retarded subjects are of low SES. Other research seeks to clarify the nature of the difficulties of scholarly retardates in low SES groups (Alric, in progress). On the other hand three-quarters of our precocious children came from what are considered to be high SES groups.

Thus the continuation of our analysis implied taking environmental characteristics as experimental variables into account. Several studies, undertaken by our research group, have attempted to analyse this same period of cognitive development in relation to different environmental criteria.

A COMPARATIVE STUDY OF SEVERAL GROUPS OF CHILDREN LIVING IN CONDITIONS OF UNDERDEVELOPMENT.

The study concerns Haïtian children from both urban and rural backgrounds, aged from six to seventeen (Robeants, thesis in preparation). All of the children attend school and live in materially underprivileged conditions (the infant mortality rate in Haïti is the highest in Latin America). This transversal research concerning two hundred children is being carried out by a native of Haïti.

These subjects show, according to our indicators, a retardation and a fixation which resembles that which we described above concerning mental retardates. With subjects of rural origins the phenomenon is even more marked: an apparent halt in their development and cognitive functioning characterized by generalized passivity and inertia. The intervention of our training provoked enormous progress in the urban subjects, but up to this point very little in rural subjects. But the study has not progressed far enough to propose an interpretation. Its interest consists in emphasizing questions raised in part by the preceding studies: the relationship between environmental conditions, and the characteristics of developmental rhythm and cognitive functioning.

A COMPARATIVE STUDY OF SEVERAL GROUPS OF NIGERIAN CHILDREN FROM FAMILIES WITH A MANUAL LABOURERS BACKGROUND.

The age range under consideration in this transversal research (Aboubakar, 1982) goes from six to thirteen, the population consisting of 600 non-scholastic subjects. The latter, from rural backgrounds, coming from families engaged in various manual labor: pottery, cattle rearing, trade, culture. It is a very detailed study carried out, like the preceding one, by a native of the region. The developmental indicators used here have been drawn and adapted from different Piagetian tasks of quantity conservation. Contrary to the expectations of the author, the order of appearance of the different invariants of quantity was identical in the four groups and in conformity with results normally obtained from European children (confirmed by Guttman's scaling). However, the rhythm of accession to the different invariants varied from one group to another in a significant manner: the influence of milieu engendered more difference between these four Nigerian groups than between the totality of Nigerian children and European children (from Aix and Geneva). Aboubakar interprets these differences in relation to the environmental characteristics which can be considered as a training system. With the aim of acting on the "natural" training conditions he proposes now to introduce (with these children), our operator inductions. He draws our attention to the importance of the various educational systems, there is a striking difference between the farmers and the other groups.

However, in so far as this latter variable was noticed only after sample taking it was not possible to treat it as a separate experimental variable.

A COMPARATIVE STUDY ON CHILDREN FROM FAMILIES CHARACTERIZED BY DIFFERENT EDUCATIONAL PRACTICES.

Cunha de Carvalho (1984), drawing her inspiration from Lautrey's research (1980), set out to treat precisely this latter variable referred to in the preceding section. To this end, she carried out two studies using children of six years of age with a high SES. The studies were conducted in France and Brazil. She was able to show that the relations between the parental educational system and the cognitive status of the child, established by Lautrey with 10-12 year old children, exists as early as six years. Families defined as flexible (the child being able to negociate when faced with unexpected situations or with parental educational rules) are more favorable to cognitive development than those with a rigid educational system which leaves the child little initiative. For each population (French or Brazilian), coming from an identical socio-economic background, this difference is extremely significant between the two groups, which were constituted according to contrasting parental educational practices. The author uses our induction of systems of rules with Brazilian children from a privileged class and divided them into them two groups according to the educational system defined beforehand. She was able to observe that if the children from families with rigid educational practices reacted only from the 5th training session onwards, they did show during the 5th and 6th sessions a brusque reorganization of their behaviour and enormous progress. From then on they could not be differentiated from their counterparts in the other (flexible educational system) group (whether or not they were subjected to our training). On the other hand they distinguished themselves very significantly from the other subjects belonging to their own group (rigid educational system) but not trained in the same conditions (they were occupied for the same time period with various logic games with an experimenter who didn't know the hypotheses). Moreover the functional modalities employed by these children had also evolved (mobility of responses, anticipation, retro-action, particularly in spatial tests).

SKETCH OF AN EVOLVING FRAME OF REFERENCE FOR RESEARCH.

The evolution of our research has led us to consider development from a pluralist point of view. This is not a question of idealistically preaching a wide eclecticism but rather taking recent contributions of psychology into account. It seems to us that today one tends to recognize that the object of psychological research is sufficiently complicated and lacking in continuity to warrant several approaches. The study of learning, for a long time a prisoner of theoretical options, apparently exclusive and divergent, could be cited by way of example. Gagné (1968), and more recently Georges & Richard (1982) insist on the diversity of the phenomena of learning and on the need, in order to understand each distinct phenomenon, to refer to an adequate model. In the case of development any attempt at theoretical construction stumbles over the same difficulties: the reference to an exclusive model is just as inadequate. Development can be approached using distinct levels of analysis: this allows each analysis to better adapt itself to its object.

However, distinguishing these levels of analysis - which is required in order to assure better knowledge of the totality of developmental phenomena - does remain an enormous problem which cannot be ignored. We shall see that, without claiming to have resolved the question, we can, from now on, distinguish partial levels.

In this concluding section we shall attempt, for each level of analysis, to specify both references to theoretical models as well as the characteristics of the methods corresponding to them. It seemed to us both difficult and artificial to put forward propositions of theoretical constructions supporting a study of cognitive development without making clear the possible operational means one has to test these models.

First Level of Analysis: Descriptive Study of Development.

    The first level of analysis that we can take up concerns the descriptive study of development. This study immediately imposes choices as to the delimitation of observed facts which necessarily refers us to a model. We chose a model which on the one hand is based on the work of Piaget and on the other draws on the recent trend concerning functional aspects of behaviour. The steps that we describe are organized by invariants which invoke the Piagetian concept of scheme. But our invariants differ in two ways from the concept of scheme. The definition we give of them implies in no way general stages, since they only have the status of indicators of development. We are not seeking to use this framework to account for the structure of knowledge and the formation of the different logical concepts (quantity conservation for example). We have tried to study the role of systems of rules in terms of rules of management. These rules of management can produce constituted knowledge (this is not our present concern); but they also concern a great many other things relative to the organization of the actions of the subject and of their regulation, within given classes of action. For example we were able to account for the organization of the different games of alternation in children of three to five years and of the representation they have of this.
    We chose the ontogenetic method in order to obtain this objective in defined conditions, described in the first part of the present article, more precisely in the section on operational procedures. The collection of all of these observations consituted for us an indispensable base of study.

Second Level of Analysis: Study of Transformations.

The second level of analysis corresponds to the study of transformations: how to pass from one stage to another? With regard to this question, Piaget's model seems to us so general as to be irrefutable. Equilibration as the main driving force presupposes as internal regulator (directed towards a higher degree of coherence), without the characteristics of that internal regulator being made explicit. Moreover the extension of changes concerns the whole stage, which is supposed to be a general structure.

We referred to another model in order to take these transformations into account: the concept of organizer that Spitz borrowed from the embryologists and that we have transposed and remodelled. Like Spitz we suggest that certain sorts of privileged behaviour have a decisive influence on the course of development; we have given them the status of organizer. We thereby recognize that all observable behaviours do not exercise an equivalent influence on genesis.

In saying this are we implying that the reorganizing action depends on the privileged behaviour considered in isolation, when it appears for the first time? Certainly not. We do not attribute this capacity to the behaviour itself as a final product. Certainly the organizer is recognized by means of observable data: such as regularities identified beforehand and for which the emergence would be the indication of the presence of a new operator. Starting from these indications (confirmed and validated within the limits mentioned), we infer a status of potential organizer to this behaviour.

However, the organizing action of this privileged (and its reorganizing action in relation to the pre-existing organizations) depends more precisely on several factors which intervene in chain during its emergence phase behaviour:

First, the phenomenon of emergence must correspond to a construction effectively stemming from the observed behaviour. Let us consider an example, reported by one of us, concerning retarded children able to reproduce, in a familiar context, a system of previously learned rules (a series of correspondence rules), but unable to abstract it in a new situation (coordination of rules of correspondence in a game of covariations). In this case no systematic generalization of the presumed system of rules can be detected in other classes of situations where it normally appears synchronously. In the same way, with five year old kindergarden children we encountered similar cases with other systems of rules. It is obvious that the diagnostic of "organizer" cannot be based on the selection of a single indication. Here, as elsewhere, a cluster of indications (in codified classes of situations) is the only means of pertinently establishing the effective construction of a new system of behaviour. We recognize the presence of a new operator when the indications from a coherent whole and express the action of rules belonging to the same category. It would seem appropriate at this point to investigate the conditions of this effective construction.

Second, the bringing into play of constructive processes depends on the functioning modalities of the last system of rules that is generated. These modalities are considered as favourable when they correspond to a very diversified utilization of this system, generalized in space and extended in time according to certain limits not yet completely defined (Orsini-Bouichou, 1982, 1986; Desprels-Fraysse & Fraysse, 1978, 1979). Here the point is to see the extended functioning of the previous system, in a zone located beyond the limits it had in the period of its formation. Let us consider, by way of example, research on the operator which engenders the relation of alternance (Orsini-Bouichou, Malacria-Rocco, Rohrer, 1985). It concerns a game of free sequential combinations (the subject has to construct dominoes, one after the other, choosing freely for each item two distinct parts, from an almost limitless stock offered to him. The first rule applied (around three or four years) corresponds to an opposition of minimal difference, generally the colour (almost alike). A year later the difference consists of a more marked degree: the associated objects differ, most often by two criteria. Towards five-six years, the dominant combinations are based on the maximum difference (the search for the opposite). Our interpretation of this data is in terms of evolution of the functioning of the most recently established system towards a greater variability. Easily mastering the previously formed and practised systems the children find themselves in a position of greater freedom. From then on they will seek to increase the variability of his behaviour. Exploratory reactions will multiply and the child will present an apparent instability in his functioning. It is for this reason that we propose, depending on the phase of functioning of the cognitive system, to appeal to two distinct and apparently opposed models: the tension induction model and the tension reduction model. The first is appropriate for taking the formation phases of the new cognitive systems into account; the second represents an attempt at identifying existing cognitive systems. Both models seem to us equally pertinent, but applicable to different moments of cognitive functioning. In each of the two phases thereby identified we claim that cognitive functioning and genesis are closely linked. The differential method will allow us to confirm this hypothesis. Retarded children (Orsini-Bouichou, 1982) maintain, after the phase of formation of the most recent system, a mode of behaviour characterized by weak internal variability. They seem to be stuck in this state and confine themselves to quasi-reproductions. On the other hand, precocious children seek variability and novelty. In support of this hypothesis we would evoke the importance of exploratory behaviour in young animals (Orsini, 1957), in precocious children (Planche, 1985) and its weakness in retarded children (Paour et al., 1985). With the multiplication of exploratory reactions the subject reaches a higher risk functioning zone.

Third, this mode of risky functioning will contribute, according to the composition of the external environment [6], to the more or less rapid construction of the new cognitive system. The environment offers a series of incentives or perturbations which will be integrated differently by different modes of functioning.

The subjects who are "explorers" seek other information contained in their environment: covariances and incompatibilities. This new information, cannot enter into the previous system, which becomes increasingly unstable. This is followed by the (provisory) destruction of the old systems of rules which are submitted to a new treatment. Basing ourselves on the study (Orsini-Bouichou, 1982) of the evolution of these systems in the child (and following the example of other biological evolutions: Jacob, 1970; Atlan, 1972) we will surmise that this treatment will consists of arranging them (among themselves) in order to integrate them into a higher system, which results in the construction of a new operator. The representation of old systems, the projects and expectations concerning the new hypothesis play a fundamental role which we are at present attempting to clarify. The subjects identified as being passive avoid, contrarily to the "explorers", "novelties" which could not enter into the pre-existing systems. The latter thus function in closed circuit which results in more or less stereotyped productions. Resorting to a plurality of methods allows us, here again, to test these conjectures. In various studies with Hurtig (work in progress) we have employed the differential method. We were thus able to note that precocious children, who are characterised by their exploratory behaviour, generally are of high SES. It would seem plausible to surmise the presence of a relationship between each of these functioning modes and the particular background, which accentuates the aforementioned functional specificities. We do not pretend to give a causal significance to this relationship, we would simply point out that at the moment we approach our subjects, at time "t", there is a significant conjunction between these two variables.

The use of a provoked intervention offers however the possibility of going beyond the simple observation mentioned in the preceding paragraph. In our research the intervention is aimed at modifying the environment in two ways: with "normal" children we offer an environment we think pertinent (Orsini-Bouichou, 1978). We propose varied games which presuppose latent new covariances. The setting up of these situations arouses expectations, explicit or not, and deceptions (retroactions, overt or not, concerning the possible failure of their attempt). With the retarded we offer a "prosthetic environment" which selects the information and progressively distributes it (following a hierarchical sequence); moreover this sort of aid facilitates all of the processes of metacognition in encouraging in the child, indirectly, the construction of individual representations. In any case, the partner-experimenter neither expresses directly, nor makes known to the subject the expected behaviour which could be generated from the new operator.

The intervention of our inductions using different populations has enabled us to illustrate the role of environment prior to (perhaps) demonstrating it. An undoubtedly heuristic field of research is presented to us.

Fourth, the new operator, during its installation and exercise, will provoke a reorganization whose rhythm and generalization will vary from one individual to another according to both the individual behavioural context and the particular background of each individual.

Thus the synchronic analysis complements the diachronic analysis. The former presupposes an open scheme of analysis framework as advocated by van Geert (1983); a multitude of terms can intervene: variables linked to age, to the different learning situations experienced by the child (in his scholastic and familial environments), to the type of language and culture related to his environment, effects due to modifications taking place during physical maturation, in his life style (familial and scholastic) and including real or imaginary events.... We are in complete agreement with Gréco when he states he is not

> "convaincu de l'idée que les schémas servant à l'analyse diachronique au niveau du temps long de la genése soient identiques aux schémas utilisés dans une analyse de type synchronique" (convinced by the idea that models used for diachronic analysis when the genesis is very extended in time are identical to models used in a synchronic analysis) (Gréco, 1985, p. 27).

However, it is clear that in pursuing the study of change, in the course of development, the researcher, being referred to the level of the individual, must inevitably come across the junction point of these two analyses. We are thus involved in a linked research undertaking which, by the utilization (succesively and in combination) of several approaches, allows us to better circumscribe the phenomena of development. These phenomena are complex and seem both discontinuous and continuous, according to the particular temporal reference one adopts. They appear to be situated at the meeting point of several types of interdependence: functioning and genesis, and functioning and environment, (environment in the sense of generalized training system or braking system). We abandon the old dichotomies: development/learning, general/singular. Henceforth it seems possible to undertake research (at a high cost) which can claim to progressively circumscribe the conditions and modalities of change, during development.

NOTES

(1) We would like to thank our colleague Michel Hurtig for his kind help and David Feltham who translated our text.

(2) Laboratoire de Psychologie de l'Enfant et de Psychologie Génétique, CREPCO (associé au CNRS), Université de Provence, 29 ave Robert Schumann. 13.621. Aix-en-Provence, France.

(3) We use the term scheme in the sense given to it by Piaget when he described certain categories of behaviour in young children (for example, circular reactions and the different forms of prehension). This use of the term corresponds to the most widely known formulation:

     "un scheme est la structure ou l'organisation des actions, telle qu'elle se transfère ou se généralise, lors de la répétition de cette action en des circonstances semblables ou analogues" (a scheme is the structure or organization of actions when that structure or organization is transferred or generalized during the repetition of the action in similar or analogous circumstances) (Piaget, 1966, p. 11).

(4) The subjects draw from a stock composed of numerous objects (more or less varied, according to the situation) and randomly mixed. They choose the objects one by one and inserts them in the apparatus: an elongated "pencil box" comprising 24 compartments of which 23 are hidden. They perform a sequential combination according to a rule they have elaborated themselves.

(5) We were able to identify only a very small number of rules whereas theoretically one could predict an extremely large number of possibilities.

(6) It should be noted that we do not mention modifications of the internal environment, the subjects' representations, their state of knowledge, what Vergnaud calls the conceptual field (1982). However, it is obvious that under the influence of cognitive activity based on the pre-existing systems, the subjects constructed new objects of knowledge and imagined the properties of the objects differently. This topic of research does not enter directly into our present concerns.

REFERENCES

Aboubakar, I. (1982). Etude comparée de l'apparition des invariants de quantité chez des enfants nigériens appartenant à différents milieux: commerçant, potier, éleveur, agriculteur. Thèse de doctorat de troisième cycle. Université de Provence (unpublished).

Ajuriaguerra, J. de (1974). Manuel de psychiatrie de l'enfant (2nd ed.). Paris: Masson, (2 ème édition).

Atlan, H. (1972). L'organisation biologique et la théorie de l'information. Paris: Hermann.

Bates, E., Beijni, I., Camaioni, L. & Volterra, V. (1979). The emergence of symbol cognition and communication in infancy. New York: Academic Press.

Bourmault, J.Y. & Meynier, G. (1982). Induction opératoire et aide psychopédagogique chez des enfants en échec scolaire. Unpublished Research Report: Université de Provence.

Cunha de Carvalho, L., Hurtig, M. & Orsini-Bouichou, F. (1984). Facteurs culturels, environment familial et apprentissage cognitif. Psychologie Française, 29, 38-39.

Desprels-Fraysse, A. & Fraysse, J.C. (1977). Induction des structures logiques élémentaires chez des enfants d'âge préscolaire et analyse fonctionelle des comportements observés. Thèse de doctorat de troisième cycle. Université de Provence (unpublished).

Desprels-Fraysse, A. & Fraysse, J.C. (1978). Analyse fonctionelle des comportements préopératoires. Cahiers de Psychologie, 21, 163-183.

Desprels-Fraysse, A. & Fraysse, J.C., Orsini-Bouichou, F., Paour, J.L. (1979). Genese et déterminants de la pensée opératoire. Bulletin de Psychologie, 340, 523-531.

Florès, C. & Orsini-Bouichou, F. (1979). Induction et formation de la pensée logique chez l'enfant. Unpublished Research Report.

Georges, C. & Richard, J.F. (1982). Contribution récente à la psychologie de l'apprentissage et à la pédagogie. Revue Française de Pédagogie, 67, 67-91.

Gréco, P. (1985). Réduction et construction. Archives de Psychologie, 53, 21-35.

Gagné, R.M. (1968). Contribution of learning to human development. Psychological Review, 75, 177-191.

Hurtig, H. & Rondal, J.A. (Eds). (1981). Introduction à la psychologie de l'enfant. Bruxelles: Mardaga.

Jacob, F. (1970). La logique du vivant. Paris: Gallimard.

Jacob, F. (1981). Le jeu des possibles. Paris: Fayard.

Lautrey, J. (1980). Classe sociale, milieu familial, intelligence. Paris: Presses Universitaires de France.

Noizet, G. (1965). Verbalisation et performance. Cahiers de Psychologie, 8, 173-180.

Orsini, F. (1957). Conduite et besoin d'exploration chez les mammifères. L'Année Psychologique, 54, 99-119.

Orsini, F. (1965). Régularités et système de relations chez l'enfant. Cahiers de Psychologie, 8, 143-155.

Orsini-Bouichou, F. (1975). Régularités dans les organisations spontanées chez l'enfant et genèse des comportements cognitifs. Thèse de doctorat d'Etat, Université René Descartes, Paris (unpublished).

Orsini-Bouichou, F. (1982). L'intelligence de l'enfant, ontogénèse des invariants. Paris: C.N.R.S.

Orsini-Bouichou, F. & Malacria-Rocco, J. (1978). Des régularités à l'induction opératoire. Cahiers de Psychologie, 21, 163-182.

Orsini-Bouichou, F., Malacria-Rocco, J. & Rohrer, B. (in press). Statut et autonomie de l'apprentissage, methode d'étude du fonctionnement et du développement cognitifs. Archives de Psychologie, 53, 513-522.

Orsini-Bouichou, F., Malacria-Rocco, J. & Rohrer, B. (1985). The same and not the same. Cahiers de Psychologie Cognitive, 5, 324.

Paour, J.L. (1975). Effets d'un entrainement cognitif sur la compréhension et la production d'énoncés passifs chez des enfants déficients mentaux. Etudes de Linguistiques Appliquées, 20, 88-110.

Paour, J.L. (1979). Apprentissage de la notion de conservation et induction de la pensée opératoire concrète chez les débiles mentaux. In R. Zazzo (Ed.), Les Débilités Mentales. Paris: Collin.

Paour, J.L. (1980). Construction et fonctionnement des structures opératoires concrètes chez l'enfant débile mental. Apport des expériences d'apprentissage et d'induction opératoires. Thèse de doctorat de troisième cycle, Université de Provence (unpublished).

Paour, J.L. (1981). Apprentissage des structures logiques et développement du langage chez les arriérés mentaux. In J.A. Rondal, J.L. Lambert & H.H. Chipman (Eds.), Psycholinguistique et handicap mental. Bruxelles: Mardaga.

Paour, J.L., Galas, D., Malacria-Rocco, J. & Soavi, G. (1985). L'apprentissage opératoire chez les retardés mentaux. Archives de Psychologie, 53, 477-484.

Paour, J.L. (in press). De l'induction des structures logiques à la modification du fonctionnement cognitif chez les retardés intellectuels. Revue Suisse de Psychologie.

Piaget, J. (1936). La naissance de l'intelligence chez l'enfant. Neuchâtel. Delachaux & Niestlé (The Origins of Intelligence in the Child. Harmondsworth: Penguin, 1977).

Piaget, J. & Inhelder, B. (1966). La psychologie de l'enfant. Paris: Presses Universitaires (The Psychology of the Child. New York: Basic Books, 1969).

Planche, P. (in press). Modalités fonctionnelles et conduites de résolution de problèmes chez l'enfant précoce de Cinq, six, sept ans d'âge chronologique. Archives de Psychologie, 53, 411-415.

Richelle, M. (1976). Manuel de Psychologie. Bruxelles: Mardaga.

Scandura, J.M. (1973). Structural learning. London: Gordon & Breach.

Soavi, G. (1986). Une analyse du fonctionnement cognitif à propos de la construction de la relation de couple (genèse observée et provoque), chez l'enfant retardé mental. Thèse de doctorat de troisième cycle. Université de Provence (unpublished).

Spitz, R. (1973). De la naissance à la parole. Paris: Presses Universitaires de France.

Van Geert P. (1983). The development of perception, cognition and language. A theoretical approach. London: Routledge & Kegan Paul.

Vergnaud, G. (1982). Cognitive and developmental psychology and research in mathematic education: some theoretical

and   methodological   issues.   For   the   Learning   of
Mathematics, 3, 31-41.

Wallon, H. (1941).   L'évolution psychologique de l'enfant (5th
Ed. 1957). Paris: Collin.

Theory Building in Developmental Psychology
P.L.C. van Geert (editor)
© Elsevier Science Publishers B.V. (North-Holland), 1986

9

Developmental Sequences

Some characteristics and an empirical demonstration

Jan ter Laak

The first section of this paper discusses
development from the viewpoint of behaviourism,
the viewpoint of the individual differences
approach and the viewpoint of the information
processing approach. It is concluded that none
of these approaches offers a genuine
developmental perspective on behavioural change.
In the second section, aspects of a truly
developmental perspective are discussed,
characterized by the study of vertical structure
of behaviour, i.e. developmental sequences. In
the final section, the developmental sequences
view is illustrated in an empirical study of the
vertical structure of a school readiness
curriculum.

The aim of developmental psychology is to describe and to
understand the changes and the constancies in the organization
of behaviour at a certain point in one's lifetime and during
the whole lifespan. No one will deny that behaviour is
organized, i.e that it is not random and that the organization
changes in the course of time. Whether a developmental
perspective is necessary or even useful, however, is sometimes
disclaimed. The reason for such a state of affairs is the fact
that three major goals have dominated psychology. The first
goal is to establish procedures and theories to modify and
explain behaviour. The second is to assess and explain
individual differences in behaviour. The third is to describe
and explain human cognition as symbol manipulation and
information processing. The description and understanding of

how behaviour changes are less emphasized. The study of
behaviour change is not absent, however, take for instance the
work of Piaget. More recently, there is a revival with authors
like Fischer (1980) and Case (1985) who have put forward a new
"comprehensive picture" of development.

In the first section of this paper, the construction of
development from a behaviouristic viewpoint, from the
viewpoint of individual differences and from the viewpoint of
functional processes will be described. Although behaviourists
would never write books on development as such, their
epistemological and methodological orientation is still
present in developmental psychology. The construction of
development as the predictability of individual differences
during the course of time is also still vivid. The most
time-honoured framework, however, is the information
processing approach. This framework plays a vital role in the
explanation of cognitive develoment.

In the above mentioned approaches, the meaning of
"development" is derived from something else or is second
order. That does not disclaim the fact that aspects of the
aforementioned approaches are useful for developmental
psychology.

In the second section, a developmental perspective will
be discussed. This perspective implies the attribution of a
direct and definite meaning to the concept of development.
This attribution is impossible without referring to the state
of biological science at the beginning of the twentieth
century, and to the work of Jean Piaget, Heinz Werner and many
others. Because of later severe criticisms of Piaget's
developmental psychology, the neglect of Werner's work and of
possibly meaningful alternatives, the developmental
perspective has been nearly abandoned. Some characteristics
of a genuine developmental perspective and its methodological
implications will be described. This perspective includes,
among other things, the study of vertical structure of
behaviour, i.e. developmental sequences, which will constitute
the main topic of the present paper.

In the final section, some aspects of the developmental

perspective are demonstrated in an empirical study of a school readiness curriculum. With many others, this curriculum shares a developmentally inspired structure. The claim is of course that the supposed structure has empirical reality, and that school readiness will indeed improve if this structure is taken into account. The major question of the study we will discuss in the third section is whether or not the developmental structure appears in the data.

DEVELOPMENT AS BEHAVIOURAL CHANGES, INDIVIDUAL DIFFERENCES AND FUNCTIONAL PROCESSES

THE BEHAVIOURAL VIEW.

In the twenties, behaviourism promised an independent science of behaviour. Philosophical questions like mind-body relations and biological problems about the evolution of organisms were abandoned.

The subject matter of psychology was defined as "matter in motion", i.e. observable behaviour. Theoretical behaviourism initially searched for general laws of learning,, much like natural laws. Studies were predominantly carried out with animals. In the fifties, learning studies with children were started (e.g. White, 1970). The aim was the assessment of the generality of learning laws. The generality became questionable because of the variety of results in children of different ages. Spiker (1966) stated that children could not learn anything at any age. This was explained by limitations of the organism at a certain point in its development. These limitations, however, were believed to belong to the biological, and not to the behavioural domain. More recent forms of behaviourism accept all kinds of learning and motivational processes, such as attention, retention, memory sensorimotor reproduction, reinforcement, motivation, etc. Despite this enlargement (see e.g. Bandura and Walters, 1963), accounts for changes in processes and behaviours with increasing age were absent.

Operant   behaviourism   emphasized   the   control   and
modification of behaviour. Bijou and Baer (1960) applied
control and modification techniques to children. Although not
oriented to any theory, Baer stated
>   "... development   is   behavioural   change   which
>   requires programming and programming requires time,
>   but not enough to call it age". (Baer, 1970, p. 245)

This and similar remarks were illustrated by research in which
training changed the age and the sequence in which subjects
succeeded in discrimination tasks.

Except in applied behaviour analysis, studies of learning
in   children   declined   precipitously   the   last   20   years
(Stevenson, 1983). Apart from the emphatic presence of Piaget,
it was caused by
>   "... an incompatibility between the basic assumption
>   that learning mechanisms operate in the same way
>   regardless of context and the mounting realization
>   that people's learning and remembering are crucially
>   affected by what they already know" (Siegler, 1983a,
>   p. 263).

Although the amount of learning studies in children
decreased   rapidly,   epistemological   and   methodological
behaviourism is still present in developmental psychology. For
example, Brainerd (1978) denied the scientific value of the
stage concept since it failed to specify any target behaviour
and any antecedent-consequent relation. Equating a scientific
approach to development with the experimental research
paradigm is well suited to a logical positivistic model of
explanation (Kitchener, 1983). Brainerd (1977) also criticized
the   hypothesis   of   interaction   between   the   organism's
developmental level and learning for methodological reasons.
He re-analyzed 13 studies in which the effect of learning was
dependent on the developmental level (Brainerd, 1977). The
author found very small differences between between pre- and
posttests   of   transitional   and   pre-operational   children.
Brainerd stated that the difference scores were too small to
warrant the conclusion of stage-dependent learning. Brainerd's
conclusion can be challenged, however. The score range was

small, mostly three classes, and few subjects participated, maximally 12. Since Brainerd used difference scores, there was, in his opinion evidence for stage-dependent learning if the means of the pre- and posttest differed, the measurements were reliable and the pre- and posttest scores were not correlated. Thus, Brainerd conceived of the conservation sequence as a classic psychometric unidimensional construct. However, the authors of the 13 criticized studies, among whom many Genevans, regarded the conservation sequence as a set of qualitative, i.e. not unidimensional steps in a coherent whole.

Behaviourism constructs development as in- and decrease of elementary responses. The adherence of behaviouristic authors to the logical positivism of the thirties -either implicitly or explicitly- has caused their rejection of central developmental concepts like stages, differentiation, hierarchical organization, orthogentic principle, qualitative change, etc. Early logical positivism, and behaviourism with it, was formalistic and static in its conception of science, and as such not well suited for the study of development. On the other hand, behaviourism did provide mechanisms of learning, and stressed justly the necessity of looking for empirical referents for theoretical constructs.

THE INDIVIDUAL DIFFERENCES VIEW.

The study of individual differences originated in Evolution Theory. This theory addressed the question of the origin of different species. Galton studied particularly the "small" variation of biological and behavioural characteristics in only one species, namely man. Partly because of his use of formulas to express the variation, Galton became the first psychometrician. Spearman (1904) took individual differences as a point of departure to test his hypotheses on the structure of intelligence. These studies were carried out with adult subjects. Binet and Simon (1905) designed tests for children. The development of intelligence was not viewed as an explicit problem. They assumed a linear relationship between age and intelligence. In the "structures of intelligence" described by Spearman, Thurstone and Guilford, a developmental perspective is absent. In short, many instruments for the assessment of behavioural characteristics offer norms for different age groups while lacking a view on the development of these characteristics. Despite the non-developmental character of the aforementioned approaches, developmentalists were still happy to have the "objective instruments" of the psychometricians at their disposal. These instruments made comparisons of behaviour at different points in a lifetime possible to a certain degree. Much research on the stability of intelligence and personality was carried out (Bloom, 1964; Mischel, 1968; Block, 1971), but there existed virtually no research on change and development (McCall, 1976, 1977, 1981).

The study of individual differences offered developmentalists further correlational techniques, especially factor analysis. The factor-analytic framework is sometimes developmentally interpreted. In course of time factors can emerge, disappear and change (Sternberg and Powell, 1983). Baltes and Nesselroade (1973), for instance, simulated with help of differing scores on five tests "differentiation" of intelligence with increasing age.

The individual difference orientation on behaviour is inherently non-developmental. The instruments and data-analytic techniques can however be used to confirm or reject developmental hypothesis which have been formulated outside the individual differences framework.

THE INFORMATION PROCESSING VIEW.

Research in cognition is presently dominated by the information processing framework. This framework contains a language to describe cognitive units like "scripts", "frames" and "representations". The course of processing information is described by means of flow charts, tree structures or production systems. The methods employed are precise and flexible: analyses of reaction times, eye movements, protocols and errors are used.

Although the "bottom up" and "top down" flow charts for the description of task activities , and the frequent use of Piagetian tasks give the impression of developmental sequences thinking, most of the research is non-developmental (Siegler, 1983b). Changes with increasing age are interpreted as differences in experience (expert-novice comparisons), or as individual differences in cognitive style. The information processing equipment is considered complete at about six years of age (Huttenlocher and Burke, 1976). Later changes in cognitive proceses are abundant, such as changes in strategies of rehearsal, semantic organization, elaboration, meta-cognition and knowledge base. These changes are however seldom interpreted as being developmental changes. With respect to the latter point, Spiker (1977) saw no difference between behaviouristic and information processing approaches. Although information processing analysis is largely non- developmental, one may profit from its task descriptions, units and methods . An integration with studies on cognitive development seems possible. The recent work of Case (1985), for instance, is a voluminous attempt to integrate develomental levels with information processing abilities.

SUMMARY.

We have seen that empirical developmental psychology depended largely upon the experimental and the individual difference approaches. Presently, the information processing approach, although partly non-developmental, provides useful tools for the study of cognitive development. Nevertheless, neither of these approaches provides a genuine developmental perspective. The meanings of change and development are derived from other approaches. Developmental studies based upon the three aforementioned approaches have no common agenda of goals and methods. A truly developmental attitude and perspective is needed.

A DEVELOPMENTAL PERSPECTIVE.

THE MEANING OF "DEVELOPMENT".

A developmental perspective consists of a direct attribution of a definite meaning to the concept of development, in order to reach specific goals. This implies that the developmental perspective is not defined by a population (e.g. children) or by certain behaviours (e.g. cognition, emotion). It also means that development is not defined as a second order or rest category, e.g every behaviour that is not learned or learnable.

The attribution of meaning to the concept of development started long before the official installation of psychology. Within the short history of psychology the definitions of development as stated by Piaget and Werner have dominated. Their definitions are partly justly criticized and partly wrongly understood. Leaning upon these authors, some characteristics of a developmental perspective can be - formulated. Because the perspective contains a demise of the individual differences and the experimental approaches, some specific methodological implications should be taken into account. The contemporary developmental perspective, on the other hand, has lost faith in the regular succession of broad stages which is believed to terminate when individuals have achieved insight into the fundamentally rational and logico-mathematical structure of the physical and the social world. The approach put forward in the present paper consists of local developmental hypotheses about circumscribed behaviours, i.e. the search for developmental sequences.

In the history of the concept of development, Aristotle is the first to have given a definite meaning to development. He saw a similarity in the meaning and course of human ontogenesis, the genesis of living beings, and the history of the world. Aristotle designed a "scale of nature" which consists of eleven steps. The steps formed an ascending progression in complexity and perfection. The scale was built up with classes, which differed by means of qualitative characteristics, for example the possession of blood, breeding habits, ability to move oneself, etc. The Aristotelian analogy tradition has been followed up through nineteenth century biology (Gould, 1977).

A second source of meaning for the concept of development is the idea of biology as natural history, stemming from the nineteenth century. Darwin (1859) stated that biological species originated gradually from each other by natural selection. This implied a radical rupture from Aristotle whose opinion was that species were qualitative, immutable, logical classes (Feldman and Toulmin, 1975). Another element of evolution theory, recapitulation, was influential in developmental psychology. For example, Baldwin (1895) wanted to study the development of children in order to get insight in the intellectual history of the human species. In biological theory, recapitulation disappeared rapidly. As early as 1888, the biologist His criticized Haeckel's recapitulationistic studies as being "rigid morphological diagrams, abstracted by pure logical operations" (cited in Gould, 1977, p. 295). In developmental psychology, recapitulation lived much longer, for instance in Piaget's use of a particular version of this notion.

A third source of meaning was the biological study of embryological development. Some characteristics of embryological development, for example the view of development as a process with a beginning, a direction and an end are applied to behavioural development. The course of development is organized: parts and systems of parts become hierarchically organized wholes. Some changes are irreversible, some cyclical, some may arrest. These and similar principles may be observed in the classical theories of cognitive and mental development.

THE MEANING OF DEVELOPMENT IN THE TRADITIONAL THEORIES.

The above mentioned sources of meaning do not directly bear upon behavioural development. The meanings can be used as fruitful analogies, which for instance Piaget, as a biologist, profited from.

Piaget attributed a specific meaning to the concept of development. He made this choice in order to serve a rather broad goal, i.e. a contribution to the philosophical question of the relation between subject and object, between the knower and the known. The founding idea was that every psychological explanation of human knowledge started in biology and ended in logic (Piaget, 1970). From the evolution theory and the embryology of his time, Piaget borrowed the idea of development as irreversible transformations of structures. Changes were understood as evolving from each other in a certain pattern without the possibility of returning to genetically earlier structures. Examples of these changes were the evolution of biological species and embryological and cognitive development. Biology also provided the notion that functions were permanent and in equilibrium, take for instance the analogy between homeostasis and the reversible thinking operations of the concrete operatory child. Logic, more precisely a certain kind of logic, namely "pschologic", had a double function: it was the end- or comparison point of thinking, and it was a model to describe and understand empirical cognitive phenomena (e.g. the logical groupings). Human thinking was at the same time reversibly permanent (functional adaptation) and irreversibly changing (it expressed itself in genetically and historically evolving structures).

Piaget wanted to be a scientist and not only a philosopher. He confronted his construction with empirical "facts". He thougt it possible to gain insight in philosophical questions by studying the history of western science and human cognitive development. The individual cognitive development was supposed to show genetically evolving qualitatively different structures. The developmental psychology of Piaget consisted of the continual identification and empirical demonstration of the transforming thought structures. The functional aspect, i.e. how thought functions are equilibrated, and under which conditions the functions expressed a structure was less thoroughly scrutinized (but see Piaget, 1975).

The theory driven search for transformations of structures resulted in the stages of development. For each stage one or more behavioural phenomena were searched in order to demonstrate the structures. Examples of these phenomena are object permanence, or the lack of it, conservation of matter, and inductive and deductive reasoning. Many tasks and tests were designed for concepts of western rational thinking, for instance life (biology), inclusion, propositional thinking (logic), and concepts from mathematics, e.g. space, time, causality, number, velocity, etc. The acquisition of the mature or complete form of these concepts was sequentially described and connected to the broad stages.

Development had a distinct meaning and a specific goal in the Piagetian tradition. There was a relatively complete theory of development. There were units (circular reactions, schemes, structures,) and basic processes (assimilation, accomodation,..). Development was viewed as a specific kind of change. Sequences in the acquisition of concepts and determinants of development were described (organic growth, physical and logico-mathematical experience, and equilibration). Finally, tasks and tests were designed in order to confront hypotheses about organization and change with -carefully selected- facts.

Werner's developmental psychology consisted also of a perspective that was applicable to a broad range of phenomena, among which behavioural phenomena. The theory also served a broad goal: the discovery of "the one in the many" (Kaplan, 1983). Werner became famous mainly because of his concepts for describing the course of development, such as differentiation and hierarchical organization. There also was a concept for "good development", the orthogenetic principle. This principle did not have the status of empirical fact, rather it made the

judgment   of   the   contribution   of   certain   factors   to
developmental disorders possible.

TOWARDS A CONTEMPORARY PERSPECTIVE.

The develomental psychologies of Piaget and Werner were
severely criticized and partly neglected. Piaget's structural
interpretation of cognitive achievements such as conservation
was regarded as unproven and sometimes wrong. All kinds of
task   variables   and   functional   processes   of   perception,
learning,   language   comprehension,   etc.,   were   considered
responsible for these allegedly developmental achievements.
Although partly wrongly understood, Piaget's statement that
structures were not "learned" provoked many learning studies.
These studies led to the conclusion that Piaget underestimated
learning   (Beilin,   1978,   1980).   Fundamental   concepts   and
notions   were   criticized: stages   suggested   a   firmness   of
organization   that   was   not   empirically   supported   (Flavell,
1977, 1982a; Kagan, 1980); stages were lacking in explanatory
power (Brainerd, 1978). The determinants of development were
vague   and   unspecified   (equilibration,   logico-mathematical
experience, etc.) and incomplete because of disregard of the
social   environment   (Vygotsky,   1934;   Bruner,   1973).   Also
Piaget's methodology was criticized: the "méthode clinique"
was unstandardized and logic and empirical knowledge were
confused (see for example Philips and Kelley, 1975).

   Much   of   the   criticism   of   Piaget's   theory   is   surely
justified. However, Piaget's attitude and epistemological
standpoint have not become obsolete. They still have to
function   in   any   discussion   on   developmental   psychology
(Beilin, 1981). Much modern structural developmental research
(Kohlberg, Selman, and Case, among others) is inspired by
Piaget. The great number of tasks that Piaget designed
continue to be investigated. It should be noted, however, that
although Piaget's tasks are still part of current research
programmes,   the   theories   in   which   they   now   function   are
considerably more modest and make fewer claims than Piaget's

theory of the inevitable course of development to an all-embracing logico- mathematical understanding of the physical and social world. Nevertheless, no modern approach to development can dispense with Piaget's perspective and the large quantity of research it inspired.

A developmental perspective must be a perspective first of all. It is a way of looking at behaviour: how it is organized, and how its organization changes. It is a way of transforming data into "facts". The use of perspective also implies avoidance of "theory". Theory suggests, even in developmental books, a number of axiomas, a calculus, empirical definitions for all concepts, and a model (see Reese and Overton, 1970). This conception of theory is allied to the logical positivistic view. In developmental psychology, theories are much more informal. There are (historically) developing networks of concepts, taxonomies and "local hypotheses". The perspective includes a goal, i.e. the beginning, direction and acquisition of mature forms. A mature form is not meant to be a universal or metaphysical entity. Rather, it acts as a comparison point for the actual organization of a developing subject.

Secondly, relations between behaviours are emphasized in a developmental perspective. Behaviours are conceived of as "concatenated patterns" (Kaplan, 1964), as organized wholes. Constructs like stage, coherence (Stroufe, 1979), structure, "Gestalt", etc. refer to patterns of behaviour. It is a continual task to critically examine whether the aforementioned theoretical constructs have sufficient and correct empirical references. The empirical mapping of these constructs is a controversial point in psychology in general. Kagan reproached developmentalists with their continual supposing "connectivity" and their eagerness to tell "coherent stories" (Kagan, 1980, 1983 respectively). These remarks are correct. Incorrect however is the suggestion that the search for coherence is illegitimate.

Flavell analysed the Piagetian stage concept thoroughly. Although he admitted that there must be some "glue" in behaviours, he doubted the existence of stages. Flavell (1982,

p. 17) gave his best guess

"...human cognitive growth is generally not very
stage like in the horizontal high homogeneity
meaning of the term" (emphasis from Flavell, 1982).
In his presidential address for developmental psychologists,
Flavel stated

"...there is really something generally stage-like
about the child's cognitive development, if we knew
where and how to look" (Flavell, 1982a, p. 9).
One can agree with this last statement.

Thirdly, because a developmental perspective does not
coincide with an individual differences and an experimental
orientation, there is the returning question of the tuning of
hypotheses, the data and the data analyses (see also Appelbaum
and McCall, 1983). One has to identify behaviours and model or
represent their organization at one particular moment and
during the course of time. In the Piagetian tradition, some
behaviours are logically modeled, which was criticized because
of the moderate empirical support. Logical positivistic and
experimental modeling demands antecedent-consequent causal
relations. This modeling is not always and only suited for
every developmental question. For the understanding of
development, other types of explanation must be allowed, such
as formal and final causes, narrative and "how-is-it-possible"
explanations (Kitchener, 1983).

For the assessment of behavioural organization modern
psychometrics is useful. It offers a lot of techniques: metric
and non-metric factor analyses, scaling techniques, ordering
theoretical models and multivariate techniques. There is
however no simple one-to-one relation between techniques and
research questions. There are many models for the hypotheses,
which are often too imprecise to allow one to choose between
the models. A pragmatic solution is either to look at
convergence of the data patterns under different models (an
example will be shown in the next section, see also ter Laak,
1983), or to choose the model with the best fit for the data.
Kingma (1983), for example, used four models of scaling
seriation responses. One of them, the Mokken scale, showed the

best fit.

Within a developmental perspective we search for the organization of behaviour at a certain point in time, and more importantly, during the course of time. In the "stages" research, the emphasis was on broad clusters of behaviour at a certain point in time (the so-called "structures d'ensembles"). There has always been a small and presently growing amount of research on the changing of rather circumscribed sets of behaviour in the course of time. So developmental sequences are described for the concept of justice (Damon, 1977), aspects of social cognition (Selman, 1980), conventional and moral rules (Tisak and Turiel, 1984), and many "Piagetian" concepts like number, life, velocity (Siegler, 1983a), formal and post-formal thought (Demetriou and Efklides, 1985), to mention but a few. In addition to the growing empirical research on developmental sequences, the literature also contains conceptual analyses aimed at defining these sequences more precisely.

Developmental sequences concern the vertical structure of behaviour. They usually refer to specific and circumscribed behaviour. Flavell (1982b, p. 18) called sequences "... the very wire and glue of development". He suggested that at present we live in a particularly exciting time for studying developmental sequences, because of the availability of statistical techniques, interesting substantive behaviours, and ongoing attempts at theory building. Current conceptual analyses of developmental sequences do not point in one direction, but future discussion will probably accomplish a more coherent and complete picture. A few contributions to this discussion will now be mentioned. Sigel, Bisanz and Bisanz (1983) consider sequences to be states, which are structured wholes with increasing differentiation and integration. Developmental sequences are invariant and one should look for main sequences. The authors put forward that little has been said thus far about transition mechanisms. The latter statement is also made by Kessen (1983) and Aebli (1984). Campbell and Richie (1983) are the most demanding authors with regard to the problem of developmental sequences.

They ask for a theoretical account of underlying processes and
for the true precursors of mature forms. They demand a
construction of sequences from the standpoint of the organism.
Thus, analyses viewing development as a process proceeding
towards a specific mature form, known only to the
psychologist, are regarded with suspicion. Analyses of tasks
and activities of the subject necessary to solve the tasks are
in their opinion not satisfactory. With regard to describing
transitions, they quote Flavell (1972), but accept only
inclusion and modification. Addition, substitution, and
probably mediation are not effective transitional mechanisms
in a developmental sequence. Fischer and Silvern (1985)
describe some criteria for developmental sequences and
characterize levels or steps of sequences as structured
wholes. They expect relations of sequences with increasing
age. The change in behaviour has to be qualitative and
discontinuous. Learning is expected to be stage-specific. The
authors put the criteria in a coherent framework. Corell and
Furman (1984) expected the transitions within developmental
sequences to be of long duration and irreversible.

SUMMARY.

    We have stated that a developmental perspective requires
a direct attribution of meaning to the concept of development.
Historically, this meaning was influenced by the Aristotelian
analogy tradition and by the biology of the end of the
nineteenth century. The traditional developmental views of
Piaget and Werner relied heavily on the Evolution Theory and
the embryology of their time. Piaget in particular has built a
complete theory of development. This theory was partly justly
critized because of - among other things - the lack of
empirical support for the broad stages and the logical
modeling. A contemporary perspective however cannot dispense
with Piaget's insights, but has to be more modest concerning
the horizontal and vertical structure of behaviour. We have
described a developmental perspective in which local

developmental hypotheses about circumscribed behaviours, relations between behaviours, and the use of a rich collection of representational models are emphasized. Taking this perspective behaviours are studied in their developmental sequence towards a mature form.

Thus far, the choice for a developmental perspective implies the assertion of relatively simple organizational hypotheses. The assumed developmental sequence has to be demonstrated in the empirical world in order to become a "fact". When the existence of a developmental sequence has been demonstrated, the sequential organization forms the background for the understanding of experimental and environmental influences and for the understanding of individual differences and functional processes.

In the next section the developmental perspective will be demonstrated. First, empirical support will be sought for the assumed developmental sequence of thirteen cognitive aspects of a school readiness curriculum. Second, the data of the thirteen aspects will be analysed in order to identify the existence of a main sequence. Finally, an attempt will be made at understanding experimental and environmental influences, individual differences and functional processes taking the developmental sequences notion as background.

DEVELOPMENTAL LEVELS IN A SCHOOL READINESS CURRICULUM.

TRADITIONAL VIEWS ON DEVELOPMENT AND CLASSROOM EDUCATION.

In designing an educational curriculum choices have to be made about goals, contents, means, teaching methods and their organization and sequencing. The selection of goals, contents, etc. does not belong to the psychological domain.
Psychological knowledge is however relevant for curricula when characteristics of pupils and teachers play a role, for example abilities, motivation and learning, information-processing and developmental processes. The contribution of psychology to curricula reflects the three major goals of

psychology. Also, developmental psychological hypotheses are
used to design curricula.

The behaviouristic experimental orientation was
influential in education. Thorndike was one of the first
psychologists who applied learning principles to classroom
education. This application caused elaboration of and change
in the learning principles (Hilgard and Bower, 1975). Later
Gagné (1965, 1968) depicted human learning as an orderly
progression of more and more complex learning processes. All
sorts of school tasks were analyzed in this way to establish
the necessary learning processes.

The individual differences orientation made tests for
abilites and educational goals available. These instruments
were widely used for diagnostic purposes and for decisions
about school choice. The instruments were criticized because
they offered no insight in learning processes. Cronbach and
Snow (1976) took these criticisms seriously and attempted to
relate individual differences in capacities and personality
characteristics to methods of instruction: (A)ptitude
(T)reatment (I)nteraction research. The results were limited;
only few interactions were found. Modern item-response
"theories" can be considered to be models for a small domain,
namely the domain of a test response. These models can be used
for curricula with specific contents and for evaluation (see
e.g. Spada and Kempf, 1977).

The information processing orientation is presently most
influential. Problem solving has even become an educational
goal. All kinds of school tasks are analyzed in component
steps and flow diagrams, trees and production systems are used
to describe the tasks (see Siegler, 1983b). Expert-novice
studies are carried out in order to discover factors
responsible for the solution of school tasks.

A developmental perspective on education was elaborated
by pupils of Piaget and by Vygotsky, the founder of the
Russian Cultural-Historical tradition. Although Piaget was
only moderately interested in school learning the broad stages
of cognitive development and the descriptions of the
development of many concepts and reasoning processes were

widely used to design curricula (see e.g. Aebli, 1961; Kamii, 1981). In the Russian learning psychology the goal was to establish "full-fledged mental actions". Gal'perin described on a priori grounds five general steps which had all be passed through in a definitive sequence in order to establish "full-fledged" mental actions. These general steps served as a framework for any schoolcurriculum. The steps or "etappes" are considered to be developmentally ordered. The developmental succession required specific educational support (see Van Parreren and Carpay, 1980). Recently several attempts have been made at relating Piaget's structural analyses of several concepts to information processing. In accordance with Piaget's way of analyzing the number concept, Case (1978), for example, distinguished developmental steps in solving addition problems.

DESCRIPTION OF THE CURRICULUM RESEARCH.

The Curriculum.

The curriculum that forms the subject of the present paper, Dumont and Kok's School Readiness Curriculum (Dumont and Kok, 1973), is partly based on a developmental orientation. This curriculum is adapted from an experimental curriculum for young mentally retarded children from Connor and Talbot (1966). School-readiness is divided in several areas, e.g. cognitive and social development, development of play, of handedness, etc. Each area contains several aspects. Each aspect in the curriculum consists of five steps. The steps are sometimes called "developmental levels" and sometimes "subgoals". The first level is named: "not school ready" and the fifth level: "school ready". Each step or level of the curriculum is described by means of achievements and behaviours of the children. The rationale for the five ascending steps of every aspect is not completely clear. Arguments for ascending steps are borrowed from the experience of teachers, from task analyses and - especially for the

cognitive aspects - from Piaget's descriptions of the
acquisition of number and space concepts, of seriation, of the
use of categories, etc.

Research Questions.

The most important question of any curriculum is: Does it
work?; Do pupils profit from participation? In our research we
confined ourselves to the question of the assumed ascending
five steps from each cognitive aspect. Are the steps
empirically ordered as assumed? A second question was the
mutual relation between the several stepwise constructed
cognitive aspects, in other words: is there a "main" sequence.

RESULTS.

The question of developmental order.

    To answer the first question 77 subjects were selected
out of 192 children attending five schools. The subjects
belonged to the lower middle- and middle socio economic class.
All subjects were native Dutch speakers. Their age was between
4 and 7 years. This range was chosen to be sure that the steps
between "not school ready" and "school ready" were present.
Five age groups were formed with age differences of half a
year. Each age group contained at least 15 subjects. The
groups consisted of boys and girls. The age groups differed by
maximally three boys more than girls, or vice versa. The sexes
did not differ significantly on any developmental level. All
chi-squares reached values with a chance of more than 5%.
    Thirteen cognitive aspects were used, such as visual
perception and memory, auditory perception: analysis and
memory, spatial orientation, number concept, etc. For the
complete list see table 2. In the original curriculum each
level is verbally described. Examples of what has to be
achieved for attaining a certain developmental level are

given. In our research we standardized each level by designing an average of three tasks, with a minimum of two, for each level. For each task there were instructions, materials and scoring rules. In designing the tasks, the description of the curriculum was accurately followed. It was however sometimes necessary to elaborate. For example the description of a level of visual memory "a child is able to remember four objects for a short duration" required choices of the objects, duration of looking and reproduction: the objects did not belong to a class, the duration of looking was 5 second and the reproduction was after 10 second. The materials for the different tasks were comparable. They were part of the materials used daily in school. All but one aspect contained 5 levels. Level 4 and 5 of visual memory were put together because no difference was observed. Table 1 gives an example of the first and the fifth level of one aspect: preparatory arithmetic (number concept).

Table 1: The tasks of level 1 and level 5 of the aspect "preparatory arithmetic: number concept".

LEVEL 1.   Ordering of objects on the basis of their relations.

    Materials: Three series of three pictures: a. 3 different puppets, b. 3 different cars, c. 3 different animals.
    Instruction: Present the child with the pictures in a random order. Say: "Put these pictures in three groups, hére the cars, thére the animals and thére the puppets" (while pointing to the required places).
    Criterion: Nine pictures divided in three groups: Level 1 +

LEVEL 5.   Operate with numbers by means of symbols.

    Materials: Paper and pencil with number problems.
                    2 + 3 = .
                    4 + . = 7
                    8 = 5 + .
                    7 - . = 5
    Instruction: Say: "How much must I add to 2 to get 4?" Say: "How much must I add to 3 to get 5?" Give paper and pencil. Say: "Do you know what these are? Put the right numbers in the rigt places".
    Criterion: Four out of six: Level 5 +

Four experimenters (students in developmental and
clinical psychology) tested 77 subjects on 195 tasks for 64
levels. Three experimenters tested subjects of all ages, one
tested predominantly subjects of 6 and 7 years. The tasks were
carried out in a room at school, divided over 5 successive
sessions of about half an hour. Children were predominantly
tested in the morning. There was no difference in achievements
before and after half past ten. All chi-squares reached values
with a chance of more than 1%. All subjects carried out all
tasks of every level.

All tasks were coded "right" or "wrong". In about 120
tasks direct scoring was possible. In the remaining tasks
(speech utterances and drawings) judgment procedures were
necessary. Two independent judges agreed 81% or more on the
levels of the tasks. For 18 of the 22 levels the interjudge
agreement was 90% or more. Subjects were considered successful
on a level if two thirds of the tasks were carried out
correctly.

Direct scoring and judgment with hindsight yielded for
every level of every aspect a pattern of 64 zeros and ones for
every subject. Scalogram analysis was used to determine how
much the empirical pattern of each aspect diverged from the
assumed pattern. Two indexes were used: the reproduceability
and scalability coefficient. The first is an index for the
extent to which the sum of the "ones" is the predictor of the
pattern of "zeros" and "ones". Usually a reproduceability
coefficient of 90% or more is required. The second index is
described as a measure of "unidimensionality" of the aspect in
the "cumulativity" sense. This coefficient takes non-
informative but "correct" patterns into account. Generally, a
minimum value of .60 is demanded (see for example Nie et al.,
1975, p. 533). Table 2 shows the values for the two indexes of
the thirteen aspects of cognitive development from "non-school
ready" to "school ready". The indexes supported the assumed
sequence in only three out of thirteen aspects. They were
spatial orientation with abstract materials i.e. geometrical
pictures and two aspects of preparatory arithmetic i.e.
arithmetic language and number concept. The aspect of visual

memory nearly failed the two criterion values. The tasks on the aspect of spatial orientation consisted of drawing geometrical forms of different complexity like circles, triangles, trapezia, etc.; the drawing on squared paper of stylized concrete objects (house, tree, chair, etc.) and deferred copying of complex geometrical figures. 94% of the subjects showed a perfect scalogram pattern: 10% of the subjects demonstrated right but non-informative patterns (all zeros on all ones). The percentage of subjects that succeeded on levels 1 to 5 was 87, 55, 35, 10 and 08 respectively. The differences between the fourth and fifth level were not significant.

Table 2. Coefficients of reproduceability and scalability of the assumed sequences of the five levels of 13 cognitive aspects.

Cognitive aspects	Reproduceability coefficient	Scalability coefficient
1. Visual perception (abstract material)	76	.25
2. Visual memory	89	.60
3. Acoustical analysis	70	.64
4. Acoustical memory	82	.03
5. Spatial orientation (schematic reproduction)	81	.44
6. Spatial orientation (abstract materials)	97	.88
7. Spatial orientation (concrete materials)	67	.00
8. Speaking in correct sentences	70	.20
9. Development of thinking (categorization)	77	.27
10. Development of thinking (seriation)	80	.20
11. Preparatory arithmetic (counting, concept of quantity)	82	.32
12. Preparatory arithmetic (arithmatic language)	95	.73
13. Preparatory arithmetic (number concept)	96	.84

The levels of the aspect of arithmetic language contained concepts like big-small, high-low, thick-thin, etc.; relations like bigger-biggest, higher-highest; place determinations in a row such as in the middle, the last one, etc.; operations like adding, subtracting and taking a part; the different coins and telling the right time while looking at the clock. 86% of the subjects did show a perfect scalogram; 13% had a pattern of all zeros or all ones. The percentage of subjects that passed level 1 through 5 was 96, 69, 71, 29 and 13 respectively. Levels two and three did not differ significantly.

Tasks for the levels of the number concept were: ordering of the same objects and symbols in groups of three elements; ordening of quantities; increasing and decreasing, comparing, insight in symbols like =, + and -, adding and subtracting with numbers smaller than ten. The percentage subjects that passed level 1 through 5 was: 88, 58, 62, 32 and 04 respectively. The levels two and three did not differ.

In summary, only three out of thirteen cognitive aspects did show the assumed sequence. From these three aspects two levels could be put together without loosing information.

THE MAIN SEQUENCE QUESTION.

To answer the second question about the relation between the several stepwise constructed cognitive aspects two explorative analyses were carried out on the 64 developmental levels of 13 cognitive aspects. The assumption was that the results of the two analyses - hierarchical cluster analysis (Johnson, 1967) and Homegenizing Alternating Least Squares (Homals, Gifi, 1980) - would converge. Finally, we investigated whether an alternative ordering of the separate aspects would fit better for the aspects which were not perfect scales. The ordering was conceived of as an acquisition and deletion sequence (Coombs and Smith, 1973).

Hierarchical Cluster Analysis.

The 64 right/wrong scored levels of 13 cognitive aspects were expressed as Euclidean distances. The minimum/maximum method of hierarchical cluster analysis were carried out on these distances. The minimum method is discussed because the results of the two methods hardly diverged. The cluster levels were arbitrarily chosen on .31, .41 and .50 values of intercluster proximity. On the level of .15 every developmental level was a separate cluster and on the .63 level all developmental levels together were one cluster. Five clusters which contained together 52 of the 64 developmental levels are further considered. Each cluster contained at least six developmental levels.

The first cluster contained 17 developmental levels. Eleven out of 17 were the a priori levels 4 and 5 of several cognitive aspects. Among them were spatial orientation, visual perception (abstract), acoustical analysis, development of thinking (seriation and categorization) and preparatory arithmatic. Examples of tasks were: the drawing of complex geometrical forms with and without the picture in front of the child, adding, knowledge of the days of the week, the ordering of objects by means of two or three independent criteria, drawing schematic pictures of concrete objects and perception and reproduction of mutual distances of objects in a field. The first cluster was interpreted as the ability to operate with self-made, instructed or discovered rules in order to put together and analyse concrete events and symbols.

The second cluster contained 13 developmental levels. Eight out of 13 were the two assumed lowest levels, 1 and 2 of several cognitive aspects. Among them were preparatory arithmatic: counting, concept of quantity, number concept, acoustical memory and analysis and visual memory. Examples of tasks were: production of two words that differ in sound pattern, keeping four different objects in mind for a short time, copying a circle, triangle and square, pointing to the animals in a string of pictures, composing groups of three of the same elements out of a collection and carrying out two different tasks subsequent to hearing a signal. The second cluster was interpreted as the ability to recognize, keep in mind and discriminate a small and simple collection of stimuli.

The third cluster consisted of 7 levels. It contained all assumed levels from 1 to 5 from several cognitive aspects. Among others, these aspects were preparatory arithmetic (counting, concept of quantity and number) and acoustical memory. Examples of tasks were: ordering different geometrical forms in a prescribed sequence comparing quantities, increasing and decreasing quantities and deferred copying of objects. The third cluster was interpreted as the ability to recognize, remember and discriminate a simple collection of stimuli, like the second cluster, and moreover the ability to carry out a simple prescribed operation on the stimuli, like putting in a row, putting in another modality e.g. drawing the perceived stimuli, ordering by means of simple relations as much as, more, thicker, etc.

The fourth cluster consisted of 11 levels. Nine were assumed levels 3 and 4 of several cognitive aspects, such as visual perception, development of thinking (seriation, categorization), preparatory arithmatic and spatial orientation (schematic reproduction and abstract materials). The cluster contained tasks, like ordering from small to big and vice versa, pointing to the place of an element in a row, dividing a set of elements into groups on two different criteria, telling a story based on pictured events, carrying out operations like adding subtracting and handling the symbols "=", "+" and "-". The fourth cluster also contained the ability to operate on simple stimuli. The operations are however more complex than in the third cluster: to handle two different criteria at the same time and to handle abstract materials and symbols.

In the fifth cluster no common features were discovered.

Although the several cognitive aspects did not all form Guttman scales the 64 levels together can be ordered in clusters from simple to complex abilities, which make developmental sense. The mutual relations depended mainly on the levels and not on similarity of contents.

Homals of the Age Groups and the 64 levels.

Homals is a programme for homogeneity analysis and an
extension of the principal components analysis to nominal
variables. The variables have categories, in our case
right/wrong. The technique orders objects (individuals) and
variables, in our case developmental levels (for a complete
description see Gifi, 1980, 1981).
The five age groups were ordered as expected. Especially
the 6-6½ years old children formed a separate group. They
received formal schooling. The differences between the other
age groups were not absent but smaller.
Plotting the 64 levels in a two dimensional space did not
demonstrate the expected horseshoe shape but a rectangular
triangle. About half of the levels were located near the
origin, indicating that the levels did not differ very much.
On the second dimension two groups were found. The first
consisted of "positive" scores and the second of "negative"
scores. The first group contained positively scored levels 4
and 5; the second contained wrongly scored levels 1 and 2. The
group of rightly scored levels contained tasks from spatial
orientation (abstract materials), preparatory arithmetic
(number language, number concept) and acoustical analysis.
More than half of these levels were also found in the first
cluster of the hierarchical cluster analysis. The groups of
negatively scored levels contained tasks from the three
preparatory arithmetic aspects, categorization, spatial
orientation and visual perception with abstract materials.
More than half of these levels were part of the second cluster
of the hierarchical cluster analysis. The results of the two
analyses converged. Both analyses predominantly showed
clusters on the base of the levels of the curriculum and not
on common content, like spatial orientation, preparatory
arithmetic, etc.

Conjunctive Analysis of the Levels of Each Cognitive Aspect.

Scalogram analysis showed that only three out of thirteen cognitive aspects were Guttman scales. Coombs and Smith (1973) suggested two dimensions to describe developmental (and attitudinal) processes. The authors considered the one-directional, cumulative assumption for developmental processes to be too limited. Development was considered as an acquisition and a deletion sequence. An empirically observed characteristic was acquired and not yet deleted and a non-observed characteristic was not yet acquired or already deleted. These assumptions made it possible to interpret more 0-1 patterns as being developmental processes than would be allowed by a Guttman scale. The Guttman scale can be considered as a special case in which the acquired characteristic did not get lost.

Table 3. Conjunctive analysis of 10 cognitive aspects which did not form a perfect scale. The numbers 1 to 5 refer to the assumed levels. Aspects marked with an asterisk are perfect scales. The numbers of the aspects correspond with table 2.

Cognitive aspects	Ordering with conjunctive analysis					Percentage fitting patterns
1. Visual perception.	2	1	5	3	4	76%
(abstract materials)	5	3	4	2	1	
2. Visual memory	3	1	4	2	5	79%
	4	1	3	2	5	
3. Acoustical analysis*	3	2	1	4	5	--
	-	-	-	-	-	
4. Acoustical memory	4	?				--
	3	2	?			
5. Spatial orientation	3	2	1	4	5	58%
(schematic reproduction)	5	2	1	4	3	
7. Spatial orientation	2	4	1	5	3	79%
(concrete materials)	5	4	2	3	1	
8. Speaking in correct	2	3	4	5	1	--
sentences	?					
9. Development of thinking	5	2	3	4	1	--
(categorization)	1	4	?			
10. Development of thinking	5	2	3	4	1	--
(seriation)	3	2	1	4	5	
11. Preparatory arithmetic	3	2	1	5	4	--
(counting concept of quantity)	-	-	-	-	-	

A conjunctive analysis (Coombs, 1964, p. 254-259; Coombs and Smith, 1973, p. 341-343) was carried out on the ten cognitive aspects which were not Guttman scales. To perform the analysis the following choices were made: within a block with the same sum of ones the most frequent pattern was chosen. The analysis was stopped when different patterns had the same frequency. In order to obtain a measure for fit the percentage of pattern allowed by the model was computed. Non-informative patterns (all zeros or all ones) were not taken into account. Table 3 shows the results. Three aspects could not be described by means of the conjunctive analysis. Various patterns had the same frequency. These were acoustical memory, speaking in correct sentences and categorization. The aspects acoustical analysis, counting and concept of quantity led to one sequence: a cumulative scale. The remaining aspects showed insufficient fit. The aspects could not be described as a two-dimensional developmental process with an acquisition and a deletion sequence.

SUMMARY AND DISCUSSION.

A developmental perspective on behaviour during the course of time implies an independent view that is different from behaviouristic-experimental-, individual differences- and information processing approaches. Such a perspective is not readily admitted. For instance, the curriculum we have discussed was not clearly designed from a developmental perspective. In our opinion it could however be read as a structure of developmental sequences.

An organizational hypothesis about circumscribed behaviours has been put forward, which we considered in two ways, first as a Guttman scale, and, second, as an acquisition- and deletion-sequence. The levels were meant as wholes, which differed qualitatively. For each level reference behaviours were sought. Although the results were not impressive, a beginning of a developmental sequence reconstruction has been made. The five levels of three aspects could be reduced to four cognitive developmental levels. These aspects have to be considered as cumulative scales. The model of acquisition and deletion was neither suited for the present three, nor for the additional ten cognitive aspects.

The explorative analysis of all the levels of the 13 cognitive aspects offered a picture that made developmental sense. The results of two different analyses of the data converged. The analyses conveyed the existence of four developmental levels, distinguished by qualitatively different abilities or skills (see e.g. Fischer, 1980). The levels can be conceived of as the expression of a differentiation process starting with the discrimination of simple stimuli and leading to the control over several ways of organizing events and symbols. It is assumed that the sequence is invariantly acquired. This does not mean that particular children always and in every context will be at the same level. The levels corresponded with age, as expected. This correspondence is a criterion, although a rather weak one, for a developmental sequence (Fischer and Silvern, 1985, p. 628). A further criterion for a developmental sequence is level-dependent learning (Fischer and Silvern, 1985). Although the curriculum designers did not offer empirical evidence, learning was considered to be level-dependent. The very reason to distinguish the levels was the assumption that learning on the assessed level and one level higher was most profitable for pupils.

The above findings and arguments render it possible to consider the cognitive aspect of the curriculum from a developmental perspective. But the picture is not complete: what are the underlying processes, what are the precursors, what are the exact mechanisms? (see e.g. Campbell and Richie, 1983; Flavell, 1972). Much conceptual, empirical and data-analytical work remains to be done.

The developmental perspective offers a specific view on experimental, environmental influences, individual differences and functional processes. In other words, the perspective adds a dimension to the behaviouristic, psychometric and information processing views.

The experimental, environmental influences distinguished in the behavioural view are understood with the developmental levels as background. This is an answer to Siegler's remarks (1983a, see the section on the behavioural view in this paper). Learning mechanisms operate in the context of a developmental level. This was a basic assumption of the curriculum. The combination of developmental level and environmental influence enriches the interpretation of the effect of training and experimental influences.

Classic psychometric instruments usually reflect a trait conception of cognition and intelligence. We compared the cognitive levels with a Dutch School Readiness Test. This test considered school readiness to be a unidimensional construct. There was a considerable correspondence between the levels of the aspects and the score on the test (Pearson r between .40 and .70). The developmental sequence conception enriches the unidimensional construct conception. The developmental conception enables one to actually make distinctions among skills that underly the differences in test scores.

Although much information processing research is non-developmental, an integration with the developmental approach is possible. Support for the distinction in levels can be found in Case's model of the development of relational control structures (Case, 1985, p. 94 and further) and in Fischer and Silvern's (1985) distinction of two levels between 4 and 7 years. The first mentioned author has explicitly stated that the integration of functional processes with developmental levels and structures may be highly profitable.

In summary, the developmental perspective can be considered to be a fundament and supplement for the three other approaches. In combination they offer a more adequate understanding of how human behaviour changes in the course of a lifetime.

REFERENCES.

Aebli, H. (1961). Grundformen des Lehrens. Stuttgart: Klett.

Aebli, H. (1984). Kognitive Entwicklung: Was entwickelt sich, un bei welche Anlässen? Zeitschrift für Entwicklungspsychologie und Pädagogische Psychologie, 16, 102-118.

Appelbaum, M.I. & McCall, R.B. (1983). Design and analysis in developmental psychology. In P.H. Mussen (Ed.), Handbook of child psychology, Vol. I: History, Theory and Methods, Kessen, W. (Vol. Ed.). New York: J. Wiley.

Baer, D.M. (1970). An age irrelevant concept of development. Merrill Palmer Quarterly, 16, 238-245.

Baldwin, J.M. (1895). Mental development in the child and the race. New York: MacMillan.

Baltes, P.B. & Nesselroade, J.R. (1973). The developmental analysis of individual differences on multiple measures. In J.R. Nesselroade & H.W. Reese (Eds.), Life-span developmental psychology: Methodological Issues. New York: Academic Press.

Bandura, A. & Walters, R.H. (1963). Social learning and personality development. New York: Holt, Rinehart and Winston.

Beilin, H. (1978). Inducing conservation through training. In G. Steiner (Ed.), Psychology of the 20th century, Vol. 7, Piaget and Beyond. New York: Academic Press.

Beilin, H. (1980). Piaget's theory: Refinement, Revision or Rejection? In H. Spada & R.W. Kluwe (Eds.), Developmental models of thinking. New York: Academic Press.

Beilin, H. (1981). Piaget and the New Foundation. Invited Address to the eleventh Symposium of the Jean Piaget Society. Philadelphia, May.

Bijou, S.W. & Baer, D.M. (1960). The laboratory - experimental study of child behaviour. In P.H. Mussen (Ed.), Handbook of research methods in child development. New York: Wiley.

Binet, A. & Simon, Th.A. (1905). Méthodes nouvelles pour le diagnostic du niveau intellectuel des anormaux. L'Année

Psychologique, 11, 191-136.

Block, J. (in collaboration with N.Haan) (1971). Lives through time. Berkeley: Bancroft Books.

Bloom, M.J. (1964). Stability and change in human characteristics. New York: Wiley.

Brainerd, C.J. (1977). Cognitive Development and Concept Learning: An interprative Review. Psychological Bulletin, 88, 919-939.

Brainerd, C.J. (1978). The Stage question in cognitive developmental theory. The Behavioural and Brain Sciences, 2, 173-213.

Bruner, J.S. (1973). Beyond the Information Given. Studies in the psychology of knowing. Selected, edited and introduced by J.M. Anglin. New York: W.W. Norton.

Campbell, R.L. & Richie, D.M. (1983). Problems in the theory of Developmental Sequences. Human Development, 26, 156-172.

Case, R. (1978). Piaget and Beyond: Toward a developmentally based theory and technology of instruction. In R. Glaser (Ed.), Advances in instructional Psychology: vol. 1. Hillsdale: Erlbaum.

Case, R. (1985). Intellectual Development, Birth to Adulthood. New York: Academic Press.

Connell, J.P. & Furman, W. (1984). Studies of transitions. In R.N. Emde & R.J. Harmon (Eds.), Continuities and Discontinuities in Development. New York: Plenum Press.

Connor, F.P. & Talbot, M.E. (1966). An experimental curriculum for young mentally retarded children. New York: Teachers College Press.

Coombs, C.H. (1964). A theory of data. New York: Wiley.

Coombs, C.H. & Smith, J.E.K. (1973). On the detection of structure in attitudes and developmental processes. Psychological Review, 80, 337-351.

Cronbach, L.J. & Snow, R.E. (1976). Aptitudes and instructional methods. New York: Irvington Publishers.

Damon, W. (1977). The social world of the child. San Francisco: Jossey-Bass.

Darwin, C.A. (1859). On the origin of species. London: J.

Murray.

Demetriou, A. & Efklides, A. (1985). Structure and sequence of
    formal and postformal thought: general patterns and
    individual differences. Child Development, 56, 1062-1091.

Dumont, J.J. & Kok, J.F. (1973). Curriculum Schoolrijpheid,
    Deel 1 (Curriculum School readiness, Part 1). Den Bosch:
    Malmberg.

Feldman, D. & Toulmin, S. (1975). Logic and theory of mind:
    Formal, pragmatic and empirical considerations in a
    science of cognitive development. In W.J. Arnold (Ed.),
    Nebraska Symposium on Motivation: vol. 23. Lincoln:
    University of Nebraska Press.

Fischer, K.W. (1980). A theory of cognitive development: the
    control and construction of hierarchies of skills.
    Psychological Review, 87, 477-531.

Fischer, K.W. & Silvern, L. (1985). Stages and individual
    differences in cognitive development. Annual Review of
    Psychology, 36, 613-648.

Flavell, J.H. (1972). An analysis of cognitive developmental
    sequences. Genetic Psychology Monographs, 86, 279-350.

Flavell, J.H. (1977). Cognitive Development. New Jersey:
    Prentice Hall.

Flavell, J.H. (1982a). On Cognitive Development. Child
    Development, 53, 1-10.

Flavell, J.H. (1982b). Structures, Stages and Sequences. In
    W.A. Collins (Ed.), The concept of development. The
    Minnesota Symposia on child development: vol. 15. New
    Jersey: L. Erlbaum.

Gagné, R.M. (1965). The conditions of learning (2nd. edition
    published 1970). New York: Holt, Rinehart and Winston.

Gagné, R.M. (1968). Contributions of learning to human
    development. Psychological Review, 75, 177-191.

Gifi, A. (1980). Niet-lineaire multivariate analyse
    (Non-linear multivariate analysis). Department of
    Datatheory, Leiden University.

Gifi, A. (1981). Homals, Users Guide. Department of
    Datatheory, Leiden University.

Gould, S.J. (1977). Ontogeny and Phylogeny. Cambridge (Mass.):

Harvard University Press.

Hilgard, E.R. & Bower, G.H. (1975). Theories of Learning (Fourth Edition). New Jersey: Prentice Hall.

Huttenlocher, J. & Burke, D. (1976). Why does memory span increase with age? Cognitive Psychology, 8, 1-31.

Johnson, S.C. (1967). Hierarchical clustering schemes. Psychometrika, 32, 241-254.

Kagan, J. (1980). Perspectives on Continuity. In O.G. Brim & J. Kagan (Eds.), Constancy and Change in Human Development. Cambridge (Mass.): Harvard University Press.

Kagan, J. (1983). Classifications of the child. In P.H. Mussen (Ed.), Handbook of child psychology. Volume 1: History, Theory and Methods (Volume Editor W. Kessen). New York: Wiley.

Kamii, C. (1981). Application of Piaget's theory to education: The preoperational level. In I.E. Sigel & D.M. Brodzinsky (Eds.), New directions in Piagetian Theory and Practice. New Jersey: L. Erlbaum.

Kaplan, B. (1964). The conduct of enquiry: Methodology for behavioural science. San Francisco: Chandler.

Kaplan, B. (1983). A trio of trials. In R.M. Lerner (Ed.), Developmental Psychology, Historical and Philosophical Perspectives. New Jersey: L. Erlbaum.

Kessen, W. (1983). Construction, Deconstruction and Reconstruction of the Child's mind. In C. Sophian (Ed.), Origins of cognitive skills. New Jersey: L. Erlbaum.

Kingma, J. (1984). A comparison of four methods of scaling for the acquisition of early number concept. Journal of General Psychology, 110, 23-45.

Kitchener, R.F. (1983). Changing conceptions of the philosophy of science and the foundations of developmental psychology. In D. Kuhn & J.A. Meacham (Eds.), On the development of developmental psychology. Basel: Karger.

Laak, J.J.F. ter (1983). Over het vaststellen van cognitieve ontwikkelingssequenties (On the assessment of cognitive developmental sequences). Doctoral Dissertation, Leiden University.

McCall, R.B. (1976). Toward an epigenetic conception of mental development in the first three years of life. In M. Lewis (Ed.), Origins of Intelligence. New York: Plenum Press.

McCall, R.B. (1977). Challenges to a science of developmental psychology. Child Development, 48, 333-344.

McCall, R.B. (1981). Nature-Nurture and two realms of development: a proposed integration with respect to mental development. Child Development, 52, 1-12.

Mischel, W. (1968). Personality and assessment. New York: Wiley.

Nie, N.H., Hadlai Hull, C., Jenkins, J.G., Steinbrunner, K. & Bent, D.H. (1975). Statistical Package for the Social Sciences (second edition). New York: McGraw-Hill.

Parreren, C.F. van & Carpay, J.A.M. Leerpsychologie en onderwijs 4: Sovjetpsychologen over onderwijs en cognitive ontwikkeling (Learning psychology and education 4: Sovjet psychologist on education and cognitive development, second edition). Groningen: Wolters Noordhoff.

Philips, D.C. & Kelley, M.E. (1975). Hierarchical theories of development in education and psychology. Harvard Educational Review, 45, 351-375.

Piaget, J. (1970). Piaget's theory. In P.H. Mussen (Ed.), Carmichael's Manual of Child Psychology, Vol. 1. New York: Wiley.

Piaget, J. (1978). The development of thought, equilibration of cognitive structures. Oxford: Basil Blackwell. Translation by A. Roin. Originally published as L'Equilibration des structures cognitives. Paris: Presses Universitaires de France, 1975.

Reese, H.W. & Overton, W.F. (1970). Models of development and theories of development. In P.B. Baltes & L.R. Goulet (Eds.), Life span developmental psychology. New York: Academic Press.

Selman, R.L. (1980). The growth of interpersonal understanding. New York: Academic Press.

Siegel, A.W., Bisanz, J. & Bisanz, G.L. (1983). Developmental Analysis: a strategy for the study of psychological change. In D. Kuhn & J.A. Meacham (Eds.), On the development of developmental psychology. Basel: Kager.

Siegler, R.S. (1983). Information processing approaches to development. In P.H. Mussen (Ed.), Handbook of Child Psychology, Volume 1: History, Theory and Methods (volume editor W. Kessen). New York: Wiley.

Siegler, R.S. (1983). Five generalizations about cognitive development, American Psychologist, 38, 263-277.

Spada, H. & Kempf, W.F. (Eds.) (1977). Structural models of thinking and learning. Bern: H. Huber.

Spearman, C. (1904). General intelligence, objectively determined and measured. American Journal of Psychology, 15, 201-293.

Spiker, C.C. (1966). The concept of development: Relevant and irrelevant issues. Monographs for the Society for Research on Child Development, 31, 40-54.

Spiker, C.C. (1977). Behaviourism, Cognitive Psychology and the active organism. In N. Datan & H.W. Reese (Eds.), Life span developmental psychology. Dialectical perspectives on experimental research. New York: Academic Press.

Sternberg, R.J. & Powell, J.S. The Development of Intelligence. In P.H. Mussen (Ed.), Handbook of Child Psychology, Vol. III, Cognitive Development (volume editors J.H. Flavell & E.M. Markman). New York: Wiley.

Stevenson, H.W. (1983). How children learn, a quest for theory. In P.H. Mussen (Ed.), Handbook of Child Psychology, Volume I, Theory, History and Methods (volume editor W. Kessen). New York: Wiley.

Stroufe, L.A. (1979). The coherence of individual development: early care, attachment, and subsequent developmental issues. American Psychologist, 34, 834-841.

Tisak, M.S. & Turiel, E. (1984). Childrens conceptions of moral and prudential rules. Child Development, 55, 1030-1039.

Vygotsky, L.S. (1934). Thought and language, Moscow-Leningrad, Soc. Econom. Ird. Translated by E. Haufman & G. Vakar. Cambridge (Mass.): M.I.T. Press.

Werner, H. (1948). Comparative Psychology of mental

development   (Revised   Edition).   New   York: Follet
   Publishing Company.
White, S.H. (1970). The learning theory tradition and child
   psychology. In P.H. Mussen (Ed.), Carmichael's Handbook
   of Child Psychology: Vol. I. New York: Wiley.

Theory Building in Developmental Psychology
P.L.C. van Geert (editor)
© Elsevier Science Publishers B.V. (North-Holland), 1986

10

Psychic Development of the Individual

A process of structuring and restructuring experience

Maria Tyszkowa

Psychic development of the individual is conceived of here as a process of structuring and restructuring of experience. Experience is defined in terms of 1) memory traces, 2) the whole of cognitive, affective and functional content of the temporal bonds in the nervous system, 3) functional changes in different subsystems of an organism. Thus it is of enactive character. The whole of an individual's experience consists of species experience, individual experience sensu stricto, and social experience acquired during the processes of socialization and enculturation. The basic unit of human experience has cognitive, affective and evaluative aspects.
The structuring of experience takes place in the processes of programming activity, in the formation of habits, cognitive structures of personality, etc. An important role in the processes of structuring experience is played by cultural patterns of behaviour, language and other systems of signs and symbols in a culture.

Developmental psychology is increasingly becoming a distinct science dealing with the processes and regularities of psychic changes which occur during the whole life cycle of an individual. This broadens the field of the discipline, in which basic questions about what the psychic development of an individual consists of and how (i.e. according to which principles) it occurs are adressed anew. A new formulation of the subject of research makes it impossible to maintain the position of all the theories of psychic development that view it as the growth of psyche as a component and a function of the processes of biological growth and development of an organism.

Assuming that the psychic development of man takes place in all periods of ontogenesis and is not completed with his biological maturity, one cannot avoid contradictions while supporting those conceptions of psychic development according to which it occurs only in the period of childhood and adolescence. Doing so, in spite of acknowledgment of the multi-factor conditionings of psychic development, one would still be of the opinion that the psyche, being a function of an organism equal to other functions (which is a true but incomplete statement), develops in a similar way, i.e. only in the ascending period of ontogenesis. Much evidence, however, has been collected to prove that psychic development takes place after the processes of organic growth have been completed and biological maturity has been reached.

Many facts revealed by contemporary research in developmental psychology prove that developmental changes in the psyche of an adult are at least equal to those which occur in the period of childhood. These changes concern both the range and depth of psychic transformations (see Gould, 1955; Riegel, 1976; Labouvie-Vief, 1982). Some scientists share the opinion that as far as the specifically human aspect is concerned, the changes in question are even more important than those which occur in the first half of life (Jung, 1967; Levinson et al., 1978).

If this is so, one must accept that this evolving system, i.e. the human psyche, is also subject to evolution (i.e. develops and forms itself) even after growth of an organism and its structures has been completed. This means that the psychic development in ontogenesis is relatively independent of biological development of an organism. To be more precise, it is independent of the growth of organic structures but not of the structures themselves and their functions. There is no development of psyche - in fact there is no psyche at all - when the functions end and organic structures break up. Nevertheless, psychic development can continue as long as the structures of an organism function; it is not confined to the period when they are being built.

This is possible when we realize that the psychic system

of an individual is (1) a functional system whose functions consist in (2) regulating its relations with the surrounding world and that they develop (3) in connection with maintained interaction and exchange between an individual and the environment. These relations and interactions, indispensable for living and development of an individual, are expanded and transformed in the course of ontogenesis while their maintenance is conditioned by the activity of an organism and the development of regulating actions.

It follows, therefore, that one can speak about the psychic development of an individual only in connection with his or hers activeness. In other words, one must assume that man is an active and not only a reactive being (see Overton, 1976; Tomaszewski, 1975).

Having stated this, we must again ask a question as to what the development under consideration consists in, if it means something different and something more in the life of a human being than carrying out a genetic programme (in terms of species and biological individuality).

This paper will present an outline of the conception of psychic development in ontogenesis. It makes an attempt to elaborate an aspect of the process which has been poorly explored so far, namely, the aspect of gaining and organizing (structuring) individual experience. In the psychological theories of development the individual experience was treated as a background for developmental changes, as a kind of learning affecting development (learning by experience or on the basis of experience), or, as regards the influence of environment, as a factor facilitating or inhibiting developmental changes in early childhood (see Spitz, 1950; Uzgiris, 1977).

For a long time, however, individual experience was treated as an essential component and factor of psychic development appearing in different forms of intuitive cognition and social practice based upon it.

In fictional literature, construction of characters and fates consists mainly in constructing the experience of a hero in the world (both external and internal) and his psychic

transformation   evoked   by   experiencing   so-called   crucial
events.

In the psychoanalytical conceptions which arose from intuitive
clinical cognition, the psychic development of an individual
remains under the influence of the overwhelming (not to say
fatalistic) experience from the early period of life (Freud,
Adler).

In the process of education there are intentionally created
situations which aim at modelling experience and its proper
structuring in the psyche of a pupil. Psychotherapy, in turn,
by means of different methods drifts towards restructuring
experience in order to acquire the ability of constructive
adaptation and development of an individual.

If we would assume that the literary gnosis, expressed in
literary fiction, was an early (intuitive, artistic) stage of
human cognition, it might be advisable to devote more attention in research and theoretical conceptions of development
to the role of individual experience, its kinds and methods of
structuring in the psychic development of an individual.

Referring to the above mentioned literary, pedagogical
and clinical intuition (psychoanalysis), in the conception
here presented, I suggest that experience in particular should
be treated as the basic material for development which is
accumulated in the whole course of life and activeness of an
individual in the world. According to the assumptions of this
conception, the experience in question becomes the object of
structuring and restructuring which constitute the process of
developmental changes in the individual's psyche and comprise,
first of all, qualitative (structural) changes. This means a
different treatment of experience from that which has been
pointed out previously. At the same time it means a different,
specific formulation of the development of an individual's
psyche.

I should like to make an attempt to present below the
outline of this conception, i.e. to formulate its basic
assumptions and theses.

PSYCHIC DEVELOPMENT AS A PROCESS OF STRUCTURING EXPERIENCE.

An essential feature of the theoretical proposal presented here is the thesis that psychic development of individuals consists in accumulating and elaborating experience which (because of the need connected with their activity in the surrounding world) is subject to the processes of structuring and restructuring in the whole course of his life. Experience is treated here as the material for development while development is treated as a series of changes which result from organizing the structures of this experience (i.e. structuring) and their transformation (i.e. restructuring) issuing from both the inclusion of new experiences and adaptation of an individual's activeness to the needs of balancing his relations (i.e. exchange) with the surrounding world.

Such an approach is of a constructivist nature in the sense that it regards the psychic development of individuals as a process of constructing (self-organizing) their psychic structures which results from gathering, accumulating and structuring experiences gained from their own activeness. Such a formulation of the problem would make it possible to consider psychic development in ontogenesis as a function of the subjects' own activeness in their relations of continuous exchange with the environment and, at the same time, as a function of their individual (which does not mean inborn) possibilities of accumulating and organizing their experiences into psychic structures characterized by internal coherence, self-control and ability to develop.

Being blended from broadly understood activist, structuralist and dialectical formulations, the standpoint in question differs distinctly from behaviourist conceptions.

The basic assumptions of the formulation suggested emphasize the dominating role of the subjects' own activeness in their psychic development. This remains in agreement with the conceptions of an active organism (see Overton, 1976; Leontiev, 1962, 1975), with the role of experience (particularly the individual one) in psychic development, and the structuring of experience as a principle of psychic development in ontogenesis.

A brief presentation and discussion of the theses in question is presented below.

ACTIVENESS AND PSYCHIC DEVELOPMENT.

The conception of psychic development in ontogenesis suggested here is meaningful only when we assume that man, in his relations with the world, is an active being. Such a thesis has definite contextual and theoretical implications which allow us to speak about structuring in ontogenetic development.

Among the contemporary psychological theories of development we can distinguish theories based upon the model of an active organism (structuralist and dialectical theories) and theories which accept the model of a reactive organism (these include, in particular, behaviourist conceptions of development). Theoretical approaches within the framework of these two models are essentially different.

The present writer accepts the assumptions which are involved in the model of an active organism. She assumes that man is born as an active being, that activeness is an immanent feature of living organisms, i.e. their mode of existence (see Tyszkowa, 1977). It is so because man can only live and develop thanks to the processes of constant exchange (at the biochemical and psychological plane) with his environment. The relations and processes of exchange between man and the surrounding world are carried out in the course of and through the activeness of an individual and require constant regulation.

The human psyche is a functional system carrying out the basic task for a living creature, namely, controlling man's behaviour as a form of activeness, regulating his relations with the surrounding world as well as the relations with the psychic system itself. The relations of an individual with the world change, expand and enrich as their activeness becomes differentiated, organized and modified. The dynamic character of relations in the system "an individual - the world" and changes occurring in both of these subsystems are responsible for the act that the processes of their equilibration must be of an active and dynamic nature (i.e. homeoresis, see Piaget, 1975).

Consequently, adaptation to the changing environment implies changes and modifications of the system regulating the relations of an organism (an individual) with the surrounding world. This refers not only to situational changes but also to developmental changes and modifications. The psychic system which regulates them must develop in order to cope with the demands of balancing the relations of individuals with the surrounding world and controlling their behaviour. This behaviour, in turn, has the nature of a functional exchange with the world and, according to Jean Piaget, it assumes "two main aspects closely linked with each other: the affective aspect and the cognitive" (Piaget, 1967, p.10).

Man's activeness in the world - his acts, activities, behaviour - is the source of various experiences connected with objects and relations in this world, with his own actions and activities, with experience gained in the course of his activeness. This experience changes and forms his psychic system of regulation but also - as a feedback - influences his activeness in its different forms.

In the course of life, the individuals' activeness becomes differentiated, enriched and organized. It is also subject to qualitative modifications due, among others, to mastering the use of tools and the systems of signs (see Wygotsky, 1971, 1978; Luria, 1976 a, b).

While being differentiated and modified the activeness of an individual assumes the form of activities of a different structure, oriented towards different spheres (areas) and goals. The basic forms of activities comprise (1) objective activity, distinguished by A.N. Leontiev, i.e. complexes of activities directed towards objects of the external world and aiming at the elicitation of changes within these objects as well as (2) social activities, i.e. complexes of different actions and proceedings directed towards other people and aimed at exercising and influence upon them (e.g. educational, artistic, political activities, and the like). Looking at the problem from a different angle, one can distinguish the main kinds of activities as those which dominate man's activeness in the succesive periods of life, i.e. play, learning, and work. All these kinds of activities are the source of experiences which constitute the material for development. They are also the source of impulses initiating developmental changes in man's psyche.

What, however, is experience? What do we know about its role in psychic development from studies of developmental psychology? We shall try to answer these questions in the considerations presented below.

THE CONCEPTS AND KINDS OF EXPERIENCE.

Individual Experience.

The concept of experience, one of the key ideas in the conception presented here, functions in psychology and in colloquial language with at least several meanings:

1. The term means actual experiencing of some event, events, or situations, contacts with the environment, one's own activities, and the like.

2. By "experience" one understands only those events, situations, contacts with the environment or one's own activities which are assumed to leave a trace in man's psyche.

3. Experience is understood as a trace of experienced events, situations, contacts, activities or sensations in memory.

4. Experience is defined as an effect, particularly a durable one, of the experienced events, situations, contacts with the environment, actions or experiences in one's own psyche, behaviour, individual activities (compare expressions such as "learning through experience", "an experienced person", "life experience"). Phenomenological

psychology treats experience as the history of all previous stimulation an individual was subject to, i.e. the history of stimuli and events as they were perceived and assimilated by this individual (see Wohlwill, 1973).

5. Experience is defined as knowledge, especially practical, acquired from one's own previously performed activities, proceedings, situational behaviour or experiences (compare expressions such as "an experienced worker", "an experienced mother", "professional experience").

6. The concept of experience was given a specific meaning by introspective psychology which regards it as a total of psychic phenomena perceived by a person experiencing these phenomena at a given moment (E.B. Titchener).

The concept of experience in introspective psychology, functioned also in behaviourism and psychoanalysis.

In the behaviourist tradition, experience is treated either in terms of stimuli and/ or events with which an individual comes into contact, or in terms of his response to these stimuli. Either case involves learning. Wohlwill is of the opinion that the·behaviourist approach is always applied when one moves from theoretical considerations to programming empirical research in which stimuli (conditions) and responses of an organism (behaviours, actions and their changes) must be controlled. Wohlwill points out that the behaviourist approach to experience has proved useful in numerous investigations on the role of experience (particularly so-called early experience) in development. The review of the results of these investigations made by Hunt (1961) and Wohlwill (1973) reveals that conclusions about the influence of experience upon development were principally made on the basis of changes in an individual's behaviour, whereas the experience itself was evoked by defined stimuli, controlled in the experiment, or by the intensification of spontaneous reactions. There probably is a grain of truth in this particular behaviourist view, because identifying experience with stimuli or responses facilitates the clear planning of research and perspicuous analysis of its results. By no means, however, do these

results   prove   that   such   a   theoretical   approach   is
well-founded.

Identifying   experience   with   stimuli   (stimulation)   or
responses   (behaviour)   is   an   example   of   reductionism   which
simplifies   the   problem   and   cannot   be   satisfying.   Such
identification cannot be allowed because even if one accepted
the theoretical model of a reactive organism (which does not
correspond with the facts), then (1) many stimuli which affect
individuals in the past leave no such trace in the behaviour
which could be ascribed to their influence and (2) responses
are provoked (according to behaviourist conceptions as well)
mainly by present, not past stimuli. Thus the concept of
experience refers clearly to the subject (organism) and his
regulating   mechanisms,   not   to   environment   (stimuli,
situations) or behaviour. Thus it must not be automatically
assumed that if someone found himself in a given situation,
then he gained proper experience related to it. Neither can
one directly ascribe changes in one's behaviour to the
influence of this situation or situations. Here the relations
of mutual dependence are more indirect and complex than they
seem to be.

In the psychology of learning one can find different
views as far as the question of experience is concerned.
Generally, however, no one neglects the role of experience in
changes of behaviour although sometimes experience is
identified with effects of learning. Wlodarski (1975, p.19)
states that experience "is understood then (...) as a result
of contact (with the environment - M.T.) in the form of
defined changes in an individual's behaviour". For us,
however, other approaches are much more valuable.

According to Hilgard (1977, p. 191) "learning can be
defined as relatively durable change in behaviour resulting
from previous experience" or as "making use of previous
experience". Linhart (1972) defines the role of experience in
a similar way. This could mean that experience is something
other than learning and changes observed in the behaviour of
an individual. Experience would be something that lies at the
base of these changes. But what?

Experience is connected with memory. Strictly speaking, it is connected with storing up traces of events in which an individual took part, traces of his or her contacts with the environment, or his or her own behaviours, activities and feelings. These contacts with environment, behaviours, activities, feelings, etc. constitute the content of the individual's memory traces. Primarily, the concept of experience refers to the traces of a subject's own broadly understood activeness. It refers indirectly also to those events, situations and environments in which activeness of a subject took place. At the same time experience also includes slight functional changes in different systems engaged in the activeness that take place in the learning processes. These slight changes are manifested in the subject's activity. They gradually become components of the modifications of a systemic nature. These modifications in turn are manifested in the change of the individual's behaviour, and his or her psychic regulatory system.

Experience understood as a trace (or an effect) of individuals' own previous activeness in their relations with the world would mainly consist in modifying their functional schemes, cognitive schemes, patterns of emotional response, and the like in the course and as a result of an individual's own activities, behaviour, and experiences. (Thus it would be relevant to understand experience as sui generis of the practical or procedural knowledge according to the conception of Winograd). Appearing in different forms, these changes can modify not only the simple but also the more complex forms of activeness (e.g. professional activity).

Experiences acquired as a result of the subjects' own activeness cause the greatest changes in this activeness when their functional (and other) schemes are at the initial stage of being organized, i.e. in early childhood. The role of these experiences in development was recognized early by developmental psychology which has thoroughly analyzed their influence (e.g. Hunt, 1961; Przetacznikowa, 1973; Uzgiris, 1977; White et al., 1977). A similar analysis has been provided by ethology which tries to find universal

regularities of behaviour (see for instance Konrad Lorenz).
Psychoanalysis, in turn, places the main stress upon the
importance of socio-emotional experiences from the period of
childhood (particularly the first five years of life) for the
formation of emotional life patterns and social interactions,
chiefly in the psychosexual aspect (Freud) but also in the
aspect of striving for power (Adler), feeling threat or
danger) (Horney), and the like.

Uzgiris, summing up the results of investigations of the
role of early life experiences in psychic development,
distinguishes four general conceptions which explain how
experience influences the development of an individual. These
are conceptions which formulate the role of early life
experience as: a determinant of anticipated further
experiences; a factor modifying the range and proportion of
their kinds; a factor modifying the pattern; and a selective
modifier (Uzgiris, 1977, p. 92). It is assumed here that early
life experiences shape, first, the perception of a situation
and the ability of selective response to external stimuli and
situations; and second, patterns and schemes of activeness
exercising influence on the course of an individual's further
development.

Experiences that are of key importance for development
can be acquired by means of different concrete forms of
activeness. This has been revealed by observations of
thalidomide and other physically handicapped children who
compensate for the lack of normal sensorimotor possiblitities
by establishing contacts with the environment by other sensory
and motor activities. Moreover, early life experiences do not
univocally determine further experiences. Neither do they
explicitly determine the course of an individual's future
development. For a long time psychology has been dominated by
a belief (implanted as a result of the dissemination of
psychoanalytical views) that the influence of early life
experience upon the development of an individual is
irrevocable. This referred especially to the harm done by
negative experiences or to the absence of certain kinds of
experience. Such a belief seemed to be justified by the fact

that the experience in question constitutes the initial programmes of action, patterns of psychic activeness, and interactions between an individual and his environment. More recent investigations do not confirm the validity of this position. Developmental psychology, therefore, is gradually abandoning the thesis that the influence of the early life experiences upon the formation of an individual's psyche is irrevocable, regardless of what his or hers further experiences would be (see Kagan, 1978). The later experience can evidently modify and transform the effect of the earlier experiences, changing the line of individual development. Experience continues and continues also the transformation of the previous experiences by the new ones.

Experience can have a conscious or unconscious character. This is revealed by the means and mechanisms through which experience influences behaviour. Thus, e.g. practical (or procedural) knowledge is very difficult to verbalize but it becomes real in the course of performing an action, in concrete situations, in acitivity. Quite frequently people are not able to answer the question "How do you do this?", but they can demonstrate how actions are performed. (Hence the importance of demonstrative instruction, apprenticeship, drills in mastering practical actions in technology, music, sports, and the like). If we have a practical experience in some field, it is not necessary to verbalize the procedural knowledge; our hands (nerves, muscles, joints), our fingers, our body "knows" how to perform given actions. We learn them, therefore, rather by imitation and drill than by fulfilling verbal instructions.

Emotional experience manifests itself in such a way that before we become conscious of it, we react with similar feelings to the situations resembling in some way those in which we had sustained definite emotional experience (Hilgard, 1977, p. 334). On this principle, different kinds of emotional trauma arise, which lead to the formation of attitudes or, more precisely, their emotional components. A person also learns to recognize a given emotional state which becomes a signal eliciting adaptational behaviour.

A human being's experience has an individual character in the sense that each individual acquires his or hers own experience, the content and formation of which are unique. The whole of man's experience consists of, first, species experience transferred in the form of structures, complete nerve connections and schemes of inborn actions constituting a part of genetic individuality; second, individual experience, i.e. this part of experience which is acquired by individuals from their own activities, experiences, events, contacts and situations in which they participate; and, third, social experience acquired during the processes of socialization and enculturation by means of interpersonal communication.

The species experience demands little - but despite appearance, it does demand some - exercise, in order to become reality in an individual's activity. The remaining two types of experience are acquired by an individual through his or her own activeness. An individual can possess only that part of social experience that he or she can actively assimilate. The assimilation can be completed only in such a way that a defined fragment of the social experience will become an object (and later, quite frequently, a tool) of an individual's cognitive activeness and experiences.

Traces of this activity and experiences are included in man's individual experience, enriching it with the content accumulated in the experience of previous generations and coded in the products of technical, usable and symbolic culture (according to J. Kmita's distinction made in 1975).

Those social transfers which are directed towards individuals but which do not become an object of their cognitive, manipulative, or other type of activeness, remain outside the range of their experience or are assimilated only superficially and impermanently (e.g. a part of the information learnt at school which is actively forgotten by a majority of pupils as soon as they get a grade).

In this way individual experience could consist of not only memory effects (traces), programmes of action, patterns of an individual's own response and activeness in the environment, but also the experiences arising in connection with the individual's own activeness and experiences which pertain to that part of social experience a given individual has contact with and actively assimilates.

Such a broad scope of the concept of individual experience is not without grounds when we accept that experience is an effect of man's activeness in his relations with the surrounding world. An important component of this world, a part of man's environment, is culture which fulfills the function of coding, storing up and transmitting essential experiences of a given society. Man's activeness in his relations with the world, and thus also his individual experience, pertains also to culture and - indirectly - to the social experience which in its generalized form is generally coded by this culture by means of symbols, values, etc. (Tyszkowa, 1983, 1984, 1985).

Experience-generating activeness of individuals in their environment aims at the constructive adaptation implying their development (see Piaget, 1967, 1981).

Man's activeness lasts throughout the whole life. Only its forms, intensity and inner structure change. Similarly, individual experience is accumulated and organized throughout man's life, enriching his activeness and providing the basis for the developmental modifications of his psyche. Seeking advantageous conditions for functioning and development, individuals seek new experiences. This expresses itself in a change of their relations with the environment, in organizing for themselves a proper stimulation, in taking up new activities and goals.

In achieving progress in development (particularly at the moment of transition from one stage to another) an individual must necessarily have experiences surpassing those which are typical for a given stage. This regularity appears even in early childhood (Uzgiris, 1977). It is described in the literature on adolescence, and can also be referred to the period of transition from adolescent to adult life (Levinson et al., 1978; Gilligan and Murphy, 1978) as well as to later periods of an individual's psychic development.

Experience comprises of the traces (effects) of all kinds

and areas of activeness important for individuals in the
course of their life. It is connected, therefore, with the
individuals' fulfillment of social roles, their activity,
experiences pertaining to the situation in the world as well
as to the changes which occur in the organism and the psyche.

An important content of experience are also individuals'
interactions with other people, processes of their own
development and also the experiences connected with culture.

Considering the fact that the physiological bases for
experiences are complex functional systems, experience can
also be designated - as W. Szewczuk has done (1979, p. 58) -
"the whole of cognitive, emotional and functional content of
the temporal bonds (in the nervous system - M.T.) which have
appeared and function in a given individual".

Being linked with a person's activeness and experiences,
experience has the character of an individual experience. Its
effects are continued (i.e. connections formed, mental traces,
multilateral functional changes resulting from one's own
sensory, motor and cognitive acts as well as from one's
behaviour and activities) which appear in the organism and in
one's long term memory in connection with one's own personal
activeness in relation to the environment (external and
internal).

Thus understood experience is individual because its
form, components and dynamics are unrepeatable. At the same
time it contains a range of common content and features
typical for people belonging to a similar age group (cohorts),
living in the context of defined events and in similar
cultural-historical conditions.

Conditions that are similar for members of a cohort
undoubtedly differentiate the individual experience of people
who live in different epochs or who belong to societies which
live at different stages of development. This fact has been
pointed out by the cultural-historical school of developmental
psychology (Wygotsky, 1971, 1978, 1980; Leontiev, 1962, 1975,
1976; Luria, 1976) which regards it as a source of differences
in the development of mental function (perception, thinking,
solving problems) as well as structures of human personality

(Luria, 1976a).

The differences in people's individual experience can also be observed in the shortening of time intervals referring to generations and age cohorts. This becomes particularly distinct in the periods of acceleration in the development of civilization, at the time of violent turning points in the history of society, etc. Varieties of development connected with the specificity of individual experience represented by members of different cohorts are controlled by means of the sequential analysis method which aims at determining the so-called pure ontogenetic change (see Schaie, 1965; Schaie and Baltes, 1975).

Universal aspects of people's individual experience are connected with the common basic periods or - according to Levinson (1978) eras - of the human life cycle (childhood and adolescence, adulthood, ageing period and old age). There are main assignments characteristic for each of these periods and also basic existential problems and dillemmas which accompany human life.

The individual experience arises as an effect of the subject's own activeness. This activeness decides the result of the interaction between the inborn characteristics of an organism and the environment which is co-defined by it. Thus the activeness influences both the process of acquiring experience as well as the essential content and formal characteristics of the individual experiences of human beings.

Sometimes experience is treated as an interpretation of the "raw data" arising as a result of the individual's contacts with the world (Smedslund). Then, however, learning and development would be determined either by the sequence of external stimulation or by the innate structures of an organism, which is incompatible with the dialectical constructivist position.

As has already been emphasized, experience has to a considerable extent an enactive character. Piaget has shown that the basic unit of experience (and activeness) includes cognitive, affective and evaluative aspects. Human beings also seek experience and organize it actively for themselves because, as Kagan (1978, p. 138) puts it, their "actions and thoughts are often directed at a goal, where a goal is simply a desired experience". This does not, however, only imply seeking new stimuli (as one might interpret it in accordance with the hypothesis of optimal stimulation) but it is also connected with the subjects' need to shape their own activeness.

Individual experience is composed of a record of the past but it also effects present experiences and the behaviour of a human being. This is accomplished in different ways but primarily by, modifying the perception of the present situation, and the way in which it is cognitively interpreted and evaluated on the one hand, and by modifying the acts in current behaviour on the other hand.

Various proposals for differentiating the categories of experience serve in trying to explain the possibility of their influence upon man's behaviour. Some psychologists distinguish two categories: record experience and conclusion experience. The record experience is connected with Penfield's hypothesis according to which all facts, events and experiences of an individual are continuously registered and thus form a kind of mental record of his life. The information which constitutes this experience is arranged on the axis of biographical time. Conclusion experience is such experience which comes into being as a result of operation, on the material recorded in memory (i.e. upon record experience). A key to the understanding of how experience affects development would be, on the one hand, the knowledge of laws which govern the functioning of memory and, on the other hand, the knowledge of cognitive bases for behaviour.

However, if we take the position that cognitive processes serve people's survival, or, in other words, their achievement of constructive adaptation, then we should rather return to the analysis of behaviour as a form of the subjects' activeness regulating their relations with the surrounding world. In an act of behaviour a specific synthesis of the results is performed, a wholly formulated situation from the viewpoint of the subject's imagined goal (anticipation) and experience. Linhart (1972, p. 372) writes: "The integration of past experiences with requirements of the current situation and attitude towards a goal is carried out in the form of different kinds of anticipation". The anticipation (e.g. of a defined state or situation) conditions the formation of a plan of activities. Thus, if one considers the fact that the mechanism of memory functions in such a way that the information is stored up in man's mind and retrieved from it selectively, then it is necessary to agree that in experience, that which is fixed (recorded), is that information which is necessary and important for an individual in the context of the situation of the moment. On the other hand, the information regarded as important from the viewpoint of the anticipated goals (around which man's current activities and behaviour are organized) is extracted.

Thus, experience effects both the behaviour participating in the mechanism of goal selection and the behaviour which accompanies the organization of activities.

Many facts indicate that the record experience is subject to reconstruction from the viewpoint of the current situation and vice versa: the current situation is perceived and interpreted in terms of previous experience. The interaction between experience and the current situation of an individual and his or her goals, activities, etc. is mutual. The current situation, in turn, is perceived and the experience is reconstructed in terms of goals realized within the subject's own activeness.

Thus the controversy on experience as a record of the past versus the subject's goals and attitudes directed towards the future can only be resolved within the framework of the theoretical model of an active organism. It is impossible to solve the problem while accepting the behaviourist approach, since activeness denotes and implies the dynamic time relations conditioned by the character of successive structures and plans of activity (see Linhart, 1972, p. 372 and Linhart 1976). The organization of experience in the course of ontogenesis may also be considered and explained in the context of the subject's activeness and in connection with modifications which occur in it.

THE STRUCTURING OF EXPERIENCE AND DEVELOPMENTAL CHANGE IN AN INDIVIDUAL'S PSYCHE.

The conception presented here assumes that the psychic development of an individual is connected with the active self-organization of experience. This proces is based on the emergence of inner relations between experiences connecting them into systems functioning as a whole and, as such, playing an essential role in the relations of individuals with the surrounding world, within their psychic systems, as well as in the construction of their current behaviour. Thus understood, self-organization of individual experience can be designated as its structuring or structuration. Since, however, experience is continually acquired anew as an effect of the subjects' activeness, their previous experiences which been already been structured in some way are subject to reorganization or restructuring resulting from the assimilation of the new experiences. In this way individual development would be connected with the process of structuring and restructuring the individual experience.

The structuring of experience can be performed according to different principles and in various ways.

Some psychologists assume that "all experience is structured" (Cofer, 1977) in as much as an indivudal imposes the inner structures of his psyche on the surrounding world. There is definitely a grain of truth in this, and yet the structures of activeness are not the only source and principle for the structuring of experience.

The simplest form of arranging experience in agreement with the hypothesis of the record-type experience is ordering them on the axis of time, i.e. in succession of occurrence, along the axis of biographical time. Another possibility of experience organization would be connected with the grouping of experiences into entireties linked by their content or by their connection with the subject's current situation and activity.

Jean Piaget, considering the question of psychological structures (1972, p. 88), distinguishes three possible solutions to the question of their genesis. These are: "... preformation, accidental creations or construction".

Here we are taking the constructivist position in the sense that individuals, having the organs of activeness supplied by nature at their disposal, organize for themselves the inflow of experiences whose accumulation implies their arrangement and structuring in connection with situational needs, life tasks and activities of the subjects. Thus, experiences are constructed in the course of activeness, and their structuration modifies activeness. The schemes and structures of activeness effect individual experience and are imprinted in it.

The formation of funtional systems in the organism and brain activity of individuals would constitute the physiological basis of those processes, together with the experiences, ordered in one way or another, which come from their own activity, the use of tools, etc. The functional systems described by Soviet psychologists and neurophysiologists are the structures of connections formed in the course of ontogenesis between various organs of the body and their centres in the brain appropriate to the particular elements of a given activity or the ability to perform it. These systems are flexible and once established, they function as a whole (see Anochin, 1971; Ananiev, 1959; Leontiev, 1962; Luria, 1976; Sokolov, 1969; and others).

The analogical systems of brain activities arise as a result of the coördination of the functional blocks of the brain according to Luria's (1976) model interpreted in relation to the psychological competence of an individual by Das and co-authors (Das et al., 1979). The formation of such dynamic organizations of activeness is also assumed by Allport (1961) in his analysis of the development of the personality of an individual. According to Allport, such a dynamic organization of the individuals' psycho-physical system lies at the base of the structure of their personality and conditions the formation of the unique forms of their psychic and social adaptation.

The expanding and organizing activeness of individuals in their environment depends also on the structuring influence of the elements of the environment. Since it is a form of interaction of individuals with the environment, activeness must form interaction and changes appropriate to its demands. Thus, an essential factor of experience structuring is the activity in which an individual makes use of socially elaborated means, such as tools and signs, particularly language signs creating a new system of the subject's own (verbal) activities.

Mastering language signs, persons acquire a tool for coding and elaborating individual experience. Language signs, being a carrier of socially established meanings and referring to the one's own experience, allow one to distinguish certain experiences which are similar and give a name to them. This has a two-fold sense for structuring experience: first, it constructs certain broader units grouping experiences, and, second, it invests these experiences with common meaning and transfers them into the sphere of reflexive abstraction ("abstraction réfléchissante") (Piaget, 1975).

Thus mastering language and other systems of cultural signs and symbols modifies an individual's experience providing him or her with the instrument for experience coding, structuring and evaluation (see Wygotski, 1980; Tyszkowa, 1984). The systems of cultural signs and symbols as well as the appropriately structured content carried by them not only construct a certain image of the world or a separate imaginative world, but also provide the patterns for structuring (categorizing, interpreting and functioning) individual human experience. Culture also provides the patterns of life, determines developmental tasks proper for the different periods of human life, promotes various kinds of experiences, treating them as proper and desirable, etc. In this way culture influences the behaviour of people, their life activeness and - indirectly - their experience. Being the social product of culture, experience creates also the criteria of acceptance and self-acceptance of the course of life and the line of the individual's development. This has been pointed out by Erikson (1950, p. 208) who writes that a growing child must have the feeling ".... that his individual way of acquiring experience is a proper variant of the group identity and is in agreement with his space-time and life schedule".

The structuring of experience can also occur in connection with the areas (kinds) of activeness important to individuals, which are the focus of their attention. Around such areas or forms of the individuals' activeness their current experiences are grouped and their previous ones are brought up to date, thus forming together structures which improve their activeness and at the same time invest it with individual dimensions.

Accumulating and organizing individual experience prepares and conditions developmental psychical changes. This becomes especially clear in case of the qualitative structural changes that signify the transition from one stage of development to the other. At that time the patterns of experience accumulation, organization and interpretation are reorganized as well (see Neugarten, 1969).

The development directed towards the new organization of activeness creates the need for experiences of a given type, while the preparation for change intensifies the effectiveness of learning, which takes place in the so-called sensitive periods of development. The processes of rapid structuring (or restructuring) are favoured in turn by the experiences which force the making of a new selection and different evaluation of previous experiences. Due to these effects, they are called critical experiences or - when referring to external reality - critical events. They find expression in developmental changes of early childhood when, as a result of experiences acquired from children's own activeness, the basic patterns of their sensiromotor activities, acting on objects as well as the basic structures of psychic activeness are formed (Uzgiris, 1977; White et al., 1979; Zazzo, 1978).

Experiences of a specific nature play a significant role

in the formation of the structures of psychic activeness and
are indispensable for their emergence. The experiences which
are essential for a child's development originate from the
objective activities the child performes in multisided
interaction with adults (Elkonin, 1960; Lublinska, 1979;
Leontiev, 1962, 1975). In the further phases of childhood
experiences resulting from the child's own activeness in
relations with peers, processes of mastering proficiency and
knowledge in intentional learning as well as experience of
responsibility connected to this take on a corresponding
meaning.

In the period of adolescence such an important role in
development is played by experiences connected with the
processes of growth and biological maturation, with the
appearance of the new functions and needs, in particular
sexual needs, with changes brought out by the mutual relations
between an individual and other people and his or hers
position among them. Csikszentmihaly showed that adolescents
spend the major part of their free time talking to others of
their own age (Csikszentmihaly et al., 1977). The experience
gained by such conversations, the itensity of which has also
been noted by other scientists, leads - as can be supposed -
one to see the relativity of one's viewpoints which leads to a
deepening of one's understanding of others. This is of
essential importance for the future ability to establish
intimate contacts with other people, particularly sexual
partnerships characteristic of adult life. In the form of
interpersonal exchange, these conversations make it possible
to arrange and interpret the experiences of the young
interlocutors, and thus they facilitate their inner
integration and development.

Gilligan and Murphy (1978) in turn have observed that the
transition from principled moral reasoning to contextual
morality requires that the young adults undergo certain
experiences in intimate relations with other people.
Experiences of this kind are also important for the
development of cognitive activities characteristic of
dialectical thinking and essential for the change of the

individuals' inner attitudes towards themselves (Riegel, 1975, 1976; Labouvie-Vief, 1982; Levinson et al., 1978).

An adequately rich and organized inner life experience generates new forms of adult thinking, such as the forementioned dialectical or metaphorical thinking, and leads to such a state of cognitive activities, thinking and conduct, which is called mature wisdom (Baltes and Schaie, 1976; Baltes, Reese and Lipsitt, 1980).

It can be said that in the process of becoming organized, experience assumes the form of structures signifying a new quality of psychic functioning, and the new organization of activeness characteristic of the new stage of psychic development. The newly organized activeness strives in turn selectively for experiences which prove to be important for it. A kind of searching and selective restructuring of an individual's experience occurs.

The reorganization and restructuring of experience can also occur under the influence of new experiences changing the position of individuals in the world or revealing to them the changes which have already taken place (e.g. in the periods of adolescence, entering adulthood, or ageing). The situations which lead towards experiences changing the selfperception of individuals and their relations with the world are purposely organized in education (also in special education, resocialization, etc.), in rehabilitation treatment of the ill or handicapped and in psychotherapy.

An impulse for a specific reconstruction of experiences and the internal integration following it is sometimes the experience of catharsis of humour, revelation, etc. The source of this reorganization of experience in all these cases seems to be in the emotions currently experienced by the subject. These emotions reveal some new aspects of the subject's situation and his or her previous experience. This in turn causes the restructuring of this experience. This mechanism works - according to Piaget - in the transformations of emotional attitudes as well as cognitive experiences and cognitive structures (Piaget, 1976). Thus, one can say that a current experience is influenced by a former experience, and at the same time restructures the latter.

Being aware of one's own experiences and past experiences forms their representation in consciousness, and subjects them at the same time to categorial reorganization and structuring. Perhaps because of this process adolescents have to devote so much time to the conversations with their peers, old people must share their experiences with others, etc. Would it be possible that only this form of interpersonal communication facilitates the structuring of their individual experience?

Most probably autocommunication alone is not enough for an adequately deep restructuring of individual experience, This process may only be carried out in the form of interpersonal communication. The effectiveness of education (in terms of facilitating an individual's development) and psychotherapy is definitely based upon a similar mechanism.

Individual experience conditioned by innate characteristics and life circumstances determining the conditions of activeness constitute the individuals' psychological biography. Undertaking particular forms of activeness, making certain life choices in accordance with value standards, people create for themselves the conditions of aquiring these particular experiences which are an essential part of their life experience. The above mentioned instruments for structuring experience are also acquired to a considerable extent from the subject's own activeness. In this sense, i.e. in the sense of creating for itself conditions for acquiring and structuring of experience, humankind is also the creator of its own psychic biography and, indirectly, in this important aspect, of itself.

REFERENCES.

Aebli, H. (1978). A dual model of cognitive development: Structure in cultural stimulation, construction by child. International Journal of Behavioural Development, 1,

221-228.

Allport, G.W. (1961). Pattern and growth in personality. New York: Holt.

Ananiev, G.B. (1959) Osyazanye v processach poznanya y truda (Touch in the processes of cognition and work). Moskva: APN.

Anochin, P.K. (1971). Principalnye voprossy teorii funkcyonalnych sistem (Main problems of the theory of functional systems). Moskva: AN SSSR.

Baltes, P.B. & Schaie, W.K. (1976). On the plasticity of intelligence in adulthood. American Psychologist, 31, 720-725.

Baltes, P.B. & Willis, S.L. (1979). The critical importance of appropriate methodology in the study of aging. The sample case of psychometric intelligence. In Hoffmeister and Müller (Eds.), Brain functions in old age. Heidelberg: Springer.

Cofer, C.N. (1977). On the constructive theory of memory. In I. Užgiris & F. Weizmann (Eds.), The structuring of experience. New York, London: Plenum Press.

Csikszentmihaly, M., Larson, R. & Prescott, S. (1977). The ecology of adolescent activity and experience. Journal of Youth and Adolescence, 6, 281-294.

Das, J.P., Kirby, J.R. & Jarman, R.F. (1979). Simultaneous and successive cognitive processes. New York, San Francisco, London: Academic Press.

Elkonin, D.V. (1960). Detskaya psychologia (Child Psychology). Moskva: Uczpedgiz.

Gilligan, C. & Murphy, J.M. (1979). Development from adolescence to adulthood: The philosopher and the dilemma of the fact. In D. Kuhn (Ed.), Intellectual development beyond childhood. San Francisco: Jossey-Bass.

Henry, W.E. (1971). The role of work in structuring the life experience. Human Development, 14, 125-131.

Hilgard, E.R., Atkinson, R.L. & Atkinson, R.C. (1979). Introduction to psychology. New York, San Diego, Chicago, San Francisco, Atlanta: Harcourt Brace Jovanovich.

Hunt, J. McV. (1961). Intelligence and experience. New York:

Ronald Press.

Kagan, J. (1978). The growth of the child. Reflections on human development. New York: Norton.

Kmita, J. (1975). Homo symbolicus. In J. Kmita (Ed.), Wartość, dzielo, sens (Value, work, sense). Warszawa: Ksiazka i Wiedza.

Labouvie-Vief, G. (1982). Dynamic development of mature autonomy. A theoretical prologue. Human Development, 25, 161-191.

Leontiev, A.N. (1962). O rozwoju psychiki (On the development of psyche). Warszawa: Panstwowe Wydawnictwo Naukowe.

Leontiev, A.N. (1975). Dieyatelnost, sosnanye, litchnost (Activity, consciousness, personality). Moskva: Izd. Polit Lit.

Levinson, D.J., Darrow, C.N., Klein, E.B., Levinson, M.H. & Braxton, McK. (1978). The seasons of a man's life. New York: A. Knopf.

Linhart, J. (1972). Proces i struktura uczenia sie ludzi (Process and structure of learning in a man). Warszawa: Panstwowe Wydawnictwo Naukowe.

Linhart, J. (1976). Cinnost a poznavani (Activity and Cognition). Praha: Academia.

Lublinskaya, N.N. (1979). Detskaya psichologia (Child Psychology). Riga.

Luria, A.R. (1976). Cognitive functions: their foundations and development. Cambridge, London: Harvard University Press. (a).

Luria, A.R. (1976). Podstawy neuropsychologii (Foundations of neuropsychology). Warszawa: Panstwowe Zaklady Wydawnictw Lekarskich. (b).

Neugarten, B.L. (1969). Continuities and disconstinuities of psychological issues in adult life. Human Development, 12, 121-130.

Norman, D.A. (1976). Memory and attention: An introduction to human information processing. New York: Wiley.

Overton, W. (1975). General systems, structure and development. In K.F. Riegel and G.C. Rosenwald (Eds.), Structure and transformation: developmental and historical aspects: vol. 3. New York: Wiley.

Overton, W.F. (1976). The active organism in structuralism. Human Development, 19, 71-86.

Overton, W.F. (1973). Models of development: Methodological implications. In J.R. Nesselroade and H.W. Reese (Eds.), Life-span developmental psychology. Methodological Issues, New York: Academic Press.

Piaget, J. (1967). La psychologie de l'intelligence. Paris: Armand Colin.

Piaget, J. (1972). Strukturalizm (Structuralism). Warszawa: WP.

Piaget, J. (1976). The affective unconscious and the cognitive unconscious. In B. Inhelder, H.H. Chipman and C. Zwingman (Eds.), Piaget and his school. A reader in developmental psychology. New York: Springer.

Piaget, J. (1975). L'équilibration des structures cognitives. Problème central du développement. Paris: Presses Universitaire de France.

Przetacznikowa, M. (1973). Podstawy rozwoju psychicznego dzieci i mlodziezy (Foundations of psychological development of children and youth). Warszawa: Wydawnictwa Szkolne i Pedagogiczne.

Reese, H.W. & Overton, W.F. (1978). Models of development and theories of development. In H.W. Reese and W.F. Overton (Eds.), Life-span developmental psychology. Research and Theory. New York: Academic Press.

Riegel, K.F. (1975). Toward a dialectical theory of development. Human Development, 18, 50-64.

Riegel, K.F. (1976). The dialectics of human development. American Psychologist, October, 689-698.

Schaie, K.W. (1965). A general model for the study of developmental problems. Psychological Bulletin, 64, 92-107.

Schaie, K.W. & Baltes, P.B. (1975). On sequential strategies in developmental research: Description or explanation? Human Development, 18, 384-390.

Smedslund, J. (1963). The concept of correlation in adults. Scandinavian Journal of Psychology, 4, 165-173.

Sokolov, E.N. (1969). Mechanizmy pamiati (Mechanisms of memory). Moskva: Izd. MGU.

Spitz, R.A. (1963). La prémiere année de la vie de l'enfant. Paris: Presses Universitaire de France.

Szewczuk, W. (1979). Slownik psychologiczny (Dictionary of psychological terms). Warszawa: Panstwowe Wydawnictwo Naukowe.

Tomaszewski, T. (1975). Czlowiek i otoczenie (Man and his environment). Procesy spostrzegania (Processes of perception). In T. Tomaszewski (Ed.), Psychologia. Warszawa: Panstwowe Wydawnitwo Naukowe.

Tyszkowa, M. (1977a). Aktywność i dzialalność dzieci i mlodziezy (Activeness and activity of children and adolescents). Warszawa: Wydwanictwa Szkolne i Pedagogiczne.

Tyszkowa, M. (1983). Zasady rozwoju dzialalności (Principles of development of activity in man). Przeglad Psychologiczny, XXIV (3), 519-531.

Tyszkowa, M. (1984). Kultura symboloczna, wartości i rozwój jednostki (Symbolic culture, values and the individual's development). In M. Tyszkowa, and B. Zurakowski (Eds.), Wartości w świecie dziecka i sztuki dla dziecka (Values in the world of child and in art addressed to children). Warszawa-Poznań: Panstwowe Wydawnictwo Naukowe, p. 24-48.

Uzgiris, I.C. (1977). Plasticity and structure: The role of experience in infancy. In I.C. Uzgiris, and F. Weizman, (Eds.), The structuring of experience. New York, London: Plenum Press.

White, B.L. (1971). Human infants: Experience and psychological development. Englewood Cliffs (NY): Prentice-Hall.

White, B.L., Kaban, B.T. & Attanucci, J.S. (1979). The origins of human competence. The final report of the Harvard preschool project. Lexington/Toronto: Lexington Books/ C.D. Heath and Company.

Wlodarski, Z. (1975). Rozwój i ksztaltowanie doświadczenia indywidualnego (Development and shaping of individual experience). Warszawa: Wydawnictwa Szkolne i

Pedagogiczne.

Wohlwill, J.F. (1973). The concept of experience: S or R? Human Development, 16, 90-107.

Wygotsky, L.S. (1962). Thought and language, Cambridge (Mass.): MIT Press.

Wygotsky, L.S. (1969). Izbrannye psichologicheskye sochinienya (Collected psychological works). Moskva: APN RFSSR.

Wygotsky, L.S. (1971). Wybrane prace psychologiczne (Selected psychological works). Warszawa: Panstwowe Wydawnictwo Naukowe.

Wygotsky, L.S. (1978). Narzedzie i znak w rozwoju dziecka. (Tools and signs in child development). Warszawa: Panstwowe Wywadnictwo Naukowe.

Wygotsky, L.S. (1980). Psychologia sztuki (Psychology of art). Kraków: Wydawnictwo Literackie.

Zazzo, R. (Ed.) (1978). Przywiazanie - ujecie interdyscyplinarne (Attachement - interdisciplinary approach). Warszawa: Panstwowe Wydawnictwo Naukowe.

PART 5

RATIONALISM VERSUS EMPIRICISM
IN DEVELOPMENTAL THEORY BUILDING

Theory Building in Developmental Psychology
P.L.C. van Geert (editor)
© *Elsevier Science Publishers B.V. (North-Holland), 1986*

11

Children's Theories and Developmental Theory

Ed Elbers

Rationalist and empiricist approaches to the
child as a knowing subject coexist in cognitive
developmental theory. This chapter explores the
implications of each approach for our
understanding of the growth of children's
knowledge about reality. In particular, Piaget's
early theory of children's ideas about reality
is discussed, in which he attempted to reconcile
the child's own intellectual activity (which
rationalism emphasises) with the influence of
the environment (which empiricism focuses on).
Piaget's theory, which still stands as a
paradigm for research on the development of
children's ideas, is criticised in the light of
recent understandings of cognitive development,
philosophy of science, communication theory and
anthropology. It is concluded that the early
Piaget, despite his intentions, is essentially a
rationalist, who saw the influence of the
environment only in children's communication
with their peers, and neglected their
interaction with adults and the social
transmission of knowledge. As an alternative it
is proposed that children's ideas originate from
the interaction of two processes: children's
using a variety of intellectual strategies to
expand their knowledge about reality and adults'
transmitting knowledge to children. As a result
of this interaction, children's ideas bear the
imprint of the culture they grow up in and
gradually approach the standards of knowledge of
their culture (which rationalism fails to
account for). This interaction also occasionally
leads to a refusal on the part of children to
accept knowledge from adults because they are in
a process of working out their own theories
(which empiricism cannot explain).

A basic problem in building cognitive developmental theory is whether the growth of knowledge should be understood as the result of spontaneous construction by the child or as the product of environmental shaping or socialisation. Some theorists, standing in an empiricist tradition (among them psychologists influenced by behaviourism and followers of Vygotsky), emphasise the role of the environment in the acquisition of knowledge. Others, representing a rationalist approach (such as those favouring an information processing theory), have explained cognitive development in terms of processes of cognitive structuring and restructuring or increasing cognitive abilities, but have neglected the environmental, and in particular the social, influences on children's growing understanding of reality. In this chapter I shall clarify the theoretical dilemma of emphasising either the spontaneous contribution of the child or the environmental shaping of knowledge, by discussing Piaget's early work on children's theories about reality. These studies are particularly appropriate in this discussion, as Piaget explicitly set himself the task of including into one theoretical framework both the child's own contribution to a growing understanding of reality and the impact of the environment. He rejected both empiricism, according to which the child's knowledge is entirely shaped by the environment, and rationalism, which considers knowledge solely as the product of structures of the mind, and he made an attempt to reconcile these positions in his theory of adaptation. I shall argue that Piaget not only was unsuccessful in reconciling the two extreme positions, but that he could not escape the charms of one of them: rationalism.

My analysis of these studies by Piaget does not stem from sheer historical interest. Piaget's early investigations of children's understanding of reality still stand as a model for contemporary studies on the content of children's thinking. By adopting Piaget's early views as a paradigm, modern investigators, as I shall show, find themselves encountering the same pitfalls as Piaget. Moreover, although the works of the later Piaget have been the object of severe criticism in the last decades, his early books are sometimes judged much more favourably. Brainerd, normally very critical of Piaget's ideas, writes in a review of the research on animistic thinking of young children, that replication studies have confirmed young Piaget's findings (1978, p. 121). I shall argue that these studies by Piaget cannot survive in the light of modern views on cognitive development. In this critique, I shall transplant recent discussions of Piaget's later works to these early studies, and, moreover, I shall confront these studies with recent insights from anthropology, history and philosophy of science, and communication theory. My criticism of Piaget implies some ideas about how the interaction of individual and social factors in cognitive development should be conceived of, and, therefore, my analysis points the way to a reinterpretation of young Piaget's theory of the representation of reality in children and contains suggestions as to how children's ideas should be understood. Throughout this chapter the term "young children" denotes children between about three and seven years old.

PIAGET'S THEORY OF CHILDREN'S IDEAS.

The early Piaget found himself in good company when he turned to the investigation of children's ideas about reality. All the great developmental psychologists of the first decades of the century - Karl Bühler, Stanley Hall, William Stern, James Sully and others - were interested in the content of children's thinking. Typically, these developmental psychologists tried to discover global orientations or dominant tendencies in the way young children view the world. James Sully (1896), for instance, describes the child's disposition to animate nature and to personify things, as in the case of a little boy who explained the wind by the idea of somebody waving a big fan. Sully was an influence on young Piaget, who investigated children's understanding of reality in two books, which could in fact be considered as one study in two volumes: The Child's Conception of the World

(1927/1973) and The Child's Conception of Physical Causality
(1927/1930). In these studies Piaget reported his
conversations with children between four and eleven years old
about subjects like: Where do dreams come from? Is the moon
alive? What makes a river move?

As my main object in this section is to show how Piaget
in these studies attempted to reconcile empiricist and
rationalist conceptions of the child as a knowing subject, I
shall begin by summarising Piaget's discussion of empiricism
and rationalism. Subsequently, young Piaget's famous theses
about children's egocentric and pre-causal thinking can be
clarified.

Piaget's argument against empiricism is his version of a
standard philosophical argument: the world children perceive
is an interpreted world and this interpretation depends on
their cognitive capacities, on their "dominant mental
tendencies" (1927/1930, p. 256). Piaget also rejects the
opposite idea: if knowledge is merely a spontaneous product of
the child's mind, why does not it appear in its completed
form? The development of knowledge, therefore, can only be
explained by acknowledging that the child's mental structures
are open to the action of the environment. In short, as Piaget
argues elsewhere (1961): empiricism explains the development
without accounting for the structure, while apriorism explains
the structure and does not understand why there is
development.

Piaget attempted to find a way out of the dilemma
represented by these two extreme epistemic positions, by
establishing the respective contributions of both the mind and
the environment in the development of thinking. To give a
precise representation of this mutual relationship Piaget
developed his theory of adaptation, which he unfolded in The
Child's Conception of Physical Causality. Every influence of
the environment is incorporated by the subject in existing
structures (assimilation), but, at the same time, the subject
must adapt these structures to this influence (which Piaget
calls imitation, and which he designated as accomodation in
his later works). The development of cognitive structures

consists of the gradual changing of these structures by adaptation: the child can adapt to new objects only partially, in so far as the structures are able to assimilate them, but these adaptations do not leave the structures unchanged, so that there is a continuous process of developing structures.

It is characteristic of the early Piaget, that he sought this process of adaptation in the child's social interaction with peers. Children come to discover that others have ideas different from theirs. As a consequence they make efforts to adapt themselves to the points of view of these others. To quote an example Piaget uses himself (1927/1930, Section IV): all young children believe that the sun follows them when they move; but eventually they realise that this is impossible, because the sun cannot at the same time follow two people going in different directions. Hence, according to young Piaget, changes in children's ideas about reality are not primarily the result of an intrinsic interest in the world, or the product of occasional clashes between expectations and reality, but they are rooted in children's need to communicate with other children and their desire to share the perspectives of their friends. Children discover that their knowledge is incompatible with the ideas of their peers, and only because they attempt to overcome these social impossibilities do they progressively coordinate their viewpoints with those of others.

When this social process of adaptation is taken into account the general course of the development of children's representation of reality becomes clear. Children begin by confusing self and world, but they have to abandon this impossible position in their interactions with other children and in the end they have constructed self and world as separate entities. The development of children's thinking, according to Piaget's early position, is a process of desubjectification, in which an initially egocentric relationship with reality is gradually given up. Piaget subsumes his theories of the growth of logical thinking (1923/1967 and 1924/1928) and of the development of the representation of reality under this broad perspective, and

consequently presents these two lines of development as
parallel processes.

At first, children up to about seven years of age show
egocentrism in both logical and ontological respect. On the
logical plane, this egocentrism is apparent in the absence of
a need to justify statements; in conversations children take
it as a matter of course that people understand them and agree
with them. Instead of reasoning and trying to make logical
inferences, they connect the things in their world according
to their affective and personal relationship with these
things. Instead of using deduction, they argue by
transduction, i.e. by associating singular cases without
referring to general laws. On the ontological plane,
egocentrism appears in their tendency to confuse psychological
activity and physical mechanisms. To denote this tendency to
confound motive and cause, Piaget uses the term
"pre-causality", which he presents as a higher order concept
subsuming the manifold manifestation of children's egocentric
representation of the world. Only in middle childhood, from
seven or eight years onwards, children start justifying and
verifying statements.

Piaget classified children's explanations of reality in
seventeen stages, which represent a gradual transition from
pre-causal thinking to physical and mechanical explanations,
the first nine being characteristic of pre-causality. I shall
restrict myself to the most important forms of pre-causal
thinking in Piaget's classification. Participation and magical
thinking are very early forms, that disappear after age five
or six. Children then think in accordance with artificialism
and animism, until seven or eight years of age, when genuinely
physical explanations gradually supplant the other forms. In
order to clarify the idea of pre-causal thinking in children
and its different, sometimes overlapping, forms, I shall
borrow some examples from Piaget's studies.

In participation children wrongly consider two or more
things as having something in common and influencing one
another:

DUG (6½): (...)- Where is the dream made?
                - In the bed.
                - How?
                - From air (...)
                - Is there something that sends the dream?
                - Yes, the birds.
                - Why?
                - Because they like the air.
                (Piaget, 1927/1973, p. 130-131).

In magical thinking children regard things as obeying the
thoughts and wishes of people:

SALA (8):   - You have already seen the clouds moving
                  along. What makes them move?
                - When we move along, they move along too.
                - Can you make them move?
                - Everybody can, when they walk.
                - When I walk and you are still, do they move?
                - Yes.
                (Piaget, 1927/1930, p. 62).

Things and events are conceived of as the result of human
creative activity in artificialism:

GRIM (5):   - Why does the water in the Arve move along?
                - Because people make oars. They push.
                - Where are the oars?
                - In the boats there are men who hold them.
                  They make it go. (...)
                - Is the Arve running today?
                - No .... It is moving along little.
                - Why?
                - Because there are a few boats.
                (Piaget (1927/1930, p. 94).

By considering things as being alive and invested with
consciousness, children manifest animistic thinking:

MONT (7):   - Does the sun know it gives light?
                - Yes.
                - Why?
                - Because it is made of fire.
                - Does it know that we are here?

- No.
- Does it know it is fine weather?
- Yes.
(Piaget, 1927/1973, p. 205).

In sum, young Piaget tried to solve the dilemma of empiricist and rationalist explanations of children's knowledge by arguing that children try to adapt themselves to the perspectives of their peers and in the course of this process intellectually construct both logic and the objective world. Children start in an egocentric state, in which self and world are confused and in which they do not doubt the correctness of their opinions. Children's subsequent interpretations of reality (participation, animism, etc.) are intermediary positions in their course from an egocentric to an objective viewpoint.

CRITIQUE OF PIAGET'S THEORY.

In this section I shall criticise Piaget's early theory of children's ideas about reality. In particular, I shall deal with four components of this theory: his characterisation of young children's thinking as inadequate, his ideal of scientific reasoning, the idea of a logical order underlying the development of a concept, and his view on the influence of the environment and social relationships. But first I want to place Piaget's theory of young children's thinking in a broader intellectual context by dealing with the ideas of the French anthropologist Lévy-Bruhl on the representation of the world in primitive societies. Lévy-Bruhl, whose main studies were published in the years that Piaget was preparing his early books, was a major influence on Piaget. A discussion of Lévy-Bruhl's work will be a help in understanding Piaget's ideas. In fact, the shortcomings of Piaget's theory are in many respects analogous to the objections Lévy-Bruhl's theory has evoked.

Lévy-Bruhl as a Source of Inspiration to Piaget.

Lévy-Bruhl characterised thinking in traditional societies with the concept of "primitive mentality" (cf. Horton, 1973). Primitive mentality is the opposite of modern thought, which according to Lévy-Bruhl is an attribute of western society. Perception and thought in primitive people are strongly invested with emotions; the world has a mystical aspect and is filled with invisible and intangible powers. Everything is imbued with spiritual and personal forces and there is no distinction between mind and matter. Instead of using causality, primitive people explain reality by magic and by the belief that two phenomena can directly influence one another, even though there is no intelligible causal relation between them - a belief Lévy-Bruhl called "participation". Dreams and visions in the primitive view of the world are not different from ordinary experience and, as a consequence, traditional people are insensitive to observations which refute their beliefs. Primitive mentality is also unable to detect and avoid contradictions, and therefore "pre-logical".

In the first decades of the century, drawing parallels between children's and primitives, thinking was a component of the intellectual climate of the West. Stanley Hall called non white people "the children of the human race" (Jahoda, 1982, p. 187). Freud, in Totem and Taboo (1913), expressed his conviction that primitive people represent the childhood of humanity, and that the intellectual development of the child reproduces this phase on an individual plane (cf. Lévi-Strauss, 1949, p. 113). In his own way, Piaget fell a prey to what Lévi-Strauss called the "archaic illusion". And although Piaget admonishes not to exaggerate, the relevant texts speak for themselves:

> "It is therefore our belief that the day will come
> when child thought will be placed on the same level
> in relation to adult, normal, and civilized thought,
> as 'primitive mentality' as defined by Lévy-Bruhl"
> (1924/1928, p. 256; other relevant texts are cited
> by Lévi-Strauss, ch. 7).

In his early studies Piaget ascribed a primitive mentality to children, and for a description of children's thinking he borowed concepts like pre-causality, participation and magic from Lévy-Bruhl. Just as Lévy-Bruhl distinguished primitive from modern mentality, Piaget opposed young children's thinking to socialised thought.

But how convincingly can children's understanding of reality be described with such global and negative concepts? In anthropology the opposition between the savage mind and the modern mind has apparently never been entirely abandoned. This argument is contained in an article by the English anthropologist Robin Horton (1973), who criticises the distinction. His critique is twofold. The first point is based on an interpretation of anthropological studies by Malinovsky and Evans-Pritchard. People in traditional cultures normally rely on a model of reality in which - contrary to what Lévy-Bruhl believed - mythical and animistic elements are absent. People, animals, plants and things according to this mental framework do not in essentials behave differently from the way we understand them: in normal circumstances animals and plants do not communicate with people, and stones or water do not carry messages. Everyday life in traditional societies is moulded on beliefs of causal relationships - be it insufficient and. often erroneous beliefs - which are to a certain extent open to correction by experience. Only occasionally, when this mental framework fails, preliterate people resort to ideas about spiritual beings populating the world, ideas which they use to explain the unexplainable. And, Horton assures us, they do so quite reluctantly, conscious of the limits of their knowledge (Horton & Finnegan, 1973).

Horton's second point is a philosophical one. The ideal of science, on which the distinction between the modern, scientific mind and the savage, primitive mentality is based, has been destroyed by modern philosophy of science. Elaborating on Horton's argument, three outcomes of modern theory of science can be distinguished. (1) The concepts of animism and participation were coined to understand the primitives' attempt to explain their world with invisible

forces. But postulating unobservable entities is objectionable
only to an inductivist interpretation of science, according to
which scientific activity must be based exclusively on
observation and observation statements. Inductivism has not
survived the recent progress of history and philosophy of
science. Modern theories of science acknowledge that in
scientific theories, too, we postulate invisible forces and
elements. Popper writes that, in science, we try to explain
the known by the unknown (1972, p. 63). (2) In the theories of
Kuhn and Lakatos about scientific achievements a tenacity to
ideas, even when the facts seem to contradict them, is
considered a rational virtue. In his famous article, Lakatos
(1970) presents examples of scientists who did not give up
their programmes despite refuting evidence, and who succeeded
in making the programme successful in the end. Therefore, the
blindness to facts which Lévy-Bruhl attributed to primitive
people does not separate primitive mentality from the
scientific attitude towards reality as sharply as Lévy-Bruhl
thought. (3) And what about the lack of logical coherence in
primitive thought, "patchwork thinking" as Lévi-Strauss calls
it: is this a ground for delimiting a primitive mentality
from the scientific spirit? In modern investigations of
scientific achievements, it is stressed that the elaboration
of new ideas is often guided by analogy and association, even
by paradoxes, rather than by strict, logical rules. Einstein
called the process leading to a scientific discovery a "free
play with concepts" (cited in Wartofsky, 1980). In this
respect, too, the difference between the modern, scientific
mind and primitive mentality must be softened.

Horton goes so far as to say:

> "traditional ideas about unobservable entities are
> most appropriately described (....) as theoretical
> concepts couched in a slightly unfamiliar idiom"
> (280).

This position, which is cited approvingly by Warren (1980) and
Jahoda (1982), does not imply a relativism in which all
differences of quality between western and traditional
societies are blurred. Horton emphasises that the distinction

between traditional and scientific theories is a matter of
degree rather than a basic contrast. Only when we have
understood that theoretical ideas have the same function in
traditional and modern societies, we can fruitfully work out
the differences between them.

Young Children's Intellectual Capacities.

    Do analogous arguments apply to young children's thinking
and the way it has been understood by Piaget? In my opinion
recent results of investigations of cognitive development show
the need for a reorientation in the field of children's
thinking, which is in many respects comparable to Horton's
plea to soften the contrast between traditional and scientific
mentalities. In the study of children's thinking, too, we must
do away with ideas of basic differences and acknowledge the
similarities between children's reasoning and adult thinking.
When we hear children talking, when we see how they discuss
problems confronting them, we are impressed that they often
reason so well. Young children, even three and four-year-olds,
already know a lot about the make up and conventions of their
world, be it a world restricted and prestructured on behalf of
them by adults. If we have forgotten this or if we have not
been astonished as parents by the cleverness of our small
children, we are reminded of it now by the growing number of
observational studies about young children's reasoning in
everyday situations which have appeared in the last few years
(Wood, MacMahon & Cranstoun, 1980; Dunn & Kendrick, 1982;
Tizard & Hughes, 1984). The same studies document children's
curiosity and their eagerness to enlarge their knowledge of
the world.
    Of course, children's understanding does fall short in a
lot of situations, but it is impossible to characterise it as
inadequate in global terms. Investigations of children's
reasoning capacities and their egocentrism (reviewed by Gelman
& Baillargeon, 1983) have revealed that children perform best
in familiar situations when they are confronted with questions

which are not altogether new for them. In such circumstances
they are often not egocentric, but quite capable of taking
someone else's perspective. Dunn & Kendrick, for instance,
when they visited families in which a second child had
recently been born, were often approached by the elder
sibling, who spontaneously began explaining the baby to them
(Dunn & Kendrick, 1982, p. 104). Tizard & Hughes (1984), in a
study based on recordings of four-year-old children's
conversations with their mothers at home and with their
teachers at school, have defended the idea that children's
arguments sometimes seem egocentric and illogical, but that
they may only be based on the wrong premises. They describe a
conversation between a four-year-old girl and her elder
sister, who is about to go to a party:

> Child: Whose party is it?
> Sister: Franny's Mum and Dad's party.
> Child: Were Franny's Mum and Dad born on the same
>   day?

(Tizard & Hughes, 1984, p. 130).

Tizard & Hughes propose, rightly I think, that this child
argues correctly, but that she uses the false presupposition
that only birthdays can be a ground for parties. In the
conversations Tizard and Hughes recorded, they found that
children had theories like: shopkeepers supply their customers
with money instead of the other way round, mother turns on the
streetlighting by operating a switch in the living room,
people with the same Christian names also have the same
surnames, adults steadily grow longer as they get older.

Tizard & Hughes found in their naturalistic study an
amazing level of intellectual activity in the children, which,
they think, can only be understood by assuming that children
are more or less conscious of the limitations of their
knowledge and actively try to fill the gaps. When children
encounter problems or unexpected events they construct
theories, elaborate on them and test them. Many theories which
children invent are wrong, but not always because they are
egocentric or completely lack the ability to reason logically
but because their knowledge of reality is still limited and

the integration of this knowledge poor.

All this does not mean that children never exhibit egocentrism nor that they can argue as well as adults. To be sure, children's thinking is clearly immature in a lot of situations, but it is certainly not always inadequate, and this makes it impossible to characterise it in global terms, as Piaget did. It is by no means justified to distinguish children's and adult thought as sharply as Piaget has done. Young children already understand a lot of their world, and when their thinking proves to be inadequate, they try to gain a better understanding of it by constructing new theories. In these respects, there is no basic difference between children's thinking and our own.

Piaget's Ideal of Scientific Thinking.

Piaget's ideal of science is embedded in the same philosophical tradition that opposed primitive to modern thought. Therefore, Horton's arguments, which were presented in the discussion of Lévy-Bruhl's ideas, apply just as well to Piaget's early theories. Firstly, children's magical or animistic thinking does not necessarily give evidence of an attitude radically opposed to scientific thinking: it may be an attempt to understand hitherto unfamiliar mechanisms or relationships between phenomena. In a later section I shall reinterpret Piaget's conversations with children, on which his books on the representation of reality are based, with the help of this idea.

Secondly, children's conservatism, their tenacity to ideas even in the light of experience or if they are corrected by adults, is not always a sign of intellectual immaturity. Just as scientific investigators sometimes have to neglect empirical counterevidence in the process of elaborating a theory and may progress despite these contrary facts, children in the course of elaborating their ideas sometimes refuse to learn from experience. At the end of this chapter I shall dwell extensively on this similarity between the progress of scientific theory (as understood in modern philosophy of science), and the development of children's ideas about reality.

And thirdly, for Piaget, the ideal of science was represented by the perspective of objective and logically consistent thinking. Hence, he could only consider children's thinking, although progressing in the direction of this ideal, as immature. Here are the roots of Piaget's lack of interest for creativity in children's thinking, a gap in his work Riegel (1973) reproached him for. Already Wallon (1945, cf. Anthony, 1973, p. 61), in his discussions with Piaget, emphasised that the different forms of pre-causal thinking give children a freedom which they need in constructing a representation of reality. Moreover, the characteristics of this immature thinking - transductions, analogies, paradoxes, associations - have, as I have shown, acquired a more respectable place in the philosophy of science since the time of young Piaget's studies. Children's thinking may often lack logical rigour and systematization, but it is impressive in its creativity and curiosity, and in this it resembles the "free play with ideas" of the successful scientist.

The Construction of a Concept as an Orderly Process.

The main reason why Piaget was attracted to the anthropological studies by Lévy-Bruhl was because he was convinced that parallels can be drawn between the development of children's ideas in ontogenesis and the development of thinking in history. When we observe animism and magic in young children, we see the cultural history of the species repeated. In fact, human understanding of nature had to go through the same process of desubjectification that each child has to go through again. Piaget discusses this idea in Play, Dreams and Imitation in Childhood (1946/1962). Criticising Jung's theory of archetypes, he writes:

> "We can (....) refer to the striking resemblances
> between the beginnings of rational thought in the

child of from seven to ten and in the Greeks. (...)
Are we then to conclude that the archetypes which
inspired the beginnings of Greek physics are
inherited by the child? In our opinion it is
infinitely simpler merely to assume that the same
genetic mechanisms which account for the development
of the thought of the child of to-day were in action
also in the minds of those who, like the pre-
Socratics, were just emerging from mythological and
pre-logical thought" (p. 197-198).

In some modern studies of children's theories the same
presupposition of a fixed sequence of ideas and a repetition
of the cultural history in ontogenesis can be observed,
sometimes explicitly, sometimes implicitly. Broughton (1980),
in an article on children's metaphysical ideas, tries to
demonstrate parallels between the development of children's
spontaneous philosophy of the relationship between the
psychological and the physical and the history of the
mind-body problem in science and philosophy. Bernstein and
Cowan (1975), in a study of the development of children's
concepts about how people get babies, sketch a developmental
sequence in which we see the growing understanding of
procreation in history repeated.

The idea underlying these studies is that there is a
logic inherent in the progressive understanding of a problem,
which is manifest both in cultural history and in ontogenesis.
Kohlberg, in his systematic presentation of cognitive
developmental theory (1969), explicitly states that children
in their developing representation of the world must go
through the same logical sequences of steps, which he - as a
true pupil of Piaget - equates to a gradual desubjectification
of the concepts involved. The order of development, he argues,
is invariant and independent of the influence of the
environment. As an example Kohlberg treats his own
investigation of children's beliefs about dreams. In
elaborating their understanding of dreams, children go through
a three-step sequence: first they must realise that dreams are
unreal; this understanding is the prerequisite of the

discovery that dreams are invisible to others and therefore inside the body; ultimately it is comprehended that dreams are psychic events, distinct from physical phenomena, and consequently immaterial. Kohlberg then writes:

> "The steps represent progressive differentiations of the subjective and objective which logically could not have a different order" (p. 359).

It cannot be denied that one concept must sometimes logically precede a second one. To use an example by Alston, quoted by Shweder & LeVine (1976): it is impossible to deliberately break a rule without knowing that rule. But Kohlberg's pretension goes much further: there is a logical sequence in the understanding of every concept. This is an exaggerated claim, and I do not find his example of the dream concept very convincing. Why is it necessary that a dream is considered unreal before it is recognised as invisible to others? Shweder & LeVine (1976), in fact, offer empirical evidence that this order may be reversed in some cases. But, more importantly, obtaining knowledge is something different from logically contructing it. Knowledge is acquired in a piecemeal way, it is at first incomplete and logically inconsistent, and only in a later stage is it reorganised in a coherent way by a subject reflecting on this knowledge. Just as the real history of a scientific discovery must be distinguished from its rational reconstruction (Lakatos, 1970), the logical structure of a concept should not be confused with the history of its acquisition by the child.

Piaget's View of Influences from the Environment.

In Piaget's theory of adaptation there is no place for the notion that children adopt ideas from more experienced persons. The theme of the transmission of knowledge from adults to children is completely ignored in The Child's Conception of the World and The Child's Conception of Physical Causality, and it is only mentioned in passing as a negative element in development. Socialisation, for Piaget, amounts to

the gradual desubjectification of knowledge, a process which
is kept in motion, as we have seen, by peer interaction, and
in which adults have no part to play. For children adults
represent authority: children adopt adult ideas out of respect
and not because they realise that these ideas can provide for
the insufficiency of their knowledge. Inspired by Rousseau,
Piaget wanted to leave development to the children themselves.
Accordingly, he rejected the idea that the adoption of
knowledge from adults contributes to children's intellectual
development.

Consequently, in his studies Piaget tried to discover the
spontaneity of children's convictions by removing the
influence of the social environment. He tells his readers so
in the very first line of The Child's Conception of the World
(1927/1973, p. 13):

> "The subject of this investigation (...) is as
> follows: what conceptions of the world does the
> child naturally form at the different stages of its
> development".

But, in my view, it is a fiction that we can find these
original convictions: spontaneous construction and social
transmission of knowledge are too much interwoven to be
distilled, even by Piagetian chemistry. Therefore, although
Piaget rejected the theory of innate concepts, he has always
given a rationalist account of children's ideas, which
explains the contents of children's thinking by the action of
the mind itself. In Piaget's account, children's thinking does
develop, but along an fixed sequence of wrong ideas which
children must go through before reaching mature thought.

Piaget's theory of adaptation must be amended to
incorporate the specific characteristics of a social
historical environment. This would require his abandoning the
dogma that development is primarily stimulated by peer
interaction and that acceptance of knowledge from adults is
merely submission to authority. The observations by Tizard and
Hughes (1984) show that Piaget's idea that children are not
interested in communication with adults is competely wrong.
These investigators made some interesting observations on the

way children use adults, especially their mothers, in the
elaboration of their ideas. Tizard and Hughes observed what
they called "passages of intellectual search", in which
children work out and test their theories in conversations
with their mothers. These investigators show how persistently
children sometimes question their mothers and how they
repeatedly return to the same subject.

On the other hand, Piaget was completely right in
rejecting extreme empiricism, which ascribes children's
thinking exclusively to the influence of the environment, and
in particular to the transmission of knowledge from more
experienced persons to the children. This position, which we
find in many learning theories of socialisation and in
Vygotskian approaches to cognitive development, is equally
untenable. Let us look at some empiricist accounts of the
development of children's ideas. Margaret Mead's study among
the Manus of New Guinea (1931) is a classic in this
discussion. Although animistic thinking had been found in
children of different cultures by the time Mead made her
investigations, she found no trace of it in Manu children. She
writes:

> "evidence was found to support the view that animism
> is not a spontaneous aspect of child thinking nor
> does it spring from any type of thought
> characteristic of immature mental development; its
> presence or absence in the thought of children is
> dependent upon cultural factors, language,
> folk-lore, adult attitudes, etc., and these cultural
> factors have their origin in the thought of
> individual adults, not in the misconceptions of
> children" (213).

Another representive of this point of view is the Russian
psychologist Tul'viste, in a critique (1981) of Piaget. This
author maintains that animistic explanations abound in the
child's environment in most cultures. Parents use animistic
elements in their speech to young children, and, more
generally, animism can be found in children's songs and fairy
tales. So, Tul'viste concludes, childhood animism is not a

spontaneous phenomenon in the child, but it is engendered by
the way adults themselves talk about reality to their
children.

This empiricist theory is not convincing because it
presupposes that children adopt more or less passively the
ideology of their parent culture. Exaggerating the
"malleability of human nature" (Mead, 1931, p. 3), these
theorists forget that children contribute to their development
by spontaneously constructing knowledge and elaborating it.
Because children actively construct knowledge, discrepancies
between their ideas and the dominant beliefs of adults are
inevitable. Children's showing animistic thinking is not
completely determined by the culture they are educated in. It
is hardly imaginable that children do not explore the
possibilities for the application of a distinction as
important as the difference between living and not living, and
so, occasionally, attribute life to inanimate things. In this
respect Mead's study is unconvincing. And against Tul'viste it
can be argued that our culture not only presents examples of
animism to children (he is undoubtedly right in that), but
occasionally also disencourages it. Scupin & Scupin (1910, p.
102) report that their son Bubi (4;3) seeing a mushroom asked
whether the mushroom wouldn't get angry if a snail came and
eat it. When the boy was laughed at because of this question,
he immediately corrected himself: "I only thought it".

Conclusion.

In this section Piaget's early theory of the development
of children's ideas about reality was criticised. In ascribing
pre-causal thinking to children, Piaget was inspired by
Lévy-Bruhl's theory of primitive mentality in traditional
cultures. The concept of primitive mentality was found to be
based on an erroneous interpretation of the mental life of
people in traditional societies and an obsolete inductivist
interpretation of the nature of science. Analogous objections
could be raised against Piaget's early studies. Modern

research has shown that children's cognitive performances are much better than Piaget maintained, especially in familiar circumstances; therefore, it is impossible to characterise children's understanding of reality in a global way as pre-causal. Piaget contrasted science as a body of logically structured knowledge with the unsystematic thinking of children, but he did not see that children and scientific investigators have much in common in the way they create new knowledge.

Piaget attempted to reconcile rationalist and empiricist interpretations of children's knowing activity in his theory of adaptation. In this theory, he equates the development of children's knowledge of reality with their gradual liberation from subjective understandings of reality. This process takes an orderly course, dictated by the structure of the concepts involved. Piaget, however, does not give sufficient attention to the influence of the environment. In Piaget's theory, peer interactions motivate this process of desubjectification. But the development of children's theories about reality can never be understood without acknowledging the influence of culture, and the transmission of ideas from adults to children. Children appear to actively turn to adults in order to have their understanding of reality confirmed or corrected.

A REINTERPRETATION OF CHILDREN'S THEORIES.

In the light of this criticism, how can the views the children exhibited in their conversations with Piaget be interpreted?

To begin with, it must be recalled that Piaget's interest was in the spontaneous beliefs of children as opposed to ideas adopted from adults. To reach this aim, Piaget carefully selected his questions according to two criteria. He avoided suggestive questions by introducing themes which children of that age already have a spontaneous interest in; for instance a question like "how did the sun begin?" can only be asked when children have shown a natural curiosity about the origin

of things. But, on the other hand, Piaget took care to ask
questions to which the children had not yet learnt a clear
answer and which were sufficiently new to stimulate mental
activity.

From the perspective of my analysis in the preceding
section, the answers of the children can be understood when
they are regarded as attempts to answer the new problems
Piaget confronted them with, as guesses originating from a
genuine motive to understand reality. These guesses are by no
means blind guesses: children make use of their partial
understanding of reality to explore the new problems posed to
them by Piaget. Their answers, therefore, manifest an
incomplete understanding of reality, full of gaps, rather
than, as Piaget thought, an underlying inclination or tendency
in their thinking. Take for example these ideas of a child:

> "The planets are living, they grow, they are born,
> and yet they have been made by man" (1927/1973, p.
> 405).

Piaget calls this a combination of animism and artificialism.
But why should we assume that a child uses any preferred
interpretative scheme in talking about things (planets in the
example), which he or she perhaps discusses for the first time
in life? Why should such a statement reveal an inclination of
thought rather than an incorrect generalization of existing
knowledge, in this case the application of a biological
understanding, to an unfamiliar phenomenon? How should a child
know that planets are not born, or that they are not man-made?
The only way the child can know this is by someone telling him
or her. This statement, therefore, gives evidence of a wrong
theory applied to an unfamiliar problem. Such statements of
children are the result of the application of incorrect ideas
rather than the manifestation of underlying tendencies of
thinking (like animism and artificialism).

It is not surprising that children, trying to elaborate
the distinction between living beings and lifeless things,
occasionally make mistakes and ascribe life to a thing. Keil
(1983) showed that learning the concept of a "living thing" is
accompanied with errors of under- and overgeneralization. In

an investigation with children between five and ten years old he found that the youngest children denied life in plants. Children of an older age did understand plants as living beings, but they attributed properties to them which should only be applied to animals (like sleeping and being hungry). Only at a still later age did children know so much about sleep and hunger and the biological properties of animals and plants, that they applied the concept of a "living being" in a correct way. Comparable errors of attribution can be expected for instance when children learn to distinguish objects and events (Keil, 1983), when they learn which things are edible and which are not, or how to discriminate between valuable and worthless objects.

Many replication studies of Piaget's observations of pre-causal thinking in young children support the interpretation of pre-causal thinking as errors of attribution, made by children being asked unfamiliar and difficult questions. In studies by Dolgin & Behrend (1984) and Donaldson (1985) the children did not show a strong tendency to use pre-causal explanations. Others (Deutsche, 1943; Berzonsky, 1971; Looft, 1973; Gelman & Spelke, 1981) have argued that the particular content of the question is important in determining the answers: questions about familiar subjects generate less pre-causal responses than questions about unfamiliar subjects. Berzonsky (1971), for instance, found that his subjects often resorted to non-naturalistic causal explanations when asked what makes the wind blow, the stars shine or the clouds move (the very kind of questions Piaget asked), but that they gave naturalistic explanations of what makes a clock tick, a care move and a kite fly. Klingensmith (1953) and Looft (1974) showed that children have an incomplete understanding of concepts like "life", "alive", "living", a finding which implies that a child ascribing life to a lifeless object may mean something different from what Piaget called animism. Children prepared for the questions by instructions about the concept of life showed less animistic responses after the instructions than before (cf. Modgil & Modgil, 1976). Huang (1943) confronted a group of children

with conjuror's tricks and simple demonstrations with a
surprising and unexpected outcome, in which fundamental laws
of nature were violated, and asked children to explain what
they saw. The children acknowledged the abnormality of the
situation, and their explanations, although incorrect, most of
the time were not pre-causal.

Nevertheless, there are studies supporting Piaget's
thesis, the most prominent of which is the study by Laurendeau
& Pinard (1962) among 500 subjects between four and twelve
years of age (for a review of early studies, see Looft &
Bartz, 1960, whose conclusion is in favour of Piaget). Faced
with the problem that so many replication studies have an
outcome negative for Piaget, Laurendeau & Pinard have proposed
an interesting explanation of the differences between various
investigators, by discriminating two general techniques used
in the study of children's ideas. According to one method, the
answers of each separate child must be assessed in a global
way, neglecting differences in the answers of the child over a
number of questions. Investigators adopting this method
generally find pre-causal thinking. The other method consists
of analysing the answers of a group of children to each
separate question. These investigators generally find results
opposite to Piaget's idea of pre-causal thinking.

It is remarkable enough, but by no means exceptional in
psychology, that two methods result in opposite conclusions.
Of course, Laurendeau & Pinard consider the first method the
only suitable one, and Piaget gives them his blessing (Piaget,
1962). My sympathy, however, is not on their side. The main
disadventage of a method that typifies the answers of each
child in a global way, is that it masks the fact that children
achieve at different levels of competence in various
situations and tasks. When Laurendeau & Pinard write:

> "In fact, wrong answers are often more significant
> and throw more light on the true level of the
> child's explanations" (p. 93),

it must be argued that such a true level does not exist (cf.
Light, in press). The interest of many investigators of
cognitive development has moved away from the quest for

encompassing capacities to the study of the variability of cognitive achievements across specific tasks. Piaget himself found deviations in performances from stage levels and he explained them in a rather ad hoc manner with his theory of "décalages". But such deviations are no longer considered as exceptions: they are rather the rule in cognitive development.

But apart from the factors mentioned (the unfamiliarity of the topic and the method of interpreting the answers) there is still another issue, perhaps more fundamental, which must be discussed: Piaget's conversations with children can be analysed from an interactional point of view. Piaget did not consider children to be really interested in talking with adults. In the Introduction of The Child's Conception of the World he writes:

> "in the society of adults, he (= the child) may ask questions interminably but without ever seeking explanations of his own (...). He is silent about them (= his own explanations) especially because he regards these explanations, being his own, as not only the most natural but also as the only ones possible" (1927/1973, p. 18).

Therefore, Piaget rejected naturalistic observations of children's conversations with adults as a suitable means for the study of children's ideas. Instead, he elaborated his clinical method, which has the advantage that the interrogator can approach a problem from various angles, and by persistent questioning can separate real conviction from fantasy and arbitrary answers.

These presuppositions which underlie the clinical method have not stood up to criticism. Children are interested in conversing with adults: as Tizard & Hughes (1984) have shown, they use adults to elaborate their ideas in passages of intellectual search. It has become increasingly clear that revealing children's reasoning achievements is very sensitive to the communicational context in which the child is questioned. Children reason best in conversations with familiar people, in familiar circumstances, about familiar subjects. The point is not so much that these persons help them particularly, but that the partners in conversation share both the motives of the interaction and background knowledge. When there is mutual interest and mutual understanding and when they know that they will be helped if necessary, children's reasoning is often adequate. Piaget's clinical interviews did not create favourable opportunities to elicit children's best reasoning level.

Compared to children's achievements in familiar circumstances, their performance is much poorer in situations of interrogation in which their knowledge is only tested, or in experiments (Donaldson, 1978; Shatz, 1983; Elbers, in press). In recent research, especially on the conversation experiment, we have learnt that young children may not be familiar with the conventions in such situations of testing and interrogation, conventions which are a matter of course for us. Children do not react to what the experimenter says, but to what they think he or she has said. For example, the repetition of a question, quite innocently meant by the experimenter, may sometimes be understood by the child as a signal to change the answer (Rose & Blank, 1974). Another finding is that children expect the experimenter to respond to their answers: when no comment is given, children apparantly think that their answers satisfy the experimenter because they proceed in the same way even if the conversation is completely nonsensical or incomprehensible to them (Campbell & MacDonald, 1983, and Hughes & Grieve, 1983 present examples). My guess is that the lack of any positive feedback in the discussions of the children with Piaget, and the absence of any help in constructing the right answer, has encouraged the children to stick to their answers and to proceed in the same way. A third example is that children do not ask for clarification when they do not comprehend what has been said to them (as Donaldson, 1978, found with children read to, and Siegel & Hodkin, 1982, found with children participating in an experimental task). We may expect the same behaviour in the children interrogated by Piaget. The observation by Anthony (1973), in which a child protests to an unfamiliar question, appears to be an exception rather than the rule:

"How did the sun begin?

Richard (5;4): What do you mean how did it begin?

I don't know. It's you that ought to tell me
that." (p. 65).

Now, Piaget was certainly sensitive to the problem of
suggestive questions and of children's ability to invent
answers on the spot, infinitely more so than many of his
followers. But he was not aware of the social and
communicational constraints of the child's answers. He was too
deeply committed to the idea of childhood egocentrism.
Therefore, we can conclude that Piaget's studies are severely
handicapped, because the children have not been interrogated
in circumstances which are best for revealing their
capacities.

INTELLECTUAL STRATEGIES IN CHILDREN.

In its essential elements this reinterpretation of
Piaget's findings is not different from the interpretations
given long ago in studies by Nathan Isaacs (1930/1974) and
Huang (1943).

In his critique of Piaget's early studies, Isaacs
underlines the "total difference" between the situation in
which a child spontaneously asks an adult for an explanation
and the interaction in which an adult makes a child explain
something to him or her. In the first context, the child is
motivated by an unexpected event or by a new thought which has
come to mind. But in the second situation children are often
not really involved. Many questions posed by Piaget are
confusing or incomprehensible for the children, but they know
that an answer is expected. Isaacs states that, as a
consequence, children say the first thing which comes into
their mind, so that what we observe is not a belief but merely
an association. For the youngest children, there is the extra
difficulty that they are habitually interrogated about their
motives or purposes, so that they easily misinterpret the
question as a request to clarify their intentions. At best,

Isaacs maintains, when children have understood the question, they fall back upon familiar knowledge, the available "stock of explanations", and try to adapt it to the present question.

Huang (1943) stresses that children in these interviews are expected to give an explanation on the spot. The children then try to find a solution by applying already familiar principles to the problem the experimenter has introduced. The resulting explanations are, of course, wrong most of the time, but they are not so much characterised by pre-causality as by an immature knowledge of the world. Animistic answers according to Huang are simply the effect of a misapplication of ideas obtained from biological and social spheres.

These reinterpretations are remarkable, because these theorists have anticipated in many repects the results of decades of research into Piagetian psychology. Especially Isaacs' critique makes a modern impression, because he has understood the motivational and communicational aspects of the interaction between interviewer and child - a theme which is central to the present discussion of Piaget's work (e.g. Donaldson, 1978; Light, in press). These early critiques of Piaget have been forgotten almost completely: they are an example of diachronic disunity in psychology (cf. Staats, 1983). Publications of more than 20 years old are hardly considered to be relevant for the latest research problems; in this way knowledge is lost in psychology (cf. Vroon, in press). In the construction of theory, psychologists have a short memory indeed, and they often have to reinvent the very ideas which have already been expressed in the past. At the same time it must be realised that we have learnt a lot since the era of Isaacs and Huang about the developmental interview as a scene of interaction (cf. Elbers, in press).

Both Huang and Isaacs explained the child's strategy vis-à-vis unfamiliar problems as the application and testing of already familiar principles to new situations. I agree with this interpretation only if it is not meant that the child's knowledge progresses according to a simple scheme of guesses, corrections, new guesses. The child's strategy must not be considered equivalent to what in philosophy of science is called "naive falsificationism" (cf. Lakatos, 1970), but this very idea is more or less implicit in the writings of Isaacs and Huang. Just as science does not proceed by abandoning every theory which is confronted with contradicting evidence, children do not necessarily give up an idea when it has not stood the test of experience or when it has been denounced as wrong by an adult. Children often stick to their ideas and cherish them, even in the light of counterevidence, because these ideas are not isolated thoughts which can be given up without consequences: children's representations from an early age on are organised in hierarchical structures. Keil (1984, p. 87) argues that knowledge of adults and children is organised in tree structures, children's representations being just quantitatively less extensive than adults' (for instance three branches instead of fifteen). Giving up an isolated fragment of knowledge is much easier than changing an element in an organised structure. When one idea is abandoned other ideas which are connected to it must be changed as well. Moreover, it seems plausible that more central ideas must be distinguished from peripheral ideas, and that the former are more resistent to change than the latter.

In the relevant literature several factors are suggested to explain refusals of a child to accept new information or to learn from experience. Some think that it may depend on the structure of the new information. Siegler & Richards (1982), for instance, mention that the importance of the new information for the problem at hand may not be clear to the child, and that the child must be helped to discriminate between the existing incorrect rules and the new correct rule for solving the problem. Piagetians, like Inhelder, Sinclair & Bovet (1974) adhere to a similar view; they maintain that new information can only be assimilated when it is not too new nor too similar to the available structures; it must be "moderately novel". Others relate the impossibility of the child to adopt new ideas to certain stages of cognitive development (Popper, 1976, speaks of the "infantile dogmatism" of young children), to the limited encoding capacity of younger children (Siegler & Richards, 1982), or to cognitive style (Kogan, 1983). Common to all these explanations is that it is judged undesirable that children are not open to new information. But in many circumstances such an attitude in children may be favourable for their intellectual development and it deserves a more positive treatment in cognitive developmental psychology.

It is by no means clear how far such tenacity in children goes: cognitive obstinacy and its contribution to intellectual development is a field totally unexplored in cognitive developmental theory, but it is a common experience of every parent that children sometimes reject new information, possibly because they want to elaborate their ideas in their own way. To quote another example from Scupin & Scupin (1910, p. 146): Bubi (4;9) had been asking a lot about thunder and he had been told that lightning consists of fire piercing through the clouds. About a month later he raised the topic again. He said that it was impossible that lightning goes through the clouds and that it is made of fire. Because clouds are wet, the lightning would go out. As evidence he advanced that when water is spilled on the cooker in the kitchen, the fire goes out immediately.

If we accept that children's ideas form conglomerates which are characterised by hierarchical organisation and that children are in a continuous process of expanding and reorganising their knowledge, some findings by Tizard & Hughes (1984) become clear right away. These investigators report that their subjects sometimes in a short period of time repeatedly returned to the same topic and explored it with their mothers in "passages of intellectual search". It is easy to see how these intellectual search activities serve as means to try out and test ideas, before replacing them by new explanations. There is, however, no reason to assume that children use the interaction with adults as the preferred way to ameliorate their knowledge: in this sense the idea of "passages of intellectual search" must be expanded. Children use a variety of strategies of intellectual search: asking information from older children or adults, interactions with peers, testing their ideas in a direct interaction with reality, making changes in their ideas on more or less theoretical grounds. On the other hand, children do not use all these strategies at the same time. The choice of a suitable search strategy may depend on the way a child poses a problem and, therefore, on the state of elaboration of his or her ideas.

Of course, this view of the child's mind is influenced by recent discussions in the philosophy and history of science, in which naive falsificationist accounts have been replaced by an interpretation of science as progressing in organised programmes. It is hard to say how far we can go in applying models from recent studies of science to the cognitive development of children. However, my view receives support from another field of child development, in which basically the same processes are found: children's drawing. Goodnow (1977) showed in longitudinal studies that children in their drawings use "formulas", particular schemes which are the basic moulds of their drawing activity for a period of time. She found that variations within such a period of time occur mainly in the accessories, but leave the formula unchanged. After some time, however, the formula is replaced by a more complex one, for instance from a stick-and-circle drawing of a person to a formula with a solid body. Goodnow observed that children over time fill in the details of a formula: using a stick-and-circle formula they gradually learn to draw the correct number of limbs and to give them the right positions, to add ears and facial features, etc. Then, after some time, children present a drawing which is based on a new formula. Goodnow suggests that these changes may be the result of playing with the accessories; for instance, the discovery of a solid body as a formula may be caused by accidently filling in the empty space between the legs of a stick-and-circle figure. I would rather propose that the adoption of a new formula may reflect that the possibilities of a given formula were exhausted. A stick-and-circle formula only gives limited possibilities to make progress; when a child has realised all of these, he or she may actively seek a new basic formula. I suggest that such a "crisis" may be the occasion for children

to increase their intellectual search activities or to apply
new strategies: they intensify their observations of people
and compare their own drawings to the products of other
children. In this manner, they try to find another basic
scheme.

CONCLUSION.

In conclusion, I shall present in a systematic way the
consequences of the reflections in this chapter for the
dilemma of empiricist and rationalist interpretations of the
child as a knowing subject. Certainly, empiricism and
rationalism must be reconciled, as Piaget endeavoured:
elements of both rationalism and empiricism must be preserved.
Rationalism teaches us that children's minds have universal
properties. These properties, however, are not revealed by
necessary processes of desubjectification, but by the
motivational and procedural sides of cognitive activity:
children's curiosity and eagerness to understand reality,
their desire to elaborate their knowledge and to organise it,
and the strategies they use in dealing with other human beings
and with nature to expand their knowledge. To call these
characteristics of children's thinking universal does not mean
that culture has no impact on them at all. Infants are
probably born with a basic interest in the world and we cannot
be wrong when we interpret the young child's intellectual
activity as a prolongation of this innate curiosity. This
primary interest, however, must be conserved and moulded by
culture. For instance, the capacity to imitate other people
may develop in children in all cultures, but cultures may
differ as to whether they encourage imitation or not.
     Though the motive to understand reality can plausibly be
interpreted as characteristic of all children, this does not
mean that the contents of their knowledge are universal as
well. This is the lesson that can be learnt from empiricism.
The problems children pose and the answers they construct bear
the imprint of the specific culture they grow up in. Children

appropriate the knowledge (or rather a part of it) which has been accumulated in their culture and, thus, they gradually meet the standards of knowledge of their culture. In this respect, children's ideas in a certain culture belong to what Harris & Heelas (1979) called "local knowledge". Enormous differences exist in ideas where babies come from between different generations and cultures, for instance in the Katz children growing up in the Germany of the Republic of Weimar (Katz & Katz, 1928), in the American children studied by Conn in the forties (1947), in the American subjects a generation later, interviewed by Bernstein & Cowan (1975), and in Margaret Mead's Manu children. It is incomprehensible that so many psychologists have in all seriousness studied the development of children's ideas, without investigating whether the ideas prevalent in the environment of the children have influenced their viewpoints: Broughton (1980), in his study of mind-body conceptions, Furth (1980), in his book on children's conceptions of society, and Munari, Filippini, Regazzoni & Visseur (1976) in their genetic study of anatomical understanding in children. All these investigators, like Piaget, assume that these ideas are constructed autonomously, and, consequently, that they are evidence of universal sequences of ideas.

Children's ideas originate from the meeting of two factors in cognitive development: children's spontaneous construction of knowledge and the transmission of knowledge by more experienced members of the culture. Sometimes this meeting takes the form of a clash, like when children refuse to accept information from adults and stubbornly stick to their own ideas, sometimes it takes the form of cooperation, for instance when children engage with adults in intellectual search activities. In this process of gradually approaching adult norms of knowledge, discrepancies between children's and adults' ideas are inevitable. They are due to children's limited and insufficient understanding of reality and of their misapplying familiar knowledge to unfamiliar areas of interest. But it is wrong to see children's insufficient knowledge only as consisting of discrepancies which will be overcome with time: children's knowledge is also the product of the tension between the individually constructed understanding of reality and the accepted body of knowledge in society. This tension will never completely disappear, and the forms in which it appears in childhood (wrong theories, misattributions, naivety, cognitive obstinacy) are also the roots of traits that we value so much in adults, such as originality, humour, and artistic and scientific creativity.

REFERENCES.

Anthony, S. (1973). The discovery of death in childhood and after. Harmondsworth: Penguin Books.

Bernstein, A.C. & Cowan, P.A. (1975). Children's concept of how people get babies. Child Development, 46, 77-91.

Brainerd, C.J. (1978). Piaget's theory of intelligence. Englewood Cliffs: Prentice Hall.

Berzonsky, M.D. (1971). The role of familiarity in children's explanations of physical causality. Child Development, 42, 705-715.

Broughton, J.M. (1980). Genetic metaphysics: The developmental psychology of mind-body concepts. In R.W. Rieber (Ed.), Body and mind. Past, present and future (p. 177-221). New York: Academic Press.

Campbell, R.N. & MacDonald, T.B. (1983). Text and context in early language comprehension. In M. Donaldson, R. Grieve & C. Pratt (Eds.), Early childhood development and education (p. 115-126). Oxford: Basil Blackwell.

Conn, J.M. (1947). Children's awareness of the origins of babies. Journal of Child Psychiatry, 1, 140-176.

Deutsche, J.M. (1943). The development of children's concepts of causal relations. In R.G. Barker, J.S. Kounin & H.F. Wright (Eds.), Child behaviour and development. A course of representative studies (p. 129-145). New York: McGraw-Hill.

Dolgin, K.M. & Behrend, D.A. (1984). Children's knowledge

about animates and inanimates. Child Development, 55, 1646-1650.

Donaldson, M. (1978). Children's minds. London: Fontana.

Donaldson, M.L. (1985). Young children's production of causal connectives. University of Reading: Child Language Seminar Papers.

Dunn, J. & Kendrick, C. (1982). Siblings. Love, envy and understanding. London: Grant McIntyre.

Elbers, E. (in press). Instruction and interaction in the conservation experiment. European Journal of Psychology of Education.

Furth, H.G. (1980). The world of grown-ups. Children's conceptions of society. New York: Elsevier.

Gelman, R. & Baillargeon, R. (1983). A review of some Piagetian concepts. In J.H. Flavell & E.M. Markman (Eds.), Handbook of child psychology, Vol. III: Cognitive development (p. 167-230). New York: Wiley.

Gelman, R. & Spelke, E. (1981). The development of thoughts about animate and inanimate objects: implications for research on social cognition. In J.H. Flavell & L. Ross (Eds.), Social cognitive development. Frontiers and possible futures (p. 43-66). Cambridge: Cambridge University Press.

Goodnow, G. (1977). Children's drawing. London: Fontana/Open Books.

Harris, P. & Heelas, P. (1979). Cognitive processes and collective representations. European Journal of Sociology, 20, 211-241.

Horton, R. (1973). Lévy-Bruhl, Durkheim and the scientific revolution. In R. Horton & R. Finnegan (Eds.), Modes of thought. Essays on thinking in western and non-western societies (p. 249-305). London: Faber & Faber.

Horton, R. & Finnegan, R. (1973). Introduction. In R. Horton & R. Finnegan (Eds.), Modes of thought. Essays on thinking in western and non-western societies (p. 13-67). London: Faber & Faber.

Huang, I. (1943). Children's conception of physical causality: A critical summary. Journal of Genetic Psychology, 63,

71-121.

Hughes, M. & Grieve, R. (1983). On asking children bizarre questions. In M. Donaldson, R. Grieve & C. Pratt (Eds.), Early childhood development and education (p. 104-114). Oxford: Basil Blackwell.

Inhelder, B., Sinclair, H. & Bovet, M. (1974). Learning and the development of cognition. Cambridge: Harvard University Press.

Isaacs, N. (1930/1974). Children's "Why" questions. In M. Hardeman (Ed.), Children's ways of knowing. Nathan Isaacs on education, psychology, and Piaget (p. 13-64). New York: Teachers College Press.

Jahoda, G. (1982). Psychology and anthropology. A psychological perspective. London: Academic Press.

Katz, D. & Katz, R. (1928). Gespräche mit Kindern. Berlin: Springer.

Keil, F.C. (1983). On the emergence of semantic and conceptual distinctions. Journal of Experimental Psychology: General, 112, 357-385.

Keil, F.C. (1984). Mechanisms in cognitive development and the structure of knowledge. In R.J. Sternberg (Ed.), Mechanisms of cognitive development (p. 81-99). New York: Freeman.

Klingensmith, S.W. (1953). Child animism: What the child means by "alive". Child Development, 24, 51-61.

Kogan, N. (1983). Stylistic variation in childhood and adolescence: Creativity, metaphor, and cognitive style. In J.H. Flavell & E.M. Markman (Eds.), Handbook of child psychology. Vol. III: Cognitive development (p. 630-706). New York: Wiley.

Kohlberg, L. (1969). Stage and sequence: The cognitive developmental approach to socialization. In D.A. Goslin (Ed.), Handbook of socialization theory and research (p. 347-480). Chicago: Rand McNally.

Lakatos, I. (1970). Falsification and the methodology of scientific research programmes. In I. Lakatos & A. Musgrave (Eds.), Criticism and the growth of knowledge (p. 91-196). London: Cambridge University Press.

Laurendeau, M. & Pinard, A. (1962). Causal thinking in the child. A genetic and experimental approach. New York: International Universities Press.

Lévi-Strauss, C. (1949). Les structures élémentaires de la parenté. Paris: Presses Universitaires de France.

Light, P. (in press). Contex, conservation and conversation. In P. Light & M. Richards (Eds.), Children in social worlds. London: Polity Press.

Looft, W.R. (1973). Animistic thought in children: Effects of two response modes. Perceptual and Motor Skills, 36, 59-62.

Looft, W.R. (1974). Animistic thought in children: Understanding of "living" across its associated attributes. Journal of Genetic Psychology, 124, 235-240.

Looft, W.R. & Bartz, W.H. (1969). Animism revived. Psychological Bulletin, 71, 1-19.

Mead, M. (1931). Growing up in New Guinea. A comparative study of primitive education. London: Routledge.

Modgil, S. & Modgil, C. (1976). Piagetian research: Compilation and commentary. Vol. II. Windsor: National Federation of Educational Research.

Munari, A., Filippini, G., Regazzoni, M. & Visseur, A.S. L'anatomie de l'enfant: étude génétique des conceptions anatomiques spontanées. Archives de Psychologie, 44, 115-134.

Piaget, J. (1923/1967). The language and thought of the child. London: Routledge & Kegan Paul.

Piaget, J. (1927/1973). The child's conception of the world. Frogmore: Paladin.

Piaget, J. (1927/1930). The child's conception of physical causality. London: Routledge & Kegan Paul.

Piaget, J. (1946/1964). Play, dreams and imitation in childhood. London: Routledge & Kegan Paul.

Piaget, J. (1961). Les mécanismes perceptifs. Paris: Presses Universitaires de France.

Piaget, J. (1962). Preface. In M. Laurendeau & A. Pinard (Eds.), Causal thinking in the child. A genetic and experimental approach. New York: International

Universities Press.

Popper, K. (1972). Conjectures and refutations. The growth of scientific knowledge (Fourth Edition). London: Routledge and Kegan Paul.

Popper, K. (1976). Unended quest. An intellectual autobiography. Glasgow: Fontana/Collins.

Riegel, K.F. (1973). Dialectic operations: The final period of cognitive development. Human Development, 16, 346-370.

Rose, S. & Blank, M. (1974). The potency of context in children's cognition: An illustration through conservation. Child Development, 45, 499-502.

Scupin, E. & Scupin, G. (1910). Bubi im vierten bis sechsten Lebensjahre. Leipzig: Th. Grieben.

Shatz, M. (1983). Communication. In J.H. Flavell & E.M. Markman (Eds.), Handbook of child psychology. Vol. III: Cognitive development (p. 841-889). New York: Wiley.

Shweder, R.A. & LeVine, R.A. (1976). Dream concepts of Hausa children: A critique of the "doctrine of invariant sequence" in cognitive development. In Th. Schwartz (Ed.), Socialization as cultural communication (p. 117-138). Berkeley: University of California Press.

Siegel, L. & Hodkin, B. (1982). The garden path to the understanding of cognitive development: has Piaget led us into the poison ivy? In S. Modgil & C. Modgil (Eds.), Jean Piaget. Consensus and controversy (p. 57-82). London: Holt, Rinehart & Winston.

Siegler, R.S. & Richards D.D. (1982). The development of intelligence. In R.J. Sternberg (Ed.), Handbook of human intelligence (p. 897-971). Cambridge: Cambridge University Press.

Staats, A.W. (1983). Psychology's crisis of disunity. New York: Praeger.

Sully, J. (1896). Studies of childhood. London: Longmans, Green, and Co.

Tizard, B. & Hughes, M. (1984). Young children learning. Talking and thinking at home and at school. London: Fontana.

Tul'viste, P. (1982). Is there a form of verbal thought

specific to childhood? Soviet Psychology, 21, 3-17.

Vroon, P.A. (in press). Man-machine analogs and theoretical mainstreams in psychology. In W.J. Baker, M.E. Hyland, H.V. Rappard & A.W. Staats (Eds.), Current issues in theoretical psychology. Amsterdam: North Holland.

Wallon, H. (1945). Les origines de la pensée chez l'enfant: vol. 2. Paris: Presses Universitaires de France.

Warren, N. (1980). Universality and plasticity, ontogeny and phylogeny: The resonance between culture and cognitive development. In J. Sants (Ed.), Developmental psychology and society (p. 290-326). London: MacMillan.

Wartofsky, M.W. (1980). Scientific judgement: creativity and discovery in scientific thought. In T. Nickles (ed.), Scientific discovery: Case studies (p. 1-20). Dordrecht: Reidel.

Wood, D., McMahon, L. & Cranstoun, Y. (1980). Working with under fives. London: Grant McIntyre.

Theory Building in Developmental Psychology
P.L.C. van Geert (editor)
© *Elsevier Science Publishers B.V. (North-Holland), 1986*

12

Getting Development off the Ground

Modularity and the infant's perception of causality

Alan Leslie

What is the role of perception in the
development of thought? If perception has its
own distinctive organisation, what are the
consequences for development? These issues are
considered in relation to the understanding of
objecthood and physical causality in infancy and
the preschool period. It is argued that the
"modular" organisation of perception has a
specially useful role in getting development
started in these areas. Modular perception is
inherently limited to analysing "appearances" in
fixed ways. This has important advantages for
allowing the rapid build up of general
knowledge, even though such knowledge must
eventually go beyond appearances to underlying
realities. It also allows the human child to
benefit from the long evolution of the
perceptual apparatus in lower species, giving
rise to a more competent infant.

I want to discuss some issues concerning the role of
perception in development. The discussion will center round
the contribution perception can make to the development of
"empirical" concepts. What I mean by this will, I hope, become
clear in the course of discussion. For the moment, let me say
that such concepts are involved in understanding objecthood
and physical causality. Fundamental to this is the distinction
between how the world appears to a perceiving organism and how
its underlying realities might be grasped (perfectly or
imperfectly) by a thinking organism.

One might hold the view that perception has no distinctive
role in development, save that of registering elementary
sensations. If so, one will see the development of perception
and the development of thought and general knowledge as simply

different ends of essentially the same thing. This has been
the traditional outlook for both empiricist and constructivist
positions. A quite different view is that perception has its
own distinctive organisation and therefore its own distinctive
role in development. On this view it becomes vitally important
to investigate what the consequences of perceptual
organisation are for development.

THE ORGANISATION OF PERCEPTION.

One rapidly emerging view is that perceptual processes
are to a significant extent impenetrable to cognition (Fodor,
1983; Kanizsa, 1985; Marr, 1982; Ramachandran, 1985; Rock,
1985; Ullman, 1985). This impenetrability may reflect an
underlying "modular" organisation. To say that a process is
modular is to assert that it is highly independent of other
processes both in terms of the information it accesses and the
computations it performs.

For example, Marr (1982) argued that the visual process
of stereopsis is modular. The main problem in stereopsis is in
reconciling two retinal images which are not quite the same.
An edge in one image must be put in correspondence with the
correct edge in the other image. The processes which do this,
however, appear to operate quite early on in the analysis of
the retinal array. In particular, they do not have access to,
for example, information about the shape of common objects,
their function, the likelihood of finding such an object in
these surroundings, and so on. Perhaps such information might
conceivably be relevant to solving some stereopsis problems.
But, even if it is, the module for stereopsis has to do
without it. Modules apply their own local solutions to their
own limited problems. They perform their task automatically
and mechanically with resources which are fixed beforehand.
They cannot call for outside help if the going gets tough.
The main advantage of such organisation, it seems, is in the
speed of computation that can be achieved when complex
problems are broken down into smaller parts and dealt with

independently (Fodor, 1983).

Just as there are advantages for the organism in this kind of organisation, so there are inherent limitations. One of the main limitations is that perceptual processes can only deal with appearances and not with underlying realities. This is because "reality" does not always fit into the neat packages allowed for by automatic modular processing (though often it does). This limitation of modularity may explain the existence of perceptual illusions (Ramachandran, 1985; Long & Toppino, 1981). Ramachandran (1985) gives a particularly bizarre example. Under appropriate conditions, we see apparent motion of a light through our own hand, despite conflicting tactile information, commonsense, and even expert knowledge concerning the illusion. Modules for motion perception automatically apply their fixed analyses, returning the results of these procedures without regard for how absurd or contradictory they are. In other words, it is left to cognition to sort out what is "really" there.

Fodor (1983) argues that the processes which are responsible for the "fixation " of our beliefs about what is really there are of a quite different character. These central thought processes can access a vast and in principle unlimited range of information, consider all sorts of possibilities, weigh them up, one against the other, and arrive at conclusions which it can always revise later. But such central processes are unable to influence the activities of the "input modules". This has the advantage of ensuring speedily available information about what is present to the senses and avoids us "seeing" just what we think "ought to be there". But it can also give rise to illusions that simply will not go away!

THREE EXAMPLES OF EMPIRICAL KNOWLEDGE.

The inherent advantages and limitations of modular architecture in perception will have important consequences for development. Some of these consequences can be seen in connection with "empirical" concepts. I shall look briefly at two such concepts: first, the question of what sorts of concrete objects there are in the world; and second, what identity particular objects have as we encounter and re-encounter them. Then at somewhat greater length, I shall discuss a third: the question of discovering what causal regularites there are in the world. These questions are faced in particularly vicious forms by scientists, but they are also faced at a more mundane level by quite small children.

Object Sorts.

    One approach to the child's developing understanding of objects focusses upon the learning of rules and definitions. To take one example, having a concept of a dog is equated with understanding definitive criteria for deciding whether an object one has encountered is a dog or not. Such a definition might be in the form of a list of criterial features of "dogginess". The issues surrounding the problems of the nature and formation of concepts are highly complex (see Carey, 1982 and Medin & Smith, 1984 for lucid reviews) and my purpose here is not to enter into that debate nor in particular into more recent versions of the classical approach such as prototypicality (Rosch, 1978) or fuzziness (Zadeh, 1965). I do want to draw attention, however, to the contrast between having a definition for a given type of object, and having something more akin to a theory.

    Definitions can be formulated without the benefit of theories. And theories do not always make criteria clear by which to judge whether a phenomenon or object belongs to a given type or sort. In fact, no one knows what the necessary and sufficient conditions are for something to be a dog. If this what a definition is, then no one knows what the definition of dog is (cf. Kripke, 1972; Putnam, 1975).

    The good news (especially for dog lovers) is that one does not need to know the necessary and sufficient conditions for being a dog in order to recognise instances of dogs, mostly with success. Our concept of dog may rule out electro-mechanical dogs without us being able to tell at a glance or even after a lot of study which are dog "androids" (canoids?) and which real dogs. Having a concept of dog implies having some general or theoretical knowledge about the nature of dogs (however partial and inaccurate). This allows us to separate the problem of acquiring the concept from the problem of learning how to recognise instances of it. Indeed, our general knowledge about dogs does not have to play any part at all in our normal processes of recognising instances.

Osherson & Smith (1981) draw a somewhat similar distinction between a concept's core and its identification procedure and suggest that prototype theory (Rosch, 1978) characterises an important identification procedure. Murphy & Medin (1985) use the notion of "theoretical" knowledge in a similar way to that intended here to suggest an organised piece of knowledge about the world. If it is preferred, we can talk instead of encyclopaedic or general knowledge.

We can link all this with the earlier discussion in the following way. The problem of concrete objecthood splits into two major parts. The first concerns the operation of a device for recognising objects (mostly successfully) by applying a set of fixed perceptual tests to perceptual input. It operates as if it possesses a definition for a given object but actually is subject to all the advantages and disadvantages of an input module. It operates fast, is cognitively impenetrable and is inherently limited to appearances. The second part of the problem has to do with a centrally constructed set of ideas, in effect a rudimentary theory, that attempts (often imperfectly) to describe realities underlying appearance (whales are really mammals...). The "attempt" is what is important since describing underlying realities correctly is something that neither nature nor culture could guarantee. The attempt surfaces in the open ended evaluation of hypotheses and in the revisable nature of conclusions reached. Object recognition in contrast may proceed as Marr & Nishihara (1978) have argued in the automatic application of a fixed algorithm. But concepts, as we are thinking of them, belong to central processes of thought and have the job of attempting to relate to what is really the case.

Object Identity.

This sort of picture can be extended to another aspect of concrete objecthood, namely, the problem of object permanence, as Piaget (1955) called it. Again, current approaches have often focussed upon the application of internal rules or definitions. For example, Bower (1982; Wishart & Bower, 1983) argues that the infant follows a lengthy developmental path before she can solve the problem of how to tell when an object retains its identity from one encounter to another. For example, a red ball goes out of sight behind a screen and emerges again on the opposite side. Bower and his colleagues have used this and other types of situation to study young infants judgements of the enduring identity of objects.

Bower argues that infants pick out persistent objects by consulting an internal definition of when an object remains the same despite changes (of position etc.) or alternatively, that the infant applies rules for reidentifying a particular object across successive encounters with it. Spelke (1982) has studied a similar problem concerned with when a stimulus configuration is perceived as a single unified object and when as a set of distinct objects. Again the infant seems to apply a set of fairly complex rules to decide this.

It seems clear that the infant is not addressing the "empirical" version of these questions. Instead, the infant is applying a sophisticated yet fixed and automatic set of perceptual rules and definitions for deciding the identity and unity of objects. I suggest that she computes the apparent identity of the objects she perceives through the automatic and fast action of an input module. But the question, "Is this object really the same one as before?" is a question the input module can neither pose nor answer. The psychologist does not expect the infant to want first to see what's really going on behind the screen before committing herself to a response. The infant, like her input systems, responds in a sophisticated way to appearances. Perhaps the three or even two year old has the competence to address empirical questions. "Could this really be my teddy? How could my teddy have got from my house to here? Did mummy bring it perhaps?" These are empirical questions for which there are no predetermined fixed rules for getting the correct answers.

Causality.

   Understanding cause and effect raises a similar dichotomy between input analysis and empirical reasoning. Current approaches suggest that the child picks out causes and their effects from the stream of events by consulting a "tacit definition of cause-effect relations" (Bullock et. al., 1982) or by applying "rules of causal attribution" (Shultz, 1982).
   Recent evidence shows that 3 and 4 year olds use a number of rules in their selection of a cause for a given event including covariance, temporal priority, temporal contiguity, spatial contiguity and so on. The child gives different weights to these different rules in different situations: in some, spatial contiguity will have more emphasis than temporal contiguity, while in other circumstances spatial contiguity will just be ignored (Bullock et al., 1982; Shultz, 1982). Three year olds can select a cause on the basis of a minimal covariance pattern (AX, B, ABX = A cause X). But even more interestingly these same children will change their minds when given mechanical information that contradicts the selection of the covariant event (Shultz, 1982). Thus, previous conclusions can be revised and in a way that contradicts appearances.
   Even the young child seems to be trying to understand the event sequences as plausible mechanisms (Bullock et al., 1982; Bullock, 1985). The "rules" of causal attribution are not used literally as rules to rigidly and definitively specify a cause. They are perhaps "rules of thumb" or heuristics to suggest a plausible hypothesis. Such hypotheses even when initially confirmed remain revisable if further considerations

crop up. Processes of this sort have the characteristics of the central processes that Fodor describes. Unlike input modules, they are sensitive to encyclopaedic or general knowledge and their conclusions remain revisable and tentative. But, of course, general knowledge is one thing small children are desparately short of.

The problem in talking of "rules of causal attribution" or of a "definition of cause-effect relations" is that it can not be taken literally. There is literally no such thing. If there was a definition or set of rules for causality then there would also be a mechanical procedure for carrying out empirical investigations. There would be a fixed and specifiable way for determining the causal structure of the world and therefore a mechanical or formal procedure for doing science. If there was such a thing, we could guarantee the "truth" of the answers we receive from it simply by making reference to the fact that we had faultlessly followed the procedure.

To think, then, of the child's development as requiring him to learn or employ causal rules or definitions could be misleading. On the other hand, flexibility, uncertainty and a willingness to change one's mind could all be symptoms of a genuine empirical approach to underlying reality.

However, some parts of human processing do appear to operate as if empirical questions can be settled definitively by applying fixed tests. These are the input systems. Input systems provide "take it or leave it" descriptions of appearances. Central processes inherit these descriptions and evaluate them in the light of further considerations. Although they operate in a quite different way, the input systems speak the same "language" as the central processes. Their descriptions categorise and identify objects and propose causes and effects. This is why input systems sound as if they are empirical.

THE ONE-SIDED DIALOGUE.

Two Dialogues.

Allow me to illustrate these ideas in terms of dialogues between input systems and central processes.
Object Recognition: a tree.
  Input Systems: "That's a tree"
  Central Processes: "Hang on, this is a desert. Trees don't normally grow in deserts. Let's see about this!"
  (Goes up close to have a look at the "tree")
  Input Systems: "That material is plastic"
  Central Processes: "So I was right, it's not a tree!'
  (Walks away, then looks back)
  Input Systems: "That's a tree"
  Central Processes: "No it's not, it just looks like a tree"
  Input Systems: "That's a tree".. etc.
Reidentifying Particular Objects: My pen.
  Input Systems: "That's my pen"
  Central Processes: "It can't be. It's the Professor who has it. I didn't give it to her and she would never steal."
  Input Systems: "That's my pen"
  Central Processes: "It can't be - it just looks like my pen"
  Input Systems: "That's my pen"

Causality: Michotte's illusion.

Michotte (1963) discovered that adults would report seeing a causal interaction between two entities despite the fact that the stimuli used were just pencil marks on paper or coloured lights projected on a wall. The adult observers knew full well how the displays were made and thus knew that there was no question of real objects really causing one another to move. But, as in the example of a light going through a hand, their knowledge and reasoning powers did nothing to prevent the illusion. Over and over again, the causal illusion was obtained, unaffected by the subject's knowledge. I leave it to the reader to construct the dialogue for this one.

I suggest that Michotte's causal illusion results from the operation of an input module. The module applies a fixed algorithm and has access to only very restricted information, probably operating fairly early in the analysis of motion. Nevertheless, it can give outputs in an "abstract" causal code. Before considering the possible developmental role of such a module, I want to summarise briefly results from a series of experiments on six month old infants that are beginning to indicate that this module might be in place and running that early.

All the experiments measured the infants' visual attention to cinematic stimuli using an habituation – dishabituation of looking technique (Leslie, 1982b, 1984a, 1984b, 1984c; Leslie & Keeble, forthcoming). This widely used technique allows one to measure the recovery of the infant's interest following a change in a stimulus that has become familiar to the infant. From the patterns of renewed interest discernable over a number of experiments involving different kinds of stimulus comparisons, it is possible to begin to make inferences about the ways in which the infant is internally representing and comparing the events presented (Leslie, 1982a, 1984b). Thus, one can make hypotheses about the kinds of structural descriptions the infant is assigning the various events.

A red brick glides across a table top and appears to impart its motion to a stationary green brick by colliding with it. In this direct launching the first brick appears to make the second one move. If a short interval of say half a second is interposed between impact and the reaction of the second brick, this impression of direct causality is lost. Infants around six months are sensitive to the difference between the continuity of motion in direct launching and the discontinuous motions in the delayed reaction sequence (Leslie, 1982b).

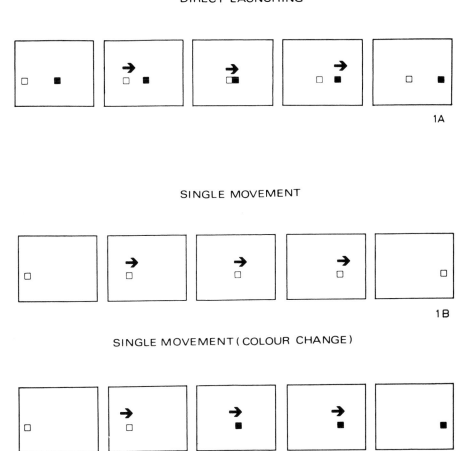

FIGURE 1: Illustrations of the event sequences used to test infants'
    ability to parse submovements in direct launching. The white square
    represents the red object in the films used and the black square the
    green object. Each sequence lasts approximately 3 seconds including
    the stationary periods at the beginning and end. For more details the
    reader should consult the appropriate reference given in the text.

But can they distinguish the submovements in the continuous direct launching or is it perceived simply as a single unanalysable "whoosh"?

Leslie (1984c) reasoned that if direct launching was for the infants an event with internal structure (i.e. composed of submovements), then reversing the event should alter that structure. The amount of recovery to this reversal could then be compared with the recovery produced by reversing an event with no internal structure (i.e. a single movement made by a single object). One group of infants was habituated to a direct launching event (see Figure 1a) shown over and over again in a single direction. Meanwhile another group of infants was habituated to a sequence in which a single red brick moved from one side of the screen to the other, again in a single direction (Figure 1b). Having reached a predetermined criterion of habituation, the film the infant had been viewing was reversed by the simple expedient of turning the projector into reverse. Now the objects moved in the opposite direction to before. For the single object group this is the only resulting change. But for the direct launching group the relative order of the submovements is also changed (red first to green first). If, then, this direct launching group distinguished and remembered the submovements, they should recover their interest more. The results indeed showed significantly greater recovery in the direct launching group.

A further experiment showed that direct launching was highly discriminable from another single movement event in which the object changed colour from red to green around the position where impact takes place in direct launching (Figure 1c). Direct launching is not simply perceived then as a "whoosh" with a red beginning and a green ending.

Incidently, these findings also show that the infants do not have to rely simply upon their pattern of eye movements for encoding these events, since both direct launching and a single movement event are tracked smoothly by infants (Borton, 1979). We can conclude then that the six month old is capable of a true perceptual encoding for the submovements in these events (Leslie, 1984c).

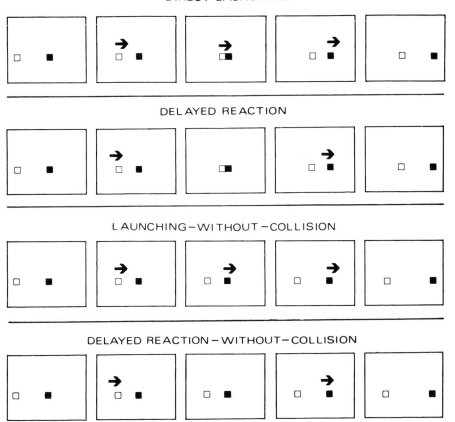

FIGURE 2: Illustration of the event sequences used to test infant's encoding of the relationship between the submovements. The nature of the stimuli is outlined in the legend to Figure 1.

Infants perceive internal structure in direct launching. But what kind of structure? Leslie (1982b) suggested two alternative hypotheses. The first was based upon the classical analysis of causality provided by the Scottish Empiricist Hume (1740). This was that infants would encode the spatial and the temporal relations between the submovements as two distinct and independent features (or orthogonal dimensions).

The second competing hypothesis was derived from Michotte. This was that the infant's recovery of interest would depend upon whether the two sequences contrasted in apparent causality or not. Direct launching is the only sequence that should appear causal out of those shown in Figure 2. A comparison of it with any of the others should produce more recovery than a "Hume-equivalent" comparison not involving it. For example, in going from causal Direct Launching to non-causal Delayed Reaction-without-collision both the spatial (contact/no contact) and temporal (delay/no delay) features change. In going from Delayed Reaction to Launching-without-collision both these features change too (the reader can check this in Figure 2). But with this latter pair neither sequence should appear causal. According to Michotte's but not Hume's hypothesis then, there should be more recovery with the causal change pair.

The results supported Michotte's hypothesis: the Direct Launching group showed greater recovery despite the fact that the contrast seen by the Delayed Reaction group was by Hume's hypothesis exactly equivalent (Leslie, 1984c: Experiment 2).

However, if it was the apparent causality of direct launching that was really producing this effect then direct launching should prove more contrastive in other comparisons as well. For example, in direct launching versus delayed reaction (delay change) there should be more recovery than in launching-without-collision versus delayed reaction-without-collision (also delay change). And so too for the comparisons involving the equivalent changes in the spatial feature. But here the results failed to support Michotte.

Each sequence was discriminable one from the other, but there was no indication that direct launching had a "special" status

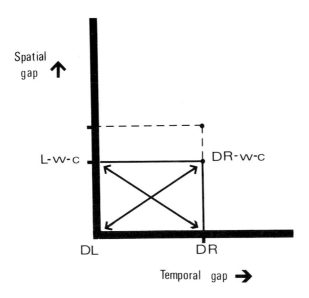

FIGURE 3: Theoretically possible 2-dimensional similarity space for the
following stimuli: DL = direct launching; L-w-c = launching-without-
collision; DR = delayed reaction; DR-w-c = delayed reaction-without-
collision. A similarity space can be used to predict subjective
similarity between members of a stimulus set. Predictions are made by
measuring the distance between the points representing the stimuli.
The closer two stimuli are to one another, the more subjectively
similar they should be.

(Leslie, 1984c: Experiment 3).

Suppose Hume's hypothesis was reformulated as two
orthogonal dimensions instead of two binary features. One axis
would represent the size of the spatial gap, while the other
axis, orthogonal to this, would represent the size of the
temporal gap or delay. Would this better explain the results?
Perhaps the size of the spatial gap used did not equal the
size of the temporal gap. Is this a problem for these results?

In fact, it is not. A glance at Figure 3 shows why.
Direct launching with zero spatial and temporal gaps lies at

the origin of the two axes. Launching-without-collision will be somewhere along the x-axis, and delayed reaction somewhere along the y-axis. Delayed reaction-without-collision is diagonally opposite direct launching. If this graph has any psychological reality, we could use it to predict the amount of recovery a given pair of films will give rise to. The rule would be to measure the distance between the points representing the sequences. The greater the distance between them, the more subjectively dissimilar they are, and the more dishabituation of looking we expect. In the special case that the spatial gap exactly equals the temporal gap, the resulting space will be a square. In all other cases it will be a rectangle. Either way, the diagonals ought to be equal. This was not what was found. Analysis also showed that there was no interaction between dimensions (Leslie, 1984c). The results thus contradict a space with 2 dimensions.

In fact, the results can neatly be described by a similarity space consisting of a single dimension (see Figure 3). This single dimension can be interpreted as representing the degree of spatiotemporal continuity between the submovements, ie. the sum of the values in the two dimensional space. We are currently testing predictions from this new hypothesis.

In a more recent study (Leslie & Keeble, forthcoming), we controlled for differential changes in spatiotemporal properties so that we could better isolate causal properties. To do this we returned to the technique of reversing events. One group (causal) was habituated to direct launching, while another group (non-causal) was habituated to delayed reaction. After reaching criterion, both groups were then tested on the same films respectively but shown with the projector running backwards (see Figure 4).

The reasoning was as follows. Reversing either event will change it from moving rightwards to moving leftwards and from red moving first to green moving first. Both will reverse spatiotemporal direction. But if direct launching is seen as causal, reversal will also change its causal direction. From red cause, green effect it will go to green cause, red effect.

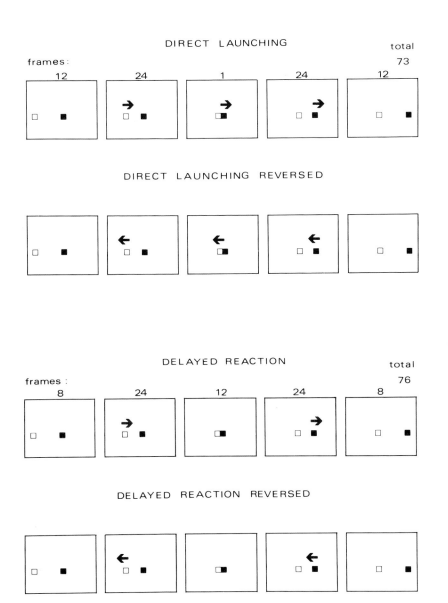

FIGURE 4: Illustration of the stimuli used to test infants' perception of causal direction with spatiotemporal direction controlled for.

So, if infants perceive causal direction only in direct launching and not in delayed reaction, they will be differentially sensitive to its reversal.

This is just what we found in two separate experiments (Leslie & Keeble, forthcoming). In both, infants recovered their looking more to the reversal of direct launching than to the reversal of delayed reaction. The six month old seems to perceive a specifically causal property of this event. We have already seen from the studies discussed above that direct launching is not simply "better" remembered than delayed reaction. Instead there seems to be a causality factor that increases the importance either of spatiotemporal direction or of the entities' causal roles. This factor appears to be distinct from the gradient discussed earlier since a sequence in reverse will have the same degree of continuity/ discontinuity it has when played forward.

The point of making these detailed studies is to arrive at precise ideas about the kinds of structural descriptions for events the infant visual system can generate. So far these seem to include:

(1) parsing of submovements;

(2) encoding of degree of spatiotemporal continuity between the submovements;

(3) encoding of causal direction in direct launching.

This is beginning to look rather similar to Michotte's causal percept. I would now suggest that the same input module is involved in Michotte's causal illusion in adults and in these results with infants. It is possible, in other words, that the module develops very little or not at all from 6 months to adulthood.

A WORKING HYPOTHESIS

The working hypothesis that my current studies are bent on testing is illustrated in Figure 5. The basic idea is that the origins of our understanding of causality lie, at least in part, in a fairly low level visual mechanism. This mechanism may be modular in nature and take its input from lower level processes of motion perception. For example, Restle (1979) outlines a model of how two dimensional motions may be coded in the visual system, extending the work of Johansson (1950, 1973). Representations of motion amplitudes, phases, orientations and so on might be the input to the mechanism we are hypothesising. This mechanism will then have the task of producing higher level descriptions of the spatiotemporal properties of the event configuration and, in the right cases, a description of (apparent) causal structure. Such higher level descriptions then constitute output, to be processed further by the visual system or passed to central processes.

One feature of the model in Figure 5 is that the module computes multiple representations for the same event, each more "abstract" than the one before. A higher level description is computed from a lower one. Thus, given two motions forming a launching event, the spatial and temporal relations between the submotions are computed and represented independently. I have to say immediately that there is still no evidence for this level in infants. The reason it appears in the model is that first, I think it a reasonable guess as to how the next level (for which there is evidence) is computed i.e. as a sum of the spatial and temporal gaps identified at the first level and second, I have the hunch that given simultaneous presentation of Launching-without-collision and Delayed Reaction infants would have no trouble discriminating them. We are starting studies now to look at this possibility.

We have already discussed the evidence for the second level. Further studies are testing this predictively but it is too early at time of writing to say how these will turn out. At least it is easy enough to see what the point of such a level would be, offering a succinct description of launching and its variants. The third level is postulated on the basis of the findings of differential sensitivity to reversal of direct launching. Description at this level would only be computed for those events having some high degree of continuity. Perhaps causal roles are described at this level.

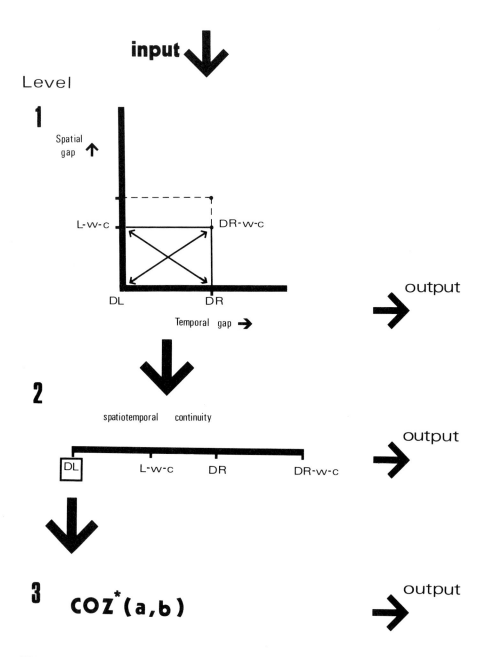

FIGURE 5: A working hypothesis: three levels of representation for direct launching computed by an input module functioning in infancy. * Note: not the English word "CAUSE"!

Again current studies are investigating this.

I find it useful to think in terms of such a mechanism in order to be as definite and precise about its properties as possible. I have come to realise that there are many plausible ways of describing launching type events. In experimental investigation we try to discover which descriptive systems the infant's visual system employs. There are other questions too. For example, what is the information in these events that visual analysis picks up? What are the lower level descriptions of motions that are used by the module we have postulated? And of course there are questions regarding the consequences for development the operation of this module may have. It is to this question that we turn next.

MODULARITY: GETTING DEVELOPMENT STARTED.

We saw that one of the advantages of breaking perceptual processes down into modules is the speed of computation which is possible. Applying limited resources to a given task means that solutions are found fast, even if, from a wider perspective, the "solution" may sometimes be defective or even bizarre. Rigidly limiting the resources also means that the module is impenetrable to cognition and general knowledge. This impenetrability has one other advantage which nature may have exploited in designing an organism like us whose development involves a large information gain. The lack of influence by general knowledge and reasoning suffered by a perceptual module enables it to operate quite happily in the absence of general knowledge and reasoning ability. And this, of course, is essential for a mechanism that has to operate very early in development, before there is general knowledge or reasoning ability.

Indeed, a mechanism which can operate independently of general knowledge to provide interlocking descriptions of the environment would be very handy for producing development. This may be the crucial point of modularity. Clearly, there would have to be other learning devices that could take advantage of the descriptions provided by such mechanisms. Ideally they should go beyond the description of appearances and place such descriptions in wider contexts of knowledge and resources. But for solving the problem of getting a little general knowledge in the first place and of thus getting development off the ground, modular perceptual devices are ideal.

As we have seen, there is a good sense in which, though they may be computationally highly sophisticated, perceptual modules perform "tricks", mimicking empirical descriptions of the world without really understanding what is going on. This characteristic of modules may be of central importance in allowing them to be biologically predesigned and built in. Their presence in infancy may give the appearance of specific innate knowledge (of particular causes, for instance). In fact, their function is to allow the process of acquiring knowledge to get started.

Thus, the module we postulated above for the perception of launching can provide "knowledge" about causal interactions without really knowing what a cause is. For the module a "cause" is just what the module says it is. But this may be just enough to get causal development off the ground.

There are a number of ways in which this mechanism could promote development. For example, although the submovements in all the sequences I used covaried equally and perfectly the infant was able to distinguish direct launching, for instance, from delayed reaction. The perceptual mechanism could therefore help in sorting causally connected events from those which merely covary or are just coincidental. It could also play a role in picking up kinetic properties of events (Kaiser & Proffitt, 1984; Todd & Warren, 1982). Visible causal chains could be followed and distinguished. All these things are important for understanding the mechanics of events and for providing thought processes with initially plausible hypotheses about them. The module could tell central processes "A COZED B". Central processes could then begin the abstraction of causal regularities by asking questions such as, do A's always cause B's? under what further circumstances?

what are the properties of A's such that they cause B's? and so on. In other words, the output of this module may provide the starting point for the development of some of the preschooler's causal "theories", in the sense intended earlier.

PERCEPTUAL MODULE VERSUS CENTRAL "THEORY".

The view that perception has a special and distinct role in development brings into sharp focus the following issue. Given that we can identify and describe a particular early competence, what aspects of it are due to the operation of input modules and what to the elaboration of general knowledge? How does the nature of perceptual descriptions influence the construction of central "theories"?

I have been arguing that a part of the child's causal competence is due to an input module. I have argued this on the basis that there is evidence suggesting that young infants are subject to a similar causal illusion as adults. On the one hand, the existence in adults of a perceptual illusion is prima facie evidence of impenetrability (and thus perhaps a module) and on the other hand it seems unlikely that a six month old would have such a percept by virtue of general knowledge and reasoning.

Findings that general knowledge and/or individual differences may play some role in the adult percept (Beasley, 1968; Gemelli & Cappellini, 1958) may simply indicate that verbal reporting of introspections in adults is not the best way to test the properties (or existence) of this module. Such reports are certainly open to "contamination" in various ways by general knowledge and attitude. Some of the rather "flowery" descriptions obtained by Gemelli & Cappellini (1958) underline this and Beasley's (1968) technique of getting subjects to write down their descriptions may not help either.

On balance, then, it is reasonable to suggest the existence of a common mechanism which explains both the infant and at least the basic adult phenomena.

These arguments and evidence are hardly conclusive but they are, I submit, at least worth taking seriously, especially if lessons learnt from them can be applied to understanding other infant competences (e.g. perception of numerosity (Starkey, Gelman & Spelke, 1983), of musical structure (Trehub, Bull & Thorpe, 1984), perhaps of faces (Maurer, 1981), and so on).

What I now want to do is briefly consider the issue of perceptual mechanism versus central "theory", bringing in some other causal events to contrast with launching.

Gruber, Fink & Damm (1957) studied (adult) perception of an event in which a "bridge" collapses. The bridge consisted of a vertical bar supported by two upright posts. When one of the posts was removed the bar would collapse depending upon whether or not the experimenter switched off an electromagnet that was actually responsible for the bar staying up. Gruber et al. manipulated the time interval between removal of the post and collapse of the bar, asking subjects to describe their impressions. As the time interval between removal and collapse was increased, subjects reported a causal link between the two less and less often. This seemed to be a direct analogue for the effect of increasing delays between impact and reaction in Michotte's launching effect.

But is it? Gruber et al. also found that a subject's temporal threshold for a causal judgement was increased by watching a series of trials with very long delays, but decreased by watching a series with no delay. This was interpreted as an effect of experience on an "immediate" perception. Powesland (1959) replicated this result. But when he made a similar study of launching there was no effect of simply watching a series with long or short delays. The temporal threshold for a causal impression remained unchanged (Powesland, 1959). Here then is an interesting difference between the perception of causality in the bridge collapse situation and in launching.

Keil (1979) used a very similar set up to Gruber et al. (1957) with a bar apparently supported by two posts but actually held up by an electromagnet. However, Keil was interested in the understanding of support and balance that 18 month olds have. Using a surprise measure, he found that the infants were clearly surprised when the bar did not collapse after removal of both supports (they were not surprised when it did). Keil interpreted this as showing that the infants had already come to expect the collapse of an unsupported object. However, the infants were not surprised at the non-collapse of the bar after the removal of a single support, even when the unbalanced nature of the bar was accentuated. Keil argued that while the infants had come to anticipate the outcome of a no support situation, a single support would suffice and the importance of balance to the outcome was not appreciated. Even 30 month olds still did not seem to appreciate the nature of balance. Keil argued that the infant had acquired a rule of inference such that no support implies collapse. Collapse, on the other hand, does not imply previous lack of support (none of the children were surprised when the bar did collapse in the balance situation).

If Keil is right, then the appreciation of support and balance involves the learning of inference rules. The perception of this causal situation then involves an important element that goes beyond the operation of input systems. This would help to explain the results of Gruber et al. (1957) and Powesland (1959) discussed above. The bridge situation and launching may differ in that one involves an (overlearned) central inference, while the other is a direct perception.

Of course, it might well be that the learning of this bit of general knowledge, this inference rule, is promoted by an input module of the right sort, perhaps even the module for dealing with launching. We need a detailed understanding of the relevant input mechanisms and the sorts of descriptions they produce for thought processes. This will provide a good starting point for the study of the central learning processes themselves. In fact, I can't think of a better one.[1]

Finally, I raise briefly some other findings on six month olds' perception of a hand picking an object up (Leslie, 1982, 1984a). I do this to draw attention to the issue of development within modules versus central learning.

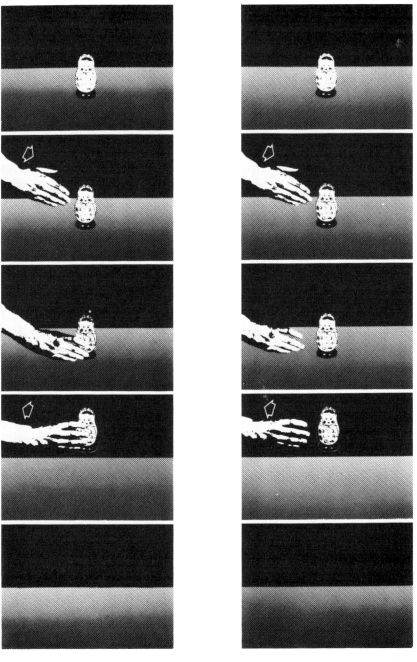

FIGURE 6: Illustration of two sequences used to test infant perception of pick up.

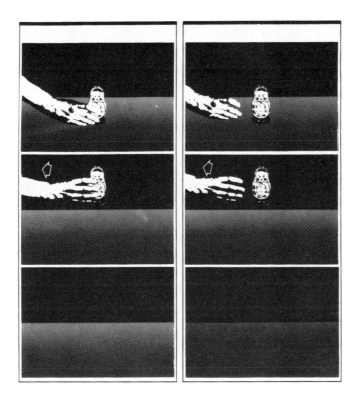

FIGURE 7a: Illustration of sequences used to test specificity of infant response to contact change in pick up (hand picking up the object).

Briefly the findings of these experiments were as follows. Infants readily discriminate a normal pick up from one in which the hand does not actually make contact with the object (see Figure 6). Such a change produces more recovery than, for example, a right-left inversion of normal pick up. More interestingly, this discrimination is only made when the hand actually picks up the object (as opposed to assuming a static relationship) and only when it is a hand picking up and not another inanimate object substituting for it and making similar movements (see Figure 7).

Michotte claimed that the nature of the entities involved

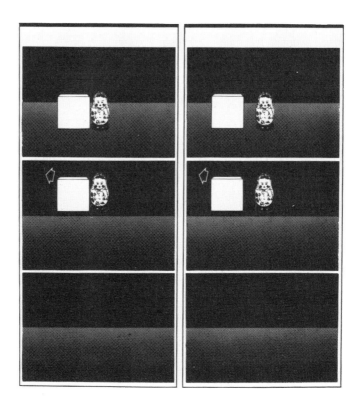

FIGURE 7b: Illustration of sequences used to test specificity of infant
response to contact change in pick up (inanimate object - cube -
substituting for hand picking up object).

in launching was irrelevant for the causal percept. If so (but
see Beasley, 1968), this could be interpreted as evidence that
the module involved operates independently of object
recognition. This seems plausible if it is part of the motion
analysis system, given the evidence for motion analysis
creating its own "objects" (see e.g. Johansson, 1950; Restle,
1979). In the case of the infant's perception of pick up,
however, the nature of the objects (whether it is a hand or
not) plays an important role.

　　This pick-up percept would have to have access to object
recognition information and so have to be organised at a much

later stage of visual processing than launching. It is suggestive that cells have recently been discovered in the visual association cortex of the chimpanzee that respond specifically to mechanical hand-object interactions but not to similar actions only mimed in the presence of the object (Chitty, Perrett, Mistlin & Potter, in press). In the chimpanzee, at any rate, such manual mechanics seems to be processed at the highest stages of vision.

The perception of manual mechanisms and object recognition may also be the product of late visual processing in the human.

Certainly, the child learns to recognise an enormous number of objects within the first few years. Probably the rate of information gain outstrips even that of word learning which averages 8 new words a day between 2 and 5 years (Carey, 1978). So, while some modules may change very little after they become functional, others may acquire a great deal of specialised knowledge.

A FINAL REMARK.

I have been arguing that perception with its distinctive organisation has a distinctive role in development. If perception is prior in ontogeny, it must make its influence felt in the development of thought. It also seems likely that input processes are prior in phylogeny. Perhaps the evolution of human thought likewise has capitalised on the nature of input descriptions.

NOTE

1. A recent study by Baillargeon, Spelke and Wasserman (1985) provides a fascinating case study for these issues. Their results show that five-month-olds believe in the continued existence of an occluded object in a particular location which should then resist the motion

of another visible object through that location. When an
"impossible" event was shown them in which the visible
object passed through this location, they were surprised
or puzzled. I would speculate that the five-months-old's
input systems already specify both the continued
existence of objects that become occluded and the
non-existence of things in locations through which an
object travels. The appreciation of the contradiction,
however, between successive input descriptions in the
Baillargeon et al. situation is surely the work of the
five-month-old's central processes. This study, then, has
interesting implications for both input and central
systems in infancy.

REFERENCES.

Baillargeon, A., Spelke, E.S. & Wasserman, S. (1985). Object
permanence in five-month-old infants. Cognition, 20,
191-208.

Beasley, N.A. (1968). The extent of individual differences in
the perception of causality. Canadian Journal of
Psychology, 22, 399-407.

Borton, R.W. (1979). The perception of causality in infants.
Paper presented to the Society for Research in Child
Development, San Francisco.

Bower, T.G.R. (1974). Development in infancy, 2nd Edition
(Revised 1982). San Francisco: W.H. Freeman and Co.

Bullock, M. (1985). Causal reasoning and developmental change
over the preschool years. Human Development, 28, 169-191.

Bullock, M., Gelman, R. & Baillargeon, R. (1982). The
development of causal reasoning. In W. Friedman (Ed.),
The Developmental Psychology of Time. New York: Academic
Press.

Carey, S. (1978). The child as word learner. In M. Halle, J.
Bresnan & G.A. Miller (Eds.), Linguistic Theory and
Psychological Reality. Cambridge (Mass.): MIT Press.

Carey, S. (1982). Semantic development: The state of the art.

In E. Wanner & L.R. Gleitman (Eds.), Language
Acquisition: The state of the art (347-389). Cambridge:
Cambridge University Press.

Chitty, A.J., Perrett, D.I., Mistlin, A.J., & Potter, D.D. (in
press). Demonstration of cells in the temporal cortex
responsive to specific hand-object interactions.
Perception.

Fodor, J.A. (1983). The Modularity of Mind. Cambridge (Mass.):
MIT Press.

Gemelli, A. & Cappellini, A. (1958). The influence of the
subject's attitude in perception. Acta Psychologica, 14,
12-23.

Gruber, H.E., Fink, C.D., & Damm, V. (1957). Effects of
experience on perception of causality. Journal of
Experimental Psychology, 53, 89-93.

Hume, D. (1740/1978). A Treatise of Human Nature. London:
Clarendon.

Johansson, G. (1950). Configurations in Event Perception.
Stockholm: Almqvist & Wiksell.

Johansson, G. (1973). Visual perception of biological motion
and a model for its analysis. Perception & Psychophysics,
14, 201-211.

Kaiser, M.K. & Proffitt, D.R. (1984). The development of
sensitivity to causally relevant dynamic information.
Child Development, 55, 1614-1624.

Kanizsa, G. (1985). Seeing and thinking. Acta Psychologica,
59, 23-33.

Keil, F. (1979). The development of the young child's ability
to anticipate the outcomes of simple causal events. Child
Development, 50, 455-462.

Kripke, S.A. (1972) Naming and necessity. In D. Davidson &
G.Harman (Eds.), Semantics of Natural Language. 253-355.
Dordrecht: Reidel.

Leslie, A.M. (1982a). Discursive representation in infancy. In
B. de Gelder (Ed.), Knowledge and representation. London:
Routledge & Kegan Paul.

Leslie, A.M. (1982b). The perception of causality in infants.
Perception, 11, 173-186.

Leslie, A.M. (1984a). Infant perception of a manual pick-up event. British Journal of Developmental Psychology, 2, 19-32.

Leslie, A.M. (1984b). Spatiotemporal continuity and the perception of causality in infants. Perception, 13, 287-305.

Leslie, A.M. (1984c). The infant's encoding of simple causal events. Paper presented at 4th Biennial International Conference on Infant Studies, New York, N.Y., April, 1984.

Leslie, A.M., & Keeble, S. (forthcoming). Do six month old infants perceive causality? MRC Cognitive Development Unit, London.

Long, G.M., & Toppino,T.C. (1981). Multiple representations of the same reversible figure: Implications for cognitive decisional interpretations. Perception, 10, 231-234.

Marr, D. (1982) Vision. San Francisco: W.H.Freeman & Co.

Marr, D., & Nishihara, H.K. (1978). Representation and recognition of the spatial organization of three-dimensional shapes. Proceedings of the Royal Society of London, B, 207, 187-217.

Maurer, D. (1981). Infants' perception of facedness. In M.E. Lamb and L.R. Sherrod (Eds.), Infant Social Cognition. Hillsdale (N.J.): Lawrence Erlbaum.

Medin, D.L. & Smith, E.E. (1984). Concepts and concept formation. Annual Review of Psychology, 35, 113-138.

Michotte, A. (1963). The Perception of Causality. Andover: Methuen.

Murphy, G.L. & Medin, D.L. (1985). The role of theories in conceptual coherence. Psychological Review, 92, 289-316.

Osherson, D.N. & Smith, E.E. (1981). On the adequacy of prototype theory as a theory of concepts. Cognition, 9, 35-58.

Powesland, P.F. (1959). The effect of practice upon the perception of causality. Canadian Journal of Psychology, 13, 155-168.

Putnam, H. (1975). The meaning of 'meaning'. In K. Gunderson (Ed.), Language, Mind, and Knowledge. Minneapolis:

University of Minnesota Press.

Ramachandran, V.S. (1985). The neurobiology of perception. Perception, 14, 97-103.

Restle, F. (1979). Coding theory of the perception of motion configurations. Psychological Review, 86, 1-24.

Rock, I. (1985). Perception and knowledge. Acta Psychologica, 59, 3-22.

Rosch, E. (1978). Principles of categorisation. In E. Rosch & B.B. Lloyd (Eds.), Cognition and Categorisation, Hillsdale (N.J.): Lawrence Erlbaum.

Shultz, T. (1982). Rules of causal attribution. Monographs of the Society for Research in Child Development, 47, No.1.

Spelke, E.S. (1982). Perceptual knowledge of objects in infancy. In J. Mehler, E. Walker & M. Garrett (Eds.), Perspectives on mental representation. Hillsdale (N.J.): Lawrence Erlbaum.

Starkey, P.D., Spelke, E., & Gelman, R. (1983). Detection of numerical correspondences by human infants. Science, 222, 179-181.

Todd, J.T. & Warren, W.H. (1982). Visual perception of relative mass in dynamic events. Perception, 11, 325-335.

Trehub, S.E., Bull, D., & Thorpe, L.A. (1984). Infants' perception of melodies: The role of melodic contour. Child Development, 55, 821-830.

Ullman, S. (1985). Visual routines. Cognition, 18, 97-159.

Wishart, J.G., & Bower, T.G.R. (1984). Spatial relations and the object concept: A normative study. In L.P. Lipsitt & C.K. Rovee-Collier (Eds.), Advances in Infancy Research, Vol.3. Norwood (N.J.): ABLEX.

Zadeh, L.A. (1965). Fuzzy sets. Information and Control, 8, 338-353.

Theory Building in Developmental Psychology
P.L.C. van Geert (editor)
© Elsevier Science Publishers B.V. (North-Holland), 1986

13

On what is Cognitive about Development

Bea de Gelder

The expression "cognitive development" means three different things. The first meaning is that of development of the cognitive functions. This meaning is complicated by the problems of finding a taxonomy of cognitive functions which is appropriate for developmental research and by the fact that the notion of function (and its corresponding term of representation) is taken in a variety of senses. The second meaning of cognitive development focusses on the development of knowledge. To clarify this meaning we look at theories of knowledge representation and knowledge dynamics in science. The third meaning we consider to be "cognitive" as a way of qualifying the kind of explanation given for developmental differences. The paper concludes with a proposal for relating these three meanings.

Cognitive development is a difficult notion. Although there may be many reasons for this difficulty, in the present paper I shall focus on only one. I shall try to show that the difficulty with "cognitive development" is explained by the simple fact that the term "cognitive", and "cognition" for that matter, is a difficult notion. There is a familiar picture of the division of labour between cognitive psychologists and students of development. It states that cognitive processes and development are two sides of the same coin. In other words, one can look at an ability from the point of view of its mature exercise and one can look at it from the perspective of its acquisition. Thus developmental research has its menu set by the way cognition is studied. Indeed, very few authors have designed a proper task for developmental research and made it an independent kind of inquiry. The most notorious example of them could be Piaget. But developmental research is no more autonomous in Piagetian perspective than it is in general, because the Piagetian notion of cognitive development inherits the ambiguity of the notion of cognition.

It may come as a surprise that I focus on an analysis of the term "cognitive" instead of paying due attention to the notion of development itself. The notion of development is a notorious stumbleblock for clarifying the theoretical and methodological issues at stake in cognitive developmentalist positions. At the core of the idea of development is the thesis of a functional relation between a specifiable pre-existing state, necessary sequences and a specifiable end state. The end state obtains as a function of the pre-existing beginning state and the necessary sequences. The idea is taken from functional explanations in biology. Nagel (1957, 1979) offers the standard analysis of biological functional explanations. But can this model of explanation be carried over to mental or cognitive phenomena? Peters (1972, 1974) claims it is possible to redefine the functional requirements and make them suitable for the explanation of cognitive phenomena. However, Hamlyn (1975) expresses scepticism. Haroutunian (1983) presents the issue of the pre-existing state as the locus of the disagreement. But this impression might be caused by the fact that the debate about cognitive development has been focussed on the innateness issue (Piatelli-Palmarini 1980). Still, how can one settle the issue of a pre-existing state when it is not clear what to put in it?

The question is not what knowledge or how much knowledge to put in the initial state. There is the preliminary question of what is the significance of putting knowledge or anything cognitive in a intitial or, for that matter, a final state of the organism. And this question looms not only behind the functionalist conception of development for which biology and physiology stand model, it is at the core of any model-borrowing in theories of cognitive development. For example in

Piaget's later theory the notion of equilibrium plays a central role (Haroutunian 1983). Piaget thereby subscribes to a long tradition in psychology which both adopts such equilibrium accounts freely to model individual-environment exchanges and extends them to intra- and interindividual cognitive phenomena (e.g. Heider and Festinger). One cannot make sense of such largely metaphorical loans from biology unless the notion of "cognitive" is unpacked.

Thus my conviction is that there is more to be gained by looking at cognition than by looking at development. The point is easy to illustrate. In an uncontroversial statement about the ambitions of developmental theories Fodor states:

> "1. The development of the child's cognitive capacities exhibits a reasonably orderly decomposition into stages. 2. These stages, though they are in the first instance characterised by reference to specific behavioral abilities that the child exhibits, are fundamentally expressions of the kinds of concepts it has available, with weaker conceptual systems corresponding to earlier stages. 3. Learning mediates the developmental progression from stage to stage." (Fodor, 1975, p. 87).

Fodor takes this statement as point of departure for his attack on the conceptual plausibility of cognitive development. Nevertheless, it is a fair rendering of the general developmentalist credo, Piaget's as well as other's. Still, such a statement is ambiguous and renders ambiguous attacks as well as defenses of cognitive development. The source of its ambiguity are the notions of cognition, knowledge and, related to that, the notion of availability of concepts. This ambiguity is present in Piagetian as well as in behavioural or information processing approaches to cognitive development.

The task of this paper is to examine this ambiguity and to trace its implications for theories of development and research on acquisition of representational and behavioural capacities. The notion of cognition must be unpacked in three different components. In one interpretation the study of

cognition is the study of so called "cognitive functions".
Correspondingly, theories of development reduce to the study
of the development of those cognitive functions. In a second
interpretation cognition means the same as knowledge. This
puts developmental psychologists to the task of studying the
acquisition of knowledge. In a third interpretation
"cognitive" indicates a kind of focus on development or a kind
of explanation for developmental phenomena. This turns
theories of cognitive development into cognitive explanations
of developmental phenomena.

A word of caution. These three aspects should not be used
as a basis for a typology of developmental theories in the
literature. As a matter of fact, these three aspects are often
co-present in the same theory. I shall try to show that each
of them creates its own conceptual and empirical problems.
This paper hopes to contribute to disentangling the web. A
bonus of the proposed disambiguation is that the notion of
cognition operative in cognitive studies becomes better
focussed. Thus before engaging in this task, I shall explain
in what sense our exercise might be of interest for the study
of cognition in general.

It should be useful to have some examples. They will
mostly be taken from two main areas : the study of object
permanence and the acquisition of reading. Both areas confront
one with reasonably well established phenomena and a more or
less large array of possible alternatives for explanation.

                                WHY CARE?

Exercises in conceptual clarification are seldom
altruistic enterprises. Most often their author has a specific
meaning in mind and wants to defend it through the somewhat
tortuous means of conceptual analysis. This paper is no
exception. But it is not so much the author's favourite
definition which the paper wants to push than some of her
reasons for being interested in development. Bluntly stated,
these reasons are related to the way in which development

challenges accepted modes of theory building in cognitive psychology. First, albeit not foremost, there is the anti-development confession of major theoreticians in cognitive research, for example, Fodor (1975). Thus developmental problems ought to challenge his cognitive (meta)theory. Next, there is Fodor's declaration that it "would be appalling" if there were any real facts in developmental research challenging his theoretical position. I do not focus on those issues. It is clear from our intention that the intended disambiguation of the notion of cognition implies that some current controversies are ill concieved. There are two more intriguing issues which might go to the core of the a-developmentalism of cognitive theories. One is the neglected aspect of the change of knowledge. The other is the neglected problem of the use of knowledge.

The first problem has received a name and a diagnosis in post-empiricist philosophy of science. In his overview of the troubles with that "Received View", Suppe (1977) mentions evolutionary and developmental aspects among the features any alternative approach to the analysis of scientific knowledge must reckon with. There are important parallels between the project of the Received View and that of cognitive science. These parallels make it understandable that the cognitivist neglect of development comes as no surprise. Much more attention is given to models of knowledge representation than to models of knowledge change. Most models start from a fixed basis of data and operations which is quickly interpreted as the innately given. Alternative proposals disagree about the extension of that basis and the way to characterize its operations (see Siegler and Klahr, 1983, for an overview).

The question of the use of knowledge is equally intriguing. The standard approach to cognitive models consists of attributing knowledge in order to explain behaviour and building a model of the way such knowledge is internally organized. Such model building is inevitably subject to various idealizations and abstractions. Take for example the case of semantic knowledge where the standard metaphor is that of the dictionary or lexicon as the place of storage. But this metaphor is not extended so as to integrate a model of a user of the dictionary.

The problem of knowledge use has different aspects. One concerns the relation to awareness. Subjects are credited with the knowledge needed for performing certain behaviours or exhibiting certain abilities. But their relation (e.g. availability, reflexion) to that knowledge is not part of the constraints on the fact of its attribution or on the model of the internal organisation. It may be perfectly acceptable to ignore constraints of that kind in some cases (depending on the domain of knowledge) and for some purposes (depending on the kind of behaviour, reflexive versus reflex-like for example). However, the very capacity for reflexive use of the attributed knowledge might start an interactive process leading to change in the knowledge basis. Another possibility is that awareness of the attributed knowledge opens possibilities for application and use of that knowledge which cannot be envisaged otherwise. The important question is of course whether the data from cognitive research prompt such a revision of models which pays more attention to use and application (de Gelder, 1986a).

The issue of change in the knowledge basis as well as that of the use of built-in knowledge are nicely illustrated by research in AI. The most intriguing problem for building intelligent systems at present is the so-called frame problem (see Dennett, 1984, for an overview). From the perspective of cognitive development the frame problem is intriguing both in its positive aspects as in its negative ones. Its positive side is obviously the relative success AI encounters in building intelligent systems by installing knowledge in them. Success at this is a function of the extent to which the adult idealization can be maintained. This idealization has two aspects. It "idealizes away" both the change problem and the use problem.

> "AI agent-creators can in principle make an "adult" agent that is equipped with wordly knowledge as if it had laboriously learned all the things it needs to know" (Dennett, 1984, p. 135).

Why then the frame problem? In preparing an action the system must consult its knowledge basis. But in addition to that, it must also go through the implications of the data in its knowledge basis which are relevant for the success of the action planned. And this is where trouble arises. It appears to be very difficult to design a system capable of evaluating what among all the things it "knows" and among all the implications of its installed knowledge is relevant for the planned action. Natural systems as opposed to artificial ones do not seem to have this problem (that is, their survival success makes the presence of the evaluation problem highly unlikely). Artificial systems have their knowledge installed in a way which is appropriate for that instant of their existence for which the researcher sets the relevant parameters. Such is not the cause for natural systems. Even if we feel like granting that nature has provided them with a generous instalment, we would still have to face the fact that they make an intelligent use of what is in their natural knowledge basis, recognizing the specific situation at hand, loading the relevant parts into this working memory, etc. The interesting problem is thus that of this use or selecting capacity. It is this problem, much more than the fact and the extent of the natural instalment, which needs explaining. What else, if not learning about the world, might explain that? If so, the frame problem would force issues of cognitive development to the foreground.

In the area of development some of these themes which are residual in a standard information processing account re-surface under the label of metacognition (e.g. Flavell, 1978). Much of the research on metacognition raises the issues of the constraints on knowledge attribution (see last section) and of the theoretical importance of the fact that the knowledge basis must change or be adapted in order to remain explanatory. Clearly, the notion of development can be looked upon as a special case of the general problems of use and application. In the three meanings of cognitive development discussed below we will run into problems with building developmental theories which might be related to this neglect of "knowledge dynamics".

ON WHAT MAKES SOME MENTAL FUNCTIONS COGNITIVE.

The first meaning of cognitive development is associated with the notion of cognitive functions. Discussion about functions is more straightforward in cognitive psychology than it is in developmental psychology. For example, many textbooks of cognitive psychology are divided in as many chapters as there are sensory modalities (Neisser, 1967). This was never as obvious in textbooks on cognitive development. For Piaget it was inconceivable that the natural taxonomy of sensory modes would contain the cue for the study of cognitive functioning and its development. But the invasion of the information processing approach has apparently encouraged developmental psychologists to bring their work in line with the task descriptions familiar in cognition research. On the other hand, information processing functions become more and more abstract. There is a shift from the study of functions in the traditional sense of faculties to a more abstract notion of function as mental mechanism. Thus the idea is no longer to accept as many functions as there are naturally given senses but to accept as many intelligent mechanisms in the mind as there are kinds of problems to be solved or, alternatively, domains of reality to be addressed. At present developmental theorizing seems to start both from natural functions and content or problem domains. The important question behind both functions and mechanisms remains that of the reasons behind the choice of taxonomy. And to answer this question we must ask why some functions or mechanisms qualify as cognitive.

The most general statement of a post-behaviourist attitude to the study of psychology is that in complex organisms the behaviour is a function of the representational states of the organism rather than being exclusively the function of either the environment or the non-representational states (e.g. the physiological ones). Thus, as the organism becomes more complex more of the explanatory burden is carried by that part of the psychological theory that studies those representational states (e.g. Fodor 1965). It is worth noting however that even in this minimal position on psychological explanation the study of representations does not replace the study of behaviour but remains embedded in it even if, in some cases (very complex behaviours, very complex organisms), it takes almost exclusive effort and attention. This somewhat trivial point of departure is neverthless representative of the ambiguity stigmatized at the outset of this chapter.

Many commentators have rejoiced over the fact that the hallmark of post-behaviorist psychology is its mentalism (e.g. Pylyshyn 1984, Fodor 1980, Dennett 1981), Mandler expresses the point in a way useful for the problems I see with the notion of "function":

> "Mentalism involves the assignment of theoretical, hypothetical functions to the human - functions that determine and guide observable behaviour" (Mandler, 1983, p. 2).

This statement suggests three different perspectives on functions: a theoretical one (the first mentioned), a naturalistic one (contained in the reference to the 'human functions') and a behavioural one. We will examine these below.

Let us return to the statement which places the burden of explanation on the internal representations. Prima facie, under this description the study of development is the study of how such representations are constructed. Whether or not there is a field of development depends on whether there is an empirical story to be told about this development. Two questions remain. The obvious one is whether cognitive development exists. It would not exist if the infant were to be born with a rich innate conceptual basis and with the means of expanding it. This at least is the standard answer. The other question is less common but is one which must claim logical priority. How can we tell whether there is cognitive development? An answer requires that we clarify the notion of cognition. There might be a different answer for each of the three meanings of cognitive development.

If we combine the general statement of the developmental
position with the definition of cognitive explanations we come
to see how crucial the issue of representation is. This fact
is widely acknowledged in the literature (e.g. Mandler 1983,
Harris 1983). But again what representations are is just as
unclear as what cognition is. Harris for example distinguishes
three theoretical issues in developmental theorizing: the role
of interpretation, the role of experience and the role of
representation. This division might create the impression that
the problem of representation and with it the problem of
knowledge is confined to an independent area. But the problem
of interpretation is the problem of representation.

Unfortunately, there are many aspects to the problem of
representation. Thus one can talk about representations and
this can be another way of talking about what the infant
knows. One can refer to representations and this can be a way
of referring to the mode of information processing in the
cognitive functions. Or, one can talk about representations as
that which is attributed in a certain type of explanations.
Clearly then, the problem of representation has important
connections to that of functions.

Here, I want to direct the discussion to two kinds of
problems with cognitive functions. First, one needs to be
clear which ones they are. This is the problem of the
taxonomy. Next, a reasonably clear and unambigous notion of
function must underly this taxonomy so that it can be relied
upon in other contexts, for example that of development. I
discuss these two problems and I will point out the
developmental implications involved.

The Basis of a Taxonomy of Mental Functions.

The classical source of taxonomies of mental powers or
faculties is philosophical tradition. Both the idealist and
the empiricist philosophers have offered catalogues of the
mind's powers. Examples are Tetens, Wolff and Reinhold.
Historically there are interesting disagreements on what does

or does not count as a cognitive function. A very convincing example is the case of imagination. This is a faculty which plays an important role in idealist philosophies, but not in empiricist ones. Current controversies over the role of mental images show how the case of imagination and its philosophical roots is not yet settled (see Block, 1981).

These differences in what to count as a cognitive faculty and how to appraise its importance in the genesis of knowledge are clearly a result of the epistemological orientations of the authors. Thus all the traditional taxonomies are epistemologically marked. As a matter of fact such taxonomies almost always appear as embedded in theories of knowledge. More complicated still, traditional theories of knowledge, not unlike their contemporary counterparts, are themselves embedded in discussions on metaphysical issues.

Such a heavy heritage raises several issues. First, it begs the question of a neutralization of the epistemological and metaphysical origins and the naturalization of those taxonomies. Second, the very plurality of taxonomies raises the issue of a choice for psychological theory and thereby one of the kind of motives for preferring one taxonomy over another. Both aspects concern the relation between cognitive psychology and epistemology. This relation is an issue which seldom comes to the foreground in the information processing theory even when it claims to be the major heir of philosophical faculty psychology. The situation is different in developmental psychology because it was Piaget's explicit motivation to offer an scientific epistemology. Traditional epistemological problems could on his view be solved if the right attention was paid to the fact that knowledge is constructed. The history of its constuction contains the justification for the objectivity of our knowledge. But as memories of Piaget's motivations fade, the philosphical ambition of his genetic epistemology gets lost. Indeed, present day Piagetians also do agree that information processing is the dominant paradigm for the study of cognitive development (Inhelder 1972). Developmental psychologists, like information processing psychologists, moved on to study

cognitive functions without worrying about epistemological
issues and assuming with them that what makes a psychological
proposition empirical as opposed to conceptual or
philosophical is that it is studied with an empirical method.

Does the empirical method in itself naturalize the
traditional faculties and does it thus thereby neutralize the
philosophical problems? In other words has a discussion of
these epistemological issues become obsolete? There are very
few efforts to draw a general picture of the issues at stake
in the empirical research on cognitive functions. Fodor (1983)
stands out in this respect. It is therefore surprising to see
how Fodor's picture of the cognitive faculties is throughly
philosophically motivated. Much as it may rest on
psychological data, the interpretation Fodor gives to them
consists in fact in an a priori argument about the possibility
of objective knowledge. His distinction between modular and
central processes is a distinction which allows Fodor to
represent the first processes as the objective anchorage of
our knowledge. Moreover, Fodor's argument ends with an
epistemological conclusion drawn form his picture of the
faculties, e.g. epistemic boundedness. But this
epistemological conclusion does itself rest on a metaphysical
argument. Fodor concludes that the way our mind works imposes
constraints on what we can know (De Gelder 1986b). His
analysis of the way the mind works (the epistemological basis
of the faculty theory) posits the need for build-in knowledge
of domains of reality (the metaphysical basis of the
epistemological argument). Thus his philosophical motivation
pays off with a philosophical conclusion. In between the two
and attached on both sides hangs the net in which Fodor tries
to catch the empirical facts. The whole issue is all the more
intriguing because both Fodorean metaphysics and theory of
knowledge serve as the background for a view which as we said
above is definitly anti-developmentalist. In the end Fodor's
refusal of cognitive development rests on metaphysics.

Fodor's view may be both extreme and of marginal interest
for empirical research. Let us assume for a moment it is and
with it the philosophical concerns we mentioned. What would be

an alternative source of mental taxonomies? In practice the alternative seems to be something like logical analysis or rational decomposition of our ordinary concept of knowledge into various (collaborating) mental powers. Our ordinary notion tells us that to know something is to have a representation. In the paradigm case, when we truly have knowledge, we have a representation which corresponds to something in the world. This requires perception of that of which we have a representation and it requires permanence of the representation. That way the idea of memory surfaces as a component of the logical analysis of what it is to know. A natural step then is to translate this logical analysis (which is an aprioristic reasoning in disguise) into a psychological blueprint, adopting as many sub-faculties as there are steps in the logical analysis. The case of memory nicely illustrates the risks of this procedure (see Bursen, 1978 for criticism of this procedure). An illustration in the area of development can be taken from the much discussed issue of stages. Brainerd (1978) has argued that the Piagetian stages do not so much represent steps in an empirical process as logical steps whose empirical reality consists in the fact that they are measurement sequences.

But let us, again for the sake of argument, grant the general validity of such aprioristic reasoning and its psychological counterpart. Can developmental research safely operate inside that framework? Without thereby wanting to settle the issue I draw attention to a problem which this time is proper to developmental research, e.g. the distinction between an ability and the ability to acquire that ability.

It is a standard assumption of research on cognitive functions that the skills needed for the mature or adult performance are the very ones that must be acquired. Correspondingly, the analysis of the adult performance will tell us what those skills are. The study of the acquisition of reading illustrates this approach nicely while at the same time stressing its problems. Rozin (1978) remarks :

> "Assuming a tight linkage between adult performance and a prescription for what must be taught is not

justifiable. The assumption is particularly dangerous when the adult task is not well understood, and yet the assumption is repeatedly made." (Rozin, 1978, p. 419).

Research on reading brings out that fluent readers decode a written page with the help of skills that are different from those the beginning reader tries to put to work and are again even in fluent readers a function of the familiarity of the words (Jorm and Share, 1983).

Rozin's remark illustrates the discrepancy between acquisition of an ability and exercise of an acquired ability or skill. But beyond that complication looms a conceptual issue. It is one thing to have an ability, for example for reading, or to be able to read fluently, or to acquire just that ability. But it is another thing to have the ability for acquiring an ability. The abilities needed to acquire fluency in reading may be unrelated to the ability to read. In other words, the logical analysis of fluent reading and the empirical research on the processes involved may shed no light on how this ability is acquired and how those processes are built up.

The obstacles we have considered so far have their origin in the ambiguity of the term 'cognitive'. The reason why all of these issues are lumped together is that all the aspects of abilities are seen as cognitive in the same sense of the term. All of them are the expression of the same underlying knowledge, they all have the same cognitive core which is revealed by the logical analysis. The major idea responsible for this is the ambiguous notion of function.

Ambiguity of the Notions of Function and Representation.

The notion of function covers a variety of meanings and is used for a variety of purposes. Moreover, the ambiguity of 'function' goes hand in hand with the ambiguity of 'representation'. This is not surprising because most often a function is characterised by its representations. We illustrate the discussion with the example of object permanence. To show how the various meanings of representation and function interact in research and theory on the acquisition of object permanence, we first briefly expose that issue following Harris (1983).

Piaget distinguishes six stages in the acquistion of object permanence. The existence of these stages, including their order of succession, has been largely confirmed by virtually all of the subsequent research. Harris summarizes the state of things by saying:

> "there is little doubt that the infant's ability to search for a hidden object becomes progressively more sophisticated" (Harris, 1983, p. 715).

This statement is meant as a summary of and conclusion about the findings. It is not yet the interpretation or explanation. Harris separates the summary of the findings from the interpretation Piaget has proposed. Thus we can take his description of the stages as one which in his view is not committed to Piagetianism. Those stages are then: (1 and 2) absence of active search but continued looking, (3) minimal adjustments to the object's disappearance and anticipation, search if the object is only half hidden, (4) search for the hidden object provided its location does not change, (5) continued dependency on full visibility at the time of change in location and hiding, (6) successful search generalized to other situations.

The point we want to draw attention to is that such a stage description may well be neutral with respect to Piagetian theory but is still not strictly observational or behavioural. The observations are embedded inside the conceptual framework of our notion of searching. Another way of talking about searching is to talk about the intention of finding an object. It is important to note that notions like intention, searching and object are conceptually interdependent. It is conceptually incoherent to observe behaviour, to consider it to be searching behaviour and then not to take it as searching for something. Thus the description of the stages consists in an interpretation which

builds upon our understanding of the logic of searching
behaviour, of intentions and of what objects are. Piaget's
theoretical explanation rests upon the same conceptual
framework but shows how this framework, from being exclusively
that of the observing adult, moves to being also that of the
behaving infant. In other words, the concepts the adult
observation puts into play must also become the infant's
concepts. Thus Piaget's explanation rests on the assuption
that behaviour is a function of representations in the much
narrower sense of available concepts. I want now to show how
there are different notions of representation and function
involved in both the observation of the facts as rendered by
Harris and the theoretical construction Piaget proposes. At
the same time the different meanings will be identified in the
information processing literature.

Functions as Coding Mechanisms.

     A first meaning of function is that of part, component or
sub-function which can be isolated through its operations.
This meaning is clearest in the information processing
approach which tries to analyse a general function, say
perception, into its component parts, subfunctions or
subparts. This kind of research would not seem to be haunted
by the old philosophical notion of knowledge. Functions are
called cognitive simply because they extract information from
the environment. The notion of representation which
corresponds to this concept of function is that of
representation as code. Thus, cognitive functions are
mechanisms that decode and encode information.
     This definition of the study of cognitive functions as
the study of the code only, seems to rest on two assumptions
which could be problematic for the idea of cognitive
development. Firstly, there is the separation of content and
code which empties the notion of representation code of all
the ordinary connotations discussed below. This separation
corresponds to the distinction between semantic aspects (the

knowledge level), and syntactic aspects (the representation
level). Secondly, the methodology seems to require that the
information is kept constant. This turns information into
something the theorist reads off from the outside world and
which can be manipulated as an independent variable in
research on the internal code. Such a conception of
information might have the disadvantage of being applicable
only to the case of an idealization, that of the competent
adult who is in Chomsky's words member of an ideal community
of competent adults[1]. Both assumptions correspond to the
idealizations made in Artificial Intellgence (see above).

Where does this fit in with the discussion on object
permanence? Both assumptions run counter to Piagetian theory
and more generally against the standard developmentalist
credo, as formulated by, for example, Fodor (see above). But
this is not the issue, at least not at present. In this
section, we want to know if this conception of cognitive
functions can lead to an alternative for the Piagetian
explanation of the facts about object permanence.

As a matter of fact, Piaget's theory of object permanence
has been challenged by researchers much closer to the
information processing approach (see Harris, 1983, for an
overview). The most important challenge has come from Gibson
and associates. The standard formulation of the clash between
Piaget and Gibson is the statement that object permanence is a
constructed notion versus the thesis that objects are
perceived as permanent because the sensory information
contains all of the cues required for establishing the
presence of object identity. It appears well established that
4 to 5 month olds can discriminate in the sense of responding
differentially to various types of object disappearance. A
paraphrase of the Gibsonian claim would consist of saying that
differential responses to various presentations of objects are
by themselves enough to attribute object permanence because
those discriminations correspond to the way the concept of
object permanence is instantiated in the operation of the
cognitive functions.
However, the study of the coding operations of cognitive

functions does not allow conclusions about the concepts the infant does or does not have available. The reason why Piaget comes to the decision about the existence of concept acquisition is that he builds the steps of concept acquisition into the developmental sequence. He does not claim, however, that at each step his conceptual interpretation of the developmental sequence maps the discriminations the infant is able to make at that moment. In other words, two things must be kept separate. One is the empirical description of what can and cannot be done. This description is formulated in the language of information and codes. The second is conceptual attribution made on the basis of (intentionalist) observation of behaviour.

To summarize, Piaget looks at behaviour through an observational framework which itself rests on a global intentional interpretation of the behaviour and from there sets out to ask when that behaviour is such that it makes concept attribution warranted. But the attribution of concepts, neither in the intermediate stages nor at the end, makes contact with data on sensory capacities. Gibson on the other hand identifies concepts with sensory operations and does not seem to be aware of the difference between analysis of the cognitive functions and interpretation in the form of knowledge attributions of their output.

"Functional" in the sense of "Teleological".

There is a second meaning of cognitive functions which is much less explicit than the previous one. We could paraphrase it as the view that cognitive functions have the role of informing the organism about the world by providing it with knowledge about its environment. This teleological notion of function corresponds to a teleological notion of representation. Representations fit into this teleological reasoning to the extent that they are copies of the world. In other words, the whole point of having cognitive functions is to obtain knowledge.

This teleological perspective is no doubt one which Piaget as well as many cognitive psychologists take for granted. It is at the basis of the whole idea of the brain containing a mental model of the outside reality of the cognitive system.

"Functional" in the sense of "Evolutionary Optimal".

An evolutionary approach would be one stating that mental functions including the cognitive ones have the properties they have as the consequence of an evolutionary process in which they were shaped. Such an evolutionary approach is inevitably brought to optimism about the adequacy of the mental powers because it rests on the premise of evolution as the optimalization of function in the teleological sense. For the case of cognitive functions this means that mental properties are optimally shaped for accomplishing their purpose, namely, the acquisition of knowledge about the environment or the attainment of thruth. The evolutionary consideration thus takes the place of a justification of the objectivity of knowledge and of an analysis of the contribution of cognitive functions to knowledge. In the evolutionary approach these two tasks, that of epistemology and that of an independent analysis of cognitive functioning, can be dispelled with.

This argument is seldom openly discussed. One of the few to discuss and defend it is Dennett (1981). At a more implicit level evolutionary optimalism is present in the view that the very operations of the cognitive functions are those which generate knowledge. To rephrase the point in information-processing terms, the sum of the products of cognitive functions are what turns environmental input into knowledge.

The optimalism argument should not be presented as one from which empirical implications follow naturally. It does not for example allow us to choose between alternative modes of functioning or rival pictures of cognitive faculties. It is purely a conceptual point that the evolutionary belief in

optimalization leads to optimism. Biologists have warned
against the use of this style of explanation as a means for
settling empirical matters in particular cases.

Is the evolutionary meaning of function present in
cognitive research? In ordinary discourse representation is
intimately linked with the optimism about the cognitive nature
of some of the mental functions. In an ordinary sense of the
words it is roughly the same to have knowledge and to have a
representation. To say that John knows what a table is, is
equivalent with saying that John has a representation of a
table. If nothing else is at stake than two equivalent ways of
putting the same point, then it is a conceptual truth that
having knowledge and having representations express the same
fact about John. It is not a very deep conceptual point
because it is embedded in nothing more than naive realism and
truth as correspondence between th content of the mind and
that of the world.

It is not my intention to discuss naive realism except
for pointing out its non-empirical status. We saw that the
equivalence between the two idioms is a conceptual one. This
means that we cannot posit an independent reality for
representations and then explain knowledge by appealing to
these representations. In other words, if to have knowledge is
to have representations then we cannot at the same time claim
that the cause of someone's knowledge is that he has
representations. There is nothing beyond or beneath the fact
that John knows what a table is. All there might be is a
different way of saying it, a different way of making the same
point, but no causal story beginning with sensory input and
ending with knowledge, and representations somewhere in
between. This fits in with our remark that evolutionary
optimalism is a conceptual claim. It is important to note
these points because in discussions on representation the
conceptual point and the empirical claim about the existence
of representations are often presented as being
interchangeable.

The study of representation as code has flourished under
the influence of research in Artificial Intelligence. Palmer

(1978) lists the huge number of codes that have since been borrowed by psychologists. In her essay on representation in cognitive development J. Mandler (1983) agrees with Palmer's pessimism in the face of such a variety of representations and so little understanding of the issue of representation itself. But her claim is that that problem is one of representation in the sense of code or in the sense of notational system. Developmental psychologists are not yet concerned with that aspect because they are at present still discovering facts about knowledge and are far from studying the way knowledge is formally represented or coded.

Mandler's view is not generally endorsed. It contrasts with an interpretation of cognitive development which considers developmental changes to be not changes in what is known, but in the way knowledge is stored. It contrasts also with the view that cognitive development is a matter of knowing more and more about the world, a matter of enrichment of the data basis of the cognitive system (see next section). We may agree with Mandler's statement that it is too early to discuss the first possibility. Just what Mandler's claim means is a matter of what one puts in the notion of code. It is an illusion to think that this focus on the code stands for a more modest and reachable goal of developmental research when there is no sensible way of separating syntactic and semantic aspects of the representation-code. In pretending there is such, the cognitive code theorists also seem to hope that there is a notion of function and a process description of functioning which can be disconnected from the other notions of function mentioned above.

The distinction between representation as knowledge and representation as code is not clear. Mandler (1983) distinguishes between two notions of representation.

> "The first of these... refers to knowledge and the way in which it is organised. This is a complex conception since it refers both to what is known and how that knowledge is structured." (Mandler, 1983, p. 421).

This meaning is contrasted with a second one:

"...representation as the use of symbols" (Mandler, 1983, p. 421). What is this contrast about? To talk about the knowledge which is represented must be the same as to talk about the symbols. The representations in which the knowledge about the world is represented must be seen as representations of the world. Otherwise there would be no point in calling them representations of knowledge. But if so, then the representations in the first sense are symbols and the symbols, in the first sense of representations are knowledge representations. Mandler seems to believe that the difference between the new psychological notion of representation and the traditional one of symbol amounts to the distinction between a representation and its semantic properties (e.g. reference and meaning). Psychologists would thus study knowledge-representations without worrying about what they represent or whether they present anything at all. Such a position would make little sense unless the concept of knowledge was given two different meanings.

To see if this is the case we must look behind the scene. Mandler's contrast between two notions of representation has two sources of inspiration. The first is Piaget's theory of the acquisition of representational thought. On this view there is no representational thought during the early stages of 'cognitive development'. Still, sensory-motor schemes can be said to represent their object, but this requires a different notion of representation. By "representational thought" Piaget seems to mean symbolic thinking or thinking in which representations of the objects are crucial. At this point a distinction introduced in AI research between procedural and declarative knowledge is brought in and allows a reformulation of Piaget's view. We could thus take Piaget to say that thinking develops out of procedural representations. If that is the distinction Mandler has in mind, it would be better to rephrase it with the help of the notion of functional representation. In its broadest sense, a functional representation is a description of the state of the organism which underlies a given behaviour. A clear case is that of sensori-motor schemes themselves. In this case the claim that a sensori-motor scheme represents the object amounts to the claim that there is a description of the sensori-motor state of the organism on the one hand and of the behaviour on the other which is such that it shows the behaviour to be a function of the so described sensori-motor state. There is no need for introducing a representation of the object in the sense of a symbol standing for the object in between the description any observer can give of the object and the description of the movements. This leaves the question of dealing with the nature of that description, the difference between a description in sensori-motor terms and reflexes and a cognitive description which is formulated in terms of cognitive contents and the need to relate those functional descriptions to knowledge attributions.

These considerations about cognitive functions seem to push us into a dilemma. On the one hand one is forced to consider the possibility that the study of cognitive functions remains disconnected from the study of knowledge. On the other hand, the focus on knowledge leads one to the risk of disconnecting from the empirical research on coding mechanisms. The dilemma opens the possibility of changes in knowledge which do not correspond to changes in cognitive functioning or, the other way round, a change in cognitive functioning which does not correspond to a change in knowledge. This could be a real problem. Various developmental psychologists have stressed that developmental theories must search for the the level of underlying representations. But at the same time they have drawn attention to the fact that there is a mismatch between behaviour and representation. In other words, there is no one to one relation between behaviour and representation (see Karmiloff-Smith, 1986, for illustrations of this point). The above gives one reason enough then to approach the issue from the other end and for looking at knowledge rather than at cognitive functions supposedly producing it.

ON WHAT IT MEANS TO STUDY THE DEVELOPMENT OF KNOWLEDGE.

In this section I want the scrutinize the idea that the study of cognitive development is the study of the development of knowledge or, that it is in other words, the study of the changes in what a cognitive system knows. This view has long been popular in the work on the child's conceptions of reality. At present, the notion of knowledge is much less in focus than it used to be. It has been replaced with the term "cognition" and thus one might have the feeling that the problems discussed here are philosophical implications of the notion of knowledge but are set aside with the scientific notion of cognition.

How can one then conceptualize the idea of cognitive development as a matter of change in knowledge? One of the first things to be clarified is understanding what it means for knowledge to change. But obviously, this approach requires an explanation of what is meant by knowledge and requires one to look for a way of representing knowledge that allows it to become an object of study. In a broad but relevant sense this is the task of the philosophy of science. It would thus be a good strategy to look at the extent to which the philosophical analysis of scientific knowledge can stand model for the psychological study of knowledge. This strategy can be defended, as for example Fodor (1983) does, on the ground that the theory of science is all one has to rely on when studying higher cognitive processes. The strategy can also be defended as Piaget does, by referring to the interaction between cognitive processes and processes of scientific theory building. One need not endorse either of these arguments for seeing the relevance for the present problems of the way the theory of science tries to come to grips with the elusive phenomenon of scientific knowledge.

There are two problem areas in the theory of science which are of particular interest. One is the disagreement over a qualitative versus a quantitative sense of growth of knowledge. The other is the contrast between context of justification and context of discovery. I will briefly look at each in turn and try to sketch the relevance of these discussions.

There is a natural or folk-philosophical view about the history of scientific ideas and theories. It consists in believing that science progresses towards an accumulation of knowledge. This view has also dominated philosophy of science during the first half of this century and has been defended as the incremental approach to scientific progress. In this picture, the difference between an old theory and its successor reduces to the fact that the new theory can answer more questions because it contains a broader knowledge basis. It is tempting to look upon cognitive development along the same lines. The difference between a young child an an adult, for example in solving physics problems, would thus be a consequence of the fact that the adult knows more about physics, has more data stored, and has concepts which the child does not yet have (e.g. Smith et al., 1985). The analogy between mind and computer makes this comparison between knowledge in an individual mind and knowledge in a scientific theory all the more plausible. On this widespread view, the mind just like the scientific theory, is what contains the knowledge and from where intelligent behaviour or applications of theory follow. The next step is then to find out how this knowledge is represented in the mind or in the scientific theory. In philosphy of science where this has been the main research programme, many alternative proposals about the representational structure of scientific theories have been defended. Given that this picture includes only quantitative changes there is no real problem of growth or development. In other words it is assumed that the same method will allow one to represent the intellectual content of the mind at any time in its history.

The alternative way of looking at the growth of science has been popularized by Kuhn. He refutes the very possibility of a comparison between intellectual contents of two successive theories. By doing so he refutes the very idea of growth itself to replace it only with the thesis that there are no standards of comparison, that two different theories

are incommensurable. His arguments and those of his followers
inevitably evoke the arguments of the defenders of stage-like
cognitive development. Indeed, the qualitative change thesis
of cognitive development is often paraphrased with the notion
of cognitive schemes or cognitive structures which have a
constitutive role for experience much in the same way Kuhn
believes paradigms do. As mentioned earlier, the very claim
that cognitive structures are constitutive for the experience
of reality carries the implication that there is no comparison
possible of intellectual content across conceptual schemes and
thus no cognitive basis to the idea of change and progress.
Must we then come to the conclusion that, if we take seriously
the idea of qualitative change, we are lead to denying its
very possibility, or at least, the possibility of
understanding it? It cannot be denied that, setting philosophy
of science aside, this is the impression one gets from the
literature attacking the idea of qualitative stages as well as
from reading those who against all odds try to make sense of
the Piagetian mechanisms for cognitive development.

These impressionistic remarks on the problem of growth
are not meant to convince, only to illustrate certain
parallels between the problems of a theory which aims at
representing the intellectual content of scientific theories
and theories aiming to represent the cognitive content of
minds. Still, what makes many expositions both of the thesis
of conceptual schemes and of that of paradigms unconvincing is
that the issue of knowledge representation itself is not
reconsidered critically. Where does this ambition of knowledge
representation come from? What makes it a desirable
intellectual goal to have a theory which represents how
knowledge is represented in minds or in scientific theories?
In looking at the second problem area in philosophy of science
we shall get closer to the heart of the matter.

The much discussed distinction between contexts of
justification and contexts of discovery is the product of the
way in which philosophy of science has attacked the study of
the intellectual content of theories. The major tool for
representing the intellectual content has been the axiomatic

method. The leading idea of traditional philosophy of science
has been that a scientific theory is an axiomatic calculus and
that all the intellectual achievements of scientific theories
go to the credit of the underlying axiomatic structure of the
knowledge represented in scientific theories and of the
specific way in which this structure is represented. Thus
observational power and explanatory force rest on this
axiomatic structure. On the other side, it is the task of
philosphy of science to represent or reconstruct this
axiomatic structure. An important step towards this goal is
the separation of the observational and the theoretical. The
latter has a status which is derived from that of the
observational.

Before going into this it is interesting to note a
consequence of the above distinction. It stands for a
demarcation between what belongs to philosophy and what
belongs to psychology. All of the aspects of scientific
discovery become the competence of psychology. But if we look
at the psychology of knowledge thirty years after its "job
assignment" (whether this was received or not does not matter)
we see that the same demarcation reappears inside cognitive
psychology. Fodor (1983) argues that only those aspects of
cognition can be studied which can be related to an underlying
logical structure instantiated in the "modules". The other
aspects cannot be studied scientifically because their
behaviour does not warrant the assumption of underlying
logical structures.

In the introduction I already referred to the dubious
success of the axiomatic reconstruction programme itself as
well as to the fact that it fails in the face of conceptual
evolution. Toulmin (1977) looks back and states the leading
intuition of the axiomatic reconstruction approach:

> "At any stage in its historical development, the
> established intellectual content of a science or
> scientific theory can be exhaustively represented as
> a 'logical system' - that is that the theoretical
> concepts and conclusions of the science are related
> to one another, and to the observational evidence on

> which they are based, in a formal network of logical
> relations - and that the consistency, richness and
> logical structure of this network determine the
> validity, and/or degree of establishment of the
> theoretical concepts and conclusions in question"
> (Toulmin, 1977, p. 603).

Toulmin asks some pertinent questions about this leading dogma
which are easily related to the problems in cognitive
development. The only case where the axiomatic method has
worked out was also the case of the science which stood model
for the programme of axiomatic representation, mechanics as
presented in Hertz' "The Principles of Mechanics". When faced
both with the intrinsic problems of an axiomatic
reconstruction and with its reduction of the dynamic dimension
of intellectual content, Toulmin asks:

> "Can the axiomatic model be used equally well in all
> cases to analyse, and judge, the intellectual
> content of any particular cross-section of a natural
> science?" (Toulmin, 1977, p. 604).

This is already dubious even when one accepts, appearances of
success to the contrary, that the axiomatic method is
apprioppriate for 'static' analysis. Translated to the domain
of cognition research Toulmin's question would thus raise
doubts about the possibility of an axomatic reconstruction of
adult cognition as well as of a reconstruction of cross
sections taken from a developmental history. For example, a
precise reconstruction of the cognitive structures at each of
the developmental Piagetian stages would thus be ruled out[2].
Toulmin's second question arises once one steps outside the
axomatic method:

> "Can the axiomatic method be used at all to analyse,
> and judge, the ways in which the intellectual
> content of a natural science develops, from one
> temporal cross-section to the next?" (Toulmin, 1977,
> p. 604).

What the axiomatic method was for logical empiricism is
what the the computer approach to mental processes appears to
be for cognition research. The leading axiom of the

representationalist-computationalist approach is the assumption that the intellectual content of the brain (i.e. for functionalists the mind), can be represented as a logical system which is in this assumption credited with the theoretical and explanatory powers recognized for the scientific (see above) or, here, for the mind (Haugeland, 1981; Fodor, 1975, 1980).

One final remark. Computationalism is largely a philosophy of cognitive science (e.g. the introduction in Haugeland, 1981). This raises the interesting possibility that, as a philosophy, it might be just as remote from empirical science than the axiomatic efforts and embedding assumptions of logical empiricism have turned out to be remote, irrealistic, and inadequate for physics. This would give a strange ring to the statements of the philosphers of cognitive science who repeat that the idea of cognitive development is logically inconsistent.

In concluding this section we must then say that rather than offering a ready-made theory of knowledge growth, philosophy of science confronts us with what is involved in such an enterprise. Rather than ruling out the possibility of making sense of knowledge development, it encourages us to take it more seriously than the received view in the philosophy of cognitive science leads us to think.

ON EXPLANATION AND KNOWLEDGE ATTRIBUTION.

In this section I shall examine an interpretation of the expression cognitive development which defends that "cognitive" qualifies a type of explanation and not a domain of reality or of phenomena. The hallmark of such an explanation is that it depicts behaviour as a function of knowledge. Obviously then the form of such explanations is that of a functional relation between a description of a behaviour and an attribution of knowledge or representation. Cognitive explanations in this sense are not restricted to psychology, but can indeed be found in biology (for example

Goodwin, 1978) and in sociology (for example Cicourel, 1973).

What is knowledge attribution? The first thing to remark about it is that it is something very familiar. In everyday interaction for example we describe/explain people's behaviour by our making a reference to what they believe to be the case or what they know, expect etc. We approach others actions as a function of their beliefs and intentions. These beliefs and intentions are attributed in an ongoing process of interaction most of which remains implicit. This mode of explaining by attributing beliefs and intentions came to be called the intentional stance (Dennett, 1978). One can safely regard knowledge attribution as fitting into that intentionalist framework and representing their cognitive aspect.

But obviously, the intentionalist stance is not limited to everyday life. Scientific observations, even the most behaviourist ones, are replete with intentionalist notions. Moreover, these notions are not just convenient fictions or accepted shorthand expressions but do play a role in the theories (see Taylor, 1964, for the classical demonstration). It would thus be idle to believe that everyday knowledge attributions do not infiltrate the search for scientific explanations. This alone is enough for making the issue of the scientific status of knowledge attributions an urgent one.

Looking at this intentionalist practice from the outside one is faced with a number of questions. Two are of particular interest here. First, one is left to wonder whether there is a question of truth or accuracy about attributions. If not, they are merely instruments for prediction. Do people really have the beliefs and intentions we attribute them, how can we tell so, and is there independent evidence to be found which does not rely upon our intentionalist interpretation? Second, how are the beliefs realized in their cognitive system? Both questions are particularly important in a developmental context. For example, in standard adult cognition the risks of mistaken knowledge attributions are limited by the fact that in most interactions participants belong to a largely shared context. But what makes this assumption of a common world and shared interpretational principles warranted is, at least to some extent, the "modelling effect" of cognitive development itself. If that is so, the attribution of knowledge to young children is a much riskier business (e.g. Van Geert, 1982) because the transaction between children and adults might be marked by cognitive asymmetry (de Gelder, 1983). As to the second question, the very idea of cognitive development forces us to take seriously the possibility that knowledge is differently realized in young infants than it is in children or than it is in adults. For example, infants as well as children and adults are capable of running in circles as well as of drawing a circle. If there is cognitive development in any serious sense (see above) then we must consider the possibility that this knowledge of what a circle is, is thus represented differentially in the three cases. Or, to put it in a more familiar idiom, infants, children and adults have a different representation of what a circle is.

If this could in principle be the case, then the possibility of a serious mismatch arises between attributed knowledge, say by an observer, and the target representation in the cognitive system considered. But what kind of mismatch is this? There might be a mismatch at the level of the first problem we mentioned. In other words, we might be wrong in attributing a piece of knowledge, a representation or a concept. For example the infant might merely behave as if it knew, as if it had the concept while, in fact, the observed behaviour is a function of motor schemes and environmental constraints or is the result of imitation. From a developmental perspective matters of truth or correctness are not the primary ones because they do not raise the issue of the instantiation of knowledge in cognitive structures. This is what the second problem is about. It forces us to address the issue not of the correctness of our attributions but of their warrantedness given our independent knowledge of mental representations, cognitive structures, categories etc. and the changes these undergo under the broad hypothesis of cognitive development.

Obviously, the issue cannot be settled unless one clarifies the nature of the relation between knowledge attributions and mental representations or cognitive structures. There is a standard picture. In this picture, knowledge attributions are taken as descriptions of the information processing system. For Gibsonians, these are descriptions of sensory discriminations. For cognitive information processing theorists, these are descriptions of the functional or representational level. The point is not usually put as one about the relation between attribution and description. But the need to stress this aspect is already clear from the possibility of a mismatch as mentioned above. Still, in the standard picture, the knowledge or competence which is attributed to the observation of a succesful performance is conceptualized as being an underlying cognitive structure or representation. Just what is put in those terms does of course depend on the particular theory. Nevertheless, the role these representations have is largely the same across different developmental idioms. In all cases statements about those underlying representations are what determines the cash value of the knowledge attributions.

However, one can see as pointed out at the end of the section on cognitive functions that there is the possibility of a dilemma arising which can be further detailed now by connecting it to the problem of knowledge attribution. A Piagetian approach seems to address the question of cognitive development at the intentional level and appears to deal with the first problem of knowledge attributions mentioned here, viz. their adequacy . From a developmental perspective the increase in adequacy implies the fact that a cognitive system over time comes to live up to the intentionalist attributions to which it is subjected. One could thus read Piaget as writing the genetic history of what Dennett calls the intentionalist stance. There is no doubt that this interpretation fits in with Piaget's biologism and his adoption for the purpose of cognitive explanation of notions like adaptation and equilibrium. But any approach which tries to isolate code from content and restricts its scope to the study of the code is likely to address the issues raised in the second question on the scientific cash value of knowledge attribution. It cannot however in itself answer that question because it pretends only to offer the element of the answer and has nothing to say about what those elements contribute to answering the problem of warrantedness.

Often, both aspects are not separated in the literature. In a comment which is typical of this confusion Flanagan mixes both levels or aspects. In commenting upon Piaget's cognitive structures he adds that that:

> " a human mind can be conceptualized, very roughly, as a system of complex mental structures that perform operations and transformations on experiental input" (Flanagan, 1984, p. 125).

As his comparison with logical and mathematical rules in computers makes clear, this is the code meaning of representation which is intended by the notion of mental structure. But following this, Flanagan illustrates his point by quoting Boden:

> "According to Piagetian theory, the child gradually develops increasingly well-articulated and interrelated schemata, or representations. It is in terms of these intentional models that the psychological subject constructs and interprets the world ..." (Flanagan, 1984, p. 125).

It is interesting to note that on our analysis the confusion between representation as code and representation as intentional scheme follows from the ambiguity of the notion of function. In the previous quotation, Flanagan notes that logical and mathematical structures in computers correspond to the notion of functions in human cognitive systems. What are the reasons for distrust in the idea that attributions reduce to descriptions and that the attributed knowledge is conceptualized in cognitive structures? A failure to raise the attribution issue for its own sake leads to tautology : the descriptions of cognitive structures that are taken to have empirical status are in fact nothing else than conceptual analyses and reformulations of the very same claims made with knowledge attribution itself.

From the above comments we can come to understand why the

problem of attribution has received so little attention.
Descriptive approaches to cognitive development, whether
descriptions of cognitive functions or descriptions of the
child's knowledge and conceptions do tend to skip the
attribution level. In practice they thus endorse the view that
attributions, to the extent that they are scientifically
valuable, reduce to descriptions of these kinds. The theories
which pretend to move from the descriptive level to
explanation do not face an attribution problem either. Two
popular candidates for such explanatory proposals are failure
driven vs. success driven models of development. I want to
make two remarks about such proposals both tending to
underscore the importance of the attribution issue.

By locating the drive for success or the awareness of
failure in the underlying developmental mechanism, we tend to
blind ourselves to some aspects of success or failure at the
surface level of descriptions. The description of behavioural
success or failure is something which has an evaluative
component. It is neither an observation of competence nor of
good performance, but an appraisal of mastery. This evaluative
component is not superordinate on a description which has
standards of appraisal at its disposal. Only in very rare
cases are there such standards and does the appraisal of
mastery reduce to a check against established criteria. Models
of failure or succes drivenness must assume that a
representation of the standards to be achieved is present as
an internal goal in the cognitive system, or alternatively in
the environment. For example, research on concept acquisition
has at times capitalized on the assumption that concepts had a
closed set of defining characteristics which the child had to
appropriate. From the observer's point of view then, the fact
that a child used (words for) concepts properly was evidence
for the fact that he or she had mastered those definitions.
But when we no longer believe in such definitions, what is it
that the child has mastered and what is it to appraise this
mastery? When taken out of the shadow of fictitious
definitions, the issue of mastery takes on a life of its own,
complicating both the theory and bringing out the attributive

aspects of a methodology which can no longer be purely descriptive.

The second aspect of attribution is related to the study of adult cognition. Often the appraisal or mastery in adult cognition has a normative component. In other words, we do not merely attribute knowledge because we believe it to be right or accurate or instrumental but because there are things one must know. If the phenomenon of cognitive development is domesticated at the descriptive level, for example that of increasingly differentiated and complex conceptions about the natural world, where does this normative aspect come in? At what point do we assume the right at making normative attributions?

CONCLUSION.

I have first discussed the cognitive nature of functions, second the development of knowledge and finally the nature of cognitive explanations. In looking at the conclusion reached at the end of each of those sections, one preceives the profile of an argument which would run like this. The problems with the study of cognitive functions require one to have a clear notion of knowledge and of development of knowledge. The problems with clarifying the notion of knowledge as needed for developmental theories require one to solve the problems with knowledge attribution. In other words, no study of the development of cognitive functions can exist without the study of the changes in knowledge. And, in turn, no study of those changes without the study of attribution. This is the profile or the sketch of an argument but this paper only exposes it without being itself that argument (see de Gelder 1986b). Still, on the basis of the present exposition, we can come to some conclusions.

Let us return to the controversial question: is there cognitive development? I have tried to contribute something to another question: what is cognitive about development? Three answers have been considered. If one takes all three together, should one answer that there are three kinds of cognitive development? It is tempting to conclude that different theories have different research programmes. Thus, cognitive development, rather than being anything like a homogeneous problem, would allow three different types of questions and corresponding answers. Or, alternatively, one might want to conclude that there is no cognitive development, not in any general sense nor in any of the perspectives we sketched.

I am not endorsing either of these general conclusions. Instead, I do believe that the problems raised in each case are real. But rather than undermining the idea of cognitive development, they do point to the need to integrate the three aspects because neither of them can, on its own, claim to be a cognitive approach. In other words, a naturalistic study of cognitive functions presupposes theories about concepts and the modalities of their attribution. A descriptive study of conceptions or evolution of knowledge must be constrained both by facts about cognitive functions and analysis of attributive practices. But in concluding like this I do not defend the possibility of integrating all those contributions. Cognitive development is no more homogeneous than knowledge or cognition. Attributions of knowledge and appraisals of mastery catch facts which are more like flags on the visible part of the iceberg or like message bottles carried by the waves. Beneath is a huge variety of things none of which are intrinsically cognitive, some of which sustain knowledge attributions. The study of cognitive attributions in developmental contexts is a way of finding out which ones those might be. Talk of underlying mental representations is just a way of streamlining too much and too soon. An in depth study of the modalities of knowledge attribution as a function of task, contex, attributor, and attributee might reveal the precariousness of the internal representationalist and functionalist level which is been accused of being the stumbling block for serious theories of cognitive development.

NOTES

1. It is clear why the study of language stands so easily model for research on the code. Linguistics provides us with a description of linguistic information and thus the natural move is to assume that the task of the information processing organism is to map or to represent the coding of linguistic information in the linguist's linguistic structures.

2. A more precise discussion of this point would have to look at different alternatives for the analysis of logical form and also ask to what extent Piagetian conceptions of logic and of cognitive structures escape the fate of the axiomatic method in philosophy of science.

REFERENCES.

Block, N. (1981). Imagery. Cambridge (Mass.): MIT Press.

Brainerd, C.J. (1978). The stage question in cognitive developmental theory. The Behavioural and Brain Sciences, 1, 173-213.

Bursen, M.A. (1978). Dismantling the memory machine. Dordrecht: Reidel.

Cicourel, A.V. (1973). Cognitive Sociology. Harmondsworth: Penguin Books.

De Gelder, B. (1983). Cognitive transactions and objects of belief. In H. Parret (Ed.), Epistemology and semiotics of belief. Berlin/New York: Walter de Gruyter Verlag.

De Gelder, B. (1986a). Phonological awareness reconsidered. Paper submitted for publication.

De Gelder, B. (1986b). On why there is not a ready-made mind (in preparation).

Dennett, D.C. (1978). Intentional Systems. In D.C. Dennett (Ed.), Brainstorms. Cambridge (Mass.): MIT Press.

Dennett, D.C. (1981). True believers: The intentional strategy and why it works. In A.F. Heath (Ed.), Scientific explanation. Oxford: Clarendon Press.

Dennett, D.C. (1984). Cognitive wheels: the frame problem of AI. In C. Hookway (Ed.), Minds, Machines and Evolution. Cambridge: Cambridge University Press.

Flanagan, O.D. (1984). The science of mind. Cambridge (Mass.): Bradford Books/MIT Press.

Flavell, J.H. (1978). Metacognitive development. In J.M. Scandura & C.J. Brainerd (Eds.), Structural process theories of complex human behavior. Leiden: Sijthoff.

Fodor, J. (1965). Explanations in psychology. In M. Black (Ed.), Philosophy in America. London: Routledge & Kegan Paul.

Fodor, J. (1975). The language of thought. New York: Crowell.

Fodor, J. (1980). Methodological solipsism considered as a research strategy in cognitive psychology. The Behavioural and Brain Sciences, 3, 63-109.

Fodor, J. (1983). The modularity of mind. Cambridge (Mass.): MIT Press.

Gibson, J.J. (1966). The senses considered as perceptual systems. Boston: Houghton-Mifflin.

Goodwin, B.C. (1978). A cognitive of biological process. Journal of Social and Biological Structures, 1.

Hamlyn, D.W. (1975). Concepts of development. In Proceedings, Philosophy of Education Society of Great Britain, 9, 26-39.

Haroutunian, S. (1983). Equilibrium in the balance, a study of psychological explanation. New York: Springer.

Harris D.B. (1983). Infant cognition. In P.H. Mussen (Ed.), Handbook of child psychology (vol 3). New York: Wiley.

Haugeland, J. (Ed.), (1981). Mind design, philosophy, psychology, artificial intelligence. Cambridge (Mass.): Bradford/MIT Press.

Inhelder, B. (1972). Information processing tendencies in recent experiments in cognitive learning - Empirical studies. In S. Farnham-Diggory (Ed.), Information processing in children. New York: Academic Press.

Jorm, A.F. & Share, D.L. (1983). Phonological recoding and

reading   acquisition.   Applied   Psycholinguistics,   4,
103-107.

Karmiloff-Smith, A. (1986). From meta-processes to conscious
access: Evidence from children's metalinguistic and
repair data (in press).

Mandler, J. (1983). Representation. In P.H. Mussen (Ed.),
Handbook of child psychology (vol. 3). New York: Wiley.

Mandler, G. (1985). Cognitive psychology: An essay in
cognitive science. Hillsdale (N.J.): Erlbaum.

Nagel, E. (1957). Determinism and development. In D.B. Harris
(Ed.), The Concept of Development. Minneanapolis:
University of Minnesota Press.

Nagel, E. (1977). Functional explanations. Journal of
Philosophy, 74, 280-301.

Neisser, U. (1967). Cognitive psychology. New York:
Appleton-Century-Crofts.

Palmer, S.E. (1978). Fundamental aspects of cognitive
representation. In E. Rosch & B.B. Lloyd (Eds.),
Cognition and Categorization. Hillsdale (N.J.): Erlbaum.

Peters, R.S. (1972). Education and human development. In R.F.
Dearden, P.H. Hirst & R.S. Peters (Eds.), Education and
the development of reason. London: Routledge & Kegan
Paul.

Peters, R.S. (1974). The development of reason. In R.S. Peters
(Ed.), Collected papers: Psychology and ethical
development. London: Allen & Unwin.

Piatelli-Palmerini, M. (Ed.), (1980). Language and learning:
The debate between Jean Piaget and Noam Chomsky.
Cambridge: Harvard University Press.

Pylyshyn, Z.W. (1984). Computation and cognition: Toward a
foundation for cognitive science. Cambridge (Mass.): MIT
Press.

Rozin, P. (1978). The acquisition of basic alphabetic
principles: A structural approach. In C.A. Catania & T.A.
Brigham (Eds.), Handbook of applied behavior analysis.
New York: Irvington.

Siegler, R.S. & Klahr, D. (1982). When do children learn? In
R. Glaser (Ed.), Advances in instructional psychology

(vol. 2). Hillsdale (N.J.): Erlbaum.

Smith, C., Carey, S. & Wiser, M. (1985). On differentiation: A case study of the development of the concepts of size, weight and density. Cognition, 21 (3), 177-237.

Suppe, F. (1977). The structure of scientific theories. London: University of Illinois Press.

Taylor, C. (1964). The explanation of behavior. London: Routledge & Kegan Paul.

Toulmin, S. (1977). The structure of scientific theories. In F. Suppe (Ed.), The structure of scientific theories. London: University of Illinois Press.

Van Geert, P. (1982). Attributing knowledge to young children. In B. de Gelder (Ed.), Knowledge and Representation. London: Routledge and Kegan Paul.

About the Authors

Paul van Geert (editor, chapters 1 and 2) is professor of developmental psychology at the State University of Groningen (The Netherlands). In the past ten years he has been involved in theory-building in developmental psychology. His most recent book on this subject is "The Development of Perception, Cognition and Language, a theoretical approach" (1983). His current research interests are theory-building in developmental psychology, the acquisition of knowledge in relation to the development of language and perception, and the problem of awareness and self-representation.

Present address:
Rijksuniversiteit te Groningen,
Instituut voor Ontwikkelingspsychologie,
Oude Boteringestraat 34,
Groningen,
The Netherlands.

Martin Atkinson (chapter 3) is Senior Lecturer in the Department of Language and Linguistics at the University of Essex where he has been involved in the teaching of various aspects of Linguistics and Psycholinguistics since 1974. Before 1974 he worked at the University of Edinburgh on a number of Language Acquisition research projects. His major publications are "Explanation in the Study of Child Language Development" (1982) and, with D. Kilby and I. Roca, "Foundations of General Linguistics" (1982). His current research interests include learnability theory, foundations of cognitive science, and Chinese language, and he is working on a book provisionally titled "Models of Mind and Language".

Present address:
University of Essex,
Department of Language and Linguistics,
Wivenhoe Park,
Colchester CO4 3SQ
England.

John Morton (chapter 4) is Director of the Medical Research Council's Cognitive Development Unit and Visiting Professor in University College London. He previously spent 22 years at the Applied Psychology Unit in Cambridge working on such topics as word recognition, reading, acquired dyslexia, human-computer interaction and memory. He is responsible for introducing a number of theoretical concepts such as logogens, PAS, P-centres and Headed Records. He has been working in London and learning about development for the last three years and his paper here is his first foray into developmental theory.

Present address:
MRC Cognitive Development Unit,
17 Gordon Street,
London WC1H OAH,
England.

Peter Bryant (chapter 5) is Watts Professor of Psychology at
Oxford University since 1980. He has written two books
"Perception and Understanding in Young Children" (1974) and,
with L. Bradley, "Children's Reading Problems" (1985). His
current research interests are the development of reading,
children's early phonological development, children's
understanding of spatial coordinates, children's understanding
of relations between mathematical operations.

Present address:
Department of Experimental Psychology,
University of Oxford,
South Parks Road,
Oxford OX1 3UD,
England.

Dieter Geulen (chapter 6) is Professor of Education at the
Freie Universität Berlin (West Germany) since 1980. His major
publication in the field of socialization theory is "Das
vergesellschaftete Subjekt zur Grundlegung der
Socialisations-theorie" (1977, 2 ed. 1986). In addition he has
written many articles on this subject. He is editor of the
book "Perspektivenübernahme und soziales handeln" (1982). His
current research interests are socialization theory, the
theory of human development and the theory of social action.

Present address:
Freie Universität Berlin,
Fachbereich Erziehungs- un Unterrichtswissenschaften,
Institut für Allgemeine und Vergleichende
Erziehungswissenschaft,
Habelschwerdter Allee 45,
1000 Berlin 33,
West Germany.

Paul Vedder (chapter 7), studied Educational and Developmental Psychology at the University of Groningen, the Netherlands. He set up research projects on cooperative learning and referential communication skills. His main theoretical interest is with the social nature of the intellectual development of primary schoolchildren. He is author of "Cooperative Learning". Momentarily he is stationed on the Caribbean island of Curacao, involved in setting up and executing research projects in primary education.

Present address:
Pasenshiweg 2,
Curaçao,
Nederlandse Antillen.

Francine Orsini-Bouichou (chapter 8) is Professor of Child Psychology at the University of Provence, Aix-en-Provence, France. She is co-director of the Laboratoire Universitaire de Psychologie de l'Enfant et de Psychologie Génétique (Aix-en-Provence) and is in charge of research team no. 1 at the Centre de Recherches en Psychologie Cognitive. Her main research interests are cognitive development and functioning, learning and enrionment and educability of intelligence. Her most recent publications are "L'intelligence de l'enfant, ontogénèse des invariants" (1982) and "Fonctionnnement et changement cognitifs chez l'enfant" (with M. Hurtig).

Present address:
Université de Provence,
U.E.R. de Psychologie,
29, Avenue Robert Schuman,
13621 Aix-en-Provence,
France.

Jean-Louis Paour (chapter 8) is Maître Assistant in Child Psychology at the University of Provence, Aix-en-Provence,

France. His main research interests are cognitive development
and functioning, learning and environment and educability of
intelligence. His most recent publications are "Apprentissage
des Structures Logiques et developpement du langage chez les
arrières mentaux" (in Rondal, Lambert and Chipman, eds.),
"Psycholinguistique et handicap mental" (1981) and
"L'apprentissage opératoire chez les retardés mentaux" in the
"Archives de Psychologie" (1985, in press) of which he is
co-writer (with D. Galas, J. Malacria-Rocco and G. Soavi).

Present address:
Université de Provence,
U.E.R. de Psychologie,
29, Avenue Robert Schuman,
13621 Aix-en-Provence,
France.

Jan ter Laak (chapter 9) is Senior Lecturer in Developmental
Psychology at the University of Leiden (The Netherlands). His
main research interests are the fundamental theoretical
aspects of development, analysis of the organisation of
behaviour, both cross-sectional and longitudinal. More
specifically he is involved in developing methodological
techniques for theory forming in cognitive development and
determining developmental sequences. His most recent
publications are, in dutch, on the assessment of cognitive
sequences, referential communication and distributive justice
in children.

Present address:
Rijksuniversiteit te Leiden,
Vakgroep: Ontwikkelingspsychologie,
Hooigracht 15,
2312 KM Leiden,
The Netherlands.

Maria Tyszkowa (chapter 10) is full professor of psychology
and chairman of the Department of Developmental and
Educational Psychology at Adam Mickiewicza University in
Poznań, Poland. Her main research interests are in the areas
of cognitive development and personality development,
behaviour in difficult situations and the theory of human
development during the life-span. She has written numerous
scientific articles published in Polish, English, French and
German and is the editor of 8 collective professional books.

Present address:
Uniwersytet im. Adama Mickiewicza,
Instytut Psychologii,
ul. Szamarzewskiego 89,
60-568 Poznań,
Poland.

Ed Elbers (chapter 11) received his training as a psychologist
at the Catholic University of Nijmegen (The Netherlands), the
University of Amsterdam and the Free University of
West-Berlin. At present, he is a lecturer of theoretical
psychology at the Department of Psychonomics of the Faculty of
Social Sciences, University of Utrecht. His main interest is
developmental theory. Among his publications are: "The
development of motivation as an historical process", in:
J.M. Broughton (Ed.), New Critical Psychologies of
Development, New York: Plenum, 1986, and "Interaction and
instruction in the conservation experiment", European Journal
of Psychology of Education, in press.

Present address:
Rijksuniversiteit te Utrecht,
Vakgroep Psychonomie,
Sektie Theoretische Psychologie en Functieleer,
Postbus 80.140,
3508 TC Utrecht,
The Netherlands.

Alan Leslie (chapter 12) received his first degree in Psychology and Linguistics from the University of Edinburgh and his doctorate from Oxford University under the supervision of Jerry Bruner and the philosopher, Anthony Kenny. After a year spent at the Max-Planck-Institut für Psycholinguistik as a Leverhulme Scholar and Visiting Fellow, he returned to Edinburgh to undertake post-doctoral research with T.G.R. Bower. He joined the MRC Cognitive Development Unit at its inception in 1982. His main interests are in the computational mechanisms of early perceptual and cognitive development, and in the representational approach to mind.

Present address:
MRC Cognitive Development Unit,
17 Gordon Street,
London WC1H OAH,
England.

Bea de Gelder (chapter 13) is professor of methodology and philosophy of psychology at the Department of Psychology of the University of Tilburg (The Netherlands) after having had lecturing appointments at the universities of Louvain (Belgium) and Leiden (The Netherlands). She holds degrees in experimental psychology and in philosophy. She is editor of "Knowledge and Representation" (1982). Her current research interests are in foundations of cognitive science, the dynamics of knowledge representation and the relation between cognitive psychology and epistemology.

Present address:
Katholieke Hogeschool Tilburg,
Subfaculteit Psychologie,
Postbus 90153,
5000 LE Tilburg,
The Netherlands.

Name Index